KURELEK

A BIOGRAPHY

KURELEK

A BIOGRAPHY

Patricia Morley

MACMILLAN OF CANADA
A Division of Canada Publishing Corporation
Toronto, Ontario, Canada

To my mother
Mabel Olive Winsland Marlow
a painter

Canadian Cataloguing in Publication Data

Morley, Patricia, date.
  Kurelek, a biography

Includes index.
ISBN 0-7715-9748-7

1. Kurelek, William, 1927-1977. 2. Painters—
Canada—Biography. 3. Ukrainian Canadians—
Biography.* I. Kurelek, William, 1927-1977.
II. Title.

ND249.K85M37 1986   759.11   C86-093864-6

Design by: Catherine Wilson
C. P. Wilson Graphic Communication

Edited by: Kathleen Richards

Indexed by: Barbara Czarnecki

Printed in Canada

CONTENTS

Color Plates

I. *The Magi*, 1965-67. Gouache, 18″ x 26″. Private collection.

II. *The Maze*, 1953. Gouache, 36″ x 48″. Courtesy the Maudsley Hospital, London.

III. *Tramlines*, 1952. Gouache, 26″ x 38″ approx. Courtesy London Transport Board.

IV. *All Things Betray Thee Who Betrayest Me*, 1970. Gouache, 48″ x 48″. Courtesy Mr. P. Isaacs, The Isaacs Gallery.

V. *Still Life With Tomatoes*, 1954. *Trompe-l'oeil*, oil, 17″ x 14″. Private collection.

VI. *Patients Working in Boiler Room of Netherne Psychiatric Hospital, England*, 1954. Wash drawing, 14″ x 18″ approx. Private collection.

VII. *Bernadette at Lourdes*, 1955-56. Gouache, 29″ x 20½″. Private collection.

VIII. *Children's Games in Western Canada*, 1953. Mixed media, 24″ x 30″. Private collection.

IX. *Easter Vigil*, 1963. Mixed media, 23½″ x 39½″. Private collection.

X. *Mama*, 1966-67. Mixed media, composite, 45″ x 65″. Private collection.

ABBREVIATIONS USED IN NOTES AND TEXT

A1	=	*Someone With Me* (Cornell University Press, 1973)
A2	=	*Someone With Me* (McClelland and Stewart, 1980)
M.C.	=	May Cutler
Ex.	=	*Exile, A Literary Quarterly*, I, 2 (1972)
A.I.	=	Avrom Isaacs
Jean K.	=	Jean Kurelek
J.K.	=	John Kurelek
W.K.	=	William Kurelek
Mss 1-4	=	four unpublished Kurelek manuscripts, self-analyses written for a Winnipeg physician, 1947-48
P.M.	=	Patricia Morley
K.S.	=	Kenneth Shorey

Unpublished letters and manuscripts written by Kurelek are held by his widow, Mrs. Jean Kurelek.

Preface

THE WRITING OF BIOGRAPHY IS AN ACT OF FAITH, THE TRIUMPH (AS SAMUEL Johnson described second marriages) of hope over experience. Initially, the difficulties are unforeseen or disregarded. Were they apparent, one might never begin.

Chance, and an admiration for Kurelek's paintings, drew me into this project. Even in commercial reproductions, in the weekend magazines of the 1960s, the paintings were striking and unforgettable. I came upon his autobiography by chance in 1973, and was impressed by the courage and vigor with which he had overcome his difficulties. Fate had dealt him a bizarre hand, and he had played it brilliantly. My admiration increased as I read and reviewed his books throughout the 1970s.

In 1980, Fate turned her attention to me. I received an invitation to a Kurelek exhibition at The Isaacs Gallery, the first such card ever sent to me by this dealer. The Gallery was some three hundred miles from my home near Ottawa, but a visit to Toronto had already been arranged for the very same week. On Easter Saturday I walked into The Isaacs Gallery and stood enjoying the paintings. Beside each was the artist's commentary, neatly typed. I began to chat with the clerk. Oh yes, she said brightly, Mr. Kurelek wrote a lot, Mr. Isaacs had bags of his writings.

Bags of his writings. It was a curious, not to say an extraordinary, phrase. The effect on me was startling. My interest in Kurelek, which had been growing quietly for nearly two decades, suddenly crystallized into the conviction that I should write his biography. After this point there was no turning back and no release from the pressures of the project for the next six years.

Masses of personal papers were indeed held by the dealer and the artist's wife. I offered my services as biographer and was accepted. This book is "official" or "authorized" in the sense that I embarked on the project with the full approval of Mrs. Jean Kurelek, who granted me the right to quote from her husband's writings and who generously made them available to me. The interpretation of those writings is my own; I could not have proceeded on any other basis.

My quest for the man behind the artist and his personal myth has been both satisfying and aggravating, but never dull. I began by believing the myth implicitly. Kurelek's power to make us see him through his own eyes is considerable. It is a power that demonstrates the artist's skill as a storyteller, his burning religious faith, and his equally strong need to be right. That need for success had been nurtured by the opposition of the father he both hated and adored. If gratitude was owing for the grit that had led to a pearl, this was a debt the son never acknowledged. As for the popular press, it was kind to Kurelek in his lifetime and took him (for the most part) at his own word. It would be years before I would question those words, that interpretation of the artist's life. Kurelek shapes his success story with the simplicity and apparent inevitability common to great myths everywhere. The reality is more complex.

My credentials as Kurelek's biographer include a lifelong love of art in all its forms, especially literature and painting. Literature has been my profession for two decades. The parallels between these two arts are more numerous than might appear at first sight. Twenty years of practising the craft of writing have stood me in good stead. Some fifty-five years of living were even more essential as a preparation and prerequisite for understanding this strange and complex man. And since my four adult children all see life (and their parents) with very different eyes from my own, I could sympathize with Kurelek's beleaguered parents.

The artist anticipated a biography and consciously prepared the ground. His own record, in the form of numerous diaries and letters as well as paintings and commentaries, sheds abundant light on the life. He was writing and rewriting his autobiography through all of his adult years. A prominent part of his makeup was a driving urge to explain himself, an urge which he believed to be part of an evangelistic witness to his faith. In thousands of paintings and drawings, dating from the late 1940s, Kurelek expressed his inner turmoil, faith, and love through the common forms of his daily world.

Kurelek was "Will" to his parents, siblings, and wife, "Bill" to his dealer and most of his friends, and "Vasyl" (the Ukrainian form of William) to a few Ukrainian friends. I met the artist only twice, but, in the course of immersing myself in his life for six years, I have come to think of him as "Bill". I have used this name through most of the book and think that Kurelek, who cared nothing for formalities, would approve. I have also retained his spelling and syntax throughout his own writings, since they help to give the flavor of the man. That flavor is utterly unique.

Patricia Morley
Manotick, Ontario
January 1986

Acknowledgements

T<small>HE</small> <small>MASSIVE</small> <small>DOCUMENTATION</small> <small>FOR</small> <small>THIS</small> <small>BIOGRAPHY</small> <small>HAS</small> <small>COME</small> <small>FROM</small> numerous sources. I am indebted to a great many individuals and institutions for help in what proved to be a six-year marathon through difficult terrain. Special thanks are due to the artist's dealer, Avrom Isaacs, who opened to me the files of The Isaacs Gallery and its other resources, including hundreds of colored slides of Kurelek paintings; to May Cutler of Tundra Books; to Mykola and Ola Kolankiwsky of the Niagara Falls Art Gallery, "The Passion of Christ" William Kurelek Collection; to Christopher Ondaatje of Pagurian Press; to Professor James Maas of Cornell University; and to the administration, physicians, and staff of two British hospitals: the Maudsley Hospital, London, and Netherne Hospital, Sussex. Both hospitals opened their Kurelek files to me after Mrs. Kurelek had given her permission for me to study the records of her husband's hospitalization there in the early 1950s. I understand that I am the first non-medical researcher to be granted this privilege. I was not able to quote from those records, but the freedom to study them provided an invaluable window into one of the most puzzling periods of his life.

I am grateful to Mrs. Catherine de Hueck Doherty, founder and director of Madonna House, Combermere, Ontario, and to the members of this lay community who shared with me their memories of the painter, who, in turn, had shared their spiritual life and found in it "the hope of the world".

I am also grateful to the Kurelek family, the artist's parents and siblings: namely Mary and the late Dmytro Kurelek; John and Helen Kurelek; "Win" (Wasylyna) and Nestor Olynyk; Nancy Black; "Sandy" (Alexandra) and Geza Takacs; and Iris Gauthier; grateful, too, to the Huculak family, siblings of Kurelek's mother, and to several of their spouses, who had known and entertained the artist for many years: Peter and Rose Huculak; William and Arla Huculak; Helen and Michael Shulhan; Kate Woychuk, and her son Alan; Alice and Nicolai Krawchuk; and brothers Steven, Samuel, Daniel, and George Huculak. Without the generous support that they have given, the portrait of their son, brother, or nephew would have been much the poorer. I met and talked with Kurelek's father once, shortly before his sudden and unexpected death in 1981.

For financial assistance, I am indebted to the Social Science and

Humanities Research Council of Canada, to Concordia University of Montréal, and to the Taras Shevchenko Foundation of Winnipeg. The SSHRCC granted me a Leave Fellowship and two major research grants. My university gave me a year's sabbatical leave and seed money to begin investigations late in 1980. The Taras Shevchenko Foundation paid part of the costs of the photography and color reproductions of Kurelek paintings. L. L. Odette of the P. and L. Charitable Foundation helped to carry the project through a lean year between grants. Without help to provide for a research assistant and travel, the book could not have been written.

A great many individuals have talked with me about the artist and shown me Kurelek letters and paintings. Any major biography is a shared effort on the part of those who knew and cared about the life under consideration. I am particularly grateful to Kenneth Shorey for making available his unbroken correspondence with the artist from 1959 to 1977, and for extended reflections on Kurelek's personality. Others who have helped include Fr. M. Abraham; Edward Adamson; Abraham Arnold; William Atkinson; Michael Audain; Edward Bader; Anna Balan; I. W. Bardyn; Fr. Michael Barida; Dorothy Barnhouse; Patricia Barnicko; Jennifer Baroni; Stanley Beecham; Mykola Bidniak; Joyce and Frank Bond; C. F. Bonnett; Bonnie Brennan; Helen Brier; Patricia and Charles Brine; Jeremy and Brenna Brown; Fr. Guy Bruneau; William Budjak; Barry Callaghan; Donald L. Campbell; Helen Cannon; Dr. G. M. Carstairs; John Champagne; Sylvia Chan; Ann Cirka, and her son John; Marie and Michael Clayton; Ruth and John Robert Colombo; Cleo Corcoran; Dr. B. Cormier; Graham Coughtry; Helen Coxe; Lois Crozier; Dr. D. L. Davies; Charles Davis; Donald DeMarco; Jan Disselkoen; Marjorie Drache; Judge and Mrs. Darrell Draper; Norman Duvell; Michael Ewanchuk; Stella Dutka Ewanchuk; Michael Fagin; Fr. J. J. Farrell; M. F. Feheley; Georgine Ferguson; Brendan Foley; Ted Fraser; Eric Freifeld; Dr. R. K. Freudenberg; Gloria and Stanley Frolick; Robert Fulford; Dr. Aimé and Mrs. Michelle Gagné; Dr. Ehor Gauk; Irene Gauk; Joseph Gay; John B. Giesbrecht; Anne Godard; John Gomez; Marie Goubran; Geralyn Hall; James Halpin; Tillie Harasymchuk; Susan Hasbury; Nancy Hawrelak; Marianne Hellwig; Lucie H. Hirniak; Jacques Hnizdovsky; Fr. E. Holloway; Vladimir Horik; Taras Hukalo; Carl Inman; Nathan Isaacs; Evva Jarmicki; Dr. D. W. Jirsch; David John; Simon Kalba; Dr. B. Kanee; Joseph Katz; Douglas Kieffer; Fr. K. Kirley; Dr. and Mrs. Zenon Kiss; Yaroslaw Kit; Dr. and Mrs. S. Klemchuk; Justin Klym; Michael Kostek; Kay Kritzwiser; Agnes Krumins; Lila and William Kudlac; Vivian and Peter Kuzina; Edna and Conrad Ladouceur; Jane and James Lanthier; Philip Lanthier; Dr. and Mrs. G. Laverty; Max Layton; Michael Leigh; Peter Lesko; Fr. L. Letarte;

M. F. Levey; Dr. R. Levy; John Loblaw; Maria and Michael Logush; Rev. S. Lucyk; George Ludski; Fr. T. J. Lynch; Emmett Maddix; Wanda and Roman Malanczak; Fr. J. McConica; A. S. McGregor; Rev. B. McLeod; John McKillop; Jean McNulty; Bohdan Melnyk; Ingrid Milic; W. O. Mitchell; Donna and George Montague; Fr. F. Murphy; Joan Murray; Dr. T. Murray; Nadia and Michael Negrich; Nadia Niechoda; Michael O'Brien; Fr. W. H. O'Brien; Gloria Ochitwa; Maria Ochrymovych; Ginny and Marc Odette; Andrew Oliver; Nadia Olynyk; Joan O'Meara; Janet Ostafichuk; Jeanne Parkin; Michael Pearson; Kathleen and Adolphe Pecoskie; Nancy and Ernie Peplinskie; Aka and Konstantin Peryma; Dr. E. J. Prokipchuk; Donna Reed; Patricia Reidy; Dan Ritchie; Jaroslav Rozumnyj; Willie Rumleskie; Terry Ryan; Kenneth Saltmarche; Abraham Schwartz; Fr. R. J. Scollard of St. Michael's College Archives; Paul Sembaliuk; Bess and Ross Silversides; Jan and George Sinclair; Stella and Henry Slaby; Beverley Slopen; Margaret Smith; W. D. Stagg; Mary and John Stefura; Peter Stitch; Louis and Joseph Stoeckle; Fr. F. Stone; Rose and Harry Streets; Lu Tasky; Jean and William Teron; John Timlin; Anne and Fred Tomyk; Olga and John Tomyk; Fr. A. de Valk; Dr. Elias Wachna; Stephany and Antony Wachna; Stan Westlake; Zena and Alex Wloch; Rose Yanovsky; Teresa and Alex Yantha; Anastasia and Wasyl Zazula; Susan and Herman Zerweck; Ireneus Zuk.

The following institutions and businesses have also been most helpful: The Art Gallery of Edmonton; The Art Gallery of Ontario; The Art Gallery of Windsor; The Art Gallery of Winnipeg; The Burnaby Art Gallery; Calgary University Archives; Canada Council; Canada House, England; The Catholic Information Centre, Toronto; Clarence House, England; The Commonwealth Institute, England; The Downstairs Gallery, Edmonton; The Agnes Etherington Art Centre; Herzig Somerville, Ltd., Toronto; Hurtig Publishers, Edmonton; Isaac Newton High School, Winnipeg; London Transport Board, England; McClelland and Stewart, Toronto; Macmillan of Canada, Toronto; The Michel de Kerdour Gallery, Québec; The Mira Godard Gallery, Toronto; The Montréal Museum of Fine Arts; The National Art Gallery Library; The National Film Board, Edmonton and Ottawa; Oseredok, The Ukrainian Cultural and Educational Centre, Winnipeg; F. A. Pollak Ltd., London, England; Public Archives Canada; The Rodman Hall Arts Centre, St. Catharines; The Royal Academy, London; The St. Thomas More College, Saskatoon; and Shandro Pioneer Museum.

My thanks also go to Kathleen Richards, my editor at Macmillan. Finally, I wish to thank Anne Erdmer, my friend and research assistant. Anne has sustained the project and the biographer for nearly five years with sorting, typing, excellent suggestions, and a listening ear. She helped in so many ways to bring the book into being.

Bill was a master finisher and expert in the exacting art of gilding, as a result of his training at Pollak's in London from 1956 to 1959. During the 1960s after his rise to fame in Canada, he continued to frame his own work at The Isaacs Gallery, often in colorful Ukrainian designs and old barnwood. A colleague observed that he had seen Bill spend eight hours framing a work he had painted in three. Courtesy Mr. Stan Beecham.

1

Kurelek:
The Man and the Myth

KURELEK'S LIFE IS ONE OF THE STRANGEST STORIES EVER TOLD. IN THE TELLING, the biographer is oddly companioned by the painter himself. This artist was compulsively confessional, haunted by his own experience and determined to understand it. I was astonished to discover, over the course of my research, that Bill was writing his own story *for thirty years*—that is, for all of his adult life. The earliest version, eight fat scribblers of handwriting, dates from 1947 when he was twenty. It was apparently written in an attempt to explain his physical and emotional problems to a Winnipeg doctor. During hospitalization in Britain in two psychiatric hospitals during the early 1950s, Bill wrote, and was encouraged to write, his life story. He also painted his traumas, and even attempted to exorcise his hatred and anger by symbolic paintings of revenge. Was it narcissism, this relentless self-examination? Or something more complex?

His autobiography was first published in 1973 by Cornell University Press by means of photographing an unedited typescript five hundred and twenty-three pages long. Bill had been revising *Someone With Me* throughout the sixties, aided by various friends. Publication became possible when a psychology professor decided to use it as a textbook. Through the last four years of his life, Bill continued to revise his manuscripts.

Obviously his own story was of primary importance to him. He saw it as both unique and typical, an encouragement to other troubled souls. The "someone" of the title is God, who is credited with saving Bill's life, restoring him to health and success, and guiding him through "this tragic, puzzling, yet wonderful world. ... And He has asked me to get up because there is work to be done" (A2 175). Soon after his death, a version of the autobiography was reprinted. It had been slightly revised by Bill and was greatly abridged by an editor.

Given the abundance of self-portraiture, there are those who

1

thought that I was wasting my time. What need was there for a biography when the subject himself had written so extensively about his life? An opposite theory is voiced by biographer Phyllis Grosskurth, who finds autobiography to be helpful to the biographer "only to the extent that it reveals displacements, condensations, and evasions." *Only?* These are strong words. Bill's evasiveness had been borne in upon me slowly, over a period of months, even years. I was unwilling to dismiss *Someone With Me* lightly, and equally unwilling to leave the last word to Bill. Biographer and autobiographer form an incongruous couple, with very different approaches to a life. The biographer's job is not to supplement or update but to see differently, freshly. And in that seeing lies the tale.

William Kurelek was an unusual individual, as most great artists have been. Yet his talent for depicting the essence of common experience led journalists to call him "The People's Painter". He is perhaps best known for his realistic paintings of farm scenes, many of them set in Western Canada where he had grown up. This twentieth-century Krieghoff loved nature, but there were nearly always people in his landscapes. His scenes of people in groups, at work and at play, are in the tradition of the medieval Flemish masters. Weddings, funerals, seed-time and harvest, in daylight or at night: nothing escaped his notice or his brush. His narrative skill turned paintings into stories. His faith made them prophetic, sometimes harsh. Like Pieter Brueghel and Hieronymus Bosch, whose works he acknowledged as major influences on his own, Kurelek's vision is both social and religious, even mystical. He caught the feeling of the richness and vastness of prairie life; of what James Bacque calls the natural terror, mystery, and abundance of earth.[1]

In his late twenties he found release from mental and emotional anguish through religious faith. His autobiography serves to witness to that faith and to encourage other troubled souls to seek help from the same source. The residue of his pain and the stern side of his faith issued in prophetic paintings which warned of judgment to come. Angered by a society he saw as secular, permissive, and materialistic, Kurelek could thunder like an Old Testament prophet or a modern Savonarola. His painted thunderings were silent, and beyond sound. A series of illustrations of the Passion of Christ intended as a teaching tool for the Church became a graphic statement of his own religious faith.

He also painted *trompe-l'oeil*, still-life scenes of coins, bills, stamps, letters, and other trivia, with a command of perspective and illusion that convinces the viewer that the actual objects are on canvas. He painted allegories of states of mind, the demons of his own suffering, and surreal fantasies; self-portraits, where the background contains a collage of autobiographical events and symbolic objects. He portrayed various ethnic cultures. In short, he painted the world as he saw it, and in that view lies extraordinary power and fascination.

Catholics, Ukrainians, Jews, and many other groups feel a personal connection with the artist through his paintings and his experience. Kurelek's life is significant because he struggled with tremendous difficulties, with madness and attempted suicide, and won. Shy and sensitive, he saw himself in adolescence as the ugly duckling cf the fairy tale, with very little chance of becoming a swan. The drive to transform that ugliness into beauty and that failure into success was very strong. He was determined to find and fulfil the great destiny he had intuited as a boy. He was convinced that, within the vast scheme of things, there must be a reason for his personal suffering. He would find it, or die in the attempt.

Out of the maelstrom, or perhaps from a precarious foothold on its edge, he found faith and his own artistic genius. He eventually achieved fame, even wealth. The story is in the torments, the triumphs, and the joy. And in the contradictions. Kurelek reveals everything, and nothing. The man who loved to write explanatory texts for his paintings remains, in the end, an enigma.

Born in 1927 to Ukrainian-Canadian pioneers near Whitford, Alberta, Bill grew up strongly influenced by the landscape, the farm routines, and the rural culture which fed the artist's imagination in innumerable ways. The first seven years of Bill's childhood were spent there, and the next dozen in Stonewall, just north of Winnipeg. The flat black farmland of Manitoba and the life of its immigrant settlers became the subject of many of his paintings and one of the deepest emotional attachments of his life.

Two periods in his life were crucial. One was the Stonewall years of youth and early adolescence, when a lack of athletic and mechanical aptitudes and a hypersensitive personality made him a target for sniping from bullies at school and a disappointed father at home. Yet the Stonewall years were also rich in joys. The joy would be recalled—and painted—later, after the pain had been cauterized and the healing begun.

The other was his time in Britain, where the bitter legacy from Stonewall erupted like an angry boil. Old hurts threatened to overwhelm Bill, to drown him in a sea of hatred and guilt. They might well have done so, had it not been for the faith which was given to him there. This vital seven-year period was critical in Bill's development. It was truly the fulcrum of his life. His hospital period, and the writing and painting that accompanied it, marked the depths of his bitterness and pain. The next few years saw his conversion to Roman Catholicism,[2] a considerable degree of healing, and the European training which lies at the root of his techniques.

Within months of his return to Toronto in 1959, there would be dramatic changes to his fortune. He met a prestigious dealer, was offered work as a framer, and had a solo show. That first exhibition at The Isaacs Gallery, in March of 1960, was an immediate success. By late 1962 Bill was established as a major Canadian painter and had married to begin his own family. In the last fifteen years of his life he painted literally thousands of paintings, achieving a degree of fame and popularity that very few have matched. It is curious that the period of "normalcy and success", as he called his last fifteen years, is given almost no room in his autobiography, even in the revisions that were written in his last years.

One of Bill's subtlest and perhaps unconscious creations is the myth of himself and his experience. *Someone With Me* is mainly concerned with his unhappy experience as a child and an adolescent; with his breakdown and hospitalization; with his religious search for and acquisition of faith. The first edition ends with his marriage and the briefest of summaries of his subsequent career in Toronto. It appears to have been written in 1962. In actual fact, his story underwent continual revisions until shortly before his death. The revisions, however, were not intended to update the story chronologically. We should ask why the portion of his life that appears to be the major one, the last eighteen years, which saw his rapid rise to fame, is ignored in fact but emphasized in theory, since the ultimate *success* of his artistic career was to him an important part of his myth.

In hospital, Bill described his problem as depression and depersonalization. He was at this time an extremely introverted, isolated personality, obsessed with his own problems and almost incapable of relating to others. His autobiography lays most of the blame for this condition on the father he both hated and adored. Dmytro Kurelek was a man whose own life had been harsh and difficult. He had survived the First World War as a child in the Ukraine, and he had weathered drought and depression in Western Canada in the thirties. He hoped to see his children achieve the security he had never enjoyed.

Tragic ironies in Bill's life include the fact that he was the first of seven children; that his younger brother John appeared to be everything in a son that Dmytro wanted and Bill was not; and that when Bill was twelve, the Second World War removed most hired men from Canadian farms. His father had to have help from his two sons. In these emergency conditions, Bill's mechanical ineptitude earned criticism which set going a vicious circle of fear and error. The symbiotic relationship between Dmytro and Bill was different from that between Dmytro and his other children: different, and very difficult.

Bill's religious faith restored his feeling of personal worth and led him into a community of caring individuals where his self-confidence began to grow. His *conscious* mythology was entirely God-centred. He credited God with his healing, and found in his Christian faith a reason for his previous suffering. He saw his painting as a God-given talent and a means to preach in the marketplace. He also saw himself as a kind of Jeremiah, although he never used this term. Firmly expecting both a coming Holocaust and a coming Heaven, he warned his audience of approaching cataclysm.

Bill's unconscious mythology reveals itself more subtly, culminating in a phrase near the end of his autobiography, "my comeback to normalcy and success". "Comeback" is a curious word, reminiscent of an athlete or an entertainer. Normalcy and success are not particularly Christian goals; indeed, the latter seems secular unless understood within a New Testament context of paradox and inversion, where a failure in the eyes of the world can be understood as success in the eyes of God. Bill's pride in achieving normalcy and success is the restored pride of an individual who has been told many times that he was abnormal and stupid, and that no one could earn a good living from painting. His psychological need to prove his father wrong and to win his admiration was a motivation that Bill understood less clearly than his Christian goals but that was operating powerfully in his life.[3] The need to succeed was also part of the immigrant experience and was thus inherited by Bill from his family's situation.[4]

The old wounds made success a necessity, one that was inextricably tied to a basic insecurity and a desperate desire to be the son his father wanted. Tragically, Bill never recognized that his own need to succeed as an artist and as his father's son was the mirror image of Dmytro's need to see his children acquire the education and security that fate had denied to him. To Bill, his father's drives were "materialistic", while his own were spiritual and therefore legitimate. He publicly condemned his father's ambition to see his children successful, but was passionately disappointed when Dmytro failed, for many years, to perceive that his son was a very successful artist. The irony was lost on Bill. There were blind spots in his view of his parents which a lifetime would prove too short to correct.[5]

His early years on the farm with his parents and the tortured climax of these years in England constitute the heart of his own story. In theory, his individual experience is important largely as exemplar. In practice, Bill found the infinite details of his personal experience to be of absorbing interest. He structures that experience as steps in the education of an artist, a portrait of the artist as a young man. He read James Joyce in his late teens, and was deeply impressed. Joyce's fiction and Van Gogh's life became secular icons in his imagination. Identifying with Joyce's Stephen Dedalus, Bill became proud of his poverty, his eccentricity, even his depression. This romantic and bohemian phase lasted till he was nearly thirty. In 1957, a magnificent self-portrait shows his new maturity and strength. It would subsequently grace the cover of the 1980 edition of his autobiography.

Self-portraits from Bill's teens and twenties depict him as a homeless wanderer on the road of life, leaning into the wind in a belted trench coat and "porkpie" hat, a touch he got (by his own admission) from an early Joseph Cotten film. From childhood he had a sense of being destined for great things. His stay in Netherne Hospital "seemed to be fated" in order that he should realize "the essential weakness and fragility of mankind". In a locked hospital ward he was touched for the first time with real pity for someone other than himself. Released from hospital, he met a sympathetic priest, "as if things were working out according to a hidden plan."

After Bill's conversion, theology transformed a secular, Joycean myth into a sacred one. Now Kurelek believed that God had permitted suffering so that good could come out of it. His suffering had broken his selfishness and pride, and had helped him to become a better artist. Now he could "start living" (A2 155). Ironically, the so-called "living" upon which he embarks after entering the Church, namely his successful Toronto years, is a period that seems to contain for him little or no autobiographical interest. Like the romantic myth where marriage is an end rather than a beginning ("and they lived happily ever after"), the act of religious commitment signified the end of the story. It completed the myth that structures the autobiography and that explained Kurelek to himself.[6] A vital part of that myth (in an almost Old Testament sense, where fat flocks reward the man of faith) is the attainment of success in his chosen career. At the end of the second edition, Bill describes himself as "a full, unqualified success", fulfilling and surpassing his parents' concept and ambition.

The Kurelek story has, in the phrase beloved by Hollywood, a cast of thousands. There are hundreds of people who knew and helped or were helped by the artist. The fascination of their stories and the reasons that drew them to the artist have become a part of the web. In the epic cast, starring roles belong to his dealer, two publishers, a Russian baroness devoted to the poor, and a British woman whom Bill credited with saving his life. Curious as it may seem to those who have approached the artist's life by way of his autobiography, his father remained the one who influenced him most and whose praise was always sought. The ambivalence felt by the artist in this relationship reveals itself only gradually, and cut to the bone. As we begin to understand it, we will begin to understand his father's son.

Bill was fortunate in having as his promoter a young dealer whose own star was rising just as fate brought them together in 1959. For his extraordinarily rapid rise to prominence in the 1960s and '70s, the artist was indebted in no small measure to the support of The Isaacs Gallery. In 1970, introducing a major Kurelek Retrospective at the Edmonton Art Gallery, Avrom Isaacs wrote of the feeling of a vast, sparsely populated land evoked by the strong lines of horizon and fences in Kurelek's western landscapes. His immigrant paintings stood alone in an area where little had been done save in documentary photography. As for his protest paintings, Isaacs described them as avant garde at a time when fashionable art was abstract and value-free. Such paintings had their own quality of abstraction in the way in which they dissected the surface into simple planes. Isaacs stressed that a unified vision underlies the entire work, no matter what the subject: "There is an intensity in his painting which converts all his work into a religious act."[7] That intensity suffused everything he touched.

His *oeuvre* consists of thousands of paintings, and a surprisingly large body of writing: fourteen books with brief texts accompanying his paintings, dozens of journals, texts to many of his individual paintings, and vast numbers of letters. His spelling is original and his syntax unsound, but a storyteller's gift and the intensity noted by Isaacs give life to his words as to his art. Novelist W. O. Mitchell found Bill remarkably ignorant of the craft of writing, while Isaacs called him a "gifted writer". The truth lies somewhere in between.

Bill cared nothing for words, save as a medium to convey meaning. He spoke as he wrote and wrote as he talked, in a colloquial idiom that reflects his rural background and the haste with which his words were set down. His diction is often unique, while his writing may induce laughter, irritation, admiration, and anger.[8] He was cavalier with regard to the facts of his own life, being unwilling to spend the time required to check. Time was a jealously guarded commodity assigned to his art. Thus dates and other facts in his autobiographical writings are often inaccurate. Some of the elegant simplicity in his published texts is due to professional editing.

Kurelek lived intensely and very fully a relatively short life span of fifty years. Occasionally his writings and talks are marred by self-pity or self-congratulation. But of the intensity of his suffering there can be no doubt. His difficulties in defining himself to himself and his father had many roots, but ethnicity remained a central strand. Had the circumstances of his home and the ambitions of his hard-pressed immigrant father been different, his life might have been infinitely easier. A less sensitive individual, a different individual, might well have suffered less in very similar circumstances. His writings and psychiatric drawings record the hell he endured for many years. He experienced his own passion, and could thus understand Christ's; having known both hatred and love, he could understand love the better. Part of his maturation involved the exploration of his roots, and his celebration of them.

The work was prodigious, the time very short. It was a heroic life, one filled with struggle and achievement, with loneliness and private modes of joy. The loneliness lay hidden, in the last twenty years, beneath a mask of sociability and family life.[9] He repeatedly observed in letters that very few people were interested in his projects or his experiences in executing them. The companionship sought in marriage had failed to meet his unrealistically high expectations. He told his publisher that only God understood him.

Why did he do three paintings a day, and glory in the tally? Why did he work seventeen-hour shifts? Kurelek himself called his work habits fanatical, obsessive. The motivation behind this punishing schedule is complex, rooted in a troubled childhood, an adult faith, and a continuing loneliness. After a painting trip, eager for comments, he would proudly display his new series in the living-room of a friend, or in his own basement. His paintings, saying eloquently what his lips could not, were his chief means of communication with other humans. Paintings were also a means of communication with God and Nature; they reflected his gratitude and awe in ways that were beyond words. Obviously he painted for money, and he painted to preach. He painted to define himself to himself as well as to the world at large. And for self-justification. Perhaps he painted to keep sane. Or to impress his father. His seventeen-hour stints may well have included an element of flagellation, especially when we remember that he lived and worked with frequent pain in his back and knees. These long work sessions gave him tremendous pride and satisfaction. *He could do it*. The power flowed from his brush and shouted his being aloud.[10]

In 1968, in the context of a discussion on building a bomb shelter, Kurelek considered the kind of death he would choose to die in peacetime. He chose cancer. Ironically, fumes from his paints may have induced tumors. In 1977, cancer claimed him.

2

The Family Story:
Kureleks and Huculaks

KURELEK'S LARGE PAINTING CALLED *PIOTR JAROSZ* (1977) CAPTURES SOME-thing of the loneliness and harshness of homesteading in Western Canada in the early decades of this century. It was common to walk sixty or eighty miles or more, simply because there was no transportation other than horse and wagon. Kurelek's settler walks on a straight road through a flat, treeless land under an immense sky. The colors are sombre, the vastness is awesome and intimidating. To reach his goal, the settler requires physical and spiritual stamina, extremes of courage and endurance. Since much of the life he has left behind in the Old Country was harsher, and what remained of value could be recovered only by re-creating it in a new land, the immigrant walks as he must: forward.

On both sides of the family, Bill's people came from the village of Borivtsi in the province of Bukovyna, a part of the Ukraine which is now Rumania.[1] His mother's father, Vasyl Huculak, came with his parents and five brothers and sisters to Canada in 1899. The Huculak family reached Halifax on May 9 and proceeded by Canadian Pacific Railway through Winnipeg and Calgary to Edmonton, Alberta.

Under the policies of Sir Clifford Sifton, Canadian immigration agents were very active in Eastern Europe between 1896 and 1914. Hardy peasants were considered well suited to breaking the virgin sod of Canada's western grasslands. The government offered newcomers one hundred and sixty acres of land (a quarter section) for the nominal sum of ten dollars. Homesteaders had to live on the land, and clear thirty acres of it within three years. In exchange, the Canadian West gained strong backs, more wheat for world markets, and a population that made the railway and national unity feasible. The immigrants gained an opportunity for prosperity and freedom such as they had never known in their original homelands. The artist's grand-father was part of the first great wave of Ukrainian immigration, while

9

his father belonged to the second wave after the First World War when young survivors turned their faces to the West. Dmytro would live to see the Ukrainian population of 150,000 (in 1923) more than triple, and become the fourth-largest ethnic group in Canada's mosaic.[2]

Vasyl, the Huculaks' oldest son, was eighteen when the family emigrated to Canada. Maria Fedorak, who would become his bride five years later, was twelve at the time, the oldest of eight children. The Fedorak family left Borivtsi at the same time as the Huculaks. They travelled on the same ship to Halifax, and on the same train to Edmonton. With the other settlers from Borivtsi, they reached Vostok by wagon. Vasyl lived with his parents for a short time, then filed on an adjoining quarter for himself. Maria's family sheltered briefly with neighbors, then took up a homestead two miles south of the North Saskatchewan River at Kahwin. In 1904, Vasyl and Maria were married in the Russo-Greek Orthodox church in Vostok, and began farming Vasyl's homestead between Shandro and Whitford some seventy-five miles east of Edmonton.

The pioneers' experience must have become very compelling in the artist's imagination, for he painted it many times. The first three scenes of *Ukrainian Pioneer*, a magnificent series of six large paintings which now hangs in Canada's Parliament Buildings, show the poverty and cruelty of an East European police state; the hope and excitement of settlers aboard an immigrant ship approaching Halifax; and "journey's end", or the new start. A sea of trees confronts a huddled family with pitifully few belongings and primitive tools, while an agent gestures, "It's yours. Go to it, and make something of it." Kurelek describes his paintings:

> The dark night in the Ukraine in the first panel symbolizes the rather hopeless lot of the Ukrainian peasantry at the turn of the last century. This plight set in motion the mass emigration to new lands. The Ukraine was a foreign-occupied, parcelled-out country, and the agricultural and social development failed to keep pace with the material and spiritual needs of the people. I have represented the poverty by the child running barefoot into the snow to beg for victuals from more well-to-do neighbours, and the oppression by the gendarmes taking away a rebellious peasant. ... The overcrowding is symbolized by the closely packed village houses.
>
> ... The first physical ordeal was the crossing of the Atlantic. He and his family had to cope with sea-sickness, home-sickness, strange food and a strange language—all new experiences.

... I have deliberately placed the family group in the
dead centre of the panel in order to emphasize the magnitude of the task facing their muscles, their intelligence
and their hearts. And the isolation![3]

Kurelek's maternal grandparents were remarkable people. If their
hardships were typical, their success was exemplary. Vasyl's story
reads like a melodrama, larger than life. In the 1920s he became
wealthy beyond his wildest dreams; he lost that wealth in the 1930s,
but by the time of his death in 1946 he had recovered much of the loss.
If he and his son-in-law Dmytro were incompatible, it was probably
because they were very alike: strong men, with the weakness of the
strong; men who could be ruthless and generous; proud, stubborn
men who brooked no opposition to their plans.

Vasyl and Maria wrestled with the full pioneer experience of turning
virgin sod into productive farmland. There were long periods when
the husband was working on the railway for cash while the wife tended
both farm and home. Like Piotr Jarosz, Vasyl once walked hundreds of
miles from southern Alberta when work was stopped because of a
strike. He had no choice but to walk from Edmonton, as the CNR was
not built through Vegreville until 1905. Pay was a dollar a day, with no
work and no pay during rainy days or strikes. After earning two
hundred dollars, Vasyl concentrated on clearing his own land.

The Huculak
brothers pause
during the
threshing, 1946.

Farming improvements chart the passage of their married years, with Vasyl in the forefront of technological advance. In 1904 he bought his first team of horses and replaced the hand flail with a circular thresher operated by horses. Around 1912 he bought a steam threshing outfit. Between 1908 and 1924 he acquired nine more quarters of land, breaking acre after acre of brush with the help of cheap immigrant labor. In 1913 he built a modern house and barn, the white farmhouse that would impress Dmytro as "palatial" when he arrived from the Ukraine in 1923. Bill's grandparents farmed in the Shandro area for over forty years, and raised eleven children, seven sons and four daughters. They were the extended family, ten Huculak aunts and uncles, whom Bill would rediscover with pleasure on his frequent painting trips in the West in the 1960s and '70s.

Vasyl and Maria's firstborn, Mary, named after her mother, would work like a man and suffer like a woman. Her own firstborn would cause her deep grief and great joy as he began to find success through his artistic dreams and to slowly resolve the deeply ambiguous feelings he had for his parents. No one who sees the Kurelek documentary film called *The Maze* can fail to be moved by Mary's sensitivity and by her suffering because she thought she had somehow failed her son. Her understanding of child care had naturally been formed by her own background. Yet Will's needs were unusual and his demands on his mother's time and strength were endless.

Grandmother Maria could neither read nor write, her parents having been too poor in the Ukraine for her to attend school. In Alberta, she had no labor-saving devices in her log home, and few enough in the frame one after 1913. Hand-dug wells provided drinking water; firewood heated stove and house. Besides caring for her children, Maria helped to clear the land, keeping babies and toddlers near by as she worked. Once she drove off a hawk that was attacking her baby. She had to feed not only her large family but also the hired help, who often numbered four or five. Harvest time meant the daily feeding of a threshing gang of fifteen or more for two or three weeks. Her family remember her as a superb cook, especially of soups and roasts.[4] Her son Peter recalls that electrical power did not reach the area until 1946 and that two massive bakings a week in the outdoor *pich* or Ukrainian oven were sometimes insufficient. Social gatherings meant more cooking for the women as the settlers gathered at weddings and christenings to sing songs and talk endlessly of the old days in the Homeland.

Mary Huculak's life before her marriage to Dmytro had been very like her mother's. Before and after marriage, life consisted largely of work. Her brothers and sisters describe Mary as "always busy: cooking, helping with the chores, feeding chickens, cows, pigs, stooking in the field. She was jack of all trades on the farm."[5] Mary herself remembers harrowing as the most difficult task in the field: "Your shoes hurt you, so I'd go barefoot sometimes, but there were stones, thorns, sticks."[6] When Mary was thirteen, her father offered to send her to high school. This, however, would have meant boarding in Edmonton with strangers, a frightening prospect to a young farm girl to whom the city seemed "foreign and threatening".

Mary's choosing to stay on the farm meant that she had to drop out of school before completing grade eight, and assume a man's role on the farm. One of her chores was to help her father shoe his own horses. Her other activities included shovelling grain, driving teams of horses, and taking charge of the horse-drawn loads on their way to the railway at Mundare in winter. The two-day journey included crossing the frozen North Saskatchewan River. Mary stayed overnight, with her father and the hired man, in a dormitory full of strange men: "When Father said you go, you go!" The weather could be thirty or fifty degrees below freezing. The artist's winter landscape *Hauling Grain*, which shows three horse-drawn box-sleighs being led by their drivers up the steep embankment of the North Saskatchewan, celebrates the work done by his grandfather and by his mother during her teens, as well as by his father in 1923-24.

Mary was sixteen when Dmytro Kurelek arrived to live and work at her father's farm early in 1923, and not quite nineteen when they married in the summer of 1925. Arranged marriages were common in the Ukraine but uncommon among Ukrainians in Canada. By all accounts, theirs was a love match.[7] For Mary, it was the beginning of a second pioneering struggle as harsh as the one she had lived through as the oldest child of Vasyl and Maria. By 1925, her father was comparatively wealthy, but the struggles of the newly married couple were just beginning.[8]

On the other side of the family, the artist's father descended from a Vasyl Kurelek, one of the "free people" on the steppes who called themselves Cossacks. After this military order had been destroyed in the late eighteenth century by the empress Catherine the Great of Russia, Kurelek had made his way west to the fledgling village of Borivtsi and built a house in a wooded valley. This legendary ancestor later survived Turkish attacks partly by his fighting skill and strength and partly thanks to a secret tunnel built beneath his house.

Vasyl Kurelek's great-grandson Dmytro married Agaphia Huculak and sired five children.[9] The oldest son, Ivan, inherited the major part of the small family farm; the second, the artist's father Dmytro, emigrated to Canada in 1923; the third, Georg, emigrated in 1937, staying

13

for a season with his brother and sister-in-law in Stonewall before moving on to farm in the Peace River country. Dmytro never mentioned his sisters, fought with his brothers, and cut all ties with his parents when he left the Ukraine at the age of nineteen. A proud and solitary man, he was sensitive and easily offended. He was also strong, and ambitious. Seeing what his father-in-law had accomplished in little more than two decades, Dmytro set similar goals for himself.

Dmytro's parents had hotly opposed his decision to emigrate. The youth, however, had experienced the carnage of war fought in his own country, and witnessed the resulting breakdown of order and morality. Besides the lure of owning land, he wanted to evade peacetime conscription into the Rumanian army. When he remained adamant, his father arranged for a sponsor: Vasyl Huculak. Dmytro's son William would later paint the family parting in Borivtsi, showing an angry father, arms akimbo, and a grief-stricken mother in front of a thatched Ukrainian farmhouse. Later, the legend wove its way into the autobiography, with Dmytro arriving at the Huculak farm with a few dollars and a small wooden suitcase: "Father was nineteen and his suitcase was light but he brought with him a heavy load of bitterness and suspicion from the troubled conditions of Central Europe" (A2 36; cf. 139). Dmytro worked for Vasyl till November to repay his passage, then stayed on for regular wages of twenty-five dollars a month. By that time, he and Mary were in love.

Their wedding in June of 1925 was a three-day gala affair with a dancing platform built beside the Huculak farmhouse—similar to the Polish scene their son would paint half a century later.[10] The platform was edged with green poplar branches to help cut the strong prairie wind. The farmyard was lined with the cars and buggies, democrats and wagons of the family's many friends. The orchestra included Ukrainian instruments such as the bandura, a kind of lute, for the waltzes and the *hutzulka*, a fast polka from the Carpathian Mountain area.

Mary, her head covered with flowers and ribbons, had chosen an ankle-length brown silk dress which she could wear again. Bridal photographs show a pretty, round-faced girl with two bridesmaids. The ceremony was in St. Mary's, the Russo-Greek Orthodox church at Shandro. Among the special Ukrainian customs followed that day was "stopping at the gate". The couple had to bribe the young men who were blocking their way with gifts of wine, whisky, or money before they were allowed to pass. After two days of celebration, the dowry was loaded onto a wagon and the couple climbed in with their belongings and drove off to their own quarter section: "There in a shacky little house they spent their first night, and were at work next day on the

(Left) Dmytro and Mary Kurelek on their wedding day, 1925.

(Below) House built by Dmytro Kurelek in the autumn of 1927 on his second quarter, near Whitford, Alberta. The property is now part of William Huculak's farm.

land" (A1 12). The artist's sketch of the scene shows the couple turning towards one another in the wagon, perhaps for the first time aware of a new interdependency amid a nearly empty landscape.

Dmytro's first quarter section lay four miles northeast of Whitford. The railway reached the village in 1927, and the grain elevators followed, so that the laborious hauling of grain to Mundare and Bellis became a thing of the past. Dmytro's rich black soil, sloping down to Cucumber Lake, was edged with woods and a little ravine. It was fine land for growing wheat, the principal crop. (Dmytro's dairy business would come later, in Manitoba.) Willows and poplars were indigenous to the region, and the spruce, pine, and tamarack planted near farmhouses in the area thrived. The land was a gift, part of Mary's dowry, but the tiny cabin in which she and Dmytro began their married life was a loan, and their first horses were bought from Vasyl. Dmytro soon became dissatisfied with his quarter, for reasons that are not clear, and exchanged it for another quarter section. The latter, also four miles from Whitford, lay to the northwest.[11] The Kureleks worked their new quarter in 1927. After the harvest, Dmytro built a two-room house.

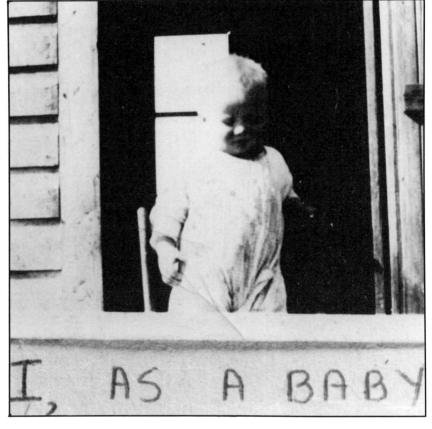

Bill as a baby. The handwriting is Bill's own.

I, AS A BABY

The artist's version of his birth owes more to his father's memories than to his mother's, and a good story was considerably more important to Dmytro than was historical accuracy.[12] But by the 1970s Bill had learned from his Uncle Peter that the midwife who had assisted his mother was his godmother, Wasylyna Hawrelak. A legless Indian herbalist had been brought in later to help with Mary's after-birth complications. Dmytro was away at the time. Mary's mother, whose tenth child was then only three months old, had sent her teenaged son Peter to check on his sister. In his haste to bring help, Peter took a short cut and got lost in the dark fields before he returned with the midwife. Thus the great-great-great-grandson of Vasyl Kurelek entered the world in a one-room shack in northern Alberta, and assumed the name of his Cossack ancestor. His battles would be different, but no less fierce.

The early years of their marriage were difficult ones for Mary and Dmytro, despite their start on a cleared quarter section. Bill writes of a mysterious stomach ailment that afflicted his father for the entire summer of 1928, when Mary was pregnant with John. Mary worked the land alone, while Dmytro kept an eye on their year-old son from his sickbed. A 1964 painting, *Illness*, shows a haggard man lying on an iron bedstead with a toddler playing on the dirt floor beside him. Through the open doorway a young woman can be seen ploughing. The contrasts of youth and age, health and illness, are symbolically underlined by the chickens pecking outside the door beside a blood-spattered chopping block. Dmytro had his appendix removed in Edmonton, but the pains continued until a doctor in Vegreville finally located the real problem.

Tales of Dmytro's harsh experiences became a part of Kurelek family history on which their oldest son would reflect and moralize:

> These and other natural calamities made my father all the
> more bitter and desperate, for he was trying to prove to
> mother's family as well as his own people back in the old
> country that he could become a successful big-time
> farmer. I tell the reader this not to justify my father's
> ambitiousness, but rather to make more understandable
> the harshness with which he treated me in later
> years—the years of the big Depression. (A1 14)

While Mary and her husband struggled with illness and a young family, her father's star was rising. The 1920s were boom years for Vasyl,[13] who had been quick to see the advantages of electricity and by 1928 had replaced all of his horses with machinery. When the CPR built the railway through his area in 1928, he borrowed heavily and built the New Willingdon Hotel, the most modern on the line. Its construction cost between forty and forty-five thousand dollars.

At the peak of his prosperity in 1928-29, Vasyl rented out all his land. He was now a power to be reckoned with in Shandro. Barred by his broken English from seeking political power directly, he acquired it indirectly, becoming a king-maker and exerting substantial influence on the election of provincial candidates as well as councillors and school trustees. A shrewd and convivial man, Vasyl was politically astute by nature. His politics changed as his fortune declined. He became less conservative and more socialist as the economic times worsened. In 1932, the year he lost his hotel, he joined the new CCF party, the Co-operative Commonwealth Federation. He was always antagonistic to communism, represented locally by the Ukrainian Labour-Farmer Temple Association. Vasyl plotted the disruption of communist meetings; his henchmen brought eggs and tomatoes to throw at the speakers, disconnected their lights, and shouted, "Go back to the Ukraine." The RCMP, who were friendly with Vasyl, turned a blind eye to this political harassment of the communist speakers.

Vasyl was a gifted leader but he had little aptitude for machinery, despite his early acquisition of farm machines and, from 1919 on, a succession of McLaughlin-Buicks. He drove his cars as hard as he drove himself and his family. When a gearshift once proved intractable, he broke it. Overhearing the comment that his car had "stood a lot", he quipped, "No, I have."

The Wall Street crash of September 1929 ruined many Canadian farmers, drastically depressing the prices of wheat and other agricultural products. Vasyl was carrying heavy mortgages. Unable to meet his obligations, he was forced to sell the Willingdon hotel in 1932—at a twenty-thousand-dollar loss—and live on the meagre income from his farm. Peter Huculak believes that had Vasyl built a smaller, cheaper hotel in 1928 he would have made money on it despite the Depression: "The other farmers lost money through mismanagement, but Father lost through ambition and a dream—a dream of a great hotel!"[14] While Vasyl dreamt of a luxury hotel, Dmytro's ambitions centred on producing successful professional sons. His first-born would prove a dreamer in the grand manner, but, unfortunately for Dmytro, becoming a doctor, lawyer, or teacher played no part in Bill's dreams.

Between 1930 and 1938, Vasyl's Huron and Erie mortgage grew from ten to thirty-five thousand dollars, while the price of wheat dropped to eighteen cents a bushel and less. Vasyl had mortgaged his land in an attempt to save the hotel. He was saved from ruin by the renewal of his mortgage for seventeen years. As things turned out, he was able to clear the debt in five years when grain prices recovered during the Second World War. His financial recovery, however, came

Bill's maternal grand-
parents, Maria and
Vasyl Huculak, near
Whitford, c. 1930.

too late to help Dmytro and Mary during their own most difficult years;
and Vasyl's financial losses played a major part in his son-in-law's
decision to move to Manitoba. Family members agree that there was
little love lost between the two men. The rupture between these two
hard-driving, strong-willed characters might well have been inevitable
at some point.

Impressions of Vasyl held by surviving members of his large family
are intriguing for what they tell us of Ukrainian culture and also
of an exceptional individual. If the artist's maternal grandfather and
his father were typical males in a culture that vested authority in its
men, we can appreciate Dmytro's expectations for his sons and see
how poorly Bill fitted the pattern. Vasyl was described as a stern, proud
man, a hard worker, "harsh", "a rough character". Neighborhood
youngsters were afraid of him, and his own children kept their distance. William and Peter marvelled that their youngest sister, Helen,
dared to sit on his knee and hug him. Perhaps Vasyl had mellowed by
the 1930s.[15] (The tenderness in his relation to Helen affords a curious
parallel with Dmytro's relation to Nancy, born nearly ten years after
her brother Bill—a tenderness Bill craved, and never experienced
from his father.) Vasyl's oldest daughter, Mary, called him an honest,
hard-working man, rather strict; to her sister Helen she confided that
Father was "mean" at times. His grandson Bill remembered "a blunt,
loud-voiced man" who drove a car, owned a hotel, and "rubbed my
father the wrong way" (A2 37-38).

The friction worsened in the early 1930s as financial pressures tightened on both men. Dmytro had been renting a second cleared quarter from Vasyl, to work along with the land that Mary had received as dowry. When Dmytro was unable to pay the rent on the second quarter, Vasyl promptly repossessed the land; worse, he placed a mortgage on the first quarter, his wedding gift, in return for money owed to him by Dmytro for machinery.[16] Torn, Mary felt the pressures on both men. Her father's debts drove him to sell the hotel at a great loss. Her husband's drove him to sell his mortgaged quarter the following year and move his family to Manitoba early in 1934, without telling his in-laws. By 1933, both men had their backs to the wall. They were in good company, as the Depression tightened its grip on the farmers of Western Canada.

Bill's memories of his Alberta days are disconnected and relatively shallow in emotional depth. It was Stonewall in Manitoba that later claimed his heart and filled his canvases with the rich experiences of a dozen years. His Alberta memories surface like the details of larger paintings: frozen stems of cabbages emerging from snow; the smell of sauerkraut; the yellow-green of urine cutting a canyon through the snow by the door; all-day socials for entire families; calendar icons on Grandmother's walls; the all-night vigils of Ukrainian Easters; and the mixed emotions of Ukrainian wakes: "In this memory I see these old country women (babeh) singing round a table loaded with food. In the next room is a profusely decorated, beflowered open coffin surrounded by burning candles. Behind that, in the corner stands a giant gilded Byzantine cross reflecting the flicker of the candle flames" (A1 24). He recalled bathing with John in a tin tub on the grass, and watching the outdoor bake oven in operation.

His grandmother's great white farmhouse with its five upstairs bedrooms was a delightful place to play, as were Grandfather's sheds and barns. There was a pleasant turmoil in the constant comings and goings of a large family. Several of his uncles were approximately his age, and an aunt was three years younger.[17] "Baba's place" is recalled nostalgically in a letter from England in the late 1950s prompted by his brother's recent travels to the old homesteads in Manitoba and Alberta. Bill remembered a trapdoor in the floor, a mysterious source of sealers of preserves and pickles; and a strong grandmother with "a will like iron" who bossed her children with unquestioned authority.[18]

Bill writes of the humor and earthiness of his Ukrainian community, and of the joy and peace of their visits to his grandparents' house:

> There were those wonderful mornings when we'd wake
> up to find that an uncle or grandfather who'd come from

20

town that evening had brought us toys or candies. We were awed too by the size of the house, by the farm with its many beef cattle, by the telephone (a luxury in those days), by grandfather's automobile. In the meat room, a cold room off the kitchen, hung a calendar with a reproduction of an old painting of a naval battle. I mention this because it was the very first inkling of my interest in paintings. I believe the very first sign of my interest in the actual production of art came at grandmother's too. (A1 26)

That first artistic interest consisted of the fascinating discovery that steps could be depicted by lines alone, and that perspective could be deceptive and ambiguous.

Bill's memories of Alberta, as reflected in his autobiography, letters, and paintings, appear to be basically pleasant ones. We might call them idyllic, were it not for the hallucinations he describes plaguing his nights as a small boy with visions of devouring monsters. Meanwhile his father seethed with resentments and insecurities, fears which his son would never really understand but perhaps subconsciously recognized. Dmytro now had two more children, Ivan (John), who had been born late in 1928, and Vasylyna (Win), born early in 1930. The bitterness of his break with his family in the Ukraine, the evident success of his father-in-law (who had emerged from extreme poverty in Borivtsi), and Dmytro's own proud, stubborn nature all made it imperative that he succeed in Canada. Bill's own overwhelming need for success was directly related to his father's similar drive. The intensity in Dmytro's nature matched the intensity evident in his son's life and in his art. Perhaps Dmytro's tragedy was his failure to find something other than himself and his family to which he could have devoted his idealism, energy, and ambition.

Bill wrote of the bitterness his father brought from Europe. This impression had been gathered from Dmytro's tales told over the years to a succession of hired men. But perhaps the bitterest could not be voiced to hired men or children: memories of Dmytro's family farm, now lost forever; of the final rupture with his father on the railway platform; of his older brother's betrayal. In Borivtsi, the Kureleks had twenty-seven *morgs* or fifty-four acres (roughly one-third of a Canadian quarter section). Much of it was let out to tenant farmers who worked small sections, ploughed and harrowed by Kurelek, in return for one-third of the crop. Up to the very moment of parting, Dmytro's father had continued to urge his favorite son to remain. When the father saw that the son was adamant, he said, "Go, and don't come back." Dmytro never saw him again. His older brother Ivan had promised (so Dmytro's story goes) to follow him to Canada within a year. If things were good he would stay, and Dmytro would share in the sale of their father's farm; if not, the brothers would return together to the Ukraine. When Dmytro wrote, some eighteen months after emigration, to say that he was going to marry a Canadian girl, Ivan replied that Dmytro had broken their bargain. Ivan's refusal to emigrate ("I've got my Canada here") meant the end of Dmytro's hope of any inheritance from his father.[19]

Dmytro Kurelek's family describe him as pessimistic by nature, a man addicted to melancholy. When I interviewed him in the fall of 1981 (shortly before his unexpected death of a heart attack), Dmytro's impressive strength was marred by a strain of self-pity. He resented the fate that had robbed him of an education, dogged his efforts with bad luck, and finally dealt him the unconscionable blows of old age and ill health. His first tale, which was both a defence of and an apology for his life, was a story of the arrival of Russian soldiers in his village at the start of the First World War. Dmytro was nine. He had had three years of primary education, which would prove to be all the formal schooling he would ever receive. The Russians took over the school as their barracks, throwing the books on the road; the building was left an empty, gutted shell. After the war, Dmytro was too old for school, and too busy. He was already doing a man's work on his father's farm. In the years to come, in a foreign land and surrounded by a foreign tongue, in a culture that emphasized education, he could not help reflecting upon it. He had indeed been cheated by fate.

The two-room house that Dmytro had built in the fall of 1927 had burnt to the ground in the early 1930s. Dmytro had rebuilt it exactly, as required by the terms of his insurance.[20] To young William, the fire meant several things, some good and some bad. The hallucinations that had terrorized his nights ceased with the flames. John had never seen the frightful creatures of Bill's hallucinations, but Win had suffered with him. His parents laughed when he spoke of them:

> My sister too saw the monsters. One was a lynx-sized cat
> clawing at the underside of our crib. Another was a gigan-
> tic grey rubber hose in the shape of a rocker. It had a
> black sheet draped over one end and kept rocking back
> and forth on the bench under our window. Most frighten-
> ing by far, though, was the huge turkey vulture that
> wanted to get at me and peck my eyes out. ... I distinctly
> felt the imprint of its feet. ... When the new house was
> built on the old foundation the creatures no longer visited
> me. (A2 40-41)

Less happily, the fire destroyed family photographs of Mary and Dmytro's wedding, of their parents, of themselves in youth. And perhaps it also destroyed his hard-pressed parents' faith: "Gone too were the religious calendars from which I had acquired anthropomorphic concepts of God and heaven. I gather Mother and Father had believed and even prayed on their knees after their marriage. Now even these vestiges of faith had been, as it were, consumed in the blaze. Never again, was I to see an icon grace their living-room walls—not in Alberta or Manitoba or Ontario." (A2 42)

By 1933, Dmytro was facing the complete loss of eight years' work. With a mortgage on his land, he found that grain prices were totally inadequate to meet the family's needs. Dmytro was in touch with his cousin who had emigrated to Manitoba before the war. John Budjak's mother was Dmytro's Aunt Maritsa, his father's sister. Budjak had told Dmytro of a large property for sale near his farm at Stonewall, some twenty miles north of Winnipeg. It was six hundred acres, just forty short of a whole section or one square mile (A1 34). Drawing on the same courage and initiative that had led him to emigrate from the Old World, Dmytro slipped secretly away to Manitoba, liked what he saw, and purchased the Kern farm for a five-hundred-dollar down payment. The farm was valued at twelve thousand dollars, and a payment of two thousand was due in 1934. Only low Depression prices had enabled Dmytro to obtain such a large spread for this low down payment. He suspected that the owner, a Swiss immigrant and retired dairy farmer, may have expected to recover the farm when Dmytro defaulted on payments, but Ernest Kern was to prove more than reasonable in the trials that followed. With the sale of livestock in Shandro for seven hundred dollars, there was two hundred dollars left for the first seed.[21]

The move from Alberta was mysterious to Bill and his siblings, not only in 1934 but in the years that followed. "Why were we children warned not to tell anyone we were leaving? Why did none of Mother's family see us off?" (A2 45) Bill's chief memories of the move were of a train seen for the first time at close quarters, of cruelly hard varnished wickerwork seats, and of a streetcar journey from Winnipeg to Stonewall.

His first sight of "Father's new kingdom" was in the dark. Years later, long after the property had been sold and the Kureleks had moved to Ontario, Stonewall would become peculiarly Bill's own kingdom, in his heart's core and through a thousand paintings which would celebrate its rich black soil and fecund immigrant culture. The emotional pain which was to be Bill's inheritance in this place would prove an essential ingredient in the artistic genius nurtured here. The move eastward was also a move into Canada's heartland and its historically dominant Anglo-Saxon culture, where to be Ukrainian was to be different. For the budding artist, it would prove a land of promise, and a land of pain.

The Stonewall farm, just
north of Winnipeg, to
which the Kurelek family
moved in 1934.

3

Stonewall:
The Crucial Years, 1934-46

WHAT DID STONEWALL MEAN TO BILL KURELEK? HALF PLEASURE AND HALF
pain, the Stonewall years were a fiery crucible of experience which
fuelled his emotions and his art throughout the remainder of his life.
The one-room public school was his introduction not only to learning
and to art but also to evil: school bullies taught the small, sensitive boy
lessons in sadism which he found deeply shocking. A mysterious spring
east of the farm, along with the entire country landscape and the
seasons' cycle, fed a feeling for natural beauty which was deep, even
mystical. Farm chores and the routines of a rural Ukrainian household
filled the senses and emotions with a thousand tactile experiences.
Stonewall represented a pre-modern existence which Bill would later
idealize, research, and re-create in his art.

But Stonewall was also the place and the time when, having failed to
meet his beloved father's expectations, Bill was humiliated and
belittled by him, till his sense of self was completely eroded and he
took refuge in silence and anonymity. When Bill, self-exiled to England
in the 1950s, painted himself returning home, his deeply symbolic
return was set not at the Vinemount farm in Ontario where his parents
had lived since 1949, but in the long lane at Stonewall. Stonewall was
home and belonging and roots. Stonewall was simultaneously an emotional wound which would never be fully healed during Bill's lifetime
but which religious faith had made bearable. Out of this deep ambivalence came some of his intensity, and a great deal of his art.

"Father's new kingdom" lay just north of Winnipeg, on the east side of
Highway 7. Today it is a short ride by car; in the thirties it was a day's
expedition by horse or car on the narrow gravel road. Victoria Public
School, long since dismantled, lay one mile north of the farm, on the
other side of the road, whose deep ditches handled the spring run-off.

25

The soil is black and the land flat, marked by the straight lines of roads and fences and growing crops. Big-sky country. Driving through it today, you feel as if you are entering a series of Kurelek paintings, so strongly has the artist caught not only the appearance of the area but its atmosphere. Stonewall was ideal country for dairying. East of the Kurelek farm, bog-land provided wild hay and free pasture. The nearby city meant a large market for dairy products and reasonable shipping costs. Dmytro turned to dairying after four years, having failed to survive by wheat alone.

To the three children, the buildings looked as enormous as Vasyl's empire at Shandro had seemed to Dmytro in 1923. The exhibition announcement for Kurelek's "Nature, Poor Stepdame" series (1970) shows the farmyard better than any camera: the big barn, chicken coop, and milkhouse in moonlight, mute witnesses to human presence in a scene dominated by open space and mystery. Bill writes: "It seemed like a quarter mile between the house and barn. All the buildings—the garage, small chicken coop, big chicken coop, big barn, milkhouse, small barn, pigpen, granary and last but not least the palatial three-story farmhouse were strung loosely round that huge open area. It took a good shout to be heard from one building to an opposite one." (A1 33) On their first morning there, the children explored the barn with its stalls for sixty cows, the enormous hayloft, the discarded treasures in the cupboards of the fifteen-room house, the full basement (a great novelty), and the kitchen water-pump, a luxury that delighted Mary. There was even electric wiring, the ends protruding from the walls in anticipation of the day when power lines would come to the area.

Bill's first autobiography devotes roughly one hundred and fifty pages to the Stonewall years; in the second edition, these have been edited down to thirty. These thirty pages are dominated by the traumas induced by local bullies and by Dmytro's mocking scorn, the relationship of father and son as it appeared to the demoralized son. There is far more of the joy of these years in the original *Someone With Me*, the joy that would find its way into paintings thirty and forty years later. Yet, even in the first edition, Bill introduces Stonewall as "the second big but unhappy chapter of my life" (A1 31).

Bill calls his first few months at school "the most traumatic experience of my pre-adult life" (A2 48). One assumes a degree of hyperbole in this strange statement, given the emphasis that follows on numerous painful exchanges with his father. Years later, however, Bill would emphasize to his British doctors the wounds inflicted at school, so those hurts should perhaps be given co-billing among the sources of his traumas. To the boy who would later understand and admit that he had been "a hyper-sensitive personality all along" (A2 51), it was simply incredible that one human being could treat another in such a heartless fashion: "Humiliation . . . gives physical pain a crueller twist. I discovered that there is a heartless mob streak in human nature that sees a fight, any fight, no matter how unequal, as an amusement." (A2 51)

Humiliation came in several forms. The first was language. The Kureleks spoke Ukrainian at home, since Dmytro had not mastered English. Bill and John, who began school together in March of 1934, discovered that there was a taboo on any language but English in the public school. Although the Kurelek children spoke no English prior to starting school, they learned rapidly and could manage by fall. Bill would eventually "love" learning English, but the first few weeks were inevitably painful. Decades later, Bill remembered the disapproval that greeted his exclamation of "Mookha! Mookha!" (Ukrainian for "fly"), and he credited the incident with inhibiting his enthusiasm for oral expression. English was the mother tongue of roughly half the students. School authorities naturally believed that immigrants should learn the language of their adopted country. Moreover, English was the *lingua franca* among the Slavic, German, and Mennonite peoples who made up the community's other half.

If language problems were bad, bullying was worse. Small, timid boys were singled out by most of the older boys for teasing, and harsher measures. Thin ice on the ditches provided one opportunity: "with barely concealed expressions of delight these fellows would half-persuade, half-force John and me and other little greenhorns out onto that ice to test it. Sooner or later we'd all break through and have to be taken, soaking wet and cold, into the schoolroom where the teacher had to undress us and dry off our underwear behind the stove." (A2 50) Gleeful when Bill and John became mired in mud in an effort to escape, bullies of both sexes attacked them with words and blows. Mary went to the school to complain. The teacher announced that the Kureleks were not to be bullied, but of course the respite was short-lived. The very sight of unequal fights were as painful to Bill as being a combatant: "Not once did I see anyone break the social code and comfort the vanquished in his humiliation" (A2 51). In 1953 Bill would paint the guilt he had felt for failing to help his brother on one such occasion.

In Bill's writings about his schooldays, the word "humiliation" occurs frequently, as do references to growing feelings of inferiority. He felt that his inferiority was proved whenever he dared to stand up to his tormentors; defending himself was useless: "there was no way out except to wait" (A2 53). Bill concealed his aggressive feelings. He seethed silently, playing the hero in an inner fantasy life. Only once did he erupt, attacking an older girl who was a skilled tormentor. He scarred the bully's cheek, and found things subsequently easier for the three Kurelek children.[1] These female bullies may well have colored his attitude to women for years to come.

Even scholastic defeats were termed humiliations. Bill turned to schoolwork as an area in which he might excel. He writes of a friendship and intense scholastic rivalry with John Giesbrecht, the son of a Mennonite farmer-preacher. The Giesbrechts lived in Manitoba from 1924 to 1937. For two years John and Bill shared a school desk. With an average of ninety, Bill was consistently at the top of his class throughout his nine years at Victoria School. Just once was he displaced by his Mennonite friend, at mid-term: "I am tongue-tied with disbelief. That night I swear an oath on the private altar of scholastic superiority: 'Never, never again this humiliation!' I did pull back into first place in June." (A2 54) The melodramatic phrasing indicates the intensity of the need to succeed. The more he failed in his father's eyes, the greater grew his need for success in other areas.

The two boys' rivalry extended into drawing. Bill recalls a particular challenge, a competition to draw the best train. Both boys claimed victory, but the real significance for Bill was his own recognition that he could draw, and draw well: "considering my many early failures and feelings of inadequacy, it hardly needs a Sigmund Freud to understand why I later developed an almost excessive creative drive" (A2 55). The two rediscovered each other in the 1960s, when Bill told Giesbrecht that he had been the cause of his earliest recognition of his talent: "Bill said he glanced at my sketch and from that point on he knew that on a comparative basis he had the edge."[2]

Giesbrecht's earliest memories of the Kurelek family are pre-school. He accompanied his father to the Kureleks' to have grain custom-ground for hog feed. The farmstead was large and imposing to visitors; it, and the grain-grinding machine, set the Kureleks above their neighbors economically. Since Giesbrecht's parents had experienced war, famine, and dispossession under Russian rule, they were leery of Slavic peoples and did not encourage contacts through their children. The climate, the distance between farms, and, above all, the chores which kept the children busy after school and on weekends also did not favor friendships. Moreover, Dmytro discouraged his children from bringing friends home. Bill seems to have spent his childhood without close friends. The friendly rivalry with Giesbrecht was as near to intimacy as he came, so his closest contacts through these growing years were with parents and siblings: John, Win, and Nancy, who was born in 1936.

In a long memoir written in 1983, Giesbrecht recalls that friendship, and the atmosphere of the one-room public school, a type that was common in rural Canada prior to the Second World War:

> It was a one-room frame building covered with wooden siding painted white, with a row of windows on the north side. ... In winter it was already dusk outside at 3 o'clock, and almost dark inside. At the back of the schoolroom was a large horizontal cylindrical steel stove with a metal skirt built around it on which we could dry our wet mittens, socks and occasionally pants. This was stoked with poplar logs 4 feet long cut from the bush the previous year and stacked up behind the school. The desks in all the junior grades were doubles and thus I happened to share a desk with William. ...
>
> The games we played at recess and noon hour ranged from drowning out gophers in spring for the government bounty of 1 cent per gopher tail, to snaring rabbits in winter in the adjoining bush. In between it was building forts with the cordwood already piled for fuel, and of course the usual playground games. Both William and I were of rather slight physical stature and thus were certainly not the first chosen for games of scrub baseball or other body contact sports.
>
> Each of us, representing one of the recent immigrant groups at school (in his case Ukrainian, in my case Mennonite), had to contend with a certain amount of ostracism from the mainstream Anglo-Saxons who were dominant, if not always in numbers then certainly in rank. This provided some commonality of feelings between William, John, and myself.
>
> I remember being forward enough to invite them over to our place on a Saturday morning in winter to play and they accepted. ... We had a large straw stack near the barn in which the cattle had already eaten large indentations which we enlarged further and utilized as forts. ... The stack itself was high enough for us to imagine as our "Everest" as we climbed it and slid down on the hard snow crust covering it.
>
> When we were cold we retreated into our very humble house, banked up on all sides with barnyard manure in fall in order to keep the wind from blowing under it in winter. I presume in order to impress my guests ... I showed them some of my father's books [a Bible and an encyclo-

pedia set]. .... Both were in the German language but I
think they caught William's fancy as at that time the
Kureleks probably did not have many books and Victoria
School library was also very meagre.[3]

Giesbrecht went on to praise the efforts of Mrs. Ethel Houghton, their
teacher in grades two and three, who provided an excellent education
in "the three R's" and displayed admirable dedication amidst very
difficult circumstances.[4] He recalled the gala Christmas concerts that
provided scope for William's artistry, and the hand-painted Valentines
that were models of economy as well as beauty. Will's hearts were
outlined with watercolors and then stippled, in a variety of colors:
"This conserved the small cakes of watercolor paints and considerably
stretched their life." The artist's perennial regard for economy in
painting techniques evidently began at an early age.

The ostracism or discrimination of which Giesbrecht writes and the
bullying of which he spoke further are widely acknowledged by all
who experienced such schools. There was a pecking order, Giesbrecht
recalls: "Big boys ruled the roost. Bill reacted more than most. He had
no corner in being picked on."[5] The artist's brother denied that Bill
was constantly bullied: "He was respected for what he could do in his
way. And for *his* respect for others. This earned him respect. Many big
boys liked Will and let him have his way. But if boys were badly brought
up, and if their parents spoke of 'hunkies' —. But we got along well with
other children. There were a couple of bad periods, several months."[6]
Classmate Peter Lesko corroborates John's memory that his brother
was admired: "Will kept to himself, didn't do much sports. He was very
smart, a real brain. He should have been the teacher. He was really well
liked. He tried to stop others from arguing, a nice guy, a peacemaker."[7]
Carl Inman, another classmate, recalls the two Kurelek brothers stick-
ing together and defending each other in fights: "We were all bullies. It
was the normal pattern. Nobody let it get out of hand."[8] Joseph Gay
remembers the artist as unusually well behaved: "The rest of us got
into trouble. He didn't."[9] Gay said a certain amount of bullying was
common, which was not surprising, considering the fact that some of
the boys in grade eight were sixteen and seventeen. Ironically, Bill
often misread his schoolmates' attitudes, and his desperate search for
success encouraged his belief that only by excelling in sports or
studies could one win admiration and approval. The strong need to
succeed stemmed from his immigrant heritage and was steadily reinforced by experiences at home and school.

Bill had five teachers in those nine years. Mrs. Lois Crozier (née
West) was in charge for one year when Bill was in grade seven or eight.

She was shocked to read Bill's version of events at Victoria Public School in *Someone With Me.* Both Mrs. Crozier and Bill's sister observed that there were only a few children in each grade in the one-room school where nine grades were covered; hence, Bill had very little competition. This makes his "oath on the private altar of scholastic superiority" look rather silly; or rather it shows how little a sense of proportion weighed in the scales against the boy's need to feel superior in at least one area. Mrs. Crozier remembers the Kurelek children as nicely dressed, neat, clean, and regular in attendance. John and Win were athletic, competitive, and more outgoing than Bill. He was "respectful, dutiful, really withdrawn". Too shy to appear on stage in the Christmas concert, he managed the curtains. He decorated her blackboard with drawings for special occasions, and was fond of handicraft periods, when the girls could knit or quilt and the boys did carpentry projects such as fretwork boxes.[10]

One unusual friendship marked Bill's school years, and that was with his cousin William Budjak, whose father, John, had helped Dmytro to find the Stonewall farm. Two years older, Budjak had several physical handicaps which affected his ability to read and to speak. By the late

Workshop class photo, Victoria Public School, late 1930s. Bill is on the far right, kneeling, and his cousin Billie Budjak is standing behind him.

thirties, "Billie" was a tall, gangling youth whose musical ability had made him a neighborhood favorite. Bill loved music but learned to play musical instruments (mouth organ and accordion) only with difficulty: "I used to envy Billie Budjak. He was unfortunate from birth, having defective speech, hearing and eyesight, and yet he played any musical instrument by ear. The accordion was his favorite; it made him a one-man band. He played at dances, and I used to love hearing in the evenings his music come across the half-mile of bush between our farmyard and the Budjaks'." (*Ex.* 69) In the forties, Budjak helped Dmytro at harvest time and worked with Bill on the farm. After hospitalization in Britain, Bill resumed the friendship in Ontario, and made a nostalgic trip with Budjak back to the Stonewall area.

Former teachers and neighbors share a view of the Kurelek parents as strict, frugal, and somewhat aloof. Harsh economic times demanded a stern hand at the family helm, but Dmytro was generally reputed to be stricter than the average father. The Kurelek parents rarely attended socials but kept to themselves.[11] Mary's role is interesting, the more so as she is rarely mentioned by her oldest son. In her own home as in her parents', she worked in the fields and the barnyard as well as caring for house and children. With a naïveté common to mothers, she expected that her children would see her efforts as an expression of her love for them. The Kureleks, like most of their neighbors, were not a family who touched or cuddled their children.[12] The cuddling that Bill needed and did not receive at home he would later find in England.

Mary was exceptional for her stamina, courage, patience, and loyalty. Bill's paintings record and celebrate her activities, though his words do not: cleaning the chicken shed, feeding the pigs, baking, making *pysanka* at Easter. John remembers her times together with them in the kitchen. Despite the fact that Bill would dedicate a painting series in 1967 to Ukrainian women's work, his writings show that he never really understood the unending effort and courage of the woman who raised him. Indeed, many who shared the immigrant experience have found him grossly unfair to his parents. Bill interpreted his mother's ability to survive and endure as mere passivity. He felt that she should have protected him from his father's wrath. Many tongue-lashings doubtless took place outside Mary's hearing. There was also a cultural factor at work: "In those times, a woman didn't stand up to her husband, especially one like Dad who was so strong!"[13] And there were times when Mary and her children might be the joint target for Dmytro's anger, "so we and she were together."[14]

Bill was, however, grateful for the sharing that farm chores involved. He writes that he had no leisure or play relationship with his parents, a statement contradicted by other evidence: "we were still lucky to have

The Kurelek family, 1936. Bill stands at the far left,
behind his father. Dmytro's brother, Georg, is seated on
the right.

a work relationship. This is one advantage farm children have, or had in
those days anyway." (A2 67) Thus there were chores that Bill considered fun, or play: transferring the chickens from one coop to another
after dark; tricking and killing rats; matching wits with the hungry pigs;
cutting wood; and harvesting vegetables just before the first frost. Joy
seems to emanate from many of the paintings of farm chores, yet Bill
always claimed to hate farm work. This was perhaps because he got no
praise or recognition for his help, or perhaps because it interfered with
his creative play: "I seemed always to be building or initiating construction projects" (A1 64). If the joy and the hatred still seem puzzling, Jean Budjak's comment may be illuminating: "We had very little
time to play, but we made fun with our work. Hauling wood, we'd fall
in the snow laughing when logs fell off the sleigh. Everybody had jobs,
but you had fun doing them. You wanted to play, but you had to work,
so you tried to combine the two!"[15]

To·judge by the paintings, there was more time for play than Bill
generally admitted. *Prairie Boy's Winter* (1973), his first book, and its
companion volume, *Prairie Boy's Summer* (1975), celebrate the
innumerable joys of a rural childhood in a northern land: school field
days, softball, reading while minding the cows, swimming in the bog
ditch, hunting for gophers or rabbits, trying archery with home-made
bows and arrows, tag, snow forts, skating, and cycling. There were
family picnics by the spring on Sundays, family fishing expeditions. The
Kurelek children had a wagon and a tricycle, skis from the mail-order

catalogue, and bicycles: luxuries in a depressed economy. The artist's imagination was fed by comic books, pulp Westerns, and radio plays like "The Lone Ranger", "The Shadow", and "Talking Drums". Playmates recall the excitement of seeing snakes in the ditch, the fun of looking for wildflowers: "We had no toys except balls. Maybe some kids had skates, or a sleigh. A few had skis; they were shared."[16] Remembering the meanness of his own father, who had broken up ice patches to ban sliding and save shoe leather, Dmytro helped his children to flood a rink. After they acquired a car, there were family expeditions to Lake Winnipeg, the first large body of water the children had seen.

A curious duet between John and his mother, long after the event, was conducted in two keys. John, developing the theme that their father's hard work had given them desirable extras, was reminiscing happily; Mary, deeply conscious of their lifelong struggle for financial survival, seemed almost bitter:

John: We went to Winnipeg at Christmas for a day, on the streetcar, as far back as I can remember. To see Eaton's, Hudson's Bay, and the toys.
Mary: You didn't *get* any.
John: We each got *one*.
Mary: Yes, *little* things.[17]

The needs of the family members varied greatly, and John thrived.

The land and the seasons provided endless amusements and fascination. The two *Prairie Boy* volumes, along with hundreds of paintings, record the wonder Bill felt for natural things. *Catching Baby Killdeer* shows a kneeling boy, awed by the fragile life in his hands. The smell of new-mown hay would return to haunt Bill in his London years. Archery seemed a way of conquering the "awesomeness" of prairie expanses. Fetching the cows could turn to enchantment in the first snowfall. Blizzards left snow in sculpted drifts. Crows marked the onset of winter and the return of spring, and the prairie teemed with songbirds.

In the 1940s, Bill had a partner in wonder, his second sister, Nancy, nearly ten years his junior. *Prairie Boy's Summer* carries this dedication:

With love for my sister Nancy
Who more than anyone else shared with me the surprise
    and wonder of prairie seasons as a child
Who has added to that surprise and wonder a sense of
    awe and love for the Creator of those wonders. Many
    call it the Living Whole—Ultimate Cause—Nature. We
    two call it: God.

Natural springs, in the public land known as the bog, were a marvel to Bill and to other youngsters. With their Polish friend Joe Gay, John and Bill explored the bog and the local limestone quarry, where a sand-pit housed thousands of cliff swallows. The area was criss-crossed with muddy roads flanked by deep ditches where jackfish and catfish could be netted. In summer, a sod dam could turn a ditch into a swimming-hole. The comic painting of nude swimmers and pranksters shows one side of Bill, while his prose reveals another:

> The bog was fascinating. It was flat and lonely and moist
> and had mysterious springs. There were no fences on the
> bog and no people and no buildings. We did not know
> what was on the other side of the bog. On clear dark
> nights we could see a glow on the horizon; I wanted to go
> into the ground. How deep were those springs? I used to
> kneel on the grass embankment; the holes were the
> thickness of the wrist. But what of the bigger holes at
> Poplar Springs, two miles further into the bog? There was
> a small brown evergreen forest there and among those
> trees were snakes of seaweed. One hour the water was
> brown, and another, it was deep aqua blue, and then lapis
> lazuli white.[18]

Some of Bill's playmates were equally captivated by Poplar Springs: "The clear spring water coming out seemed a kind of miracle. Where did it come from, so clear and bottomless?"[19]

Among Bill's amusements, the game for all seasons was drawing. He had begun to draw and paint in the first grade. Crayons and boxes of Reeves watercolors were provided to each student by the school, but paper was not, and was always in short supply. Bill loved bright colors, and the smell of plasticine. Sketching seemed to come naturally to him, and an admiring audience was balm to his spirit. Special holidays brought fresh opportunities yearly as he competed with himself in drawing and painting: "I was able to see if I could do a better Santa, a better Shamrock, or Valentine or Witch than the previous year" (A1 82).

Playmates remember Bill "forever drawing", while his parents kept urging him to help with the chores. His father considered art a waste of time at best, and at worst a perversity. Dmytro was upset to discover his son covering the walls of his upstairs bedroom with garish designs of priests and angels, nurses, snakes, tigers.[20] The images that could frighten a grown man came from many sources: radio melodrama,[21] comics, Westerns, Jehovah's Witnesses literature, even illness. Bill recalled fantasies suffered during a painful period of trench mouth: "It was as if I were choking on big spiky balls. . . . Of course many of these images eventually became symbols in my more surrealistic works." (A2 66) Illustrations in the literature given out by Jehovah's Witnesses fascinated the boy: "A blood-dripping Monster silhouetted against a burning sky, striding across a landscape of mangled soldiers, the War, and the second coming of Christ; and pictures of Adam and Eve in all glorious nakedness (except for their necessary foliage), walking in Paradise, and greedy, wizened Popes, cloak-and-dagger priests, and Witness words of hatred for all other churches and civic leaders. I daydreamed." (*Ex.* 67)

Dmytro's own tales of war in the Ukraine, first experienced when he himself was an impressionable boy of nine, were doubtless added grist for Bill's mill of horrors. Actual fighting, even the pillow-fights of childhood, made Bill wretched; transformed by art, violence became a source of fascination. His creative play was also violent: a woodpile became a pirate ship, the chicken shed a machine-gun nest. By the late 1960s, Bill had apparently forgotten the violent fantasies of his youth, for he saw no connection between them and the macabre strain that persisted in his adult imagination: "Recently, I found a portfolio in my parents' attic: cowboys, pirates, planes; people with heads torn off by cannon balls; bullet-like baseballs that terrified the players; an arrow that plunged through a knight's shield, stabbing him in the eye" (*Ex.* 68).[22] By his own statements, then, violent fantasies were Bill's artistic staple and earned him the admiration he craved. His desk was full of such works: "I did them every chance I got, even on the sly inside the desk during class hours. At recess, and in art periods on Friday afternoons, I began to get the recognition I so badly needed." (A2 60) Students would even stand on desks to watch Bill at work as he drew, slowly, seriously, painstakingly.

Bill's talent for art was only one aspect of the many differences between himself and the brother who was twenty months younger. There had been friendly rivalry between Bill and John from their earliest days, and marked contrasts. John was more active; Bill, slower and quieter, a dreamer. John actually wore out pants and shoes twice as quickly as his brother.[23] Bill's strong sense of duty made him a good berry-picker, a task John despised, but since their father considered this women's work, Bill's skill earned him no praise from Dmytro or even, years later, a place in his memory:

Mary:	I remember picking wild strawberries with our first three children. John was up in a tree, Will was picking.
John:	That was a bad part of summer, picking chokecherries

and saskatoons. If Dad wanted me, I could get out of
berry-picking.

Dmytro: But you were a mechanic, better for the horses and
tractor and everything.[24]

A Stonewall playmate, the "Patsy" of the first autobiography,
remembered Bill as "a little on the meek side".[25] He was afflicted,
however, not by a lack of courage but by a hypersensitivity. As a
three-year-old, curious and unafraid, Bill had once come to his mother
with a snake around his fingers.[26] As an adult, his courage would prove
remarkable in many areas.

Most siblings fight from time to time, and the brothers' memories of
their quarrels seem unremarkable. More significant is Bill's jealousy,
and the deep wounds to his self-esteem. John was twenty months his
junior, yet in the same grade at school. Far more painful was Dmytro's
preference for the son who shared his skills:

> We were constant companions from then [John's birth]
> until our university days. But we were rivals at the same
> time. I was early seen to be different—a dreamer—while
> John was practical and naturally brighter. I was jealous of
> the affection and praise he seemed to get from my parents
> which I, being older, thought I had first claim to. ...
> Besides his brightness, my brother's courage was also
> praised by Father. (A2 39-40)

> John was luckier than I in being talented mechanically.
> This aptitude came in very handy on the farm in Manitoba.
> I have already described the losing contest with John for
> my father's respect and affection in Alberta. (A2 65)

> We were different; I was a dreamer, and my more practi-
> cal, sensible brother, well, he seemed brighter and I saw
> him stealing affection from my parents. I had first claim to
> that affection. ... My father preferred my brother. He
> praised his courage, his luck, his hard work. I vacillated
> between terror and timidity. I envied my brother. (*Ex.* 55)

Bill's sense of his rights as first-born comes out of Ukrainian culture
and seems even biblical.[27] Ironically, had he not been the first-born, his
father's expectations and demands would likely have been lighter. Bill
bore the full weight of Dmytro's hopes for his children's advancement
and of his scorn and anger when those hopes seemed blocked. Had
John been born first, Bill's life would very probably have been easier.
The war was to provide another irony. Had it begun earlier or later,

Bill's life might have been vastly different. Strange luck, strange destiny.

The onset of the Second World War tightened the screws on the Kurelek family by making it difficult or impossible for them to hire help on the farm, although the same war would eventually prove a boon. High prices for agricultural products lightened Dmytro's debts and gave the Kureleks a measure of the financial security they had craved for so long. Of these benefits Bill says little or nothing. Just as nine years of school came to be characterized by the painful events of the first few weeks, so the hard times of a grasshopper plague in 1937 and the onset of war in the fall of 1939 represented all the agonizing years of adolescence. Earlier, Dmytro had had the help of Bill Dutka as hired man and, for a season, of his brother Georg. In 1939, Dmytro had no one to turn to but his two sons, both small for their age. The First World War had ended Dmytro's childhood, and the Second was to end Bill's:

> My father's dislike of his eldest son came down on me
> with all its weight in 1939. Two events conspired to bring
> it on—the outbreak of war and a grasshopper plague.
> Almost overnight every able-bodied single man was
> drafted into the army or went to work for the war effort
> in city factories. ... John and I, small and scrawny as we
> were, had to step into a man's shoes. I was twelve, John
> only ten years old, but Father impatiently dismissed the
> age factor: "When I was nine in the old country, I had to
> plow all day by myself. ..." (A2 71)

Bill's tendency to focus on and magnify disasters may stem from a naturally pessimistic cast of mind, or may simply reflect the artist's freedom from fact in the higher interest of narrative. A case in point is the description of the family's diet in 1938, the winter that followed the grasshoppers and the drought. In *Depression Diet* (1964), the artist shows the Kurelek family in the 1930s seated at a bare table spread with a pan of small potatoes and a bowl of gravy. The gloomy kitchen is dimly lit by an oil lamp. The mood is sombre, the faces are grim. Van Gogh's *The Potato Eaters* comes to mind as a possible influence. Bill writes that their monotonous diet that winter consisted of small potatoes and "the grease of an old cow" (A2 72). His source is doubtless an identical version given by his father to a journalist in the year of the painting.[28] His mother scoffs at the story of the potato diet. In her memory, there were always fish, berries, mushrooms, vegetables, eggs, chicken, and milk. Potatoes were served several times each day because the family liked them.[29]

The loss of the big barn by fire in 1935 had proved to be a blessing in disguise when insurance money paid the mortgage due in that year. Dmytro's difficulties had continued, and by the spring of 1938 he had made the reluctant decision to become a dairy farmer. He infinitely preferred growing wheat, but his neighbors were surviving by mixed farming. He purchased forty cows and three milking machines with gasoline suction engines. Things rapidly improved, to Dmytro's way of thinking if not to Bill's.

The memories of 1937-43 in Bill's last autobiography focus almost entirely on encounters with his father that resulted in failure and humiliation for the son. Dmytro turned more bitter, morose, "ruthless" in times of crisis: "Father drove himself and us mercilessly. ... What bothered me was that he was so impatient with us not because we were lazy—we weren't—but because we were inexperienced. Perfection, immediate perfection, was simply what he expected." (A2 72) The Kurelek parents were not alone in considering error culpable. The Budjaks thought Bill's experience more typical than he realized: "Parents worked so hard in those times, if you got hurt, you got a beating, not sympathy. A lot of families were like that."[30] Company, however, was no consolation to Bill.

As farming became increasingly mechanized and complex, John's mechanical aptitude brought praise, while Bill's fear of failure set up a further psychological barrier that made those fears a reality. Dmytro's McCormick Deering tractor was seen as a black monster which he was expected to master in a day, at the age of twelve. He writes that he feared physical punishment, yet clearly tongue-lashings were Dmytro's chief weapon: "This terror of some as yet unknown physical punishment from him hung like the sword of Damocles over me.... At times I had the uncanny feeling that I was actually sabotaging farm operations. As if some secret part of me wanted to harm both me and Father. The time I froze the waterpipe line to the barn was a case in point." (A2 73)[31]

To the British doctors in the early 1950s, Bill would express feelings of guilt and anger: guilt because of his anger, and also (one suspects) because of a lurking suspicion that he had failed his father in these years. "Sabotaging" is an interesting choice of word in the passage quoted above. One winter Bill had absent-mindedly left water in the pipes and it had frozen. The entire pipeline had had to be painstakingly thawed by blowtorch, inch by inch. He writes of the terrible guilt he felt as he watched an angry father and brother working to rectify his error; and he later depicted himself as crucified in the winter wind, thawing the overhead pipe on which the cattle depended. Another time an error with the tractor's oil crankcase induced the vicious circle of fear and paralysis that made the fears come true: "Petrified, I just stood there doing nothing. He was furious at the loss of oil he eventually discovered and once again dismissed me from the job with a swift kick in the backside. In my intense misery, I was developing a kind of concentration camp mentality called 'depersonalization'. In it, a person need not feel hurt, or not hurt nearly as much, because he is not a person." (A2 74)

The depersonalization phenomenon became Bill's most frequently applied label for the mental and emotional problems that would reach crisis proportions in the 1950s. Constant worry made him sleepy and withdrawn; deaf, dumb, and blind by his own description, he became afraid even to ask for food at the table. When things on the farm went wrong, Dmytro's anger must have been partly directed at Fate, and perhaps at himself, but it was always interpreted by Bill as contempt for his particular failures: "This contempt stayed with me nearly all my years," he would write in 1972. The trauma also made Bill angry, but his anger, unlike his father's, was concealed: "Like a packrat, I stored his wrongs inside my head for the future, when I too would be strong. It was only years later that I discovered that this was a well of poison, that it was immoral, but then, in those days, I knew nothing of faith and morality and that too was a kind of sleep." (*Ex.* 72)

In the autobiographical excerpt published in 1972, Bill makes Dmytro more admirable: "The war brought prices that were miraculous. My father drove us mercilessly. He was heroic. He worked himself like a bull, single-minded, possessed by his one chance to seize success from the maw of disaster." (*Ex.* 72) Dmytro's heroism is found in the long 1973 edition, but it has unfortunately been edited out of the third version.

Neighborhood feuds are another theme in all three versions of the autobiography. Bill's handling of each varies significantly. In the 1972 memoir, feuds are a feature of rural life amid hardships generated in the 1930s: "In those Depression years, the feuds and no-speaking times broke out: a wagon of grain was stolen; . . . after a wrong word over the fence, we find neighbor G—— had hidden iron bars in our wheat sheafs, hoping to ruin our thresher." (*Ex.* 69) In this version, neighborly affairs included pranks, as well as the "lovely old-country rituals" which Bill would later paint.

In the 1980 revision, the emphasis shifts and the feuds become Dmytro's fault. Dmytro's allegedly unreasonable treatment of his neighbors seems somehow related to his unreasonable treatment of his son: "Nothing could surpass his ability to antagonize our neighbors. The feuding got so bad that some of them resorted to underhand ways of getting even." (A2 60) Versions of the feuds have passed into local history or myth and are still current in the Stonewall area, where assignment of the blame tends to vary with the informant. Evidently Dmytro, annoyed by neighbors' cows in his grain, was responsible for obtaining a municipal pound bylaw, and on several occasions drove his neighbors' cows and horses to the pound, where a fine was required before they could be redeemed.

This revised version, edited by Max Layton after Bill's death, reduces Bill's manuscript to one-third of its original length. Selection and deletion are powerful editorial tools. The choice of incidents is sometimes unfortunate, since some material which shows Dmytro in a better light has been excised. The text is Bill's, yet both writer and editor share responsibility for the resulting emphasis on material that denigrates the father. The son's struggle to forgive his father's treatment of him would go on at many levels, conscious and unconscious, throughout Bill's life.

In the late 1930s and the early 1940s, the sheer size of Dmytro's acreage, the size of his herd, and the shortage of help made for intolerable pressures all round. The family worked late and rose early.

From left to right: John, Dmytro, and Bill at Stonewall, late 1940s.

Bill, exhausted as much by anxiety as by physical labor, began to feel sleepy as he worked; the tension of maintaining a constant alert exhausted him further, and responsibilities were dreaded because of the constant opportunities for failure they provided:

> It seems I was now bungling something or other every week, if not daily. And I was painfully aware that, with each slip I made, I was moving further and further from any possibility of closeness to my father. It was like getting deeper and deeper into financial debt until one despairs of ever being free. Knowing his dislike for me made it impossible to approach him through conversation. I found myself on the verge of breaking into sobs whenever I was alone with him. ... So intense was my fear of him that I could not even venture the words "Please don't close the latch—I'm going in." I just stood dumbly to one side until he'd turned his back and I unlatched the door and entered. He obviously reported this to Mother because later that day she said, "Why don't you talk to your father? You know he has your welfare at heart."
>
> But it was obvious to me that, except for my good standing at school, I was in no way fulfilling his concept of what a son should be. No matter what the circumstances, what I said disappointed him. "Stupid" was the most common adjective I was branded with. "Deaf", "dumb", "blind" were close second-favorites, heaped on my head as it hung in shame. It got so bad that the mere sound of my voice roused his contempt for my intelligence. (A2 76-77)

Bill's siblings hold a view of their father which is different and the same. The shifting perspective is fascinating, given the fact that so much of Bill's life hung on his tragic relationship with his father. The Kurelek children emphasize that their father's efforts were admirable: "We were better off than our neighbors. Some of them didn't have shoes. There was no way that Will could have had it much better by what Dad could do. I was fortunate in that it suited me."[32] John admitted to hating his father at times, and finding him most unreasonable. "Dad was intelligent enough to know that you shouldn't deride your children." He observed that their father's behavior came out of a Slavic tradition where the father is always right, and that in that context his harshness was not extraordinary, nor, John implied, were his brother's difficulties: "But perhaps he felt it more."

Win stressed that their father's struggle on behalf of his children was

Bill's siblings John, Nancy, and Sandy at Stonewall, July 1946.

not simply for financial security and an easier life in material terms but for the self-respect that some Anglo-Saxons sought to destroy in them: "Father fought tooth and nail to establish us as equal. We had to get an education to achieve this. He didn't have it, so we had to."[33] She considered her father a very unhappy man, "a real pessimist", and conceded that he had been "miserable" to them at times. With a genuine tolerance and understanding that one looks for in vain in Bill's talk of forgiving his father, she added, "We all, *all* give our kids a hard time."

Several of the younger Kurelek children had shared something of Bill's experience in a softer key. They believed that their father had been able to enjoy his younger children more, because by that time financial pressures had eased and the shock of cultural adaptation was largely absorbed. Iris, born in 1948, was cooler than Bill had been; perhaps she needed Dmytro's approval less: "I was afraid of him too. When he was whistling he was angry. His eyebrows bristled. You learned to look at his eyes. He was the kind of guy you had to *read* before you approached. He'd play records and we'd dance. He enjoyed his later children more than his first."[34] Alexandra ("Sandy"), born late in 1944, was also afraid of her father during childhood, but came to pity him in the 1960s as she recognized his desire to be loved.[35]

The widow of Dmytro's hired man provides another glimpse of the Kurelek parents. Bill Dutka worked for Dmytro in the mid-thirties, left, married in 1939, and returned in time for the 1940 harvest. For fourteen months and two harvests, at a wage of twenty-five dollars per month, Bill and Stella Dutka lived with the Kurelek family before departing for their own nearby farm in the fall of 1941. By Stella's testimony, the Kureleks ate well and were generous to their help. Shortly after their departure, Dmytro and Mary came to visit, bringing a year's supply of potatoes, cheese, and butter as a gift to the Dutkas. Stella, who had helped Mary in the house, had found her quiet, uncomplaining, and warm, "like a mother to me".[36] Loving emotions were not openly displayed in the Kurelek household, but were demonstrated through work and the struggle to provide an education. Stella was very familiar with this pattern among European immigrants. Children were to be seen and not heard. During the long winter evenings without electricity, Dmytro would tell stories while the children listened silently. "The Kureleks were kind to us."

These varying facets of Mary and Dmytro are important if we are to assess the artist's experience, both as it was to him and as it might have been to someone with a different temperament. To deny Bill's suffering would be untrue; conversely, to blame his parents, as he did during the 1950s and later, is simplistic and misleading. The suffering was real, and Bill would eventually learn to convert it into works of beauty and mystery. His anger may account for some of the violence that lurks in so many Kurelek paintings.

By the time the 1939 crop was in the barns, Bill had garnered his own bitter harvest of self-contempt, anger, and guilt. As an adult he slowly came to see that the grudge he bore both parents for what he considered "unjust, disrespectful treatment" had poisoned him internally and bred habits of resentment that affected other relationships through much of his life. He lived for the day when he could make a "comeback": the word is used again in a different but related context at the end of the second edition of *Someone With Me*. Years later, he realized that he had been hurting only himself with thoughts of revenge, and that the Christian counsel of forgiveness, thus heaping coals of fire on one's enemy's head, was morally superior. Still, one looks in vain for the expression of pity for Dmytro that Sandy would make with great simplicity in 1983.

Bill continued to live for the day when he might hear from his father the praise he had coveted as a youth and never received. His need for success was the need to receive that praise from the man he both "hated and adored", in the words of the gloss to *The Maze* (1953). The depth of his admiration made it intolerable when his idol failed him and imperative that he should eventually find a loving father he could serve without ambivalence.

In 1943, after nine years at Victoria Public School, Bill and John were sent to Winnipeg to attend Isaac Newton High School for grades ten, eleven, and twelve.[37] The decision had been Dmytro's. His announcement took the boys by surprise, and astonished Bill. It was, of course, an indirect compliment, indicating Dmytro's confidence that his children were university material. But the compliment was too subtle for Bill, who continued to crave the overt praise that was denied.

Isaac Newton, in Winnipeg's North End, was an exclusively academic school in the 1940s. Principal A. E. Floyd, reputed to be "somewhat strait-laced", maintained high standards. The matriculation program, a preparation for university, included English, science, history, language, and geography. The community had a large ethnic population of Germans, Jews, Poles, Hungarians, Ukrainians, and other Slavic groups. Dr. Joseph Katz, one of Bill's former teachers there, emphasizes the cosmopolitan atmosphere in the school and in the city in the 1940s. The *Winnipeg Free Press*, published and edited by John Dafoe, promoted multiculturalism long before the word became popular: "There was a very harmonious atmosphere in the school generally. They accepted one another and their special holidays."[38] Bill's experience at Isaac Newton supports this observation: there was none of the feeling of second-class citizenship he had sometimes felt in the Stonewall school, despite the fact that most of the Isaac Newton teachers were Anglo-Saxon.

From years of counselling, Dr. Katz recalls some characteristics of the rural students who formed slightly less than half of the school's population in the 1940s. They tended to be responsible, having helped for years in a family economic unit. One-room schools had made them capable of learning independently, but many had trouble socializing; farm chores had taken up the time when city children, less isolated and less busy, were learning social skills. Some of Bill's difficulty in socializing, then, was common to his group.[39] His hypersensitivity and his fragile self-esteem exaggerated his difficulty.

Mr. Floyd's influence could be seen in the conservative nature of the school uniform. Girls wore a knee-length, box-pleated navy-blue tunic, black stockings, black cotton bloomers and a white or blue blouse. Boys were required to wear a jacket or sweater over a shirt, and most wore ties.[40]

The Kurelek boys entered school a week late, having been retained to help with the threshing. It was a poor introduction to a strange milieu. Bill makes much of the initial confusion, but before long the brothers knew the ropes. They found the city school, big and impersonal as it was, less cruel than Victoria School had been. Lodgings had been found for them near the school. They boarded with two different families in the first year, changing in January when the fare in the first home became intolerable. When their sister joined them the following year, Dmytro bought a small house at 834 Burrows Avenue.

Then, as now, the street was lined with small, brightly painted houses of frame or stucco with gabled roofs. Furnishings were sparse and the living was Spartan: "We had a two-burner hotplate, two tables and chairs, a few pots and dishes, a supply of coal in the cellar and a little spending money each week for basic essentials" (A2 86). Chores were shared, and quarrels over them flourished. The three ate lightly and irregularly, consuming food brought from home. Dmytro's purchase of a house for his children's education seems a remarkable step, but to Bill it was simply evidence of his father's shrewd peasant sense of husbandry (A2 85).[41] The reluctance to give credit where credit was due seems to have worked both ways in this relationship.

834 Burrows Avenue, Winnipeg, the Kurelek home during Bill's and John's high school days. Photo by author.

Here Bill studied in front of a wall plaque he had made that read "Meta 90%" (*meta* is Greek for "pursuit" or "quest": i.e. "goal"; Bill aimed at a 90% average).[42] As Bill saw it, strangers on a tight budget could do little but study. John thought differently, and explored the city with friends while his brother worked. Descriptions of the two boys, in the notes on individual students written by classmates for the 1945 yearbook, characterize both as "book-burners".[43] Most of the students hoped to attend university. Before and after the war, the North End seethed with social mobility or "inward migration", aimed upward. Bill's personal dedication to study came from a motivation by now deeply entrenched. His only feeling of self-respect came from his ability to excel in artwork or scholarship.

Every second weekend, Bill and John took a bus to Stonewall to help on the farm, and Dmytro and Mary paid occasional visits to Winnipeg. These links allowed the parents to scrutinize academic progress and monitor career plans. Dmytro's primary ambition was to see Bill become a doctor. The notion of a doctor's physical intimacy with strangers was distasteful to Bill, but he dutifully took the Latin that was a prerequisite to studying medicine. The unavailability of Latin as a subject at Stonewall meant that Bill was behind in this subject. Summer schooling in Winnipeg offered three years of Latin in six weeks. Fuelled by praise, Bill managed it "handsomely" in 1944. The summer, however, was a sad, lonely one as Bill wrestled with the whole problem of his future plans and the dependency on his parents which he now recognized as excessive.

In the second year, his study habits became more extreme and precipitated a breakdown. The competition was vastly different from that of a one-room school. Moreover, Bill's home room that year was composed of the school's best scholars. Desperately long hours of study in a poor light earned him seventh place in December, and brought disaster in April: "I cracked. I just couldn't do more. . . . I would launch ambitious study and review programs but never complete them. I shirked algebra which I hated. . . . And so exam time came—and I FAILED! My whole world seemed to collapse." (A2 86) Again Bill writes of "humiliation". He passed in June but vowed to kill himself with study the following year. Meanwhile, the war was ending, but Bill makes no mention of it, then or earlier, except to note that it was responsible for the drastic shortage of hired men in 1939. He existed in a world of his own, preoccupied with visions of personal failure and success.

In October 1945, Bill made fourth place in class; by December, third place. When his eyes rebelled at the obsessive reading, he tried an "eye rationing program", covering first one eye and then the other as he read. Fear of going blind was now added to his anxieties.[44] He stood second at Easter, but fell just short of an eighty average in June. Instead of feeling pride in his accomplishment, he felt only bitter disappointment that he had missed his goal, the public presentation of an Honours Certificate at graduation. If Dmytro drove Bill hard, he drove himself harder.

A different view of the brothers in those years comes from Norman Duvell, their classmate and John's friend. Duvell had visited overnight at the Stonewall farm and knew the Kurelek parents. He saw Dmytro as a stubborn autocrat who took life seriously and ruled his wife and children with an iron hand: "John had a bit of a temper and wasn't afraid to stand up to the old man."[45] Duvell's sketch of the two brothers, so different in nature, illuminates both and reminds us of the personality Bill lived with for two decades and with whom he was constantly compared. For a quiet, shy youth like Bill, the younger John was a hard act to follow. Norman contrasted John's natural ability in sports with Bill's bumbling. His ineptitude was compounded by poor equipment, whereas John, "more employable", earned money for good sports equipment through various jobs. When the three went skiing at Snow Valley, John's and Norman's skis had steel edges which Bill's did not. Unused to large hills but not lacking in courage, Bill skied straight down a steep, icy slope, ending up in a bush. Hurt by their laughter, he spent the balance of the day skiing by himself.

Duvell found Bill a strange, odd youth. With a sallow complexion and thin physique, he looked unhealthy, but Duvell sensed an inner toughness: "He was not weak; he had a tough grip and you couldn't push him around. John was twenty pounds heavier but John couldn't push him around. He had a mental toughness." To Duvell, part of his strangeness was his naïveté. Then, too, he was frequently drawing or painting. This in itself was unusual, to a youth who shared Dmytro's low opinion of art. The actual drawings were even worse: "I didn't like Will's art in the forties, the faces were creepy. He'd paint a bush with a devil's face behind it. There were satanic faces behind every tree!" While Norman and John were acquiring the ruthless wisdom of the city streets, Bill dreamed alone. Duvell found him an innocent, naively idealistic about people and good intentions: "He was a dreamer, he believed in sugarplum fairies. The harsh reality of the world just bounced off his head like rice at a wedding. He didn't mix with people, wasn't practical like John."

Bill's own account of his high school days stresses two other factors. One was his new interest in things Ukrainian, fed by Ukrainian-language school and a priest at the Ukrainian Greek Orthodox Cathedral near Bill's house. His love for and knowledge of his Ukrainian heritage in the 1960s and '70s matured through his paintings in that period. The other was his crush on a local girl called Natalie. Tongue-tied, Bill worshipped from afar. It was three years before he could write of his love, by which time Natalie's affections were otherwise engaged. Had his bad experience with female bullies given him a complex? Bill mused. Over the next decade, Bill would see and paint women as angels or whores, the complementary archetypes of Western culture. His sexual feelings would be expressed through masturbation, an activity that induced strong feelings of guilt even during his agnostic days.[46] There is no doubt that his sexuality was also expressed through his creative work. It would be 1962 before he would know a woman in the biblical sense.

Bill closes the tale of his pre-adult years with a rhetorical quotation from Browning on the pursuit of excellence: "A man's reach should exceed his grasp/Or what's a heaven for?" The same mood of poignant longing is captured in his first great self-portrait, painted in 1951 and re-worked in 1953. Over the next thirty years, Bill's reach would exceed his wildest dreams, while success would continue to surprise and delight him.

4

The Lonely Road to Creativity,
1946-52

DURING THE SIX CRUCIAL YEARS THAT FOLLOWED GRADUATION FROM HIGH school and preceded the years in England, Bill completed his formal education, broke away from his family, and established emotional patterns that would last the balance of his life. His view of himself as an artist was also established at this time, thanks more to the inner or psychological drama of the period than to the drawings and paintings actually produced in it. His need to act radically and independently, to have his actions proven correct, and to earn his father's recognition and acknowledgement of his success would mark his remaining years.

In the fiction of James Joyce and the life of Vincent Van Gogh, both encountered for the first time in 1949, Bill found models that made sense of his harsh experience and, in a sense, sanctified it. These secular models continued to inspire him long after his religious conversion and despite his habitual denunciations, during the Toronto years, of the Gospel of Art. Writing of these influences later, Bill mocked his romantic pose of rebellion as "phoney". Yet the emotional patterns went deeper than his latter-day theories. In Joyce's fiction and Van Gogh's life, Bill found that he had not suffered poverty, bitter humiliation, and family opposition for nothing. Any true artist had endured similar difficulties. Indeed, seen in the light of these models, his sufferings marked him as one of the Chosen.

Bill's autobiographies record the tremendous effect made on him by the reading of two books, *Portrait of the Artist as a Young Man* and *Lust for Life*, Irving Stone's biography of Van Gogh. Bill credits Joyce's early fiction with having a more profound influence on him than any other single book during his time at university: with being, in fact, the sole book he would remember from the period in years to come: "I seemed to identify so completely with the hero—Stephen Daedelus [*sic*]. It convinced me to rebel good and proper this time. ... Like Stephen Daedelus, I determined to travel the road to creativity alone." (A1 205; cf. A2 103)

Stone's life of Van Gogh, which Bill discovered during his first months at the Ontario College of Art, added to his dreams of adventure and glory: "In my money-tight circumstances he was the ideal hero to imitate." Bill had diaries from the late forties at hand as he was writing *Someone With Me*, and he quotes from one:

> I have rebelled as I understand a proper artist is com-
> pelled to—if he is worth his salt—against convention. I
> will face the contempt and poverty that being such a
> social outcast entails. It seems that I must live as full,
> intense and varied a life as possible to gain a store of
> experience that will be my subject matter for works of
> art. I am trying hard to fashion my life on theirs (Joyce
> and Van Gogh). I am proud of my poverty, of not eating
> the right food or enough of it, of wearing shabby clothes,
> of not bathing or shaving regularly, proud of chumming
> with Communists and eccentrics; proud even of suffering
> periods of depression because I believe that out of this I
> am destined to produce great art. (A2 111; cf. A1 220)

In the 1960s and '70s, Bill would call his adulation of these artist-heroes a false assumption of a costume not his own. Public masks, however, not only reflect but form secret personalities. Bill's stubborn independence, forged in the smithy of his soul during the early years of adult life, would stand him in good stead throughout a lifetime of difficulties and would enable him to walk his own way, in art as in life.

His artistic influences would be abstracted not from twentieth-century secular ideas but from older European traditions which he found infinitely more satisfying. Joyce's revolt was against the church-dominated culture of his time and place. Bill's revolt (not surprisingly, when we consider the deep idealism that marked his nature from the beginning) would ultimately be against a secular and technological culture that seemed to have lost touch with its religious roots. Bill remained proud of his frugality, of wearing shabby clothes, and of defying the conventions of bourgeois gentility in general. The lonely rebel had started down a road that he would never really abandon.[1]

The revolt, and the budding independence, began with the summer jobs that preceded his years at the University of Manitoba in Winnipeg. His father had no objection to his first venture, painting signs. During the summer of 1946 he lived at home, bicycling eighteen miles each way to his job in Winnipeg. For a youth who described himself as a weakling, his stamina was amazing. The following summer proved to be a turning-point. Bill wanted money, but he wanted freedom more. Despite the high school years in Winnipeg, he had lived his first twenty years within a family womb that dominated everything but his dreams. Early in 1947, he signed up for a summer in the bush at a lumber camp near Neys, Ontario, north of Lake Superior. He did it, he writes, "to prove to my father (and myself) that I could make it on my own."[2]

Sensing trouble, Bill kept his plans secret until April. When he finally confessed his intentions, a storm broke in the Kurelek household. Dmytro had worked in the bush. He described its hardships and dangers with all the strength of his forceful personality. He had always instructed his children to seek white-collar jobs. Bill was not only "ruining his good name among the neighbours" (A1 180) but, infinitely worse, defying his advice, leaving home, and being ungrateful. Bill chose the occasion to attempt to confess, for the first time, to ten years of repressed resentments, "the whole ugly, smelly brew".[3] In such a context, both sides saw the decision to leave home for a job that Dmytro opposed as the very major step that it was. Dmytro said that his son needed a good spanking; the son agonized that he had never imagined leaving home would be so tough. Little wonder that he would feel drawn, soon after, to Joyce's tale of rebellion.

That summer was Bill's first real success, leaving aside, for the moment, his scholastic honors at Victoria Public School. It was his first exposure to Canada's wilderness, to the variety and vastness of a land he would later record in paint with loving fidelity. The northland had been part of the lure of the job. Bill saw it in mythic terms, as a place where he might find "peace of mind and strength of body" (A1 179). He was not to be disappointed. In the bush he found nature "fresh and strong". He writes with a poet's sensibility and an artist's eye of mists over the lake in the early morning, of rain clouds round the hills, and of the heart-tugging sound of a train whistle so far from civilization. The lake was vast, the forests were bold: "I'd never seen a mountain before."

Even better were the rough-and-ready social conditions which suited such social skills as Bill possessed: "I was shy and timid, but from the first I found myself drawn into the hearty camaraderie that prevailed. At all camps there was the same yarn-telling, back-slapping humor and feast-sized meals, the same admiration for physical prowess, skill and productivity."[4] Bill's values were similar, his rural humor right in style. He welcomed regulations such as "No Women" and "No Liquor". As he watched the city youths fold and fade, he realized he had been "lucky" to have been raised on a farm. The foreman, whom Bill admired as manly, had a soft spot for the awkward youth and did what he could to help him. For his piecework, Bill earned a reputation as a hard worker. By summer's end he had made over six hundred dollars, along with return train fare. Not only had he survived, he had prospered.

These photographs of Bill (left and below right) during his lumber-jack months appear in his personal scrapbook of his life under the heading "The Artist as a Young Man".

Bill (below left), in a lighter moment, 1947. From his scrapbook.

Best of all was his new-found confidence, the fruit of his first decisive step into the world beyond his home. His father's habitual criticisms lacked something of their old sting, now that Bill knew he could earn his own living: "What I felt I really was working for all that summer was my independence, my manhood."[5] "Manly" is a word that recurs in Bill's early writings. He took pleasure in expressing his manliness by wearing his lumberjack boots on the farm and around Stonewall. To Bill, they signified the summer's success; to Dmytro, the refusal of his advice and (no doubt) the end of an era. At his parents' insistence, Bill took off the noisy reminder that he had been right, but he retained the lessons learned.

In later years he realized just how rich had been his exposure to traditional lumberjack life. In 1951 he returned to camps in northern Québec and Ontario for seven or eight months to earn a stake which would carry him to Europe. Then, as in 1947, he experienced the last of a dying way of life, before technological innovation would radically alter it. In the Foreword to *Lumberjack*, Bill writes that camp life had remained relatively unchanged for two centuries prior to 1951, and that after that time it changed rapidly: "As a painter, I felt very lucky to have experienced traditional lumber camp living before it disappeared forever." His lumberjack paintings record the old ways, along with the depth of feeling they had evoked in him.

Bill's third summer job was as a laborer with the Commonwealth Construction Company in Port Arthur at the head of Lake Superior. The project was an extension to one of Fort William's terminal grain elevators. Many of Bill's co-workers were "D.P.s", or displaced persons, European refugees, among them a pair of brothers from the Ukraine. This provided opportunities for Bill not only to practise Ukrainian but also to hear at first hand of atrocities under Stalin's Soviet Union and Hitler's Germany. Bill would later become a relentless foe of communist regimes, which he saw as anti-religious and materialistic. In his impressionable twenties, the Klymenko brothers' horror stories and a reading of Orwell's *1984* vied with pro-communist pressures exerted by student friends in Toronto. His summer co-workers also revived in Bill an older interest in Europe and family roots: "For the first time, I felt I was close to the real Europe where our fine cultural roots were, and I knew I'd have to get there one day" (A1 196).

Religion was also on Bill's mind throughout this period, despite his description of himself as an atheist prior to his conversion in England. Bill had flair, and one suspects that he found the conversion of an atheist a more striking and dramatic posture than the homecoming of a religious seeker. In Port Arthur, he was fascinated by the religious faith of the Ukrainian immigrants. Another co-worker, John Champagne, recalls that religion was Bill's favorite topic of discussion: "he was always asking questions about religion."[6]

Champagne, like Bill, was a student at the University of Manitoba, although they had met on the construction job rather than on campus: "We'd eat lunch together. He played the violin, sitting on the window sill and oblivious to everything. He played very well." (Ironically, and typically, Dmytro's gift of a violin had been resented earlier.) The two went sketching, but neither one, according to John, saw himself as an artist. Champagne remembers Bill as "an odd type, very much a loner". They felt an affinity, since both had grown up in small farming communities, and both had a fear of heights and were attempting to overcome these fears on the construction job. John sensed that Bill admired him, was looking for role models, and might cling if encouraged.[7] Other interviews from the period substantiate this suspicion. At this vulnerable time in Bill's life, friendship had to be all or nothing. His autobiography suggests that he eventually withdrew from Champagne, in Winnipeg and later in Edmonton, because he felt outclassed, both socially and professionally (A1 199, 228).

Bill's statements seem wildly inconsistent in these years. It is startling to turn from the relatively confident tale of this period found in both versions of *Someone With Me* to the earlier unpublished autobiography written for an unknown Winnipeg doctor in the winter of 1947-48. With his own money in his pocket for the first time in his life, Bill sought professional advice for a host of problems ranging from depression and anxiety to severe acne. Several interviews led to little more than "a huge bill". Disappointed and suspicious (another trait that dogged Bill for life), he returned to his programs of self-help, self-analysis, and good resolutions. Paradoxical? In his second year at university, he was appealing to a strange physician to structure his life and teach him "how to become a normal, sensible person" (Ms 1); and in his third, he was boasting of Joycean rebellion against society. The youth who, earlier, sought advice on grooming now claimed to be proud of his poverty, his shabbiness and eccentricities. Beneath the bravado one senses a painful loneliness as he tries to make a virtue of necessity. And turn an ugly duckling into a swan. The metaphor is Bill's.

The early manuscripts make painful reading. They are incredibly long and detailed. Writing them must have taken large amounts of time away from studying, or from the social activities that so intimidated Bill. He writes that he felt anaemic and worn out: old, weary, weak, a victim of insomnia who was always sleepy. He blames his anaemia on his parents' failure to give him cod-liver oil, despite a doctor's recommendation. Visits to several eye doctors led only to the discovery that his eye pain was eased neither by glasses nor by ointments.

Emotional problems loomed larger than bodily ones, although Bill connects the two, describing "the sinister effects" of ill health on his behavior. His lack of self-esteem seemed to poison relationships, or strangle them at birth. Guilt and self-hatred extended to the body he despised: "I feel intensely angry with myself for not being strong and healthy as others are" (Ms 2). He writes of his face, posture, and carriage giving him endless mental pain; of a lack of control of facial muscles, and a "hangdog sickly expression"; of being pale and skinny: "I am stooped and lack that manly chest." Photographs indicate that Bill was by no means the Dickensian grotesque of this self-description. Yet no one studying these early manuscripts can doubt the reality of his misery.

The second manuscript focuses on grooming and etiquette. It reads like one long appeal to Ann Landers. Poverty compounded the rough-and-ready habits learned on the farm. With a curious twist, the poverty of necessity becomes a poverty of choice as Bill boasts of surviving his 1947 summer in the bush without buying any clothes. First he patched his own, then he patched the cast-offs of others. His pride in being able to do without co-existed with a belief that being well-dressed adds to one's self-confidence. In a portion of his story which he deleted for publication, he complains of bad habits acquired early, and humbly begs for advice to help him become socially presentable. Throughout the appeals runs a counter-theme of defiance which surfaced in his last year at university, encouraged by two unexpected allies: James Joyce and thyroid pills: "For the past two or three years I have begun to pay visits to doctors yet at the same time the spirit of determinism that has seized me makes me neglect my health in preference for achievement and success." By "determinism", Bill seems to mean his personal sense of fate as an artist *destined* to become famous. By the late forties, that sense of destiny was an important part of his personality.

The second manuscript shows that Bill suffered acutely from adolescent worries. He writes of clothing and grooming as major problems:

> My early life on the farm has given me some very bad hab-
> its along that line. I washed once a day, bathed once in
> two or three weeks, had a haircut once in three or four
> months, wore whatever clothing I could find, and in gen-
> eral led a life of great freedom. In the first year of city life
> I was irked by the loss of that freedom yet at the same
> time felt my inferiority to the city boys in the matter of,
> grooming.

Manners, or etiquette, bothered him even more. Here, as in so many things, he casts blame at his parents' door. Bill's inability to cope with the simplest of social situations, such as entering or leaving a room, evoked painful insecurity and an obsession with trivia. Problems were compounded by an idealistic abhorrence of repetition and hypocrisy. A similar hatred of idle chatter and gossip encouraged his habit of silence. This hatred of repetition, prominent in the second manuscript, is ironic when we remember his later practice of copying his own paintings. In the forties, this aversion acquired through years of performing farm chores made him agonize over using common social expressions most people accept without thinking: "Above all, what on earth am I to say when I wish to leave his or any other persons home" is one of many such appeals to the omniscient neurologist, who represented Science to Bill before their first meeting and a fallible human being after their second.

Since childhood, silence had been a retreat, a refuge and a defence. Patterns of silence are elaborated in his manuscripts. Unfortunately for Bill, Dmytro was a forceful debater: "I know that argument was useless. Gradually mutual hate developed between us and I was afraid to talk to him even when he appeared friendly for fear of arousing his anger in some way." (Ms 2 15) Silence had long been the social expression of his insecurity. He felt it unkind to inflict himself on someone who had doubtless rejected him in advance. Silence, he believed, staved off the trouble he might otherwise make for himself with an ill-judged remark. When emotions threatened to overwhelm him, control could be reestablished by silence: "Pride commanded me to avert the escape of my emotions through crying before my parents and the easiest method of accomplishing this was to remain perfectly silent" (Ms 2). Naturally, his silence irritated his parents and alienated prospective friends. "I am not made for society," Bill concludes, "or for communicating with it by means of my speech organs." He fantasized about speaking while practising writing. Idealism made him crave a precision of language which he rarely heard among family or friends: he would talk "purely" or not at all (Ms 2 33). Mercifully, Bill finally learned to communicate through his painting. In the forties, he took refuge in his scorn of easy chatter and his conviction that silence denoted a superior character.

Concern with success is another recurring theme in these manuscripts. Social failures made Bill long to be the centre of attraction. Daydreams—of being strong enough to conquer his enemies, of winning love, of freeing the Ukraine—only emphasized a miserable reality. He fought these fantasies in pursuit of another dream, the destiny or "determinism" that marked him for success (Ms 2 37). Fear of failure he termed one of the most potent forces in both his parents and himself. This fear fuelled his stubborn independence, and his competitive drive in school. "Ambition," he wrote in 1948, "has a strong hold on me. I admire it in others and envy them if they succeed. I admire people who can indulge in many activities and excel in all. Leonardo da Vinci is my ideal." (Ms 2 41) Success is seen as a *necessity*: "Success is food and drink and sleep to me. The criticism of me by father and his prophecies that I would be 'kicked around by people' fired me to a fierce hot desire to prove that he was wrong. This strong ambitious feeling and delight in action seems at times to conflict with the dreamy side of my nature. Which should I follow to get [the] most enjoyable life?" (Ms 2 42)

Ironically, Bill sees no similarity between his own ambition and his father's. The latter is condemned as materialistic, a word Bill extends from the literal pursuit of wealth to his father's hope that his children will have successful careers. Bill's own ambitions, he insisted, were different: "My ambitions however are more on the cultural and spiritual side. I wish to have my name preserved after I have passed away in some great work. I look more for pleasure in the future, pleasure derived from fame not from material wealth." (Ms 2 53) Bill was more like his father than he ever admitted. Or knew.

Thyroid pills may have been the most significant help the medical profession gave Bill in these university years. The family doctor, diagnosing his lethargy as the product of an under-active thyroid gland, prescribed a booster for his basal metabolic rate. The pills, which Bill called BMR tablets, had a startling effect. He described the euphoria they induced in his diaries:

> The flame of life that had flickered anaemically in me
> before now has begun to blaze forth in violent spirits. ...
> Now I'm capable of great accomplishments. Particularly in
> the hot peak of each cycle do powerful romantic dreams
> and idealistic planning come upon me. Yes, alas, there are
> lows too. ... I'm in despair. But wait, I'm on a peak again.
> I'm overwhelmed by a powerful urge to drop everything
> and plunge headlong to my ultimate goals. I want to travel
> and learn and feel and live fully. NOW, in preparation for
> a great destiny. (A2 101)

Twenty-five years later, Bill spoke of his BMR "addiction" with ironic humor. He observed, shrewdly, that the tablets probably intensified the effects on him of Joyce's portrait of an artistic rebel and of the beauties of nature (A2 103, A1 226). The prescription was perpetually renewable. Bill failed to note the actual period during which he took the tablets, or whether a later diagnosis ever confirmed a thyroid deficiency. Whatever the case, given the artist's unhappiness in these

Pencil sketch of a
friend, 1948. From
Bill's scrapbook.

years, the tablets seem to have been providential.

Bill graduated with a three-year Bachelor of Arts degree in 1949.
The university did not seem at the time to be one of the seminal
influences in his life, nor did it succeed in teaching him to spell. One of
his professors wrote on his essay on Milton: "Some excellent material
and much good sense marred by sloppy style, spelling errors and
cluttered organization." Readers of Kurelek's manuscripts will concur.
During his last year at university, Bill began to enjoy his studies more,
especially literature.

Experiences in these years, however, ran deep. In a January 1949
diary, Bill writes that education, by introducing so many controversial
issues and ideas, had only increased the tremendously painful pressure
of doubts and uncertainties on him. His grades were uneven, although
he succeeded in winning two awards: the Sellers Scholarship (1947)
and the Richardson Scholarship (1948), worth one hundred and two
hundred dollars respectively. He majored in Latin, English, and history,
since he had told Dmytro that he would eventually teach these subjects. Two single courses interested him more: introductions to psy-

chology and to the history of fine arts. The university's calendar described the latter as "a critical survey of the development of the visual arts of painting and sculpture from primitive to modern times *with special reference to the influence of religious, intellectual and social thought and customs on art*" (italics added).

From psychology, taken in the first year, had come the realization that his health problems, including severe eye pain, could be psychological in origin and might be cured by psychotherapy. This led to an entirely new game plan, which would eventually take him to British hospitals and to the years in London which became his advanced art education. Art history, in Bill's second year, awakened an abiding interest in the European art tradition, especially that of the late-medieval period, and the conviction that art should belong to the life and the society from which it sprang. These ideas would be reinforced in Toronto in 1949-50 and, more deeply, in the European years.

Bill later defined the underlying assumptions at the University of Manitoba as humanistic: "All the while my real interior convictions were being conditioned by the intellectual spirit of the university which—nobody made any bones about it—was primarily secular humanism" (A2 100). This was the spirit he later rejected as inimical to religion. The word "humanism" always meant *secular* humanism to Bill, and became, in his usage, a biting pejorative. This usage may puzzle those who think of Judeo-Christianity as one of the great humanistic traditions of mankind. Bill's attitude towards the word can only be understood within the rigorous context of his faith and the religious dogmas he came to accept in the mid-fifties. Paintings such as *Harvest of Our Mere Humanism Years* depict the Canadian university system in the twentieth century as an empty shell, a grasshopper eaten by ants who represent students in search of meaning and satisfaction:

> Their parents, sheltering under the grasshopper monument, are the well-meaning, hard-working previous generation. Often they gave up their religious view of life after immigrating to the new world. To make their own hard lives useful and meaningful they set as their goal the higher education of their children. They are portrayed worshipping the professor and the institutions of higher learning (the chocolate replicas of our universities and collegiates in the dish). ... One of the tragic deviations of mere humanism (man sufficient unto himself) is the revolt against legitimate authority. It ends up in the insecurity of anarchism—the destroyers destroy themselves.[8]

The reproof to his own parents is transparent. This monument to what

Bill saw as secular humanism is surrounded by deep earth fissures and dangerous precipices; over it hangs a nuclear bomb while monsters gnaw at the suspension device. In socio-didactic works, the artist liked to underline his points.

One more important development marked Bill's university years: the first deep friendship of his life. In Zenon Pohorecky he found the kindred spirit for whom he was starving. He met Zenon in February of his second year, in 1948, and described him in his diary as a person with "spirit-like dimensions ... a creative and interpretive artist; the very incarnation of what I dreamt of for myself" (A2 97). Rereading his own journal in the 1970s, an embarrassed Bill admitted that it sounded like a homosexual attraction but that the experience was indeed "like falling in love". The intensity of his inner life made for intense relationships. When a human being broke, even briefly, through his abiding loneliness, that relation was never casual. Zenon proved to be the first of a long line of confidants who would nourish Bill's spirit along its lonely way.

Zenon's father was the editor of a Ukrainian nationalist newspaper, and Bill found in their household a continual ferment of ideas. Zenon's art, described by Bill as "Time Magazine cover-style paintings", he acknowledged as an influence on his own style (A2 98).

The attraction was partly one of opposites. Zenon disregarded time, was impulsive, dramatic, and outgoing—a social being. Bill was time- and work-conscious, cautious, and secretive. He had set himself an extraordinarily rigid weekly schedule which governed his actions from 6 a.m. to 9 p.m., "bedtime" (A2 96). Six o'clock duties included polishing his shoes, one of the many rules made and abandoned during his pursuit of good grooming. His brother's mockery ended the polishing. There were slots for Ukrainian school homework and for studying the Ukrainian language. Only two hours a week was allotted to drawing. Other curiosities in this 1947-48 schedule include a single hour per week (early Saturday mornings) labelled "try writing poetry". Saturday and Sunday evenings were left free. The electrifying effects of Zenon's friendship freed Bill from his self-imposed schedule: "With some timidity I threw my rigid timetable to the winds and followed him to meetings, concerts, films, record shops and café discussions. I actually returned home to bed at times like two or one in the morning" (Ms 4). Zenon introduced Bill to philosophy and music. This exotic glimpse of café life in Winnipeg is missing from the published autobiographies, doubtless because the friendship had long since turned sour.

Bill judged himself dull and insensitive in Zenon's eyes. Roles were reversed in the spring when Bill passed respectably and Zenon failed.

61

The relationship was further upset by Zenon's borrowing money and failing (according to Bill) not only to repay the debt but even to take the loan seriously. Disgusted, Bill felt used. His self-confidence was higher in the third year, when he was beginning to "feel his oats" as an intellectual and an artist. He had outgrown the relationship. The two parted with a cryptic written exchange of affection.

The feeling of ending and of new beginnings which naturally attends a student's final year at university was augmented for Bill by the sale of the Stonewall farm in late 1948. He was commissioned by his father to keep the record of the farm machinery auction, an auction he would later paint. Strangely, his contemporary journal records no feeling of loss at the sale of the property which would be painted so many times in years to come and would always represent his real roots to the artist. In 1948-49 his antagonism towards his parents was actually lessened by the sale, which made him (he wrote in January 1949) better able to understand them. The remark is contradicted by numerous others of the same vintage that indicate Bill's almost total lack of sympathy for Mary and Dmytro. After the sale, the entire Kurelek family crowded into the small house on Burrows Avenue for the winter. In early spring, the four youngest Kureleks moved with their parents to their new farm at Vinemount, Ontario, near Hamilton. The older three remained to finish school. In a Joycean gesture of rebellion, Bill refused to attend his own graduation.

The reason for the sale of the Stonewall farm remains mysterious. Neither Bill's writings nor the surviving Kureleks clarify the matter. Like his famous son, Dmytro was secretive by nature or habit. Perhaps wartime prices for agricultural products had made it possible for him to opt for a pleasanter climate and a much smaller farm. As with the earlier move in 1934, he chose an area where many Ukrainians had already settled, as post-war immigration continued to alter population patterns. Bill was astonished by his first sight of Southern Ontario and describes it in superlatives: "Having grown up on the monotonous prairies this was like eating a banana split after years of plain bread and butter. It was so beautiful, so warm, so quaint, so lush, so picturesque, so civilized, so interesting, so mature. ... (A2 105) None the less, in years to come, it would be the "monotonous" prairie that would elicit much of his best work.

Bill's decision to study at the Ontario College of Art in Toronto seems, according to the 1947-49 manuscripts, to have been made quickly, early in 1949. Naturally it provoked a fresh confrontation with his father. Finding himself unable to reject Dmytro's philosophy of "prestige plus security", Bill stressed that money could be made in

(Left) John Kurelek and his wife, Helen, 1949. From Bill's scrapbook.

(Below) Bill's siblings Paul, Sandy, and Iris at Dmytro's third farm near Vinemount, Ontario, in the early 1950s.

commercial art. He began a search for summer work in Toronto which proved discouraging. His university degree seemed useless for temporary work, and he was over-qualified for manual labor. He soon learned to conceal the degree. Toronto's face became grubby, not quaint, during that long and difficult summer. In every job, from construction to waiting on tables, he suffered social ostracism. His differences included a refusal to talk about cars, women, drinking, and sports. Washing cars taught him that he had "two gears", and could shift into the higher one once he reached a certain speed or intensity of concentration (A2 108). Later, he would paint in high gear during long, isolated days and weeks of creativity.

In the fall of 1949, Bill found himself the only student entering OCA with a university degree. Most had come straight from high school. University grades are confidential, so Bill had allowed his competitive instinct to hibernate. Now he felt again "the old tug of competitiveness" and was relieved to find that, in his own judgment, he belonged in the top half of his year with regard to artistic talent (A1 215).

OCA had opened its doors only three years earlier. It had some impressive teachers at this time, and talented students (such as Graham Coughtry and Richard Williams) who were destined to become famous. Bill's teachers included John Martin, Carl Schaefer, Frederick Hagan, Harley Parker, and Eric Freifeld. Bill fondly dubbed the latter the Three Musketeers. Hagan taught costume, Parker color, and Freifeld life drawing (A2 110). Hagan initially awed Bill but is credited with loosening him up creatively. Parker floored him by asking the class to illustrate a recording of classical music: "No objective images were allowed. I was completely, utterly at sea." It was Freifeld's classes in life drawing and anatomy that stood out in Bill's mind as the place where he made real advances. This class provided his first exposure to a nude woman. Bill writes that he felt reverence rather than lust, and found the classes inspiring.

His relationship with Freifeld is both unique and, in a strange way, typical. It belonged to a pattern apparently begun with Zenon and continued through a long line of confidants, including Margaret Smith, David John, and Helen Cannon. Years later, after his conversion, his pattern of regular confession in church no doubt filled at least some of his need for this kind of relationship.

Like Bill's father, Freifeld's father had come from Eastern Europe, and the artist had grown up in Western Canada. Bill was moved by his watercolors of Alberta skies, while Freifeld found Bill a very promising student with a natural grasp on perspective and a talent for figure drawing. Bill began to attend all of Freifeld's classes, at the cost of cutting others in which he belonged. An epidiascope was used to

The artist at work during a
trip to New York (above) and
in Toronto, 1949-50. In later
decades, Bill would find the
camera an invaluable aid to
producing his art. From
his scrapbook.

project color prints of the European masters. Bill volunteered to operate the machine for Freifeld in all eight of his classes. The teacher was surprised by Bill's tolerance of the repetition this involved, but Bill assured him that he found it "very interesting".[9]

By the end of the first term, Bill had found a new opportunity to rebel. In his opinion, OCA lacked "the creative ferment or atmosphere ... for a dedicated fine artist, and that's what I thought I was" (A1 217). At a dramatic session in fellow student Gustav Rueter's home, attended by the Big Three among others, Bill announced his decision to abandon OCA for a "better" art school. In the second term he followed his own interests rather than taking the courses prescribed for first-year students. These classes included Schaefer's, Hagan's, and (above all) Freifeld's.

It is clear from Bill's first autobiography that he felt a sense of empathy with Eric Freifeld. "He gravitated towards me," the teacher recalls.[10] On his part, Freifeld was attracted by the unusual student, older than most, who obviously admired him and sought his advice: "Bill was much more interesting to me than other students. He came to me as a kind of counsellor. He initiated this." Bill told Freifeld that he had no intention of going on for a degree; he knew he would fail

Photographs of Bill during his OCA year, 1949-50. From his scrapbook.

because of the courses he was choosing to attend or ignore. Freifeld encouraged him to follow his own direction, to work on his own, and "get away somewhere". Together with Harley Parker, and sometimes with Gus Rueter (an older student, and a veteran), the friends went sketching in Toronto. Old houses, a cemetery, were all grist to the mill.

Freifeld observed that Bill loved literature and music, and the arts in general. Their relationship, he felt, was based on mutual respect and affection. Bill's interests were narrow but deep. He had no interest in politics, Freifeld recalls, and he was ambivalent about religion:

> He wasn't worldly. He was keenly interested in himself
> and in art, in the role he could play as an artist. He had a
> sense of destiny. He didn't define it, but he emphasized
> that he had a role to play. We discussed Bosch and
> Brueghel, two of the greatest artists who ever lived. We
> both admired them. Bill wasn't much of a communicator,
> he'd screw up his face when you proposed an idea to him,
> and put his head on one side. But when he did answer,
> finally, his reply would have significance. He seemed naïve
> in politics and world affairs, but he knew Ukrainian and
> Russian literature and he made interesting connections,
> psychological deductions, insights. He never sugar-pilled.
> He was a little like a figure out of Dostoevski, cryptic and
> mysterious. He saw himself as an enigmatic figure, a dra-
> matic figure. He identified with Dostoevski's fictional
> protagonists.[11]

Bill's feeling that he was marked for a high destiny is apparent throughout his writings. His strong reaction to reading the life of Van Gogh concludes with his stated belief that out of his suffering he was destined to produce great art. It must have been important to him that his confidants share that view. In Mexico, during his first trip abroad some six months later, he wrote to Freifeld with a proposal that the latter could not accept. In twelve pages of crabbed handwriting, Bill wrote to say that he was intending to make a trip, an odyssey that would change his life. He would like Freifeld to be his serious corre-spondent, the recipient of his secret thoughts. Freifeld, who was ill at the time, declined the honor. Like John Champagne, he sensed a need with which he could not cope, a responsibility beyond his resources. The letter was intimidating, even terrifying. "It was overwhelming," Freifeld recalls thirty years later.

He seems to have been drawn to the School of Fine Arts in San Miguel chiefly by the hope of studying under a Mexican artist such as

Orozco, Rivera, or Sigueros. The dream of apprenticing to a master in an atmosphere of "creative ferment" possessed him for nearly a decade.

To earn money for the anglophone art school in Mexico, Bill worked in Edmonton for some five or six months in 1950. He lived briefly with his maternal uncle, Steve Huculak, working at a variety of jobs. He painted, and experienced ecstasy, aided (he admits) by his thyroid tablets: "There was a delicious sense of complete abandonment to nature" (A2 117). He was hungry, tired, and shabby, but Joyce and Van Gogh were company enough.

In late fall, just ahead of the snow, Bill set off for Mexico, wearing the raincoat, "Joseph Cotten" hat, and work boots that are featured in so many self-portraits of the period: "My satchel carried an extra shirt, a scout knife, a loaf of bread and some apples. I'm amazed, thinking back on it now, that I set out with no provisions whatever for sleeping out in the open, something I did intend to do." (A2 118) A sleeping-bag would be added later, after many nights of hardship outside. His journey, by bus and hitch-hiking, took in the San Francisco art gallery and the city of Los Angeles, where he stayed three days with the Ukrainian Orthodox priest who had taught him to love Ukrainian language and culture during his high school years. Father Mayevsky seemed different. Perhaps the difference lay in Bill, but at any rate his idealistic view of the priest was deflated by the visit, despite the latter's kindness.

The trip was marked by another important event in Bill's life, the first of a number of mystical experiences. This incident, in the Arizona desert, would later provide the title for his own story of his life. The luck of the road left Bill stranded at night in a place where he naïvely expected to be warm. He tried sleeping under a culvert, curled up on bare ground:

> Suddenly I was aware that there was someone with me. He appeared to be a person in a long white robe and he was urging me to rise. "Get up," he was saying, "we must look after the sheep or you will freeze to death." I obeyed and set off at a near run down the road shaking violently from the chill. Presently I noticed that the sheep crowding before me had become nothing but those ragged fluffs of mist floating across the road. And the other person beside me had somehow blended into me and was gone. (A2 122)

In other ways, too, the Mexican affair proved to be a significant chapter in Bill's life. Two drawings from the period (one, a Mexican street scene; the other, a striking interior of a flophouse, with rows of iron cots and dejected-looking men) show the high degree of sophistication he had already achieved in this tradition. He had heard of contemporary Mexican artists in discussions at OCA, and his curiosity had been piqued. In Mexico he might really be challenged, might even discover the "roots" of his artistic talent (A1 225). A photograph of his first major self-portrait, done in Edmonton that spring, had won him entrance and the promise of a scholarship from Sterling Dickinson at the Institudo Allende. Bill says very little in *Someone With Me* of the work he accomplished there, choosing instead to focus on his reactions to the country and to the expatriate community whose life he shared for half a year. In San Miguel, the expatriates had time and occasion to discuss politics, art, religion, and sex. Bill was in his element.

In San Miguel, he found that the School had broken up shortly before his arrival and had been replaced by the Institudo. There were five teachers: Sterling Dickinson taught Spanish; Jack Baldwin, lithography; and Jim Pinto, life drawing. A local physician taught anatomy; and a local craftsman, picture-framing. "Only craft," Bill writes, having yet to learn that framing could be an art in itself. His insistence that craft and art should not be separated would come later.

In years to come, Bill would emphasize that he was "self-taught". By his own admission, he would eventually be forced to abandon his search for schools and masters and concentrate on teaching himself. Almost two years of study at OCA and the Institudo Allende would be forgotten, and Kimon Nicolaïdes' book—encountered in Mexico but not studied closely until 1952—would be credited with being his chief teacher. The influence of Eric Freifeld was once acknowledged by Bill in a Toronto talk in the 1970s, but more frequently a bootstrap mythology of self-help gave him solid satisfaction.

He described his time in Mexico "a great growing-up experience". It was his first exposure to the Third World, "the under-developed lands with their teeming poverty and handicapped peoples" (A2 126). Sympathy for the poverty came first, and a genuine appreciation of their culture second. He recognized that Mexicans had a "non-materialistic" culture and religious faith, which was more than he could say for many of the expatriates there. He did not see the culture's dark side, its graft and violence. A side-trip to Mexico City, in search of major Mexican artists and an eye doctor recommended by Pinto, proved fruitless on both counts but gave him a chance to see the capital. He prowled the grimy side-streets, appalled and fascinated by the openness of the prostitution trade.

Much of Bill's Mexican chapter, in the second autobiography, is taken up by anecdotes of personal encounters, many of them with homosexuals. The trip to Mexico had served as Bill's introduction to the latter. Homosexuality seems to have been almost unknown among the immigrant communities of rural Western Canada in the 1920s and '30s.[12] He had been crudely propositioned, and appropriately scandalized. In San Miguel he became friendly with a writer whose *casa* he shared. Forgetting Zenon, Bill calls Peter the first person who ever showed an interest in his interior life.[13] Their friendship was eventually broken by Peter's sexual advance. Peter accused Bill of lacking human warmth. Bill would later concede the accuracy of the charge at the time. His reaction was the fault, he claimed, of his parents: "Having received no love I had none to share out" (A2 132).

Bill's supposed appreciation of his parents' difficulties, which he claimed to have felt in 1949 after the sale of Stonewall, seems to have been short-lived. And what of the twenty years of intimacy with siblings John and Win, who were close to Bill in age and who had shared so much in the intimacy of farm life and the little house on Burrows Avenue? What of his sister Nancy, now a teenager, who shared her big brother's reverence for nature? No love?[14]

In the revisions to the autobiography made near the end of Bill's life, it is sad to see the hardening of the old interpretation which had erupted so bitterly in hospital in the 1950s and had been healed, he believed, by grace. After Mexico, fear of homosexual advances from male acquaintances added one more barrier to the many that made friendship difficult for Bill.

In May of 1951, Bill had a last fight with his would-be lover and headed north via Mexico City. He used buses and his thumb. Highlights of the gradual journey back included spreading his sleeping-bag in the bushes behind Ottawa's Parliament Buildings, and an ideological argument with his Toronto friend from OCA days, Communist Bob Cheng. He arrived at Vinemount with Mexican gifts for his family and hoped to make peace.

Bill had written a long letter to his father from Mexico explaining his many grievances against him. He describes this as the first of its kind.[15] The attempt to reveal "the whole ugly smelly brew" in the spring of 1947 had been aborted by Bill's reluctance to speak up, especially to his father. Writing was always easier for him than speaking. Letters could not be interrupted.

Despite the harsh letter, Bill actually hoped that his father would finance his proposed trip to Europe. This kind of naïveté is typical of the young Kurelek, and was never entirely discarded. On the one hand, he refused to accept his parents' hard work and financial sacrifices on his behalf as evidence of love, and on the other he continued to consider their sacrifices his due. Dmytro found the Mexican letter so painful that it had taken him months to read it. He had been unable (he wrote to his son) to swallow more than two or three pages at a time, "because something choked me in the throat and my eyes became wet and I could not see further."[16]

Dmytro had educated three children and now, in semi-retirement, was still responsible for a teenager and three pre-schoolers. Not surprisingly, he refused the request for money for what Bill called (with typically romantic phrasing) "my next artist's voyage of discovery—to Europe. . . . Feeling half-sorry for myself at this rebuff to my proffered hand, I resigned myself to one year's hard labour." (A2 136)

The "year" of hard labor was six months as a lumberjack in two camps in northern Québec and Ontario. At Camp Wilson Lafontaine, run by the Canadian International Paper Company near La Tuque, Québec, Bill found conditions "fantastically primitive". What was he here for? he asked himself while slugging it out in the sun. First, to prove he could do it. Second, to earn the precious stake for further travel. If his relations with his family put him in an unfavorable light, a gentle friendship with a fellow student restored the balance. Georgine Ferguson, met at OCA the previous year, lived in Montréal and had befriended Bill. His letter to her, written on June 11, 1951, from the Québec camp, is quoted in full:

> Dear Georgine:
>
> I am dropping you the line I promised. Though why you before all my other friends?
>
> The memory of the supper at your house is getting to be 2 weeks old. It will be many years old before it dies. It was so particularly significant because that was the first time I had anything to do with a woman. A feeling of contentment and peace—just from sitting in the house alone with you and talking. And Cathy—singing, "Haylo, everybody, haylo" and rechristening me "Weezel". I wished I could have a Cathy of my own.
>
> As for what has happened to me since then well I've given up hope trying to cure myself of the habit of idealizing a situation before I meet it in reality. The only comfort I have is that I have begun to anticipate setbacks. I came tearing out to the bush burning with enthusiasm to rake in $15 per day. I figured to return in the fall with a 1000 and a half. The first day I went to work singing the vast and silent forest said nothing. Only to me it seemed to draw back with gasping faltering steps of consternation as I felled tree upon tree.

Two days later the tables were turned. Literally I'd had it. When I dragged myself into the bunk of nights I was so exhausted my muscles and joints so wracked with strain and pain I could not even fall into the blessed rest of slumber. This wasn't the first time I'd worked in the bush but then the camp had been created for students exclusively and care was taken by the management to break us all in gradually. Now my hands—delicate "artistic" fingers shredded and blistered on the harsh bark of spruce logs thicker than my waist. Sweat—I drank gallons of water in the hot sun between laboured pants of breath. Flies— fanatical bits of blackness like Jap Kamit Kazes crawling over the bodies of their own dead to get at me dashing straight at my eyes into the caverns of my ears and my mouth.

But don't mistake me I'm not complaining—just laughing at my foolhardiness. Things have improved immensely. I'm beginning to see things besides myself for example a wonderful painting of the interior of my bunkhouse which I'm arranging in my mind day by day. And have I ever developed an appetite!

Well I began with food so I may (must) end on food. I'm too lazy to write more than a leaf anyway. Adios to Christmas.

Vasyl Kurelek

The confession that such a family supper was his first contact with a woman is amazing for a man of twenty-four. The general tone is both childlike and poetic. He would use the Ukrainian form of his name again in England despite the mockery of it found in *Someone With Me*.

In the second camp, near Fraserdale south of James Bay, most of the men were Estonian and Bill experienced national specialities such as saunas and a Finnish sour drink. He drove himself mercilessly on a twelve-hour, seven-days-a-week schedule. Unlike the others, he worked in the rain, wearing a rubber raincoat. Even Bill called his performance "fanatical". Defeated only by waist-high snow, Bill left the bush in early December with eighteen hundred dollars in cheques—a very sizeable sum for the time, as he notes.

The next six weeks were spent in Vinemount, two-thirds of that time going into an enormous Cossack painting, a historical illustration of Gogol's *Taras Bulba*. The panel was prepared with a white base of gesso by Gus Rueter while Bill stayed briefly with the Rueters, whom he calls "second parents". He describes the painting as a "precalculated geometric composition", yet it seethes with energy and bright colors. It was offered to Dmytro and was accepted—reluctantly, Bill felt.

The countdown to embarkation had begun. The first quarter of 1952 was spent in Montreal waiting for a Cunard cargo ship which would carry a handful of passengers to England for very low fares. On the $14.50 paid weekly by unemployment insurance, Bill managed to buy painting supplies and even to save money.[17] He prided himself on a "rational" diet of bread, margarine, grapefruit, and cold pea soup, and gloried in his cheap room on rue de l'Inspecteur in the docks area.

His time was not wasted; indeed, his management of that valuable resource was even more impressive than his handling of money. In some fourteen weeks, Bill made a good start at learning French (aided by only fifteen hours of classes), and applied himself rigorously to the exercises in Nicolaïdes' *The Natural Way to Draw*. His enthusiasm for the book is found in his autobiography, and in a letter to Georgine:

> The Nicolaides course began with two divergent approaches to drawing. In the first, the essence of a pose or action or the shape of a thing is captured with a quick scribble called a gesture study. The second is a slow, painstaking contour drawing and is done without looking at the paper. ... Gradually ... the two approaches meet and marry. ... Essentially, the Nicolaides approach gets the student to appreciate the inner reality of things—their weight, their hardness or softness, their texture, and so forth. ... I'd have written a letter expressing my sincere gratitude to him had he not already been dead for some time. (A2 138)

To Georgine, he wrote that the book should be "lauded and advertized to high heaven". He had done some ninety-five hours of work in the form of thousands of drawings of himself, his belongings, and people in railway stations, libraries, and construction sites. Efforts to qualify for cheap art supplies and models by joining an evening art class had met with rebuffs, both at the art gallery and at "that beautiful asylum for the elite—the Ecole des Belles Artes [*sic*]".[18] Bill was obviously paying more attention to his drawing than to his French.

There were also letters, though much of the correspondence proved disastrous. The rift with his father was deepening. A letter from Dmytro, full of hurt and anger, is quoted at length in *Someone With Me*. Bill read George Orwell's *1984*, a fictional portrait of political tyranny, at this time and it made a deep impression; he wrote recommending it to his Communist friends at OCA, only to find that his letter had terminated their friendship. Anguished, Bill walked the streets of the city he had begun to love and would later paint: "Chinatown, Harlem, the Market place, the bundled up policemen in their white caps, the streets full of children playing on a summer's evening and families sitting on the doorstep after supper (reminding me of Mexico), the two languages, all give it character."[19] In mid-May, his ship sailed for Southampton. The great adventure had begun.

5

A Bold Venture:
London, 1952-53

IN THE REWRITTEN VERSION OF HIS AUTOBIOGRAPHY, BILL SPEAKS OF GOING
to England with two conscious aims: to further his art schooling (Bill's
phrase is to "complete" it) and to find, through hospitalization, a cure
for his chronic depression and inexplicable eye pains. Here, as elsewhere, he oversimplifies.[1] Perhaps he found it less admirable simply to
admit that he very much enjoyed travelling. Like many young North
Americans, he was also in search of experience, eager to see the Old
Masters and the Old World. Both had taken on new faces for him at
university and at OCA. Perhaps he travelled to escape his conflicts.
Perhaps he hardly knew what he sought, but, mercifully, he was to find
it.

His search for an art school was extremely half-hearted, as he
admitted. Informal schooling was another matter. London became
Bill's art school: London and the cities of Western Europe. Their
venerable buildings were themselves works of art. Their galleries were
filled with paintings by Bosch, Brueghel, Blake, Van Gogh, Spencer—
and by a thousand named and unnamed artists in whose works Bill
discerned a tradition he was proud to share. The framing shops where
he would later be employed for four years after his hospitalization
were directed by European specialists who possessed secrets of gold-
leafing and other ancient skills largely unknown in Canada at the time.
At the evening college where he would take courses in framing and
book design, the instructors were the inheritors of the medieval guilds,
many of which survive today. To the boy from a prairie farm, the Old
World was a revelation and a delight.

But to the youth fresh off the boat, the city must also have been
bewildering and frightening. Four days after arriving in England, Bill
presented himself at the Maudsley Hospital in the southeast of London.

He tells it this way:

> To my amazement, within minutes I was being inter-
> viewed by a doctor. That doctor arranged two very impor-
> tant things for me: one was temporary lodgings near the
> hospital and the other was a definite date for me to move
> into the hospital for observation. During those pre-
> hospital days I began a half-hearted search for an art
> school in London. I guess my half-heartedness could be
> traced to my attention-starved childhood for, in art
> school, I would also have to compete for attention and I
> wasn't sure I was talented enough to deserve it. In the
> hospital I was guaranteed attention, albeit clinical. (A2 8)

In his earlier version, he writes that he soon abandoned the hunt for an art school, deciding to "learn to paint by painting". His strongest desire at this time was for hospitalization, where people would pay attention to him (A1 289). At this point in his life, hospitalization represented a security, psychological and economic, which Bill obviously needed and welcomed. He found the British kind and generous, and he was grateful.

Conversation with Dr. D. L. Davies, a consultant or senior physician at Maudsley in the 1950s, gives us another window on the scene. How had Bill come to the hospital?

> Dr. Davies: I got a letter from Canada one day, a young man
> had heard of the Maudsley. Could he come and get
> treatment? I told him no, he wasn't eligible unless
> he *became* ill *while* in Britain. Six or twelve months
> later, my registrar called me to see a patient he'd
> just admitted. He'd been found a few weeks earlier
> wandering in the hospital corridors. He was living
> in Penge. Dr. Brian Ackner considered him severely
> ill and admitted him to one of my beds. Kurelek
> told me he'd written previously and been refused
> admission.
>
> P.M.: *Was* he severely ill?
> Dr. Davies: Yes, very.

That Bill should have encountered the man to whom he had written and by whom he had been refused on his first day as an in-patient is one of the fascinating and providential coincidences dotting his life. That he neglected to mention, in his own story, his initial written request and its rejection hints at another side of the artist's complex personal-ity: *Fox Mykyta*, the sly one. Years later he would illustrate a transla-

Part of the Maudsley Hospital, 99 Denmark Hill, London. The psychiatric art collection was stored in this building.

Dr. D. L. Davies outside the Maudsley Hospital, 1981. He was the senior physician in charge of Bill's case during his stay from 1952 to 1953. Photos by author.

tion of Ivan Franko's famous political allegory of the same name. Secrecy had long been part of his strategy for survival.

Dr. Davies emphasized that he had never considered Bill to be schizophrenic; rather, "a man with a very introverted personality, a shy man, with periods of depression". The combination of depression and introspection could give the *impression* of schizophrenia. Psychiatric diagnosis, Davies added, is "very imprecise". Bill was first seen on June 4, 1952, was given an out-patient's appointment for June 18, and was admitted on June 23.[2]

The Maudsley, built on Denmark Hill in 1913, was founded as a psychiatric centre for university teaching on the German model. By 1939 its reputation as a post-graduate training centre was international. Vacated during the Second World War, it reopened in 1946, when its patients included shell-shocked soldiers. The Bethlem Royal Hospital, an ancient institution with a venerable history dating back to 1247, had been joined to Maudsley in 1948, when the National Health Service came into being. In 1952, the combined hospitals lacked a formal program of art therapy but were by no means disinterested in the therapeutic and diagnostic aspects of patients' art. As early as 1936, serious interest in psychotherapeutic art had been shown by Drs. Guttmann and Maclay, who began to collect the work of patients at the Maudsley.[3] The care that Bill received and the conditions he was given were influenced at both British hospitals by the interest many psychiatrists had in psychotherapeutic art and by the artistic talent Bill himself was soon to demonstrate.

Admitted to Maudsley for observation and treatment, he was given a bed in Ward Four, a dormitory for seriously disturbed men. The famous psychiatrist Sir Aubrey Lewis, whose features can be recognized in *The Maze*, saw Bill in these rather dismal surroundings. Its bunkhouse camaraderie was familiar to Bill from his logging days in Canada. He notes that a casual observer would have seen "nothing abnormal" about any of the patients. Davies remembered Bill at this time as a tense man who looked younger than his years, with a bad complexion and a furtive, anxious manner. He frowned and grimaced, but spoke coherently. He complained of eye pain, and chronic sleepiness. He had photographs of his paintings, and an autobiography in three large scribblers—part, one suspects, of the manuscript first written in 1947. In conversation he tended to depreciate his own importance. The earliest prognosis was unfavorable, because of Bill's unstable work record and family conflicts. But he was soon transferred to a convalescent ward, and the doctors became more optimistic about his prospects. The reason? His paintings. Bill's very real talent would provide an avenue for self-respect, and an invaluable means of expression and communication.

Bill writes of eating in a common dining-room, and sharing in routine chores like washing and polishing floors, of socials, which included dancing, and of sports like tennis, field hockey, cricket. Suspecting that he was under close observation, Bill pitched into the chores with a will. He took occupational therapy six days a week, where he worked well and appeared more at ease.

He made two friends, Ken Staunton and Frank Edwards, although his relations with men for much of his life seem to have been marred by the fear of homosexual advances. Serious and close human relationships, he writes, were "woefully foreign to me" (A29). He would store his belongings with Staunton on first leaving Maudsley, would stay with him briefly prior to his European tour, and would see him on and off over the next one and one-half years. In April 1953, Staunton informed staff psychiatrist Dr. Bruno Cormier that Bill was "agitated" and should be readmitted to hospital. It is probable that his anxieties and suspicions were aggravated by financial worries.

Soon after his first admittance, Bill found—by luck or by providence—relief from the chronic eye pain that had plagued him since adolescence and that had hampered his ability to paint. Bill calls it sheer coincidence. He had found an article on psychosomatic illness in a reading rack in his ward. The piece stated that psychosomatic eye pain could never actually lead to blindness in its sufferers. When staff physician Dr. Charaton confirmed the point the following day, the pain (Bill writes) disappeared within an hour: "I did a lot of paintings in that hospital, many with fine detail, but there was no eye pain. I was exultant" (A2 11); "'if only the depression and de-personalization could likewise be removed,' I sighed wistfully." (A1 294) Doctors' memories of his eye pain diminishing more slowly (although with considerable improvement from that point) suggest that Bill could dramatize and foreshorten, by artistic licence, when it pleased him.

Bill had brought with him photographs of some of his paintings which remained in Canada. From his earliest days in hospital, he impressed his doctors with his artistic talent. They soon sought a professional opinion, sending photographs of his work to a Swiss-trained artist and engraver with an established reputation in Europe. Golf Rieser, the artist who assessed Kurelek's work very favorably in July of 1952, wrote to a Maudsley physician that Kurelek's paintings demonstrated an exceptional talent and that the artist had great potential.[4] He also believed that Kurelek was not the kind of man to benefit from further formal art training.

Rieser's insight was rather remarkable for that date. Bill had already told Maudsley doctors who had gone to the trouble of investigating art schools on his behalf that he did not wish to enter a formal school; rather, he wished to meet congenial artists and to find his own level. His tour of galleries on the Continent was clearly the primary purpose for this three-week trip in August 1952, although he continued to tell himself and others that he sought an art school, possibly in Paris.

Just after his first discharge from Maudsley, Dr. Davies (who obviously took a personal interest in his Canadian patient) wrote to English artist Stanley Spencer on Bill's behalf. On several occasions Davies sought general help, advice, and connections in the art world. Bill was described as something of a misfit, a man with personality difficulties who was "anxious to find an individual Master".[5] He had, Davies observed, a great admiration for Spencer's work, for that of

Pieter Brueghel (his current "master"), and for traditional art in general. With great kindness, Spencer replied that he would be happy to meet the young man and to help him if he could.[6] No further correspondence survives, but art therapist and Bill's friend Edward Adamson believes that the meeting never materialized, possibly because of Spencer's ill health. What is clear is that Bill, by the summer of 1952, knew and admired Spencer's work, and perhaps sought in this British genius the contemporary master to whom he could apprentice.

Immediately on leaving Maudsley in August 1952, Bill headed for Europe. He continued to tell himself and others that he was seeking an art school, possibly in Paris, but his primary goal during those three weeks was to see the great collection of Brueghels in the Kunsthistorisches Museum in Vienna. During this pilgrimage (Bill's word), he spent three entire days "feasting" his eyes on details in Brueghel's paintings, concluding that Brueghel was "one of the greatest painters in history. Every brush stroke reveals his genius." (A2 14) In 1952 this was a depressing conclusion for Bill, since he believed that his own brush strokes had revealed absolutely nothing to date.

While travelling, Bill stayed in youth hostels, nursing his small Canadian savings. He had brought nine hundred dollars to England, earned in the bush. As well as his visit to Vienna, highlights of the trip included Belgium and Holland, where he saw more paintings by Bosch and Brueghel. He was moved by the great Van Eyck altarpiece, and by the countryside of Flanders. In Paris, he searched briefly and fruitlessly for an art school. He found the atmosphere there depressingly foreign.

He told Dr. Cormier that he had made a mistake in going to Europe. The trip had been a failure, from which he had learned nothing, a conviction that reflected his depressed state at that time. In fact, the works of Brueghel and Bosch had afforded him schooling of the highest order, but the full realization of this was to come later.

Travel took courage, especially in areas under Communist domination in the days of the Cold War. Part of Vienna was Russian-occupied. Bill writes: "I've always been scared. ... All my life my father had painted a frightening picture of Europe—the Old Country—as a place where people were malicious, deceptive, and thieving. England had helped dispel some of that image. But behind the Iron Curtain?" (A2 13) Scared or not, Bill ventured. He calls himself immature, and begins to see his home life as over-protected (A1 297).

Back in London, Bill took lodgings in Sydenham at 8 Jews Walk, and began work as a laborer with the London Transport Commission. In Brixton, the rails of the defunct streetcars had to be lifted, the roads rebuilt. Bill stuck at this physically demanding job for two months. The LTC story reveals a great deal about his character, and is unintentionally comic to read in his own account. Faced with Cockney, Scottish, and Irish laborers who took the longest possible breaks and thought nothing of petty graft, Bill experienced culture shock. His puritan values had always included hard work: "I couldn't stand *not* working—that is, wasting company time—and they'd drag the tea break out as long as possible" (A1 299). Throwing scrap iron onto the rubble truck for a covert kickback from metal dealers was even worse; Bill flatly refused to co-operate. When he gave these reasons for quitting, Transport officials pretended not to believe them. He had also been offended and alienated by the workers' dirty stories, a situation experienced in his laboring jobs in Canada. Bill believed these conflicts to be tied to class, whereas they seem to reflect largely ideological and personal differences.

The London Transport job resulted in *Tramlines*, one of Bill's great paintings, and his first sale. In Canada, he had already begun to use his camera as an aid to painting, and photographs were to become one of his main technical tools. Uncertain of his reception by the workers on whom he had informed, he sent Ken Staunton instead to photograph the job site and the work in progress. The result was a magnificent large painting of a London street-scene, bursting with vitality and detail.[7]

Amusingly, when the London Transport Executive proved interested in buying the painting, Bill computed its value according to the cost of material and the man-hours he had put in, at the rate of pay he earned as a navvy on the road gang, lifting rails. (In the sixties, he initially attempted to follow the same pricing system in Toronto for those sold through The Isaacs Gallery.) The Maudsley's Senior Registrar, Dr. Morris Carstairs, had written to the LTE to propose their purchase of *Tramlines*, saying that the painting gives "a very vivid and realistic picture" of a busy South London street where a gang of workmen are taking up the tramlines.[8] Carstairs believed it would appeal to a general audience. He mentioned Bill's asking price of "just over thirty-two pounds", noting (with Scottish thrift) that since his patient was by no means a mercenary character, the satisfaction of selling a picture to the LTE might compensate him "for any difference between the sum stated and whatever sum you feel able to offer." LTE officials may also have had Scottish blood. The deal was closed at thirty guineas, which translated into the oddly uneven sum of thirty-one pounds tenpence.

Ignorant of the niceties of social class, where guineas were used to price paintings and expensive clothing, Bill was puzzled by the sum, but grateful to Carstairs for having approached the Executive. It was (he wrote from Netherne Hospital) his very first sale, and it had boosted his morale, as it proved that his work was marketable: "It's supposed to be a big event in an artist's life and I should be excited but I'm still in an apathetic condition. However, I *was* excited Saturday evening and have been showing the cheque to my friends."[9]

C. F. Bonnett, Director of Civil Engineering for the Transport Board, was impressed with the painting's engineering detail. He stressed that the detail of the rails themselves, a type used only by London Tramways, was "absolutely accurate", and that the painted figures are all doing the right jobs in the right places: "It's almost a draughtsman's drawing."[10] Viewers enjoy the homespun, often humorous detail: a sign in a store window, "Tea off ration only"; the numbers and names on the red double-decked buses, all correct; the eager faces of children in a bus delayed by the construction work; the detailed cobblestones, forerunners of the thousands of stones in hundreds of Kurelek paintings over the next quarter-century; the colored bands at the wrists of jackets worn by some laborers and one bus driver, denoting second-hand uniforms pressed into service in post-war London where clothes, rationed during the war, were still in short supply.

This "realistic" painting, like other Kureleks, is strongly symbolic, impressionistic, and autobiographical. The foreman, described by Bonnett as "every inch a foreman", is the quintessential overseer and boss. He is set apart from the rest of the crew in their parkas by his collar, tie, and suit—the latter bedraggled, but still making its statement. An idling laborer, a powerful man who looks belligerent and somewhat stupid, bears a distinct resemblance to the artist's father. In this parody of Dmytro, Bill takes a secret revenge, as James Joyce did in his fiction. The workers' faces are impressionistically distorted, like those of some Ukrainian-Canadian farmers Bill painted in the 1960s. His objection to the endless sexual innuendoes in workers' conversation, and perhaps his own unease with sex at the time, are treated symbolically (and farcically) by the critical positioning of a large tool in front of one man.

Bill painted several personal statements into the scene, and two self-portraits. One is a man down a square manhole, trying desperately to get out, clawing upwards from the trapped space. His big, awkward gloves resemble the ones on the puppet figure in *Despair*, painted at about the same time and described below. The other is a trick, or secret, face, which comes into focus only when the painting is studied for some time. In the lower right, one sees first a strong nose, and a left eye, the forehead frowning in concentration, the mouth emerging after more study. Many a painter, including Michelangelo, has enjoyed fitting himself into a scene. The trick was to become a favorite with Bill. Once glimpsed, the face cannot be ignored. It is the face of a secret observer, watchful and intelligent.

I
The Magi, 1965-67.
Gouache, 18″ x 26″.
Private collection.
(see pages 219-20)

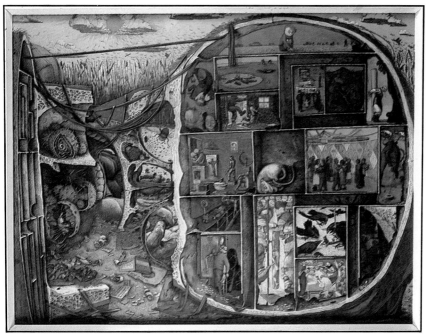

II
The Maze, 1953.
Gouache, 36″ x 48″.
Courtesy the Maudsley Hospital, London.
(see page 89)

III
Tramlines, 1952.
Gouache, 26″ x 38″ approx.
Courtesy London Transport Board.
(see page 81)

The painting's final statement lies in its composition, a cruciform shape. Cruciforms are common in Bill's paintings of the 1960s and '70s but are remarkable at this pre-conversion date. The configuration of the intersection of the tramline and a crossroad is raised to unnatural prominence. The resulting cruciform suggests the scene painted by so many Renaissance painters of the cross on the ground, not yet raised. The cruel faces of several laborers resemble workmen in traditional scenes of the Crucifixion. Two men are playing a mean practical joke on a third, hitting his head and upsetting his riveting. Bill must have been the butt of such jokes many times.

As an out-patient during his stint with the Transport Board, and throughout the winter of 1952-53, Bill came under the care of Dr. Bruno Cormier, a psychiatrist from Québec who was extremely interested in painting and in psychotherapeutic art. In the 1980s, Dr. Cormier believes he may have chosen Kurelek as a patient for this reason.[11] Like the pioneers, Guttmann and Maclay, Cormier was already collecting patients' art, and had exhibited some of their paintings in Paris at the International Congress of Psychiatrists (1950). In Europe at this time, the idea of art therapy was in the wind.

Bill's anger and frustration are evident in a note he wrote to Cormier, *demanding* some evidence of a cure and seeking "a deep emotional experience" rather than the talks he found trivial: "SOMETHING HAS TO BE DONE. The interviews are too few, too short. ... Solid advice, if there is any, is buried under words. Tell me what to do during the rest of the week; give me some hard work to do." (A2 17) The same angry hostility, greatly intensified, is evident in the nightmarish drawings he made while he was seeing Cormier. These drawings, which are currently in the collection of the AGO, are probably the most horrible ones Bill ever drew. They inspired fear even in his doctor.

The prevailing pattern is that of an inert Bill-figure, pictured as helpless victim, and a rapacious male figure, pictured as aggressor. Some of the sketches are composites, combining several scenes, a technique that was to flower in his paintings and drawings over the next few years. These scenes include: a man buried to his shoulders in sterile, stony ground while a vicious, monstrous bird pecks out his eyes with one claw while the other clamps shut the victim's mouth; a psychic rape, with a sadistic, powerful male burying his hand and forearm in the chest of the prostrate male figure beneath him (the hand is a sword); a blind man groping at the edge of an abyss, his cane tapping over the chasm, his coat muffling his mouth; a ship's hull with a tiny ladder extending a short way up its bottom side, leaving a man stranded in limbo; and a curious chart, in Bill's printing, which begins "Return to the womb. *Why?*" and includes self-descriptions as

Detail from *Remorse*, painted while Bill was in the
Maudsley Hospital. From his scrapbook.

"Desire to be as inert as possible. . . . I lie in bed til 10 or even 11 before
I get sufficient will to get up."

Despair, a fine watercolor from this period, depicts a humanoid
puppet in an amphitheatre, its walls just too high to climb, its doors
locked. The empty maze contains a large clock on the wall with a chair
below, the human puppet and its shadow, and a pattern of footprints
indicating continuous circling (with stops before clock and doors).
The figure has a strip of adhesive over its mouth on which a key is
superimposed: a double lock. It has button eyes and large gloved
hands, awkwardly extended. Colors and composition mark this as a
mature painting, one that prefigures both *The Maze* and *Lord That I
May See*. Its emotional impact, like so many Kurelek paintings in the
1950s, is very strong. The pain, the confusion, the mute pleading are
tangible. A bag over the head, tied at the neck, suggests ruffles. This
clown motif recurs in the hospital paintings, as does the image of the
blind man with groping, outstretched hands.

Bill found the Canadian doctor distant and unsympathetic, apparently
unmoved either by written communications or by an ineffectual attempt
at suicide. Cormier remembers a very inward person with a derelict
appearance, the grubby effect doubtless caused by the fact that the two
months of Bill's hospital appointments followed hard on his job with
the Transport Commission: "My impression is that he knew he was a

painter and intended to be one—he was sure of his talent in 1952. He was a great illustrator."[12]

Cormier's memories reinforce Bill's published ones with regard to his growing confidence in himself as a professional artist. Three weeks of work in an agricultural camp followed the tram-rails job. His hazy memory of the land-army work is perhaps due to memory damage from the electro-shock therapy he later underwent at Netherne. Following the November harvest, he took lodgings with the Newmans, a pleasant family living at 49 High Street in Penge. Bill called his new residence "proper" lodgings, and was amazed at his own financial daring. His unheated attic room must have seemed a "proper" place to paint, for at this point Bill decided " 'This is it. Now I am an artist by profession.' " (A1 301)

He put his new conviction to the test by doing three large works in three different mediums that winter in his fourth-floor garret: an oil, *Nature Versus Printed Matter*; the gouache *Tramlines*; and *Penge East*, a wash drawing of the view from his window. He found his three accomplishments vastly reassuring: "I could see I'd arrived as a productive artist" (A1 303). But would they sell? And if not, could he cope with a working world? Bill writes of painting at a small table in a very tight style so that his expenses were negligible, and of taking evening classes at a local art school. Here, as elsewhere, details vary or clash. According to his earlier version, he took a single two-month evening class in life-drawing (A1 304); in his revision, he attended "some half-dozen evening classes . . . but I dropped out when I found I wasn't making any impression on the teachers" (A2 16).

The teachers must have been blind, or Bill's need for praise bottomless, since the three large works done at this time are among his finest. *Penge East* is an incredibly detailed pencil drawing of back yards, storage sheds, and lower-class row housing.[13] Through an overall amber wash, minute touches of color are found in a small red gate and the orange chimney-pots. Washing is pegged to branches, individual implements can be seen through the windows of the shed. A dog watches a cat-fight.

The owner of the drawing today finds it grim, its details obsessional, its landscape desolate. But the drawing is eerie, detached, and utterly fascinating: a crowded slum with no human figures, though there is abundant evidence of human activity. The only emotion expressed in the painting is anger, shown through the animal conflict; in *Nightmare*, some months later, Bill would also use animals to suggest human antagonism. As in *Tramlines*, the composition is cruciform. There is also the suggestion of a road, one that leads to two poplar trees and a tiny church spire. There is no actual road but only an impression of one, through composition and color. As in so many Kurelek works, *East Penge* reveals its creator as secretive, observant, and detached from human activity: a seeker on the road of life. Trees and church spire suggest the direction of that quest.

Still deeply depressed, and frightened by the sharp decrease in his financial resources, Bill sought re-entry into Maudsley as an in-patient. Both versions of the autobiography reveal that economic worries aggravated his emotional disturbance. In the small room he was given soon after readmittance on May 11, 1953, Bill painted as if his life depended on it. In many ways it did. For one thing, he wanted to persuade the doctors to keep him in hospital long enough to effect a full cure. He hoped to do this by writing and painting: he would *prove* he was a "psychologically interesting" artist (A2 18).

Writing had always been important to Bill, as a means of communication which came to him more easily than speaking. Prior to 1970 he had written letters and the endless versions of his self-analysis that would eventually become *Someone With Me*. In his last decade, his writing blossomed in the simple texts that accompanied his paintings in book form and were to delight millions.

At Maudsley, Bill describes himself as writing continually in a free-association method: "I've looked back on these notes recently and I must say that I find them rather disgusting. There's a sick preoccupation with sex and an over-riding note of complaint and self-pity. Again, I was play-acting the role of a patient in the hope of effecting a break-through." (A2 18) In fact, Bill told his doctors more than once that he was acting a part. Years later, Dr. Carstairs emphasized that Bill exaggerated horrors in a melodramatic way, a characteristic typical of depressed people. A tendency to self-pity and, later, to self-congratulation continued to affect his self-image.

The latter half of his Maudsley experience is marked by a lasting relationship Bill had formed with one of the physicians, by major paintings such as *The Maze* and *Children's Games in Western Canada*, and by a budding friendship with an occupational therapist who was to be a catalyst in his search for security and faith. He was fortunate at this time to come under the care of two people, both with a keen sense of professional responsibility, who were willing to give individual attention to patients. Dr. Morris Carstairs took over from Dr. Charaton as Senior Registrar on Bill's case by late June. He followed the progress of his paintings with interest, and even invited Bill to his London home. Miss Margaret Smith, the Maudsley's Occupational Therapist, was an attractive and refined woman in her early thirties, some six years older than Bill. She was particularly generous to him with her time. She would visit him in his room, to talk and listen, to encourage. She held informal folk-dancing sessions in the Occupational Therapy Room during lunch hours, until Bill could be persuaded to join a larger group. Smith remembers literally "having to hold him at arm's length, by the shoulder, you know".[14] He was fearful of the most casual physical contact, yet was at the same time incapable of imagining mere friendship between a man and a woman. He had apparently been conditioned, on the Canadian prairies, to believe that all such relationships had to be sexual. Smith remembers that he presented an "almost" schizophrenic aspect in the spring of 1953: "he literally couldn't look anybody in the face. He had difficulty in talking to people, in making any sort of contact at all. .... My brief was to socialize him."

In years to come, Bill felt a tremendous gratitude to this caring woman. His autobiography tends to beatify the Margaret of his memories. The first edition includes a large drawing of a maternal Margaret comforting Bill beside his hospital bed. The foreshortened male figure, childlike and child-size, is bent nearly double with misery. He wrote of looking forward eagerly to the hour of her own time which Margaret would give him at the end of her working day. Since she was obviously a busy woman, that daily hour must have represented a considerable sacrifice. We can only presume that Bill interested her strongly, and that he had his own low-key brand of charisma.

Margaret Smith, occupational therapist at the Maudsley, on right, with her sister, Joan, and Bill's wooden figure, "William", carved during his months at Netherne Hospital. From the artist's scrapbook.

There was always something in Bill which made others eager to help him. He wrote of his confidence and trust in Margaret, and of their mutual fondness for verse. In Smith's view, the trust came slowly during the next year while Bill was at Netherne. But poetry and music were their first points of contact. In Maudsley, she lent Bill a favorite anthology of English verse, wrapped to protect it. The latter touch proved providential, for the homemade jacket caught Bill's eye. It was made from a Catholic newspaper. Bill claimed to have been "a staunch atheist at the time", "still preaching atheism" (A2 26, A1 330). In response to direct questioning, Margaret admitted that she was praying for him. The admission, and her serenity, strength, and faith, intrigued Bill.

Morris Carstairs confirmed that Margaret practised an informal kind of psychotherapy; put in psychiatric terms, "Bill had a positive transference for his therapist, attributing to her the qualities of an ideal young woman."[15] Margaret expanded on this:

P.M.: Bill says in his autobiography that he thought he was in love with you. Dr. Davies said the same thing.

Smith: Well, Morris put it differently, and this amused me greatly. He sat down beside me in the canteen and said cheerfully, "How's your counter-transference?" Counter-transference is when the therapist has a transference back.

This jocular treatment of a touchy topic pleased Margaret, who emphasized (decades later) that she mothered Bill: "My own feelings were mother-hennish."[16] It was a tactful comment by a thoroughly professional woman.

In the small, high-ceilinged room that served as bedroom and studio, its tall, narrow window overlooking the lawns and trees behind Maudsley, Bill began work on two strangely diverse pieces. One was a wash drawing entitled *Nightmare*, the other a large panorama of children's games in Western Canada. The latter drew on his own childhood memories and was inspired by Brueghel's treatment of games. The former was the bitter fruit of a hard winter, bad dreams, and a lifetime of anxiety.

Years later, for his Toronto exhibitions, Bill began to write detailed descriptions of his major paintings, noting their circumstances and intended meaning. The first such texts to survive are for *Nightmare* and *The Maze*.[17] He describes the drawing as a loose association of symbols, dreams, and actual incidents, and proceeds to list and comment on its seventeen scenes. The prevailing mood is one of horror, despair, and disgust: a cyclist rides along a narrow, crumbling cliff path;

a blind monk, taunted by children, is unable to enjoy or understand life; sex is polarized into sentimental worship from afar, the coupling of dogs and wolves (some with human faces), and guilty masturbation; chickens devour one another, a phenomenon of cannibalism witnessed in his youth which symbolized "my being set upon by the community I lived in because I was shy and diffident"; a row of seven Lombardy poplars, six of them healthy, is Bill and his siblings: "the stunted one represents me having been tied in a knot in my childhood."

The drawing vies with *I Spit on Life* and with several of the drawings shown to Cormier as his most horrible, in terms of subject matter. Indebted to both Blake and Bosch, it is a technically sophisticated and impressive work. Its element of hope, of which Bill was probably unconscious, lies not only in that artistic competence of the whole, but in the drawing's grim humor, a survivor's humor which cuts through the self-pity and seasons the bile. A dead rat, its slit belly bulging with worms, is described as "my father's unhealthy ambitions". (It may also be a product of Bill's preoccupation with death at the time.) His ambivalence about friendship, feared and desired, is depicted as a mouse running along the rim of a cooking pot, "caught between the frying pan and the fire". "Courage" is a medieval dragon with an ignobly truncated tail. And, as in *Tramlines*, Bill teased his viewer with a secret face (top left), not of himself this time but of a venerable, patriarchal male.

The Maze, less bitter, is also leavened with humor. Black and satiric as it is, the humor indicates intelligence and courage. Bill painted this large gouache on hardboard in approximately six weeks in July and August of 1953. *The Maze* became famous, but Bill never spoke of *Nightmare* after leaving Maudsley. In his autobiography, he calls *The Maze* "a kind of pictorial package of all my emotional problems in a single painting. . . . It was my firm belief that my problems stemmed in the main from my father's farm failures, his habit of taking his frustrations out on me because I was so useless at farming. My helpless dependence on the doctors was represented symbolically by a white rat knotted up in the middle of the maze. I had picked up that idea from the two-unit course in psychology I took at the University of Manitoba." (A2 18-19)

Carstairs, who had encouraged Bill to paint his painful memories in chronological order, remembers Bill's comments on his painting technique: "He explained to me that he liked to think about a painting and visualize every detail. It matured gradually in his mind. He said he wouldn't start to paint until he saw the whole painting in its entirety, each compartment and detail. After that, it was as if he was painting from a copy, he had visualized it so fully."[18]

Brilliant in its composition, *The Maze* shows a man's skull in cross-section lying on a barren plain before a field of wheat. The plan was inspired by a drawing of a skull seen in a medical textbook. As for the background, Bill's memory was conveniently bolstered by a wheat field which adjoined Bethlem in the 1950s. On the left, the cross-section (seen at right angles to the viewer) becomes a maze with no exit, its chambers filled with scenes of horrors past and present; on the right, the fore-shortened matching half is empty, while symbolic objects from the outside world are seen through eye sockets, mouth, and nose.

Bill's text describes his maze under seven headings. The white rat curled in the centre "represents my Spirit (I suppose) ... curled up with frustration from having run the passages so long without hope." "Home" is depicted as violent rejection by his father and brutal bullying at school. "Politics" is the Ukraine being raped by Russian soldiers, and Orwellian placards: "War is Peace", "Slavery is Freedom", "Wrong is Right". "Sex" is "the merry-go-round string of rag dolls and wall-flowers" (so much for the hospital socials), or the chained bull straining to get at some cows in heat. "Social relations" are a lizard pinned down by a flock of crows, or Bill as a hospital patient flanked by curious doctors. He is, alternatively, in a test-tube under scrutiny, or in bed being offered grapes, roast chicken, and a voluptuous maiden while doctors peer from behind screens.

Bill called these companion scenes benevolent and malevolent conspiracies. The painting's underlying humor increases with study. The flanking doctors are satirical portraits of Maudsley physicians, including Sir Aubrey Lewis and Morris Carstairs, recognizable to those who knew them.[19] Plied with delicacies of every kind, the bedded Bill wears a grin of delight. Yet these relatively light-hearted satires adjoin scenes of a man strapped to a conveyor belt moving inexorably towards "the roller Death"; of a Museum of Hopelessness where the Future is a mushroom cloud and "courage" consists of hitting one's head against a wall; and of a ghastly self-portrait where Bill slices the flesh from his own left arm in an experiment which attempts to prove "I am really mortal."

The outside world has an ominous yellow sky and a horde of locusts hovering over the wheat, representing the drought and insect plagues that tormented the Kureleks during the 1930s. The Kurelek text concludes:

> The *thorny*, stony ground is a kind of T. S. Eliot Waste-
> land, spiritual and cultural barreness, the pile of excre-
> ment with flies on it represents my view of the world and

the people that live on it. The loosened red ribbon bound together the head of a kind of T. S. Eliot Hollow Man and was untied by psychotherapy (Dr. Cormier) but since the outside world is still unappealing the rat remains inert. Before the head was opened burrs (bitter experiences) choked the throat ... and when it was opened the sawdust and shavings (tasteless education) spilled out ... equally tasteless Art, painting, literature and music. The burrs also represent, in the eye socket, the successive evaluations of my character by any friend during the process of acquaintance, all repellant but hopeful until the last when the heart is discovered a grub.

Bill shows his family, where his early relationships had been prickly at best, as burrs. The last sentence of his text is highly significant, as he describes a scene in the painting's right-hand corner. A burr in cross-section is another maze, echoing the larger one. Inside its circle, suspended on long thorns, is the figure of a little boy. Two profiles of his father, like crescent moons, surround the figure within the burr. One is a handsome man with white teeth, smiling; the other visage is demonic, with bulging eyes, frowning brows, hooked nose, grim mouth. The child holds out his arms beseechingly to the smiling father. And the text? Bill identifies the child as himself, "trapped painfully between the two aspects of my father, the one I hated and the one I worshipped."

Worshipped? The word is strong, the painted image even stronger. The same conflicts that had sealed Bill's lips drove him, relentlessly, to paint. The painting's emotional impact begins with the forlorn little figure on the Canadian prairie with the face of an old man and the eyes of a haunted child. It is developed through the scene of the helpless lizard ringed by crows who somehow suggest doctors, and climaxes in the small figure caught between two fathers in a frightening world.

Maudsley physicians, whose interest in psychotherapeutic art had been formalized in the 1950s in the Guttmann-Maclay Art Collection under Dr. Davies' management, had been at pains to obtain a professional assessment of Bill's work in 1952. On his readmission in 1953, Cormier suggested that an expert opinion on Bill's work should be sought from the Council of the Royal College of Art. The verdict from painter William Coldstream was mixed. Coldstream admired the draughtsmanship but found Kurelek's work lacking in originality and color sense. The judgment is puzzling, since we do not know which works were submitted to him. Shortly thereafter the doctors decided that Bill would profit most from an extended stay at Netherne Hospital in Coulsdon, Surrey, where every encouragement would be given him to paint. The fact that Carstairs was leaving for Edinburgh that fall may have influenced the decision.

In October 1953, Dr. Davies wrote to the senior physician of Netherne, requesting admission on a long-term basis for a highly talented artist. Bill was described as a Canadian of Ukrainian origin who had had a very difficult and disturbed childhood under a strict father. His problems were minimized; indeed, for someone in need of a lengthy period of hospitalization, they sound quite mild. No doubt Davies was hoping for preferential treatment. Bill was described as having a schizoid or introverted personality. He was not schizophrenic but was extremely shy and introspective; he suffered largely from a personality disorder. His second period of hospitalization at Maudsley had confirmed in his physicians a general view that he could achieve "a satisfactory equilibrium under sheltered circumstances".[20]

As a teaching hospital, the Maudsley was intended for fairly rapid turnover. Patients in need of lengthy periods of care were normally consigned to county hospitals. One suspects that had Coldstream's verdict been more favorable, Bill might have been retained in London. Both of the hospitals in question, however, were interested in exploring the therapeutic possibilities of art; and both were, in effect, ready to play patron by providing a promising artist with what amounted to the ideal conditions of a sheltered workshop.

Davies went on to praise the patient's unusual degree of artistic achievement. He noted that some ten paintings had been done prior to or since admission to Maudsley, and enclosed a photograph of one entitled *Self-Portrait*. He prophesied that the patient might eventually earn a very handsome living through his art. Dr. Freudenberg at Netherne was pleased to co-operate, and the die was cast.

Bill standing outside the Maudsley with the paintings he had executed during his time there. *The Maze* stands to the left behind the artist. From his scrapbook.

6

Sliding Down:
Netherne Hospital, 1953-54

KURELEK ARRIVED AT NETHERNE, HIGH ON A HILL OVERLOOKING THE
Brighton Road, on November 3, 1953. He had been sent to the county
psychiatric hospital because it had an art therapist, a new art therapy
program, and a chief medical administrator who enthusiastically supported both. Netherne even had a gallery for displaying patients' art.
Bill was to remain there less than fifteen months. Before he checked
himself out (as he had checked himself in), he had been, by his own
testimony, to hell and back. Bill would get worse before he got better
and would experience at Netherne what may well have been the most
painful period of his life.

Soon after his arrival, Bill painted a self-portrait in sombre browns
and ochres entitled *Where Am I? Who Am I? Why Am I?* It vividly
portrays his inner landscape. He stands, sightless and groping, in a
windy wasteland with one dead tree. The scene is one he painted and
drew many times, especially in the fifties: himself in baggy flannels and
old oxfords, trench coat and brimmed felt hat, walking the road of life
with a knapsack on his back. In this version, however, there is no road.
The posture is that of the suppliant, with the greatest detail lavished on
the groping, outstretched hands. And the face! Centred, poignant, with
empty eye sockets and furrowed brow, the face is obviously indebted
to Brueghel's blind men. A lost soul. Figure and horizon form a cross,
the cruciform shape echoed in the small dead tree and reinforced by
thorny twigs which suggest a crown of thorns. A slight suggestion of
hope lies in the deft handling of light and wind.

Netherne Hospital in 1953 was at the forefront of psychiatric treatment in Britain. In Dr. R. K. Freudenberg (Physician Superintendent,
1951-73) it had a pioneer in rehabilitation, a man with an international
reputation and a broad humanitarian vision. Established in 1908,
Netherne's central red-brick building resembled a private Victorian
mansion more than an institution. Its windows were edged in orna-

mental white stone, and its façade was dominated by a large clock-face, an imposing arched doorway, and a covered entrance with Grecian pillars and an ornamental balustrade. Two magnificent Cedars of Lebanon completed an effect calculated to impress and reassure.

Bill, however, was not reassured. His description of the hospital complex refers to "the villas of the deranged and the depressing Netherne watertower and smokestack" (A2 21). He did appreciate the country quiet, the space, the room for long walks. The gardens, in the early 1950s, were probably the most beautiful hospital grounds in Britain or Europe. The patients participated in gardening as a form of therapy, and there were many gardeners on staff. In the 1980s, the grounds form an arboretum, with a great variety of beautiful trees and shrubs, including silver birch, oak, beech, maple, chestnut, magnolias and other flowering trees, and many types of evergreens. Dozens of small buildings and numerous winding roads give the complex the appearance of a village, complete with a Protestant church, a Catholic chapel, a library, greenhouses, and private residences: a self-contained world. The grounds are isolated at the top of sweeping grassy downs next to parkland known as Coulsdon Common.

Its almost idyllic appearance in the 1980s belies the grim realities of the hospital atmosphere in the early fifties, before the changes introduced by the British Mental Health Act of 1959. Prior to that date, such hospitals operated under the Lunacy Act of 1899. Now the wards are unlocked, the corridors filled with light, and the patients wander freely and are sometimes indistinguishable from staff. Then there were locked doors and dark corridors. Six-foot iron fences discouraged unscheduled departures, and the atmosphere (as described by a Nursing Officer who began to work at the hospital soon after Bill's departure) was bleak and uncompromising.

In an environment where the gap between patient and staff was absolute, and the sexes were rigidly segregated, patients were dehumanized, and mere daily existence could be more harrowing than active treatment. Nursing Officer Noel Duffy praised Dr. Freudenberg for alleviating the rigidity of routines, for "opening the doors". Duffy showed me the baronial Recreation Hall where Bill would have gone for music, dances, and other social activities:

> See that chair? It was for the Chief Male Nurse. See that
> chair on the other side of the hall? It was for the Chief
> Female Nurse. The male patients filed in here, beside the
> male nurse's chair. The female patients filed in over there,
> beside the female nurse's chair, and lined up along the
> other wall. When the band struck up, the male and female
> patients moved forward in two lines, and danced.[1]

(Top) Main entrance of Netherne Hospital, and (bottom) the grounds, surrounded by the original six-foot-high spiked iron fence. The gazebo in the background contrasts ironically. Photo by author.

One thinks of those two warders, grim parodies of Victorian chaperones, and of Bill's several versions of dancers as wooden puppets on strings. A more apt metaphor would be difficult to find.

Bill was more fortunate than most in having greater freedom of movement and special regulations during much of his time as a patient at Netherne. He was free to walk where he pleased, in the hospital grounds and the adjacent parkland. In Highfield Villa he had a small room as a studio where he could paint without interruption. (Originally for linen storage, this windowless room sounds curiously like the space he later chose as a studio in his Toronto home.) The resulting isolation may have slowed his recovery. Conversely, painting seemed to offer an avenue of escape from the maze as Bill painted his suffering and his pleas for help. Here was a medium that gave him self-respect, an avenue of communication he was to make uniquely his own.

Bill was encouraged in this self-therapy by Edward Adamson, the hospital's art therapist. Soon after the Second World War, Adamson had volunteered to talk with Netherne patients about the reproductions in a circulating picture library sponsored by the Red Cross. He was subsequently hired by Dr. Cunningham Dax as the hospital's first art therapist. The discipline was then in its infancy, and Adamson was to become one of its founders. Himself an artist, Adamson set up a studio workshop in a small hut on the hospital grounds where patients could come to paint, draw, and sculpt.[2] He gave to their work neither direction nor interpretation, simply support and encouragement. In Adamson, Bill found a friend. And, in the context of Adamson's work, Bill's paintings took on greater importance in the eyes of the hospital physicians.

Adamson recalls the intimidating atmosphere of British psychiatric hospitals in the late forties and early fifties, and his own apprehension about working in such institutions. He remembers long corridors, locked doors, and post-operative patients with shaven heads, bandages, bruises, and black eyes. Dr. Anthony Stevens' description of a conventional mental hospital of the time reinforces Adamson's:

> ... The architecture speaks eloquently of the attitudes governing its construction—a huge, impersonal fortress, standing in an isolated location, and surrounded by high iron-spiked walls. The intention behind such a repository for human misery was far from therapeutic. ... It was a concentration camp for the imprisonment of unfortunates who had become an embarrassment to a society that preferred to keep them out of sight and out of mind.[3]

Stevens credits Adamson with providing, or creating, an "enabling space".

When Adamson came on staff, Netherne Hospital had about 2000 resident patients. He felt that it had neither the will nor the ability to cope with individual needs. Those in the locked wards wore hospital clothes, slept in iron beds in long, uncurtained rows, washed in communal showers without privacy. In such a setting, artistic expression offered an oasis for individuality and creativity. After more than thirty years at Netherne, Adamson firmly believes in "the extraordinary efficacy of Art as healing".[4] He saw the art therapist as a "catalyst" to facilitate this healing flow.

Through Adamson's influence, an art gallery was built in the hospital, where patients' paintings were used as a teaching tool for medical students. The gallery was a long, white, windowless room with a high sloping ceiling dominated by four large skylights. Large panels hung from the ceiling and could be raised or lowered for displays. Here Bill's paintings and drawings were hung. In a space filled with startling images, his were often the most startling and are so remembered by hospital personnel.[5]

Bill's use of graphite seemed to show another perspective. Several strong drawings from this time demonstrate his keen draughtsmanship, intelligence, energy, and humor. *Hospital Ward*, for example, shows Netherne Commonroom, with some half-dozen patients lounging or reading, anxious or resigned.[6] Two touches break the serious mood and the classical technique. On a table in the fine old high-ceilinged room stands a book, *How to Win Friends and Influence People*. Through a window a stick figure can be seen running away. Dale Carnegie's advice was not for Bill. *Patients Working in Boiler Room of Netherne Psychiatric Hospital, England,* in a more impressionistic technique, shows two men shovelling coal while a third supervises.[7] This very symbolic drawing incorporates objects such as a large wheel and a ladder. The ladder, like the ship's ladder in one of the Maudsley drawings, leads nowhere. The wheel may be a treadmill or a trap, as it so often seems to be during Bill's hospital period. A third drawing, of Netherne's workshops, impressed Adamson as being particularly fine.

In his first month at Netherne, in November, Bill was upset by his removal from Maudsley, where he had begun to feel thoroughly at home, and from Margaret. He suspected that he had been demoted as a patient. Whereas the prospect of an indefinite stay at Netherne meant security, he could sense that "the 'fun' of being a patient was over" (A2 21). *Fun?* Three days after his transfer from London, he wrote to Dr. Carstairs that the transfer had not gone as smoothly as he had expected: "I'm rather lost, to put it tamely."[8] He was established in Highfield Villa, which Bill described as a two-storey brick building isolated in a cabbage patch.

The cabbages were destined to become famous. Soon after entering Highfield, Bill underwent a mystical experience which to him was extraordinary and awe-inspiring.[9] He connected it to his new-found interest in religion, sparked by Margaret. He woke past midnight one night to see the moon shining brightly on the cabbage field and the distant pine woods. All was peaceful, yet Bill experienced "a sense of complete and utter abandonment", a desolate sense of being lost and alone in the universe. Finally, thinking of Margaret, he began to pray— for the first time since he was eleven. Years later his mammoth painting of the vision was to be titled *All Things Betray Thee Who Betrayest Me* (1970): in a room lit faintly by moonlight, a man sits in a hospital bed, his face intent and rapt; through the large window of his mind shine hundreds of cabbages, row on row, beneath a luminous sky. A glass of water on the inner window ledge symbolizes divine grace. The work is almost as disturbing and enthralling as the experience must have been.

Meanwhile, the depressed artist was finding his various doctors well intentioned but ineffectual. *Help Me Please Help Me Please Help me—Please Help* (1953) shows Bill as a bird with its head in a bag, flying across the Atlantic in hope of finding help: "Instead, a figure in a clinically white coat clips my wings, puts me in a cage and hangs [it] . . . on the white cliffs of Dover" (A1 334-35). His revision identifies the smocked figure as Dr. Carstairs. At Netherne, Bill came under the care of Dr. Sybil Yates, whom he terms a good woman, though no more effective than the other doctors had been.

Dr. Yates had been trained as a psychotherapist. All winter long, she and Bill talked of his childhood, apparently with mutual frustration. Dr. Yates observed an improvement in her patient's social behavior, but believed that his sense of alienation and suspicion remained the same. As for Bill, he had little faith in talking. He followed his analyst's advice by constructing several dolls to represent himself in infancy:

> I am seeing Dr. Yates only an hour a week now having
> what I think is psychotherapy—the two of us sit in chairs
> by her fireplace and chat "seriously". She has traced my
> main trouble right back to early babyhood from some free
> style drawings I did for her (so she says) and today I
> made a little baby about four inches long out of plasticine
> which I am to carry in my pocket and "nurse". Till I see
> her with it on Wednesday I've made it safe by putting it in
> a wrapping within a wrapping within a wrapping within a
> wrapping within a big egg within a steel drum within a
> box.[10]

The latter sentence is perhaps the strangest Bill ever wrote. Adamson remembers him walking the hospital corridors with a paper doll, looking lost.[11] Margaret, whose professional training had been vastly different, had no sympathy with Freud's regression theory and believes that Bill's emotional state worsened during this treatment.[12] The doll's final form was as a two-foot wooden puppet with jointed arms and knees, carefully carved by Bill. He took the totem with him from Netherne, and carried it back to his parents' Ontario farm in 1956. By then, Bill must have recovered his sense of humor and viewed the doll ironically. It eventually disappeared, but not before Bill had placed its photograph in one of his albums.

Like many of the doctors in Maudsley and Netherne during Bill's tenure, Dr. Yates was interested in psychotherapeutic art. As Carstairs had done, she encouraged Bill to paint his problems. *Where Am I?* and *Please Help* reflected his darkening mood. *The Maze* was a hard act to follow, but in the winter of 1953-54 Bill produced two equally complex panoramic paintings whose grim themes mirrored his inner turmoil. One contains a ray of hope, through a section which was purposely left unfinished at the time. The other, a Swiftian satire on the world at large and Bill's family in particular, was to be retitled *Behold Man Without God* in his Toronto years.[13]

Despite the bitterness of the paintings, Bill later discerned in them the gradual shift "to images with spiritual connotations". At the time of renaming *Behold Man Without God*, Bill also repainted its most repulsive parts. He imagined a future revelation of its original horrors. Restorers would find, under the anthill and the beehive, "two giant women in labour spawning the teeming masses that make up the cannon fodder of the world's warring armies. Under the dead, wormy rat is a pile of human excrement. And the weeping child is really a boy wiping his bottom using Shakespeare for toilet paper." (A2 19) Among the horrors that remain are a rickshaw cart pulled by Bill and driven by his father, complete with whip; and a street hawker whose poster reads, "The William Kurelek Theatre presents William Kurelek in William Kurelek, an epic tragedy by William Kurelek. Continuous Performance." If Bill was once termed obsessive and narcissistic, one can see why. Yet the ironic self-labels also suggest a measure of distance and objectivity.

I Spit on Life is another version of Bill's life, seen—and the qualifier is important—by the artist at what was doubtless the lowest point of his life. Its indictment of his parents and of himself is neither a balanced view nor a final one, but is rather the view induced by depression and by an illness that may never be understood. This extraordinary medley of a dozen scenes linked by stones and chains is actually a second maze. Like the first, painted six or eight months earlier at Maudsley, it represents chambers of the mind. The skull is by now a stone tomb. The prevailing theme is entrapment, entombment, and death. Most of its self-portraits are tied or imprisoned in some way, many by chains that link the manacled ankle of one Kurelek figure to a similarly manacled figure in another scene. In this painting even his friends Dr. Carstairs and Margaret Smith have deserted him. Years later, Bill described it as a montage of memories and social comments. Adamson calls it an intensely realized iconography of despair.

Dmytro is featured twice, hideously: first, as a demonic father at a family meal in the thirties, cuddling John while threatening William; second, as a furious farmer, frustrated by the collapse of an overworked horse, bludgeoning the beast to death.[14] Bill is not much kinder to himself. He shows two schoolyard bullies hurting his younger brother while a booted leg, leaving the scene, indicates Bill's failure to come to the rescue. He shows himself in a crib, terrified by the turkey-vulture poised to strike through the rails; himself in a library, suffering from eyestrain; himself struggling to escape from a coffin whose lid is held down by the recognizable figures of Morris Carstairs and Margaret Smith; himself as a faceless puppet holding a stack of posters and a book labelled "My Lost Youth: Wm. Kurelek". The puppet's placard reads: "Free: Take one (or else). Now available in illustrated book form, 'My Lost Youth', a play based on the real life story 'Life Was Beautiful'." This puppet is chained to another one near by with a seam up the back of its head. It hangs by the neck from a dead tree. Below the gibbet is a zoo-like enclosure with a sign: "*Notice*: the animals to be seen in their grotto are a freak species found in a Canadian jungle. The origins of its habits have been depicted in each case for the interest of the visitors. *Beware*. These animals have self-pitying suicidal tendencies. Visitors are requested not to humour their egotism."

At the centre, Bill painted himself painting himself in a mirror. Chained by the ankle, he wears prison or hospital garb. His identical self-portraits repeat, and regress, to infinity. (So much for psychotherapy.) Echoing this motif is the shadow thrown by the hanged puppet, adding a second victim to the scene. The entire painting is filled with meaningless repetitions: bars, walls, ropes, spikes, and chains. No exit. Most curious is the depiction of Death as the traditional skeletal figure of medieval art. Bill's Death holds an axe in preparation for decapitating him, wears a wristwatch, and bears a placard: "Go away you don't exist."

In his autobiography, Bill writes of an unfinished corner of this painting, a scene originally intended as a satire on religion. It shows an ape-like humanoid with a devilish resemblance to Bill tiptoeing away, finger to lips, from a billboard on which is sketched "Come to

Church". The church is a whited sepulchre. Another legend announ-
ces "Willie the Christian Clown was here." Chained by the ankle, the
figure may not believe in the Church but he is obviously not going to
escape. The most interesting point in this 1954 portrait is his identification of himself as Willie, the Christian clown. Even in this darkness,
Bill suspected light at the end of the tunnel. If he could endure till then.
By the spring of 1954, his mental powers seemed stretched to the
breaking point. As he later wrote, "it was only religion that was as yet
unfinished in my life, and only religion that saved me."[15]

Had painting helped Bill? To a layman, it may appear that by causing
him to dwell on his problems and by encouraging what Bill himself
labelled self-pitying tendencies, painting may actually have made him
worse. Bill's own writings seem to concur with this suspicion. He
writes of disproving to his own satisfaction "the theory that a patient
can relieve himself of aggressive feelings by painting them out. ... No
matter how intensely I painted out my accumulated store of fears,
hates and disillusionments, they still remained with me as an immense
psychological burden." (A2 22)

Educator John Timlin observes that art is "a safe and constructive
medium for aggression".[16] Adamson, who well remembers Bill's fearful, pathetic state in 1954, firmly believes that "painting got that man
better. ... He externalized all those feelings ... into a very concrete
form."[17] Playing devil's advocate, however, Adamson admitted that art
may intensify violent feelings in some individuals instead of being
therapeutic.[18] Psychiatrist Vivian Rakoff, in conversation with Adamson, spoke of art as a possible sublimation of, and substitute for,
physical violence, yet agreed that art may intensify some individuals'
hostility.

Whatever theory one adopts, it is clear that Bill's most serious
suicidal gesture followed after some eighteen months of depicting his
pain and fear through art. The paintings may actually express the
paradox that hatred becomes self-hatred. They mirror Bill's duality as
victim and aggressor. Suicide is a gesture both passive—a refusal to
fight—and active—as self-directed anger. Yet as Bill began to plot this
bizarre demonstration and to deliberate on the philosphic meaning of
suicide, his painting activity slowed markedly from ten hours a day to
two, then stopped altogether. Margaret noticed his increased despon-
dency, and his conviction that he was making no progress.[19]

Bill's gesture, on August 11, 1954, involved eight sleeping tablets, a
new razor blade, and two months of planning. He called it a "half-
measure", describing himself as "too listless to do it in a clean-cut,
definite way" (A1 342). He was found in a cupboard. His stomach was
pumped, and his numerous shallow cuts were cleaned; he woke up in a

locked ward. His earlier comment on leaving Maudsley seems more relevant here: the "fun" of being a patient was definitely over. Bill's ordeal by electroconvulsive therapy was about to begin.

The gesture, a plea for help and a form of protest, reflects the double pattern that runs throughout the hospital period. On the one hand Bill's troubles, brought to a head like an angry boil, appear to have worsened. On the other, there is an almost imperceptible upward movement as Bill stumbles towards faith. In May he writes to Dr. Carstairs that he is reading books of a religious nature nowadays. First there had been Margaret, then his midnight encounter with cabbages and Something Else. Soon there would be the magnificent statement of *Lord That I May See*. This double movement is reflected even as Bill contemplates suicide: "*Since I was also considering religion*, the question of life and death came up to stare me in the face. . . . If there was no God, no after-life, no final justice, then suicide was reasonable." (A2 28-29, emphasis added)

His psychotherapy ended abruptly with his act of self-mutilation. Understandably, doctors felt it a terrible stigma to lose a patient to suicide; Dr. Yates was left with her memories of their fireside chats and with *Penge East*, a painting that delighted her.[20]

Soon after his suicide attempt, and indeed as a direct result of it, Bill was offered electroconvulsive therapy, called ECT or shock treatment. He readily agreed, having seen a marked improvement in the behavior of patients who had had it.

In the early 1950s, electroconvulsive therapy was relatively new, and was commonly given to patients for restlessness, aggression, and depression. Its effects were not really understood, but those who underwent it seemed to become more cheerful. Theory and practice had developed from the observation that people who suffered from epileptic seizures were rarely depressed. The logical conclusion was that the artificial inducement of a seizure might help. In the fifties, Netherne averaged one hundred treatments per week.[21] Mr. Alison, a Charge Nurse at the hospital for thirty years, remembered that ECT was commonly given without the muscle relaxant scoline in the fifties, whereas Noel Duffy and Margaret Smith claim that unmodified ECT was uncommon even at that time. Over the next three months, Bill would have twelve treatments, only nine of them modified by scoline. Duffy and Smith both thought that omission of the drug in Kurelek's case must have been accidental.

Duffy confirmed that the experience would be horrible without scoline. His description of the general hospital environment in the 1950s, noted above, brought the ordeal to life. Nothing was explained to the patients. Herded in from a locked ward by male nurses, the patients were "obviously terrified". How did one feel on regaining consciousness? "You'd have a helluva headache," Duffy responded cheerfully, "and feel pretty shaky. How would *you* feel if you got a belt in the head?" It was, he added defensively, the best treatment available at the time. Adamson, who had seen post-ECT patients staggering about like punch-drunk boxers, considered the practice barbaric. In clinical observation, ECT reduced short-term memory, usually leaving long-term memory untouched. Short-term memory returned gradually over the next few months.[22]

Shock treatment affects people differently, and the patient's emotional suffering is always unique. Bill seems to have undergone the torments of the damned. He compares the treatments to being executed in a Nazi gas chamber or the Spanish Inquisition. Each coming ordeal was dreaded more than its predecessor. Yet in this Valley of the Shadow, he found Someone with him: "It is said that sorrow remarries us to God and how true that is. Here was an experience horrendous enough to knock the cocky self-sufficiency out of any man. One prays best when one is really and helplessly up against it. That is when I, too, resumed prayers. I've been praying ever since." (A2 32)

The first treatment, unmodified, sprained his back. After one such session, he found himself convalescing in a ward for incurables. These crippled, senile, barely human patients touched Bill deeply. And his sense of destiny, always an integral part of his self-image as artist, stirred: "My being there seemed to be fated, as if I personally had to realize at last the essential weakness and fragility of mankind. Here were men who to outward appearance seemed nothing more than suffering vegetables, and *for the first time in my life I was touched with pity, real pity for someone else besides myself.*" (A2 30, emphasis added) The breakthrough is highly significant: the wall had been breached, the bag torn, to use the images of separation from other human beings which Bill had been employing in his paintings for two years.[23] The experience may also have marked the beginning of an interpretation that Bill was to give to his pain in years to come: he had been allowed to suffer so that he might share in Christ's suffering, and depict it in his work.

Freudenberg remembered only superficial improvement in Bill after his shock therapy, but Bill gives more credit to this than to any other hospital treatment: "I must consider my suicide attempt in some ways fortunate, if only for the ECTs and the blessed relief they afforded me from the crushing load of depression I'd carried all those years. In my case they really worked." (A2 33)

By late November, Bill was back in Highfield Villa, feeling somewhat shaky and physically dazed but none the less cheerful. He still suffered, though less acutely, from feelings of alienation. There was no private room, Bill having betrayed the trust this had represented. He painted in the back lobby under the eye of the nurses in conditions similar to the ones he had had for working in the locked ward. There, he had painted an exquisite gouache, *Still Life With Eggs and Tomatoes*. Describing it as tight, disciplined, and super-realistic, Bill marvels at its execution and timing: "no one ever guesses it was painted at my lowest ebb" (A2 33).

Earlier, Adamson had encouraged him to paint still life as a change from personal themes. Accordingly, Bill had done several. By late 1954, still life must have seemed the answer to the problem of creating paintings that would sell, as Bill began to plot his return to the outside world. *I Spit on Life* was not exactly marketable; *Eggs and Tomatoes* was. Still life offered another advantage: Bill was still incapable of handling criticism, but still life was a medium he had mastered, and his works in this genre had been widely admired by those who saw them in Netherne's art gallery—medical students, professionals of many kinds, visitors, hospital staff.

Margaret encouraged Bill to leave hospital, promising to help him make a fresh start. Adamson was also supportive. Throughout Bill's period at Netherne, he had been allowed frequent weekend parole (the intimidating word is the hospital's) to stay with his two friends. His visits with Margaret had been weekly or bi-monthly. During his incarceration after his "gesture", Margaret had visited his ward. His two hospital Christmases, 1953 and 1954, were shared with both friends as Bill went (for one or two days each) from one to the other. Following his Christmas 1954 leave, Bill requested discharge from Netherne. He had arranged for lodgings in London's West End. The impulse that had led him to seek shelter in Britain's hospitals had exhausted itself, and his self-image, newly forged in the same hospitals, was clear. Occupation: *Artist*.

His inner state, as always, was expressed in his art. *Lord That I May See* is a striking variation on *Where Am I? Who Am I? Why Am I?* It shows the distance Bill had travelled in the year and a few months that separated the self-portraits. The figure is still blind, still groping and suppliant. The eye sockets, still Brueghelesque, are empty, but the face is more finely detailed. Intelligent and sensitive, it contrasts with the earlier face, which resembles a crudely painted mask.

In color, setting, and structure, the painting reflects the hope that Bill had begun to find in religious faith by late 1954. Instead of a flat, dark, lifeless plain, the groping figure kneels at the foot of a grassy hill topped by a small, living tree. A path winds up towards the tree, a skylark soars above. The blue sky is filled with light. On the horizon,

One of Kurelek's most haunting paintings, *Lord That I May See* (1955), watercolor, 47″ x 29½″. The Saidye and Samuel Bronfman Collection of Canadian Art, The Montreal Museum of Fine Arts.

hurrying uphill, are two small figures, the artist and his spiritual guide. A shadow falls on the path in front of the kneeling figure. Like so many of Kurelek's works, the painting makes a tremendous emotional impact. In a Kurelek snow scene, one feels the cold; in *Lord That I May See*, the longing, hope, and budding faith are tangible.

In a letter in 1964 to Dr. Evan Turner, Director of the Montréal Museum of Fine Arts, Bill explained its symbolism and circumstances. He connected it with 1954 (the finished work is labelled 1955), and with a time of depression and bitterness at Netherne Hospital:

> *The Idea.* This is essentially a prayer in paint. I depict myself as the blind man in the Bible who called to our Lord as He passed by. And when He asked him what he wished he said "Lord That I May See." Physical *blindness* here stands for spiritual blindness. I used Pieter Brueghel's gaping socket depiction of blindness to more forcefully get across the idea of *real blindness* rather than closed eyelids or glazed eyeballs. *I put the man on his knees to represent humble petition, the limp gesture of the hand to represent helplessness.* The cinder path represents the road beside which the blind man in the Bible was situ-ated. *The shadow represents Christ approaching. The lark represents beauty heard but not seen.* The woman leading the man up the hill represents Margaret Smith guiding me *up* the hill to the faith, the overlarge clothing is supposed to represent the *pathetic* condition.[24]

The emphasis is Bill's own. To describe the work as merely "realis-tic" is misleading and naïve. Its effect is achieved largely through symbolic and formal means. The tops of high hills or mountains are traditionally places of spiritual enlightenment; birds suggest freedom, peace, holiness; the road or path is one of the oldest metaphors for the human journey; and the healthy tree represents life. To these arche-typal symbols, which make the scene a microcosm of human expe-rience, Bill has added his own: an outsized ear, straining to catch the Word; distended nostrils; a disproportionately large hand, grasping an unseen presence; the total concentration of the furrowed brow. Echoes of Brueghel, along with biblical and universal symbols, indicate a considerable degree of artistic and literary sensibility, while the fineness of the artistic technique points to patience, self-discipline, and talent of a very high order.

The incredibly fine details in the material objects depicted become more profound as a reminder of the biblical injunction that even the hairs of one's head are numbered. Bill painted the details of this world in the assurance that there was another world in and beyond it. In *Lord That I May See*, he painted the stitches around buttonholes, the individual knitted stitches of the sweater, every stitch and crack in the leather oxfords, the pores of the skin and the hairs on the head. There is dirt under the fingernails and cracks in the skin of these working-man's hands. The stones and the grasses around the figure are exquisitely done. To Dr. Turner, Bill added, "*I suppose I may guess too that my emphasis on the reality represented by detail is an emphasis on the reality of the spiritual crisis.*"

As I walked on the sweeping Surrey downs in 1984, seeking to understand Bill's experience, the sun shone and a skylark darted overhead. I felt I was walking into *Lord That I May See*, not because the landscape resembled the painting superficially, but because Bill had caught its essentials: the feeling of space, of height, of fresh air, of possibility. The greenness. He had no need to paint the full line of trees which tops the downs in generous profusion. By late 1954, he had had one tree, and that was enough.

The painting as a whole carries a great deal more affirmation than the figure alone; more, indeed, than Bill's letter— written ten years after the fact—seems to indicate. It marks a turn in the road, the beginnings of recovery and new life. Soon the struggles were to be manageable, the pain bearable, the joys stronger and more frequent.

7

Moving Up:
England, 1955-56

DISCHARGED FROM HIS HILLTOP FORTRESS ON JANUARY 28, 1955, BILL WENT down the winding avenue of chestnut trees, heading north to London and a new life. He was never to be hospitalized again till cancer claimed him in 1977. Still painfully introverted, he was nevertheless prepared to function in society and to be economically independent. He was making friends, some of whom were to last a lifetime. He was receiving an art education willy-nilly through every pore as he walked and worked in London, a subtle and ancient metropolis filled with the art and architecture of past masters. He stayed briefly with Edward Adamson until he could move into his chosen "digs" near him and near the galleries where Bill hoped to sell his work. He would stay at 48 Baron's Court Road until his trip home to Canada in the spring of 1956.

Earl's Court Road, where Adamson lived and where Bill had been a frequent visitor during his stay in Netherne, was in London's fashionable West End. Dating from the late nineteenth century, its terraced brick houses and their converted coach-houses were softened by balconies and old chestnut trees. Bill's area in Hammersmith was considerably less elegant but still pleasant. Flowering trees and bow windows graced the old yellow-brick rows. Bill's tiny room on the top floor boasted a gas stove for cooking, and plenty of mice. It was so small he could stand in the middle and touch both walls. From here, he could walk over a railway bridge to Adamson's studio in the Earl's Court area, which is now part of Kensington.

Although Bill had a small cache of savings, and was well versed in the habits of frugality, financial survival remained a pressing and intimidating problem. At Netherne, Adamson had introduced Bill to an art dealer and philanthropist named Alfred Hecht, who was interested in art therapy. Hecht had donated reproductions to adorn the hospital walls, and had provided a sheltered working environment for several people with various handicaps. In Hecht's small gallery on King's Road, Chelsea, Bill found his first work as a framer. Later, Hecht was to provide Bill with a reference for work at the Blue Ball Yard, where he was later employed as a framer. Bill was also studying framing and graphic design in evening courses, in the hope that these would eventually provide him with "steady bread and butter jobs".[1]

Meanwhile, Bill was painting a very specialized type of still life, a profitable activity which brought in a regular if modest income averaging four pounds per week. He describes his *trompe-l'oeil* quite simply as "very realistic paintings of coins, stamps and dollar bills which you feel you could pick up" (A1 351). Here, as elsewhere, he tends to diminish these extraordinary little works which earned him a place for three successive years in the Royal Academy's Summer Exhibitions. Margaret Smith recalls his distaste for this type of work: "He considered it a prostitution of his art, really beneath his dignity."[2] She felt that this attitude stemmed from his rather idealized idea of the artist.

A sample of Bill's *trompe-l'oeil* work between 1955 and 1958. Private collection.

Kurelek's pejorative attitude to *trompe-l'oeil* is reflected in some, but by no means all, of the commentaries in dictionaries of art. Harold Osborne calls a *trompe-l'oeil* an artifact rather than a work of art, noting that the term is sometimes applied in a derogatory sense to highly skilful paintings that lack artistic interest. Kimberley Reynolds takes a similar stance, acknowledging the skill required and the admiration generally evoked but calling this type of painting "no more than a technical trick" that tends to lack artistic profundity. Attitudes vary, while definitions are constant: a *trompe-l'oeil* is a painting that, by

virtuoso control of perspective and chiaroscuro, deceives the specta-
tor into thinking that the objects in it are real, not merely represented.
It is the ultimate in illusionism.[3]

The form was common in antiquity as well as in Renaissance and
baroque art and architecture. Bill may have seen S. van Hoogstraten's
peep-show cabinet in London's National Gallery. Since he refers to
American artists in a letter, he may have known of the nineteenth-
century Philadelphians who excelled in *trompe-l'oeil*, William Harnett
and John Frederick Peto. He would have delighted in the story of
Rembrandt's students painting coins on the floor of his studio for the
pleasure of watching the master bend down to pick them up. Stories of
Bill's obvious pleasure in watching spectators finger his own *trompe-
l'oeil* are numerous.

Trompe-l'oeil were Bill's first "potboilers", a term that becomes
important in his Toronto years. In October 1955, he wrote to a friend
that he had "recently" sold fifty pounds' worth of *trompe-l'oeil*, which
would support him for the next half-year and which had boosted his
morale.[4] These fascinating illusions were sold, unsigned, to Bond
Street dealers for five pounds, and resold at sixteen. The rent for Bill's
tiny room was one pound, and he was living on bread, margarine,
apples, bacon, and brussels sprouts for a total of three pounds per
week. There was little to share with the mice.

From his garret, Bill ventured out to explore the cultural riches of
the city. His love affair with London could well have begun at this
point. Art and faith were nourished jointly in venerable churches such
as the London Oratory on Brompton Road, where Bill frequently
attended Mass with Adamson in 1954 and '55. With his two special
friends or alone, Bill began to haunt the galleries. At the Tate, he would
have seen one or two giant paintings by Stanley Spencer, who had set
New Testament scenes in his Berkshire village, just as Bill was later to
set them in contemporary Canada. At the National Gallery there were
Van Goghs and a single Bosch. Adamson remembers a Brueghel exhibition at the National, in 1954 or '55, where Bill spent an entire
afternoon looking at one large work, possibly *The Mocking of Christ*.
The photographs from OCA and from the art books in Netherne's
library were coming to life.

He went as Adamson's guest to concerts in the Albert Hall. Favorite
composers included Beethoven, Brahms, and Mendelssohn. Concerts
were his favorite entertainment. The two friends also attended operas
at Covent Garden, and the occasional ballet. At Festival Hall, a national
film theatre and cultural complex, they took in concerts and films,
although Bill disliked and was frightened by violence in the latter.

The Albert Hall, where Bill and Edward Adamson attended many concerts (above), and the London Oratory (left), both London landmarks. Photos by author.

Music and paintings were providing a rich supplement to a diet of bacon and sprouts. The boy from Stonewall, Manitoba, had come a long way.

In his lodgings, Bill was painting (he was *always* painting, save for that brief period in 1954 prior to his grand gesture) and observing his neighbors. Painting and observation went hand in hand. *The Batchelor* (Bill's spelling), an amusing work from this period, features the fourth-floor baron from whom Bill sublet his room. In this kitchen scene, Mr. Meyer is shown reading a newspaper, one slipper on and one off. The *Catholic Herald* on the floor and a cross over the door suggest a Catholic home. Details include underwear drying on a line, a hot-water bottle, peeling plaster, loose wallpaper, and a jar of marmalade labelled "Golden Garbage" ("Golden Shred" is a popular British brand). A ball of wool with a needle in it stands ready for darning, beside socks that are overdue for attention. Bill's sense of humor was in good working order. As in most of the paintings from the British period, the painstaking technique is close to illusionist.

Bill was thorough by nature, even meticulous. He began a systematic study of the Catholics he had known or who shared his current lodgings. They were, he soon realized, an uneven lot. His fellow tenants included a hot-tempered Irishman, and a mortician's assistant who regularly fought with his neighbors and his wife. Bill's idealism was strained to its limits.[5] *These were Catholics?* Clearly, charity was needed: "in this study I launched of Catholics I found I had to accept the standard Christian approach. ... Leave the final judgment of every individual to God. ... I was fresh to the Faith and all starry-eyed." (A1 359-60) The general lack of charity at 48 Baron's Court had, however, a curious consequence. Charity should begin at home. Bill began to reflect on his attitude towards his parents: "If I were to become a Catholic someday, then I, too, would have to learn to face anger, rage and impatience, which I'd experienced at home" (A1 361).

The Guild of Catholic Artists and Craftsmen, a London-based association for professional artists, was part of the fabric of Bill's post-Netherne life. He joined in 1955, and was a member for four years. As a national society of artists and craftsmen united by faith and vocation, the Guild was conceived in 1929 and began life with the blessing of Cardinal Bourne under the presidency of Glyn Philpot. Its aims were to bring together Catholic professional artists and craftsmen in spiritual fellowship and social intercourse, to hold exhibitions of members' work, and to organize lectures on Catholic art. By 1955 it had some two hundred members from the visual arts, including architects, sculptors, painters, silversmiths, potters, and gilders. Michael Leigh, a painter trained at the Royal College of Art and a founding member of

Bill's lodgings at 46 Baron's Court Road, London, 1955-56. Photo by author.

the association, was president. Sculptor David John was honorary secretary. Bill was so impressed with the Guild that he planned to organize one in Canada, but this never materialized.

David John was the only lasting friend Bill made through the Guild. John remembers with amusement that Bill had hesitated to join because he judged himself unworthy of the high standards represented by Guild members. The relationship was to be significant to both men. The two artists—a cradle Catholic and an aspiring convert—shared a rapport, "an awareness", a world view. Margaret Smith and Edward Adamson were kind and supportive, but Bill must have been longing for a friend who did not see him as a patient, for a relationship of equality. The sculptor, a man of subtle intelligence and sophisticated training, was full of admiration for the Canadian illustrator: "I learned a lot from seeing how he could live so simply, and with so much deprivation, and yet have such tremendous hope and inner strength. He went so quickly from being a dependent sick person to being independent."[6]

David lived with his wife, Marianne Hellwig, a painter, in a small cottage in Berkshire not far from London. Bill began to visit their home. He was awkward with Marianne, idealizing her as a Catholic mother while ignoring her as an artist and an individual. His attention focussed on David. The two men talked in his studio while David worked at religious sculpture or finely crafted furniture, surrounded by the tools of his trade.

Bill's conversation with David ran more to religion than to art. The

Church loomed large in his mind. But why Catholicism? "He was impressed by the Church's history, and by its strictness, which he liked; the dogmatism, yes, the authority. He liked to know that his confessor would have the *right* answer if he had a problem."[7] In the fifties, David belonged to the Cell Movement, a group of radical Catholics who believed in studying the Gospels by themselves and applying them to their own lives. Their motto was "See, judge, and act". Their emphasis on the individual conscience, their social concerns, and their openness to outsiders or non-Catholics contrasted sharply with British mainstream Catholicism, which was extremely conservative prior to Vatican II.

Here, as in many situations in years to come, Bill was more Catholic than cradle Catholics, more Catholic (in the old phrase) "than the Pope". He would have none of David's liberal theology, despite the mutual respect on which the relationship was based. In David's workshop, the debates went on:

> He thought he had a long way to go in terms of his faith, to reach the perfection he aimed at. I was astonished at his tenacity in pursuing dialogue, doggedly, to its conclusions. It was amazing that someone so reticent, not too successful in his university career (he indicated he'd not been well educated), who'd been ill, and who felt a novice in the faith—it surprised me how far he'd got. He could carry a debate with a fund of understanding drawn from his experience. He used his personal experience well, he had a keen natural intelligence. I could imagine

Bill's friends, sculptor David John and his wife, painter Marianne Hellwig, at their home in Woodley, Berkshire. Bill enjoyed their hospitality many times during his years in England. Photo by author.

IV
All Things Betray Thee Who Betrayest Me, 1970.
Gouache, 48″ x 48″.
Courtesy Mr. P. Isaacs, The Isaacs Gallery.
(see page 98)

V
Still Life With Tomatoes, 1954.
Trompe-l'oeil, oil, 17″ x 14″.
Private collection.
(see page 104)

VI
*Patients Working in Boiler Room
of Netherne Psychiatric Hospital, England*, 1954.
Wash drawing, 14″ x 18″ approx.
Private collection.
(see page 97)

him surviving in extraordinary circumstances by inge-
nuity. I was Jesuit-trained, yet couldn't cope with his mental constructs.[8]

As Christmas approached, David and Marianne asked Bill to share
the holiday with them and their two small children at Gorse Cottage,
Bucklebury. Marianne tells a blackly comic story concerning this
Christmas visit. To her, the incident illustrated Bill's extremism, and
his insensitivity. It was painful at the time, but became humorous years
later. Marianne recalls:

> We were living on eight pounds a week, four of us, and
> that was *not* funny. Without Bill, we'd have had a very
> plain Christmas. But with a guest, we *had* to get some-
> thing better, and I splurged. Bill was very critical. He
> arrived in the kitchen just as I was unpacking the grocer-
> ies. "What do you need all that food for?" That was his
> very first remark. He said he was living on forty-nine
> pounds a year, doing some framing, and painting. I didn't
> say anything but I was hurt. And the groceries were
> pathetic. It was the bare minimum to look hospitable!
> There were five of us.[9]

David remembers Bill's fierce pride in living on the small amount
earned from the sale of his *trompe-l'oeil*. Neither husband nor wife
would have suspected the financial anxiety with which Bill had left
hospital eleven months earlier. His pride at surviving economically is
perhaps more excusable than his insensitivity toward his hostess. Food
was not one of Bill's priorities. The puritan tradition which was to
make Bill feel "guilty" about enjoying French cooking at Lourdes a few
months later was foreign to David and Marianne (A1 363). The comi-
cal dénouement to this affair was that Bill wrote to thank David for the
best Christmas he had ever had, and to express the hope of enjoying
Marianne's cooking again at Easter.

The Guild of Catholic Artists and Craftsmen was to prove a strong
and permanent influence on Bill's attitudes towards art. Guild social
activities included recitals at the Newman International Centre in
Portman Square, sometimes in co-operation with the Royal College of
Music. Lectures were sometimes held at Spode House, a Dominican
community. London was a city full of guilds of all types. Bill's ideas on
art as part of the fabric of a Christian society, ideas first formed through
studying the later Middle Ages at university, were finding support at
Guild affairs. Even when Bill was antagonistic to Christianity, he had
been impressed by the work of Bosch and Brueghel, who were deeply

religious artists. Now his convictions—that artists were craftsmen, that tradition was more important than innovation, and that art existed to glorify God—were beginning to coalesce. In Bill's Toronto years, a favorite target of attack would be "art with a capital A", art created for galleries and for the glory of an individual.

Michael Leigh does not remember Bill personally, but the striking similarity of many of their ideas suggests that the Guild was a formative influence on Bill at this impressionable time of his life. In 1959 he would be disappointed to find that no such organization existed in Toronto. Even in England, the Guild was fighting a rearguard action within and without its ranks. In the 1960s, it split into two separate groups (the Society of Catholic Artists and the Guild of Craftsmen), reflecting the contemporary cleavage between fine and applied arts.

Bill was carefully nurturing the religious faith that had first begun to burn at Netherne. He wanted, he told Adamson, to forget the hospital experience and let his old self die so that a new one might be born. It would be February 1957 before he would take the plunge and formally join the Church; at that time, he spoke of the decision as the result of *three years* of study and prayer. In 1955, he began a correspondence course from the Catholic Enquiry Centre. The lessons came in plain brown wrappers, once a week: no cost, no exams, no pressure (A1 354). The next step was personal instruction with a priest. For Bill, the stumbling block was basic belief in the existence of God: "we bogged down after two sessions because although I seem to be quite well disposed to the Church and Christian doctrine I just haven't got the *real* conviction in God's existence on which to build a sound Catholic faith."[10]

In his autobiography and letters, Bill connects this difficulty with his state of "depersonalization", the central emotional problem which had not been cured in hospital. He called it, variously, a trance-like state and a "trance handicap", connecting it with childhood fears and seeing it as a protective device, "a kind of yoga ability to avoid facing physical reality or what I feared to be physical reality".[11] Since the fall of 1954 he had been praying that his mind be cleared. If this boon was not to be granted, he was prepared to limp into Heaven rather than be cast whole into Hell: "Apparently more important is to pray for the Faith so that I can enter the Church and get the right to confess the sins that have accumulated on my head over the years. ... I believe I'm only trying to *explain* why I failed by my human efforts to arrive at the conclusion of God's existence by reason alone with the help of Father Norton."[12]

The instructor's personality was unfortunate for this particular seeker. Father Norton's approach combined back-slapping jocularity with intimidation. His severity reminded Bill of his father and commanded a temporary agreement, "like brain-washed communist prisoners give in just to be left alone." Bill knew that such a profession of faith was worthless. His three-year struggle towards religious certainty, given his emotional handicap, is part of the heroism of his life.

Despite these setbacks, Bill seemed to intuit that his search for the Absolute would be successful in the end. By 1955, he had chosen a goal for his life: "religious propaganda". Unconcerned with modern sensibilities, Bill took the technical meaning, a scheme for propagating a doctrine or system. He wrote to his new friend and sounding-board, David John:

> I've arrived at last at a knowledge of what my life work is
> to be. I've never been satisfied with the thought of paint-
> ing for art's sake or fame's sake. I've always wanted to dedi-
> cate my talent to a cause. ... This summer I think I arrived
> home with my decision to turn it to religious propaganda.
> I would in fact be giving God back the talent that He gave
> me in the first place provided I did receive the Faith
> (unless I believe strongly enough in the Christian cause I
> doubt I could stick to this project). ... Paintings would be
> seen by too few people. I decided to illustrate completely
> the New Testament. ... Why not a slide film illustrating
> the Gospels sentence by sentence? ... I would need to
> collaborate with a Bible expert and make a trip to the
> Holy Land for on the spot information in atmosphere,
> architecture, topography, costume (I want it as compell-
> ingly realistic as possible). But so far this is a dream
> project."[13]

Bill asked for David's reaction and advice, "a line or two". The logistics were bothering him. He had to earn his living while pursuing his dream. At the rate of one "decent illustration" per fortnight, it would take one hundred and sixty years to cover the four Gospels. (With such communications, David may be excused for thinking of his friend initially as an illustrator.)

Marianne was impressed by Bill's technical expertise. As an aid to teaching, slides were still rare in Britain in the mid-fifties. Bill seemed both simple and sophisticated. She remembers his firm conviction, at the time of their first meeting, that he would carry out this religious project: "I was overwhelmed by his certainty."[14] The dream, conceived in a room barely six feet wide, was cosmic. Bill was finding another home and a faultless father. His idea would ripen during the balance of his years in England, and bear fruit in the hundred and sixty paintings of

117

the Gospel according to Saint Matthew.

Margaret Smith had met Bill's new friends and was impressed by this Catholic family. The honeymoon phase of Bill's relationship with Margaret was now over, although he continued to acknowledge her help. To David he wrote, "When I met her first three years ago I idealized her as a Florence Nightingale but as you say humans aren't gods and I now see she is not the ideal person I'd hoped to have for a friend someday. ... But she is the best friend I've ever had in that she stood by me when I needed a friend most."[15] His faith, he adds, has shown him that "the Ideal Person does exist." And the Church to which Margaret has introduced him "may as she claims hold the truth to life."[16] Strange phrases for a man who had just impressed Marianne with his overwhelming certainty. In his post-hospital years, Bill was obviously subject to considerable ambivalence on several fronts.

In the autobiographies, there is no such criticism of his faithful friend. Bill calls Margaret his "main study", in a joking comparison with the correspondence course. He speaks of frequent visits to her home, once he is back in London (A2 144). He credits her with giving him the affection he had missed as a child and with nurturing the emotional maturity needed for marriage: "she firmly drew the line in our caressing" (A1 331).

Bill was nothing if not systematic during his extended courtship with the Church. In the summer of 1955 he began to attend Mass regularly, despite the fact that he found the services boring and mean-ingless: "I had conceded that if God existed and Christ had founded the Church and five hundred million Catholics attended Mass, then obviously the Church wasn't going to abolish Mass just because it bored me, William Kurelek. I also had decided that it wouldn't kill me to give it a year's trial period just as I'd given Nicolaides a try and made a breakthrough." (A1 141) Bill's humor could be heavy-handed at times.

While giving the Mass a year's trial, and reading religious books such as Alfred Noyes's *The Unknown God*, Bill came across an article on Lourdes and decided to extend his research. At the end of March 1956 he was in the Pyrenees, almost surprised to find that Lourdes really existed. It was his first vacation, the first week spent without working. Bill naturally felt guilty about this situation, but he soon found work to do. True to his nature, he took up the spiritual task he had set for himself, turning prayer and religious inquiry into his week's work.

The healings at Lourdes intrigued and challenged him. There were so many miracles. Could they all be faked? The evidence for their validity seemed indisputable: "if I persisted in being suspicious and skeptical I would end up believing in a giant web of conspiracy between the Catholic Church and literally thousands of patients and pilgrims. In a word, it was almost easier to believe in the miracle itself."

(A2 146) He considered and rejected the possibility of psychosomatic pain such as he had experienced with his eyes. This would not account for healings in babies or unconscious patients. He was impressed by the carefully documented medical records kept by an international panel of doctors, some of them unbelievers. The matter of miracles was important to Bill; if one had happened at Lourdes in 1858, then more could have happened in Palestine in the time of Christ.[17] Bill was still sceptical, but Lourdes had moved him one step further towards the Church. While his intellect wrestled with the problems of miracles, his emotions were engaged by Bernadette. Later, he would paint the peasant visionary, ringed by the doubters, the credulous, and the pious.

Soon after his week in Lourdes, Bill returned to Canada for the summer. He gives four reasons for this visit. He wanted time away from Margaret to discover his true feelings for her. He needed to rest his eyes, strained from more than a year of painting *trompe-l'oeil*. He planned to make a stake, money that would enable him to research the life of Christ in the Holy Land in order to paint it. Finally, he felt a grudging desire to see his family again, after the traumatic searchings of the hospital period. He was still not prepared to *like* his parents, but he now knew that as a Christian he was obligated to *love* them. The love, at this point, seems to have been very theoretical. Bill intended to return good for ill—his biblical phrasing—but he was still preoccupied with the "ills" as he saw them. He apparently recognized no sins of commission, or even omission, on his part; he had told David John that he believed he had been "unfortunate rather than wayward".[18] His emotional need to tell the world that his parents had hurt him but that he forgave them was becoming entrenched as a pattern that would continue throughout his lifetime. By the spring of 1956, Bill was convinced that he might describe his parents' sins "to psychiatrists and confessors or in a matter-of-fact way to friends if it were really necessary but no longer could I run them down before everybody" (A1 369). The fine distinction between "friends" and "everybody" was lost on Bill as he sorted his way through thickets of theology.

In Margaret's view, the necessity for a reconciliation with his parents was the primary reason for his 1956 visit to Canada. She had been urging such a reconciliation on Bill for some time, and believed his failure in this regard to be the cause of his difficulties in the faith. Intellectually he was already convinced, she believes; after the summer spent with his parents, "suddenly he had faith."[19] If her view seems facile, the criticism is not of grace, or of faith. To a student of Bill's life, it may well appear that he struggled for a lifetime to forgive his father. By the fall of 1956, that forgiveness was only partial. But the first step had been taken.

In a long letter to David John, Bill revealed the state of mind in which he approached the return home. He described his family as a Slavic patriarchal one which had lost religion, where parents took the place of God and ruled with an iron hand; where "face" was important, and family honor a prime consideration. His father's ambitious hopes for his children were so high that their failures were intolerable. Bill's three-hour session with Father Norton on the evidence for God's existence as the First Cause of the universe had broken down because the priest's manner had reminded him of his father: "I felt the old terror of disappointing my father creeping over me until at the end I was stiff with fear of him. He kept asking me if anything was wrong and just as with my father I was tongue-tied."[20] Even the bitterness which Bill felt towards his family had been—irony of ironies—learned there: "I've trained myself to harbour a grudge so that I can 'get even' someday (a regular feature in our family and neighbourhood too, by the way)."[21]

The weight of Dmytro's ambitious hopes was compounded by his son's desire to please a man he admired as well as feared, a man whose praise he desperately coveted. That tiny corner of *The Maze* tells so much: the boy trapped between two Dmytros, "the one I hated and the one I worshipped".[22] His bitterness, he told David, was welling up far less frequently since Netherne, and shock therapy had been "a decided blessing as it knocked some nonsense out of me." As the *Île de France* steamed across the Atlantic, Bill's resentment wrestled with his new Christian intentions.

Arriving at Hamilton, Bill found that his father had mellowed. The Kurelek family were overjoyed to recover the prodigal son, so nearly lost to them in 1954. They spoke with care, and expressed a cautious interest in Margaret. Marriage, to the Kureleks, had always been a mark of normalcy and success. John and Win had taken this step, and Bill found "a new kind of friendliness" in them and their partners. His youngest siblings were delighted with their big brother. A sketch shows Bill with the farm dog watching Iris, Paul, and Sandy playing baseball beside the Vinemount farmhouse (A1 370). The chief irritant, the flaw in the family togetherness, was Bill's new-found faith. Although he avoided preaching, he refused meat on Friday and faithfully attended Sunday Mass.

Everyone felt a little strange despite goodwill on both sides. Bill had been away for five years, a critical period during which he had replayed family experiences in his mind many times, often from angles dictated by depression. Eighteen months later he would remember John's reaction on seeing him for the first time in five years: "'I have the feeling you're an impostor.'"[23] His easiest relationship was with his youngest brother and sisters, the three Kureleks born in the 1940s, with whom Bill shared at this time a joking camaraderie and physical ease that was perhaps unique in his experience. Sandy recalls: "He was a lot older, and he used to tell us that he never was a baby like we were. We'd argue with him on this point. We played with him roughly, wrestling on the ground, rough-housing, and we loved it."[24]

Through John, Bill obtained a job at his brother's company, Standard Tool of Woodstock. Company layoffs eliminated the position a few weeks later. Farm work filled the gap until Bill found himself another job with Grimsby Brick and Tile through Hamilton's Employment Office. He speaks of this job as infamous, "a foretaste of hell, like something out of Bosch" (A1 371). His first assignment was to act as a human conveyor belt, picking up hot tile without gloves and loading it onto a truck. Even outside the brick kilns, the summer heat was oppressive.

His second job was removing cold tile from machines. Speed was essential, and Bill soon realized he was causing delays through his nervousness. His back ached, his spirits groaned: "I thought I was tough and had already sampled the worst possible jobs."[25] Fired at the end of the week, Bill was left with time to reflect on the divine sense of humor; his efforts (had the Almighty forgotten?) were in pursuit of a stake to get him to the Holy Land. His third job involved pick-and-shovel work for septic tanks and weeping-tile beds. It amused Bill to find that he had not escaped from the tiles. His back, sprained by the unmodified shock treatments, continued to cause him pain. Bill passed a driving test for a chauffeur's licence and drove the company truck, despite his farm-bred fear of machinery. This work lasted for the season.

Throughout the summer, Bill lived at home, helping his father in off-work hours. It had been a bad year for farmers in southwestern Ontario and Bill was not blind to the pressures on Dmytro. Forbidden to talk of religion, he felt incapable of offering other consolation.[26] After helping his father to harvest corn amid flood conditions, Bill was on his way once again. His own harvest, after ship-fare, was a stake of some six hundred dollars from his various jobs. And a reconciliation with his parents, imperfect though it might be.

The Grand Design:
England, 1956-59

HE HAD DONE IT: BITTEN THE BULLET, TAKEN HIS MEDICINE, SPENT FIVE months with his father, and survived. Now Bill was eager to start carving a bright new future for himself.

Back in England, Bill took lodgings at 45 Kingsmead Road in Streatham Hill, southeast of London. Near there he had lived as an out-patient at Maudsley, had worked on the tram rails at Brixton, and had painted the view from his window in Penge East. The significance of the opening sentence of the second version of his autobiography is clearer in the context of his life: "The year 1955, when I was twenty-eight, was the turning point of my life." Why did he refer thereafter to 1955 as the year of his spiritual birth when he was not to take the decisive step of joining the Church until February 1957? Bill's emotional problems had made certitude a necessity and had turned his religious inquiry into a three-year struggle. This time there must be no mistake. By 1954, he had begun to pray. By the summer of 1955, he was attending Mass regularly and had found both an inner home and a life work: a giant project, "the illustration of the Gospel of St. Matthew sentence by sentence, eight hundred and some-odd paintings" (A2 146).

His grand design involved several stages. He knew he had more to learn abroad, and must plan his biblical research carefully. In Canada, he still seemed qualified only for laboring jobs; in Britain, framing was a specialized craft and indeed an art, one that was not yet established back home. London was therefore still necessary to Bill. But he was already plotting his return to Toronto. The plan apparently took shape during his trip home in 1956 when he foresaw his parents getting older and needing his help. Bill writes of his initial difficulties with that city in 1949-50. Toronto might be an acquired taste, but he had eventually become quite fond of it: "In fact I made a vow in back of my mind that I'd settle there one day and now it seems it will come true after all."[1]

Bill in September 1956.
From his scrapbook.

The paintings, however, could only be done on a foundation of faith. As he had written to a friend twelve months earlier, he doubted whether he could stick to the project without this basic precondition. He was *almost* ready to take the decisive steps of joining the Church. First, though, there was Margaret. Bill made what he calls a tentative proposal of marriage, and was promptly refused. He seemed vastly relieved: "I had been afraid all along that I was seeking the faith only to please her. Her rejection of my proposal revealed my fear to be unfounded. I had really been after the faith for myself." (A2 149) If relief was the primary emotion, one assumes that the relationship was no longer close. His remaining years in London would be marked by other friendships.

There would be less than a month between Bill's return from Canada and his finding work as a framer at the Blue Ball Yard. In that interim period, he was painting, job-hunting, and praying. Just around the corner from Kingsmead Road was the parish church, St. Simon and St. Jude. Here Bill stopped to pray on most days, and here he met Father Thomas Lynch.

The two men liked each other almost immediately. Bill accepted an invitation to talk, perhaps with the intention of furthering his religious instruction under this priest. He had anticipated resuming such study since late 1954. Referring to it in his first autobiography, he wrote *if I should*, and, in the second, *when I do*. He found Father Lynch very approachable: friendly, conscientious, generous. They could even joke together. The priest sought the artist's opinion on his collection of curios.

There were some months, perhaps six, when this friendship was central in Bill's life. He was unconsciously comic in his stance of intellectual superiority. Father Lynch was not a professional theologian, although he would introduce Bill to one, as a general physician may recommend a specialist. This priest did not make him feel "small or dull" as Father Norton had, and Bill felt that "things were working out according to a hidden plan" (A2 149). He always had a strong sense of personal fate or destiny, even before he became a Christian. The priest took a compassionate interest in Bill as a human being and was intrigued by a man so very different from himself. An original.

The two met frequently, praying together in Bill's lodgings or in the rectory. They talked of art as well as religion. They visited the Tate, where Bill enjoyed the paintings by Blake and Toulouse-Lautrec, "especially the Blakes because they were religious."[2] Once the priest had been introduced to the grand design, he obtained for Bill a second-hand set of James Tissot's two-volume *Life of Christ*. Bill had been unfamiliar with the work of the French artist, and he greatly admired his realistic and historical approach.

St. Simon and St. Jude on Hillside road is an attractive small church in grey stucco with romanesque windows and a yellow brick interior. For the church, Bill painted portraits of its patron saints, and a crucifix in the illusionist technique that was proving so saleable. The painted Christ appears to be wrought in metal sculpture.[3] Blood drips from the pierced feet into a chalice. The elaborate wooden frame and backdrop, in dull red and blue, features the four beasts of the apocalypse at the ends of the cross: lion, bull, eagle, and man, all winged. The double-barred cross is Orthodox.

For Father Lynch, over the course of their friendship, Bill did drawings and paintings which are personally revealing. *The Ride of the Valkyries* in graphite is a Germanic version of the Last Judgment, an apocalyptic scene executed with incredible energy and detail. *The Artist* is a composite drawing of Bill's experience in the early 1950s, showing the Wanderer on Life's road, along with a torturous scene of maidenly purity and male lust. This maze does have an exit, as two men (both Bill?) stride towards a distant light. Beside a small graveyard, a dejected figure hunches over a bedroll. The brim of a hat, covering the eyes of the largest self-portrait, suggests Bill's secrecy, his reluctance to look his companion in the face. In the medieval scene of lust in his shadow, the man's grasping hands and arms resemble the branches of

The Church of St. Simon and St. Jude, London, where Bill met Father Thomas Lynch in 1956. Courtesy of the author and Father T. Lynch.

the tree he is attempting to scale to reach the dreaming girl.

In gouache, his typical medium of the fifties, Bill executed a *Nativity With Magi*, a *Nativity With Shepherds*, and *The Apparition of Our Lady to Bernadette at Lourdes*. His versions of the nativity reveal both a knowledge of the traditional European treatment of the scenes and a striking originality. A personalized still life (1956) is based on an old Italian Madonna which Father Lynch treasured. The composition includes the small painted statue of Mary, a pewter pot with four daisy-shaped flowers in soft reds and pinks, and a tiny blue bowl with greenish cherries. The composition and color harmonies are masterly. Had Bill continued in this direction, he would certainly have been remembered for his exquisite still lifes. The Madonna sits on a narrow table by a wall. Table and wall are covered by a small piece of used decorative paper done in illusionist technique, its creases startlingly real. "Realism", however, was never the focus of the artist's interest. The paper's creases make two subtle cruciforms, one behind Mary aligned with her shoulder: the mother, crucified by grief.

Thinking that Bill might have a vocation for the priesthood, Father Lynch took him to visit a Carthusian monastery at West Grinstead, and a monastery at Aylesford: "I thought it might be his life, the contemplative life. He was too good for this world." Although Bill was impressed by the medieval customs of the monks who lodged pilgrims free of charge and trusted to God to provide, he felt no call to the priesthood,

The Artist, 1956-57. Graphite drawing, approx. 11″ x 14″. Private collection.

except the Joycean one of art. To settle his difficulties over the existence of God, Father Lynch next took him to Father Edward Holloway, a theologian trained at the English College in Rome.

Two long talks with Father Holloway were to prove decisive for Bill, who greatly admired the theologian's learning: "The fact that he knew science as thoroughly as his theology and wasn't afraid of it finally persuaded me it was 'safe' to become a Catholic in our scientific age" (A2 150). To his brother some eight months later, Bill would write that he had been impressed by Holloway's freedom in matching science and theology.[4] The priest assured him that the Old Testament, unlike the New, is a mixture of history, theology, and myth. Other problems were solved to Bill's satisfaction. Most importantly, both Holloway and Lynch concluded that he actually possessed Christian faith, a conclusion which a study of his writing, painting, and behavior over the previous two years certainly supports. Bill was reassured: "The whole issue seemed to hinge on authority—professional authority. They were the official representatives of the Church, the link between God and man, just as surely as a doctor is a representative of the medical profession or a lawyer of the legal profession." (A2 151)

Father Holloway remembers Bill as very "Canadian", by which the priest meant hard-headed and practical. He found him intelligent, "rational as a scientist, yet mystical".[5] Bill craved intellectual certainty. What did they talk about? The existence of God and of the spiritual soul, mankind's relation to a personal God of love, and the links between religion and science. Holloway considered the latter his specialty. Kurelek told the priest he was dissatisfied with both parents but "hated" his father. He said that he had been consumed by thoughts of sex in his teens and was still greatly troubled, knowing that he knew nothing of love, disgusted with himself, yet unable to escape: "He thought of himself as a tethered bull." For Bill, Holloway felt respect and affection. He found him not eccentric but unforgettable.

The theology of Bill's teacher was, by all accounts, conservative. No one who reads the book which is considered his life's work would dispute it. In *Catholicism: A New Synthesis*, Holloway's view of our decadent and materialistic society sounds extremely close to the one Kurelek later expressed in didactic paintings and in talks throughout the sixties and seventies. In "Thoughts about the Times", the priest foresees the breakdown of Western society through agnosticism and lust, if not through secular totalitarianism: "For the West is a confusion of empty arrogance, humbug and sensualism divorced from creative ideal. It has long been led by its social prophets, the rationalists, the agnostic, and the scientific humanist so-called, deep into the interior deserts of the soul. ...."[6] The word "humanism" is used pejoratively, as Bill used it. Marxism is the work of the Devil. A *last* war is predicted, the just reward of secular men. Authoritative and infallible religious authority, which Holloway sees as essential to mankind, had been undermined by the Protestant Reformation. In his view, this meant that the way was thrown open to human interpretation and human weakness, "with all the doubt and loss of authentic tradition" that entailed.[7] Overall, the similarity with Kurelek's theological convictions is unmistakable. Were the teacher's views particularly influential, or was the student already convinced of their truth and hence pleased to find

Interior of F. A. Pollak's Limited, London, where Bill
found his first regular employment following his discharge from Netherne (photo by author), and the
exterior, facing onto the Blue Ball Yard (courtesy Mr.
Stan Beecham).

them confirmed? In the end it was Holloway's version of Catholic
theology which Bill chose, not David John's gentler and more humane
beliefs. Nor did Vatican II appear to influence Bill's theology, except
in its emphasis on social justice.

Holloway and Kurelek have a common inspiration: Jeremiah. The
Old Testament prophet's name has passed into the language, making a
jeremiad a lamentation, a denunciation, a prophecy of punishment to
come. In ancient Judah, the word of the Lord had come to Jeremiah in
visions. He had seen a cauldron on fire, fanned by the wind. He spoke of
coming punishment, brought by the people's rebellion against God.

Their wrongdoing had upset nature's order and provoked His wrath: "I must pour it out on the children in the street." Friends and neighbors would perish together and the world would "burn unquenched". In righteous anger, God was preparing an inescapable disaster.[8] Kurelek believed it as contemporary truth. In the years to come, he painted the coming apocalypse many times.

The talks with Holloway, and the priests' conviction that Bill already had the faith, proved decisive.[9] The search begun in Maudsley, with Margaret as catalyst, had come to an end which was also a beginning: "It was every bit as exciting a journey of exploration as my adventures of self-discovery as an artist had been after leaving university" (A2 152).

Bill asked Father Lynch to instruct him in catechism. Six weeks later, in February 1957, he entered the Catholic Church by a ceremony of conditional baptism, the procedure called for because of his infant baptism in the Orthodox Church in Whitford.[10] Father Lynch officiated. Margaret Smith and David John were godparents the latter being unable to attend. With his flair for drama and narrative, Bill writes that it was a dark and windy night. Outside, there was rain; inside, an island of light at the altar rail, on the Feast of Our Lady of Lourdes: "I'd arrived home at last. Now I could start living." (A2 155)

By the time Bill joined the Church, he had been working for some three months at F. A. Pollak Limited, an elegant framing shop in the shadow of St. James's Palace. The business, at 20 Blue Ball Yard, occupied the rambling second floor of an eighteenth-century coachhouse down a cobblestone alley. Inside and out, the atmosphere was old-world, European. On the stairway, then as now, a sign declared, "Members of the Fine Art Trade Guild". Bill was still a member of the Guild of Catholic Artists and Craftsmen. The ideas of its members were compatible with the atmosphere at Pollak's.

Bill was extremely fortunate in finding regular employment with this firm, perhaps the best in London at the time.[11] His twenty-five months of work there constituted an important part of his training as an artist. Pollak's became for Bill an informal but highly professional art school. Frederick Pollak, an Austrian Jew who had fled from Germany in the thirties, was a painter and a fine craftsman. He had made frames for the Louvre before settling in London and establishing, in 1938, his shop for framing and the restoration of antiques.

In Europe, framing was an art dating back to the Renaissance and beyond. Frames were actually a branch of sculpture in which master carvers might choose to specialize. A single frame could cost hundreds, even thousands, of pounds; the restoration of such a frame could require many months of work and would be undertaken by a specialist such as Pollak only on open-estimate terms. The coloring of antique frames and furniture was also a subtle and sophisticated craft. Bill credits Frederick Pollack with having a true instinct for the right color, and a fine knowledge of exactly how to mix colors to obtain the desired result. He himself had had no such training. Many of the techniques learned at Pollak's (such as spattering, smudging, sealing, and gessoing the base) eventually found their way into his painting techniques (A2 159). Finally, the paintings whose frames were being restored or replaced were an education in themselves, sometimes surprisingly personal. On one occasion, a three-hundred-year-old Pietà inspired a deaf-mute framer to mime the whole of Christ's passion in the shop (A2 161).

Bill was an avid student as well as a hard worker. The sharp rise in his wages, from four and one-half pounds at the start to eight pounds two years later, shows that his work must have been highly satisfactory. His *trompe-l'oeil* had served as a reference, for they proved that he was capable of fine and disciplined work. Fellow framer Stanley Westlake recalls that he frequently made notes in a looseleaf notebook.[12] Perhaps he found his memory unreliable. The procedures were complicated, and Bill was taking no chances.

In the design for his life, framing had assumed a major role. He methodically lists three reasons for his choice of career: It would assure him a regular income, as painting "obviously" would not; it was easier on his eyes; and it afforded the possibility of a partnership with his father when Dmytro became too old for farming (A2 157-58). Letters confirm the latter point: "I feel my first duty is to my father and mother who need some kind of a break after all their years of relentless work and I thought of taking my father into the business once I do get established, if I do. He of course would be able only to do rough work. …"[13] Bill imagined a partnership in this "dream shop" with Stan Beecham, a framer and cabinet-maker with whom Bill had worked at Pollak's for six months and who had emigrated to Toronto, encouraged by Bill's "rosy view" of opportunities in that city.[14] They would go in for quality, Bill insisted, even if their high principles brought in less money.

At Pollak's Bill became a master finisher.[15] Gilding is a difficult technique whose secrets were prized in Europe and closely guarded. In time, it became his chief work at the shop in the Blue Ball Yard. As an apprentice, he began by stripping and repairing antique chairs and frames, and painting decorative borders on ornamental tables. The stripping was done with dentist's tools; two inches a day might be considered good progress. Ten months after joining the firm, Bill wrote that his work was becoming specialized. No more priming or cleaning: "I've been put exclusively on restoration work for some time now painting screens, figures and other odd things and stripping precious old frames...."[16] Bill's dream shop in Toronto never materialized, but the techniques he learned at Pollak's were to prove invaluable in his career. He was very conscious of this, both at the time and later, and thanked God for it.

Sometimes the work took an unexpected turn, and the weirdly diverse worlds of Stonewall, Manitoba, and Pollak's London suddenly coalesced. A harness belonging to an antique model of a coach and six, for example, had rotted away and the piece was urgently required in perfect order. Bill knew the principles of harnessing but had had no experience with a triple pair. Using copper wire, gold paper, string, and thin black leather, assisted by glue and a razor-blade, he found that harnessing came naturally. He was pleased with the result, his employers were enchanted, the client was charmed: "I got another ten shilling raise."[17] This is by no means the only evidence to suggest that Bill's mechanical abilities were good as long as no one was making him nervous.

Bill and his fellow framer, Stan Westlake. From Bill's scrapbook.

The original owners (now dead) were stern and authoritarian. Their "Prussian" treatment of their employees unfortunately reminded Bill of his father (A2 158). To Stan Beecham he wrote mockingly of "Herr" Pollak's nasty mood, but by 1957 he was sufficiently sensitive to other people to observe the pressures that provoked moods. He suffered under the delusion that *schweinerei* meant "pig shit" and was being applied to himself as a term of abuse. Scandalized, his former colleague Hans Roeder explained that this common German expression literally means "a piggery" and is a term often applied to a badly done job: "Mr. Pollak was an Austrian *gentleman*, he would *never* have insulted a worker like that!"[18] Bill was to find that his employers improved with the passage of time: "they're not so bad, the two of them, as I thought at first. They just have their 'days'. Mrs. Pollak asked me not to regard her as my enemy just the other day."[19] Were the Pollaks mellowing, or was Bill? He decided that their policy was to try newcomers by fire, then to welcome them into the family.[20]

And a family it was. A large family. By the 1950s, the Pollaks employed nine or ten workers. Bill's letters testify to a warm and friendly atmosphere among the craftsmen in the shop: "the slapstick, practical joking and wise-cracking goes on though in you [he writes to Stan Beecham] we lost our most sophisticated member." It was an atmosphere he would miss badly when he left. His friendly relations with co-workers were beginning to extend outside the shop into walks and home visits. With Stan Westlake, Bill found himself in the famous old department store of Fortnum and Mason: "I never knew such a place existed. It's fascinating like a museum except that you can not only look at the things on display you can actually buy them and eat them."[21]

His co-workers recall a very quiet man with whom it was difficult to make conversation but who became friendlier as time went on. Sometimes he showed them paintings from his hospital period but spoke very little of his past. The framers remembered frightening paintings, such as one with an open-mouthed man shouting for help.[22] Bill had given *trompe-l'oeil* paintings to several colleagues: a wedding gift, a favor returned. Hans Roeder observed that some craftsmen were never capable of the difficult work of gilding but that Bill became good at it. Stan Westlake found him a thoughtful man, very considerate of others, who enjoyed his work in the shop and who seemed to have his life "all mapped out".[23] The map at this point, the grand design, included leaving framing and gilding in England, visiting the Holy Land, and returning to Canada to earn a living as a framer "with a bit of painting thrown in". He claimed to have no expectation of earning a living through painting, an attitude Westlake attributed to Bill's modesty. Together they attended museums and galleries. Bill seemed to be a tireless student, "building up his mind all the time". Stan Beecham remembered Bill playing his harmonica for the others at lunchtime, and confirmed Bill's view of their employers' sternness and high standards. Work had to be accurate to one-sixty-fourth of an inch![24]

Outside work, Bill was also making friends in the Little Club, a Catholic group that met weekly in the basement of an eighteenth-century church in Warwick Street, Soho. The Church of Our Lady of the Assumption and of St. Gregory is a plain red-brick structure with

The Little Club was the Catholic social group Bill joined in the late 1950s. Meetings were held in the basement of an eighteenth-century church on Warwick Street, London. Photo by author.

romanesque windows. Its baroque interior features old icons, devout parishioners at prayer throughout the week, and an atmosphere rich in history.[25]

In the low-ceilinged basement reached by rickety iron stairs, pillars and arches convey a faint flavor of catacombs. The Little Club was a Catholic Action and social group started in 1952 for Catholics living in and around London. It welcomed visitors. Like the Catholic Information Centre in Toronto, where Bill would meet Jean Andrews some five years later, its active members were largely young, single adults, and it served very informally as a kind of marriage bureau.

Marriage was definitely part of Bill's design for his life. He actually took dancing lessons before joining the Little Club. He writes that being Christian is not the same as being puritanical; that while some self-denial, even of good things, develops moral strength, God intends His gifts to be enjoyed: "Wine, friendship, dancing, joking, sports, sex, and so forth, are good things. Since a normal life for most Christians is to marry and raise a family, the least I could do was get out of my introverted shell and meet the opposite sex." (A2 162) By 1958 Bill was dating and contemplating marriage with its promise of "a wholesome, physical relationship with a real woman" (A1 450).

In the 1950s the group had sixty to eighty men and women members from different parishes and many nationalities. For weekly socials, members went straight from work, bringing food by turns. From 6:30 to 10:30 on Friday evenings they could feast on bread and butter with scrambled eggs and baked beans, dance to records, sing around the piano, and talk. They played games like charades and planned amateur theatricals. Weekend jaunts sometimes included outings with orphaned children, or visits to famous religious centres, such as the Aylesford Priory. In this friendly, charitable atmosphere, Bill blossomed. Here was acceptance, kindness. His letters speak of rambling, dancing, swimming, touring, and having the occasional pint with the group, of attending Mass and going on retreats with them: "I look forward to such company now whereas it used to be misery before"; "I never thought that someday I would be happy and socially 'at home' as I have been with those people. ... I shall remember with pleasure especially their Friday night dances and square dances."[26] Only on country walks did he feel lonely even among friends, when other club members seemed insensitive to the natural beauty which affected Bill so strongly (A2 163).

One of his friends from the Little Club remembers Bill and the group with pleasure. The world seemed simpler then: "Coffee was the rage. We headed for espresso bars." Liquor? "Good heavens no!" Patricia Reidy recalls a quiet man, sincere and unassuming. He once brought a painting of a dollar bill to the club as a matter of interest; members were impressed, yet did not think of its creator as an *artist*. He did not speak of painting, although he spoke openly of having been "mentally ill". The dancing was "the old-fashioned kind. We always ended the evening with the record 'Give me five minutes more, only five minutes more.'" It *was* a simpler world, and in many ways Bill would carry its innocence with him to his dying day.

Trompe-l'oeil, in gouache, continued to supplement Bill's wages as a framer and to add to his savings for a trip to the Middle East. Since they were widely admired, they must also have been good for his ego, despite his disclaimers that they were not "art". Summer exhibitions at London's Royal Academy were arranged by open competition. For three years running, beginning in 1956, Bill had submitted *trompe-l'oeil* which were successful in competition and were shown at the Royal Academy. Margaret assisted with the first, on Bill's request, while he was with his family in Canada. Called *Thirty-five and Five*, this Kurelek *trompe-l'oeil* was a composition based on thirty-five shillings and five pence. *Dollar With Stamps and Coins* was exhibited in 1957, and *Odds and Ends* in 1958.[27] They sold for thirty and fifty pounds respectively. Stan Westlake had suggested the higher prices to Bill, beginning in 1957. He was of course delighted to find that they sold for these sums.

Kurelek's *trompe-l'oeil* cannot be dismissed as more artifact than art, strong on technical skill and weak in emotional, spiritual, and aesthetic content. Through composition and color, they form very pleasing still lifes. Bill also managed to personalize them and to add the depth that some *trompe-l'oeil* may lack. *Odds and Ends*, for example, is composed from a pound note, a sixpence, a burnt match, and a newspaper clipping of "An Airman's Prayer". The wartime clipping shows four verses. One reads: "I ask no help to strike my foe/I seek no petty victory here—/The enemy I hate, I know/To Thee is also dear." The printing, minute but legible, is all done by brush. Did Bill have a personal antagonist in mind?

To a friend who had lent him a penny, Bill later returned not the penny but a painting of it in *trompe-l'oeil* technique: two life-sized coins, the penny and an old 1939 farthing with a lark, have been laid on a checkered blue cloth in a composition only six centimetres square. The rich copper tones of the coins complement the blue cloth and the red frame. The effect is charming. In general, if a *trompe-l'oeil* was intended for a friend, Bill went to great pains to use objects that would have a special significance for that person. His choice of objects and his handling of them indicate a professional knowledge of the *trompe-l'oeil* tradition, as well as incredible technical skill.

One of his most fascinating paintings from the British period depicts an amusement arcade on a pier on England's south coast. The pier's owner had purchased a *trompe-l'oeil* through the Academy show and had subsequently become friendly with Bill. The two men, patron and artist, had both had domineering fathers and were similar in other ways. As the acquaintance grew, and a second purchase followed the first, it occurred to the patron that his two dreams were coming together.[28] Two of the passions in his life were his amusement arcade and his love of art. Now, for the first time, he actually knew an artist. He would have *his* artist paint *his* kingdom. Bill was shown the arcade, encouraged to view it from a ladder at the rear, and urged to get "everything" in. Intrigued, he accepted the commission and took photographs.

The pier painting is remarkable for its detail, its humor, and its observation of humanity. The human groups and situations that one sees at a fun fair are accurate and archetypal: mothers with children, old male cronies, elderly women alone, a worried customer attempting to shake a machine that has taken his coin but refused to play. The owner recognized that his observations of a lifetime had been caught, that everything *was* in. A bingo game dominates the foreground; Bill painted the faces of the regular players, many of which were recognized and identified locally when the painting hung in the arcade that had inspired it. One recognizes Bill's debts to Spencer and Brueghel, but the painting—down to the sign on the fortune-telling machine—is pure Kurelek. "What has life in store for you?" it inquired. What indeed.

The patron's memories included a trip with Bill to Mme Tussaud's Wax Museum, where he attempted to interest the artist in painting the Death of Nelson and the Sleeping Beauty. The latter's chest heaved gently, thanks to a machine, but not even this inducement could persuade the artist to tackle either Nelson or the Beauty, to the patron's regret. Bill was more interested in the onlookers than in the wax figures.

The moped that had carried Bill to the pier was another part of his grand design. Like a master draughtsman, he attended to every level; nothing was beneath his attention. Bill hoped that this mechanized bicycle, purchased in the spring of 1958, would carry him to Europe and the Holy Land: "it remains to be seen how we get along" was the way he put it to his brother.[29] He envisaged accessories such as a windshield and panniers for luggage. Of French manufacture, the bicycle was called a Mobylette. A sort of Rocinante to Bill's Don Quixote, it fed his romantic fantasies of cheap and speedy transportation to distant places. Unfortunately, the beast was to prove moody and intractable.

The Mobylette involved many new challenges for Bill, one of which was driving on the left side of the road. He described it in detail to his brother, imagining an engineer's pleasure in its workings. He envied John his mechanical sense; he found changing a tire difficult: "I like the machine when it's running properly. It gives a real firsthand satisfaction the way it eats up the road . . . but I don't like tending the thing."[30] With diabolical timing, the bicycle broke down just before Bill was to take his driver's test. Arriving late and very nervous, he was further upset by the system of secret watchers marking his progress along the designated route. Not surprisingly, he failed the test. His plan to make "the Big Trip" by bicycle had to be scrapped. Bill called the test a "nightmare experience", but he remained philosophical. Heaven had other plans for him, and disappointment could be offered up to God.[31]

With a learner's permit, the moped carried Bill as far as Brussels and Cologne in the summer of 1958. He went with Brian Cummings, a friend from the Little Club who would later accompany him in a sentimental journey to the London haunts of his Maudsley days. At the World's Fair in Brussels, he concentrated on five pavilions: Soviet, American, Canadian, British, and Vatican. He was most impressed by the Vatican's exhibit, which had something none of the others had: "It dealt with man himself rather than his achievements, his suffering, fears, hopes, work for his daily bread, and community life, and it did this by means of huge photographs."[32]

It was the Pollaks' custom to close for four weeks in August. Bill had filled his previous summer holidays with writing a hundred-page personal manuscript, painting three pictures, and visiting Ireland for six days. His admission that he finds himself unable to relax comes as no surprise. The manuscript, mailed to David John later that year, was one of the many incarnations of what would eventually be published as *Someone With Me*. The painting he did that season included the magnificent 1957 self-portrait which graces the cover of the 1980 edition of his autobiography. The subject's facial expression shows the distance Bill had travelled since he painted the large self-portrait which was re-worked at Netherne (1950, 1953). The first, against a Gothic arch, portrays the artist as a young man, wistful and timid; the second shows a mature artist, quizzical but confident. Six years and an ocean of experience separate the two.

The Irish trip was highlighted by a mystical experience at Glendalogh which Bill would later paint in a series called "Fields". He found Dublin grey and depressed, while Ireland in general was "dishevelled green". At Glendalogh, where a high wind heightened the natural beauty, Bill was in ecstasy: "I even recall doing a dance on a pathway out of sight of the other tourists. It's a state of soul that demands physical involvement too." (A1 447-48) Glendalogh was not to be Bill's last mystical experience.

The completion of his English affairs included a second trip to Lourdes in November to give thanks for his conversion at the place which had been crucial to overcoming his doubt. The weekend trip was an all-night vigil, a penance offered to God for protection from a third world war: "Peace seemed precarious just then because above-ground experiments with hydrogen bombs were very much in the news" (A1 454). The fear of such a holocaust would be with Bill for the remaining nineteen years of his life and would become intricately linked with his painting and his plans.

At Lourdes, Bill was pleased to be able to stay awake, and was deeply moved by the torchlight procession as thousands encircled the great domain with a sea of song and lights. To his brother John he wrote: "It was supposed to be a penance and brother! it certainly was, seven hours on our knees, all night with not a wink of sleep. And during our torchlight procession in the Domain outside it poured with rain. It almost had me beat but surprisingly I found myself in good spirits especially after the night was over. And my respect for British Catholics went up a few notches. The only way we were spoiled was with the wonderful French cooking."[33] After such an ordeal, one wonders why a good meal should qualify as "spoiling". Despite Bill's theory that God's gifts were to be enjoyed, pleasures frequently evoked feelings of guilt.

Christmas day, however, seems to have been one of pure enjoyment. Bill spent it with David John and his family at Wimbledon in the home of David's mother. Out of a half-dozen invitations he had chosen this particular one, cheerfully concluding that his company was "at long last beginning to be desirable". It was a large party, since Mrs. Anita John has six children, and by 1958 the David Johns had four. To this happy confusion were added two foreign students, a Nigerian and an Indian from Zanzibar from the Catholic Student Centre in London. Mrs. John found Bill silent and withdrawn that evening, "completely uncommunicative".[34] She felt that he related only to David, who had his confidence, and that he was overwhelmed by the size of the group.

Bill, however, enjoyed watching the others. He wrote to his brother of his pleasure in a gathering where everyone was made to feel at home in the Catholic family spirit. The Africans were strange and wonderful to Bill, despite the international nature of the Little Club. He channels his own wonderment through the reactions of David's young son, who kept touching the Nigerian's curly black hair. Bill's experience of ethnic diversity in North Winnipeg had not included Africans or Indians. The international attitudes prevailing in the John family were part of his introduction to Catholicism and soon became his own. They would bear fruit in years to come.

At the end of December, Bill left Pollak's, following the plan conceived three years earlier. To supplement his savings for the trip, he then carried out four weeks of work at St. Simon and St. Jude church. In a letter, he spoke of "redecorating" the church: "oddly enough it called for pretty well everything that I had learned in my two years at Blue Ball Yard." He also wrote of doing "murals" in his parish church. Today, the only identifiable Kurelek work in the church in Streatham Hill is the crucifix in *trompe-l'oeil* style. The puzzling references apparently refer to the crucifix and portraits of St. Simon and St. Jude. The work was done in isolation, and Bill was keenly conscious of the loss of the camaraderie he had shared at Blue Ball Yard.

The training at Pollak's had been supplemented by numerous evening classes throughout the five years spent in London outside hospitals. Most or all of the courses had been taken at the Hammersmith School of Building Arts and Crafts. Then, as now, instruction was offered in the modern application of a thousand ancient skills, and the intimate relation between art and craft is taken for granted. Bill studied framing, cabinet-making, and book-designing. The latter course led by a circuitous route to an encounter with a microscope. The beauty of ocean coral reduced Bill to tears and reinforced his belief in a divine creator (A1 443).[35] The addition of two or three evenings a week to full daytime employment meant a taxing schedule. Yet even as he returned home on the Underground, tired from evening class and longing for bed, Bill would write letters in order to save time.

The grand design involved more travel in Europe, where Canadians and Americans (as Bill wrote to his brother) could see the origins of their own cultures. The moped, before completely disgracing itself and Bill, had carried him to northern Europe in the summer of 1958. The next stage of his carefully planned tour involved overland travel through France, Switzerland, Italy, Yugoslavia, Bulgaria, Turkey, and Syria to Jordan and Israel. This time it was John's turn to be envious; he was tempted to join his brother.[36] Bill's anticipated three months in Jordan and Israel, however, would become six weeks, and April 4 would find him back in London planning the pier painting which was to pay for his passage home.[37] It is not clear whether his money or his energy ran out; he may simply have felt that the job had been accomplished. He now had a working knowledge of the area in which Christ had lived and died.

Bill (front row, right) with a tour group on his first trip to Lourdes, France, in 1958. From his scrapbook.

It was difficult to reach Jordan overland in 1959 because of the recent crisis at Suez. Bill had hoped to be carried on the Orient Express as far as Damascus, but the train took him only to Istanbul, where the effort to get a transit visa for Syria became a nine-day nightmare.

Bill's mood is buoyant as he embarks on this great adventure. Letters describe the journey to Istanbul (February 1-4) as a romantic comedy underscored by black humor as the train moves east. He seems outgoing, even talkative, as he struggles in four languages (English, French, German, and Ukrainian) to communicate with fellow travellers. Yugoslavia provides his first look behind the Iron Curtain.

The frequency of police checks and other delays is disconcerting: "I had always thought of the Orient Express as being full of intriguing passengers bound from Paris to the Middle East but travelling like a shot out of Hell with no stops and a minimum of formalities."[38] Bill is perturbed by Yugoslavia's "backwardness"; by its poverty, and ironic contrasts between shabby villagers and uniformed soldiers. Even so, the romantic side of his nature is fascinated by the army greatcoat, which reaches almost to the ground: "There is something cavalier and gallant about it."[39]

Physically, the trip was something of an ordeal. Bill got little food and less sleep on the train. The constant surveillance east of Italy was nerve-racking, and by the third day he was violently nauseated. Dysentery was added to his miseries in Turkey and during the weeks that followed. In Israel and Jordan he suffered from Asiatic flu, and encountered both snow and extremes of heat. A German doctor, noticing Bill on a boat crossing the Sea of Galilee, told him that his illness could be fatal if he did not get care soon. Bill was delighted when their paths crossed again by accident some weeks later and he could tease the doctor over his prognosis. He stayed in the cheapest lodgings available, usually in youth hostels, and carried his own baggage. This was a man who disciplined his spirit and punished his body. He had neither the time nor the money to be sick.

Turkey reminded Bill of Mexico, his introduction to Third World conditions. Some impressions were to remain with him for life, such as the sight of an old man rolling a heavy wheel up a cobbled street. He encountered the man twice that day, and he felt that the wheel symbolized the shackles of poverty to which the man was bound. He noticed more than poverty, however. Here, as elsewhere, he would remark on the people's spirit, which surmounted their difficulties. He was also struck by the cultural links between Turkey and the Ukraine. Turkish music reminded him of Ukrainian songs sung by old women at drinking parties and of Dribni folk dances: "In fact I realized soon just how much of what I always thought a peculiarly Ukrainian culture is in fact derived from the Tartar and Turkish invaders."

Bill was fortunate in meeting two men in Istanbul who shared his destination, Jerusalem, and his visa difficulties. A Canadian and a New Zealander became his travelling companions for the next eight days. He had been living what he calls "a pretty settled uneventful life" for several years; faced with major difficulties in language and red tape, he felt "rather helpless" and was relieved to share a car in a triple partnership. He was upset by their contempt for local people and by their purchase of black-market dollars. The three men were finally forced to bribe the steward of an American grain cargo boat which carried them from Iskenderum to Beirut. It is a beautiful irony that Bill approached the Holy Land as an illegal stowaway.

Jerusalem was only a short plane trip away. To a person of such sensitivity and religious faith, being in the Holy Land was overwhelming: "Seeing the very places before my eyes which have been so very much in my mind for the past three or four years and in the mind and heart of all Christendom for the past two thousand years is almost too stupendous to take in. Never have I been so delighted to see a new place as I was yesterday. I would say the most enlightening aspect of this visit so far is getting the geography of the New Testament events straight."[40]

Bill had already endured ordeal-by-visa, and was now to be plagued by beggars and would-be guides. Child beggars attacked him in packs, like wolves. Bill had several narrow escapes and was very nearly downed and stripped (A1 465). With a failure to appreciate the people's desperate economic plight (a failure which is atypical), he found the guiding business "hideously bad taste in a sacred place". After being reduced to tears by clamorous followers, he tried wearing an Arab head-dress but the disguise was obvious. Beggars evoked a variety of responses as Bill's defensive mechanisms warred with pity: "I asked my confessor the next day just what alms am I bound to give in good conscience. He told me what I'd been thinking. Give in proportion to one's means and preferably through the right channels."[41]

Life in the Holy Land still seemed close to what it had been in New Testament times. Women carried loads on their heads and bartered in markets. The narrow cobbled streets looked as he imagined they had looked to Christ. Camels and donkeys were everywhere. Bill proceeded to ration his time and money with the utmost precision. He had a list of places taken from St. Matthew's Gospel and was determined to see them. The sites of Calvary and Christ's tomb had been combined in the Church of the Holy Sepulchre. He seemed surprised and irritated by changes, despite the enormous difference in time: "If only people had left Holy Sites in their natural state as the Grotto at Lourdes has been preserved! . . . It's an awesomely holy place when you realize that the whole salvation of mankind actually took place within those four walls." (A1 468) Other sites included the Upper Room, scene of the Last Supper; the Garden of Gethsemane, where Christ prayed in agony; Lazarus's tomb in Bethany on the other side of Mount Olivet; and Bethlehem, with its Church of the Nativity. To many of these sites Bill walked, in frequent danger from gangs of boys and even a group of teenage girls, who took him for a Jew.

After three weeks in Jordan he walked, carrying his baggage, over the strip of no man's land into Israel. Walking, he got the feeling of the country into his head and hand. He would paint the Judean landscape many times in the years to come. Everywhere, Bill was conscious of traversing holy ground: the road the holy family had travelled, the site where Christ was born, the road that inspired the parable of the Good Samaritan.

Here there were no more beggars, but Bill missed the informal Arab hospitality he had frequently encountered and he felt terribly alone. He travelled to Beersheba, Nazareth, Cana, Tiberias, Capernaum, Galilee, and Mount Tabor. The Mount was the site of Christ's transfiguration and the place where, after His resurrection, He commissioned His apostles to go and teach all nations. This commissioning seems to have been one of the main reasons for Bill's choosing Matthew over the other gospels.[42]

"On the Jordan River where Christ was baptized" Bill wrote in his scrapbook. Bill's spring 1959 trip to Israel supplied him with information and visual images for his Passion paintings.

Bill's methodical approach naturally included photographing the scenes he planned to paint. He disliked the tourist aura created by a camera and kept it hidden whenever possible, yet he felt "forced" to use it to gather information for his project.[43] In addition to personal photographs and drawings, he purchased photos from a newspaper in Tel Aviv. His comments in this regard are interesting in light of the criticism after his death of the Semitic qualities of the faces in some of his Passion paintings: "I also got a good batch of press photos of Jewish types while I was in Tel Aviv. These I need for the apostles and the crowd scenes in my project. They cost me almost a hundred dollars." (A1 480)

A letter to John indicates that the purchase must have been made later by mail; his autobiography is often inaccurate on factual details: "So I am writing this while doing 'guard duty' at art show outdoors on the Thames Embankment near the Houses of Parliament where I have hung a picture for the day. . . . A buyer is all I'm interested in as I could do with a 100 dollars for some photographs I selected in Israel without being able to buy."[44]

A shortage of money probably hastened his return to England. His plans seem to have changed frequently in Israel during March. Eventually he took a ship to Italy via Athens and spent the Catholic Easter in Rome. (The Ukrainian Easter fell much later that year.) The Holy City depressed Bill: "I could not stand the Vatican. Its opulence, I feel, is a drag on real Christianity." (A1 481) Bill seems never to have been tempted by wealth or physical luxury, and to have maintained a life-long suspicion of affluence as a barrier between man and God. He returned to London by third-class coach, his sole regret being that he had failed to see Florence.

In London, Bill returned to his lodgings at 45 Kingsmead Road. He had seven weeks in which to wrap up the affairs of seven years spent in and near that city. Most of April went into the detailed painting of the amusement arcade, whose price had been set at seventy pounds because that was the cost of his passage home.[45] The *trompe-l'oeil* mentioned to John had been set at thirty-five pounds because that was the sum required for the Israeli photos; it had also been the sale price for the one in the Royal Academy Exhibition of 1957. Its fate is unknown, but the thought of Bill with a *trompe-l'oeil* on the Embankment is engaging. The painting attracted great interest, but the office workers had little money to spare for art. Since the photos were purchased, a painting must have been sold. He told John that he was now painting "with greater facility" than ever before.[46]

Just at this time, a leading British Sunday newspaper reproduced *The Maze*, painted in Maudsley Hospital in 1953, in an article entitled

"Labyrinth of the Sick Mind". Kurelek's name was not mentioned. He promptly responded:

> I would like it to be known that there was a happy ending to the story. Although I left hospital after various treatments not fully well, I had while there made an English friend who through good example introduced me to the Roman Catholic Church. Later, after much study, I received the Faith and it has helped me to bear with the remainder of my trouble and to begin a normal life.
>
> I am returning to Canada next month, so I would like also to take this opportunity to say "thank you" for all the social security, kindness and respect which I came needing and have been treated to during my six years stay in this country.   William Kurelek.[47]

Gratitude, and the sense that a phase had now been completed, are the tonic notes of Bill's writings at this time. For over a year his letters home had been growing nostalgic. Stonewall was in his mind, even Whitford.[48] A walk through Green Park in Central London in the early morning reminded him of haying time on the farm with the grass newly cut and the air full of its perfume. In Israel, he had even felt the lack of a letter from his father, a state of affairs he would never have believed possible four years earlier. In England, he had also been noticing children, and casting himself in the role of a lonely bachelor in need of a wife. In response to a warning by John of recession in Canada, he had written: "I myself wouldn't mind remaining here. I feel more secure and more in my element (culturally) here, but I'm going back because I hope to start up a business into which I could take my father and save him and mother from toiling their way into the grave. Or at least be on hand in their old age in some other way.... Things may get tough but I myself don't believe in luxury living so I'm sure I'll get by."[49]

More secure? More in his element culturally? Was Bill going home because things were becoming too comfortable in London, because he craved greater challenge? His sentimental journey with Brian Cummings to his old London haunts had reminded him of the vast distance he had travelled since he had painted *Help Me Please Help Me* and *The Maze*. "Seven years of my life had gone by in this country which I'd come to love. Partly because of the loss of memory from hospital treatment, it seemed even more than seven. I'd very nearly remained in England for good, having been so much happier there than in Canada," he would write in 1972 (A1 482). As for the Canadian recession, that was a bogey which held no terrors for Bill. God would provide, he reasoned. If he was destined to have a framing shop in Toronto with his father, then God would make it possible.

9

In the Lions' Den:
Toronto, 1959-62

"In the circles in which we were moving,
he was certainly an oddity."
—John Robert Colombo

BILL HAD BEEN AN INSIGNIFICANT INDIVIDUAL IN THE METROPOLIS HE WAS
leaving. As a craftsman and a secret observer, he had had a small niche
in three social units (Blue Ball Yard, the Little Club, and the Catholic
Guild of Artists and Craftsmen), but to the city at large he meant
nothing at all. In the city to which he was returning, however, he
would soon establish himself as a family man, a member of the
Ukrainian-Canadian community, and a recognized artist. Bill anticipated and sought the first and the last of these changes.

However, he did not anticipate that his life in Toronto would be
both more provincial and more sophisticated than his London life, nor
did he realize how basically rural his habits and attitudes had
remained. The radical discrepancy between his burning religious faith
and a society where many individuals were nominal Christians or
agnostics was not yet apparent to him. Armed with faith, the man from
Stonewall was prepared to give battle, but his antagonists and their
arena were still unknown.

Early in June 1959, Bill returned to Canada aboard the Cunard liner
Ivernia. Photographs show a smiling man in grey flannels and dark
blazer at the ship's rail and in the bar, apparently happy and confident.
A fellow passenger later described him as shy, boyishly charming, and
intelligent; in short, "immediately attractive".[1] By a strange stroke of
fate, another young Canadian whose tastes were oddly similar to Bill's
was on the same ship. Kenneth Shorey, an actor and a writer who was
ten years younger but mature for his years, would become Bill's friend
and correspondent for the rest of his life. Neither man could know this
on the *Ivernia*, but both had a sense of destiny and both were determined to make their mark. "I think the *Ivernia* was our reference

Kenneth Shorey (left) and Bill (centre) with a fellow passenger in the ship's bar on board the *Ivernia*, 1959. During the voyage, Shorey read a draft of Bill's autobiography, which marked the beginning of a long friendship in Canada. From Bill's scrapbook.

point," Shorey would later write, "a convenient landmark, or water-mark, as you will. We were nobodies aboard the *Ivernia*, nobodies who later went on to find success and a measure of happiness."[2] Both men were keenly concerned with music, literature, art, and religion; both were adult converts, one Catholic, the other Protestant.

The two soon discovered that they shared an interest in the St. Matthew Passion, though for different reasons. Shorey aspired to produce it on stage; Bill had dreamed, since 1955, of illustrating it as a teaching tool. Each took the other's dream seriously, and each was impressed by the odds against such an encounter as theirs: two strangers in mid-Atlantic discussing the St. Matthew Passion without a text. The discovery called for a celebration. Shorey writes: "We were not drunk but elated—like finding a nugget of gold in a handful of sand. In a very real sense, I think that what we experienced aboard the *Ivernia* carried us through the next eighteen years."[3]

In the ship's bar, Bill produced photographs of his paintings from his wallet. He then asked his new friend if he would care to read his autobiography. Shorey thought that Bill was referring to a distant future, but the artist promptly produced hundreds of pages, held together by an elastic band, from a small valise under the table: "it was wholly handwritten, and a Godawful mess to read. ... Different coloured inks changed virtually from page to page."[4] Astonished, the actor retired to his cabin to read the manuscript. Shorey had joined the Baptist Church a few years earlier and could sympathize with Bill's "conversion story", although the colored inks continued to amaze him. The autobiography impressed Shorey. A friendship that would prove significant for both men had begun.

Back in Toronto, Bill began to pick up the threads of his life. Soon after returning he called Eric Freifeld, his old friend and mentor from

Shorey, who met
Bill during the
overseas crossing,
described him as
shy, boyishly
charming, and
intelligent —
"immediately
attractive".
Courtesy
Mr. E. Adamson.

the Ontario College of Art. No correspondence had passed between them in the long interval. In late summer Freifeld spent an evening with Bill at his Huron Street room. The two talked far into the night, Bill attempting to convey the essence of the decade he had just passed through and of his new faith, while the older artist observed a man both different and the same. More than twenty years later, Freifeld recalled the small room filled with paintings, and Bill's intensity:

> He said he was doing a painting a day from St. Matthew, in the service of God. He intended everything he did there-after to be a genuflexion to the God who had emancipated him from bondage by grace. He told me of his odyssey. He still had the sense of destiny, indeed he was determined to vindicate it. I felt friendly towards him, and I later went to his first show with Isaacs, but he may have resented my refusal to correspond in 1950. He seemed ambivalent. I sensed that he was making a point.[5]

Freifeld, with little sympathy for Bill's ambition to produce religious propaganda, was disappointed in the Passion paintings. He also disapproved of the speed at which Bill was then working. He much preferred Bill's romantic work done in 1949-50, "old houses with dark clouds and threatening birds: moody, like an illustration for a fairy-tale or a Slavic folk-tale." Bill talked that evening of his parents, of the reasons they had given him to hate them and of his resulting self-hatred and guilt. He was trying, Freifeld felt, to be "positive and healthy", and evidently needed to speak of these feelings. Bill was clearly seeking Freifeld's friendship at the time, but the older man was repelled: "He was too self-involved. He wanted to be known, and to be vindicated. He was humble with the 'h' dropped, a Dickensian humbleness: very self-confident, even arrogant in certain ways. There was always a central narcissism."[6] (Perhaps there always is, with committed artists.) Freifeld saw Kurelek, then and later, as a neurotic personality, fuelled by "a strong dynamic of resentment and hate and guilt" and with a character very similar to the one he had exhibited at OCA a decade earlier.

During his first months back in Canada, Bill had been helping his parents at their Vinemount farm. They were happy to see him but still displeased by his conversion. He was also visiting old friends from his OCA years, Gus and Julie Rueter, and laying plans. A framing business would require capital, and the only means of acquiring the money seemed to be through a teaching job. Accordingly Bill registered for teacher training at the Ontario College of Education. He was devastated to be rejected on the fourth day as psychologically unfit for the profession. The odd affair loomed large in his imagination and contributed a severe blow to his ego.

The OCE fiasco brought him closer to his family. It also illustrates the naïveté which Bill never lost and which co-existed with his common sense and his peasant shrewdness. Bill was still uneasy with strangers and unable to look them in the face. At parties in the 1960s he enjoyed talking with individuals but avoided group situations. Did he really think he could teach a large class of adolescents? No doubt he trusted to willpower and to God. They had not failed him yet, and would carry him far.

In order to be near OCE, Bill had taken lodgings at 588 Huron Street, in a boarding-house run by a Hungarian couple, Stephen and Mary Szombathy. Called the Annex, the area north of Bloor Street and south of Davenport Road had come down in the world as large private mansions had become rooming-houses owned by immigrants and occupied by students and transients. Photographs of Bill's room show a small desk littered with painting supplies and a wall covered with postcards and other memorabilia. Bill described it to a friend as "one bulb, a desk, bed, paints and canvasses". Another friend recalls a crucifix, and a Ukrainian doily on the back of a chair, the latter a rather touching gesture of gentility. The room would be home for three years, till his marriage in late 1962. Here Bill would paint the Passion series, although roughly a decade would pass before it would be shown as an entity, sold, and permanently hung. While here he would meet Av Isaacs and mount his first two solo exhibitions with this impressive young dealer who had established himself in the Toronto art world only a few years before Bill's return.

Stories from the period suggest just how hard-pressed Bill was during his first year back, with money in short supply and the future uncertain. Writer John Robert Colombo, who met Bill early in 1960, remembers a man "obsessed with religion, sexually inhibited or frustrated, socially ill-adjusted and undeniably talented. He had little sense of how he was seen by others, or how he affected them,"[7] Colombo and his wife Ruth invited the artist to dinner in their Rosedale flat, after the writer had seen and admired his Bosch-like painting *Behold Man Without God*. Bill had bought a white shirt for the occasion, but, being caught short on time, ended by carrying it in its cellophane wrapping. Colombo recalls:

> We discussed premarital sex. Bill strongly disapproved of
> it, thought of marriage as a sacrament, and said he hoped
> to marry soon. Psychologically he was virgin: he didn't
> know sensuality, he projected a sense of someone unful-

Bill's room at 588 Huron Street, Toronto, where he lived until his marriage in 1962. From his scrapbook.

(Opposite page) Pencil and tempera sketch of the artist's room, Huron Street, Toronto (1960), 17" x 23". Private collection.

filled. In the circles we were moving in, he was certainly an oddity. If he believed that his suffering was providential, giving him insight into Christ's suffering, I think that was rationalizing after the fact. He found the perfect image for his sado-masochism in crucifixion. I think it was his talent rather than his faith that enabled him to overcome his neuroses.[8]

Since Colombo was a lapsed Catholic with a Jewish wife, the circumstances were not calculated to put Bill at his ease. Nor did the Colombos seem to be aware that, as urban radical avant-garde intellectuals, they were quite as foreign to Bill as he was to them. Nothing is more subjective than "normalcy". Colombo's memories were largely conceptual, while Ruth's were often physical, though equally severe:

Bill was terribly stiff and ill at ease, carrying his packaged white shirt and offering to change for dinner. I said What, in this attic? He'd tried to clean himself up, but his hands were the hands of a labourer. There was dye and engrained dirt under the nails, though his hands were obviously scrubbed. He wore a blazer and grey flannels and a horrible maroon tie with grey stripes, and his hair was all askew, nothing but cowlicks. The clothes were

badly cut, didn't fit, and they didn't suit him: he wasn't
WASP.

I've known many Ukrainian labourers, through my
father's clothing business in a small town. Some seemed
to have an artistic soul which didn't fit with the rest of
them. Bill was like that, unbalanced, split, the two halves
of artist and labourer not coming together.

He was so ill at ease he seemed like a programmed
robot, and made *me* nervous. He tried so hard to be
socially correct but he was disjointed, he hadn't come
together. He looked older than his age. And he kept apologizing for everything. No self-confidence. He was like a
peasant dressed in city clothes. There was something very
European about him.[9]

This was the man whom Shorey had found boyishly charming, immediately attractive. Obviously Bill responded to different people and
social contexts like a chameleon.

Colombo offered Bill his first Canadian commission, the illustration
of a suite of apocalyptic poems called "Lines for the Last Day". After
consulting his priest, Bill accepted, and produced a striking black-and-
white poster which ranks among the most startling and disturbing of
his works. Colombo's poetic images of bloody days, funereal skies, and
cities "pyred like chaff" are illustrated by erupting mountains, fiery
buildings, demons, and angelic spirits. Worm-like demons are splitting

a brick wall to which the poems are fastened. In a border, a mushroom cloud prefigures the atomic holocaust scenes Bill frequently painted in the 1960s and '70s. Colombo was pleased, astounded, and impressed: "it was a marvellous meeting of minds, combining words and visions both thematically and graphically. Seldom has the apocalypse come alive so spontaneously."[10]

Peter and Vivian Kuzina come from a rural background in Manitoba similar to Bill's own, yet in the fall of 1959 they found the artist almost as unusual as the Colombos had done. Peter had been John Kurelek's friend at the University of Manitoba. John must have given Bill the Kuzinas' address, for the artist appeared at their door one morning shortly before noon. He volunteered the information that he did framing, that his plans to illustrate the New Testament would require twenty years, and that he sometimes painted for two days in a row without eating: "I just forget about eating and sleeping" Bill said in a monotone.[11] Apart from these comments, he spoke only when spoken to.

Peter Kuzina, suspecting that the man was starving, urged Vivian to empty their freezer. She eventually cooked twelve pork chops, and Bill consumed eight of them along with other food. He ate in silence, and left soon after the meal without expressing thanks. He did leave his address. The Kuzinas considered him "not reserved but withdrawn," and found twenty-year plans overly ambitious. They subsequently called at 588 Huron and would remember a poor area, a huge old house, and dark, rickety stairs. Bill had not been in.

The kindly Szombathys accepted paintings as temporary security for Bill's rent, set at six dollars a week. Several hung in the dark halls. Phil Lanthier, a fellow lodger, recalls that one was a *trompe-l'oeil* of Bill's first dollar earned, another an early self-portrait, and a third "a frightening apocalyptic painting of a train hurtling off a smashed trestle, its occupants oblivious to their impending annihilation. . . . It was a hell of a picture to come home to."[12]

Brendan Foley and the two Lanthier brothers had rooms adjacent to Bill's on the top floor. Foley remembers infrequent and awkward meetings:

> Neither of us was garrulous or gregarious. He was working on the St. Matthew Gospel then, obviously driven by a religious fervour which I didn't share. When our conversations went beyond the banalities of polite discourse, they centred around our disagreements on Catholic dogma. These discussions were never acrimonious. I still respected the tradition and recognized that, for Bill, the

Roman Catholic faith was a haven from madness. I loved
the man and his dedication to his art. . . . He was skimping
by, making frames. . . . [13]

Bill's talent, self-discipline, and dedication were almost universally
admired at the start of his Toronto career, even by those with little
sympathy for his beliefs.

He remained an enigma to most, a puzzling paradox of a man whose
parts, as Ruth Colombo observed, did not seem to coalesce. Phil
Lanthier found it difficult to connect the silent, hesitant, gentle man
and his impish smile with the doomsday painting in the hall or the
scenes of the Passion according to St. Matthew, which he was executing with painstaking detail. Lanthier noted "a strangeness in his eyes,
which indicated a strong concentration on some continuous inner
event. . . . This medieval passion for submitting art to the service of faith
while one remained humble and anonymous could only inspire awe
even in the sanctimonious Toronto of the late '50s. Awe and a certain
amount of bewilderment: how on earth could Bill Kurelek and Harold
Town occupy the same city at the same time in history?"[14] Bill's eyes
were red, and appeared to be strained. Phil Lanthier saw him as a man
still struggling with his demons.[15]

James Lanthier's room was next to Bill's and the walls were thin.
Lanthier could hear Bill talking in his sleep: anxious talk; nightmares. A
single hot-plate served the top-floor roomers. None of them had much
money, but Bill's budget seemed the tightest: "We were all struggling.
He'd take my pot-cleaner pad when I was ready to discard it, and use it
for another month. He had pretty meagre food."[16] Jane Lanthier, James's
wife, remembered Bill as a kind, gentle man with a great sense of
humor, many anxieties, and spiritual depths; he projected an impression of intensity, and a curious combination of fragility and strength: "a
physical, Slavic, almost peasant feeling of strength".[17]

Bill had numerous acquaintances but few close friends. Since the
late forties the friends to whom he had opened his heart included
Zenon Pohorecky, Eric Freifeld, Margaret Smith, and David John. Then,
in the summer and fall of 1959 he had Kenneth Shorey. Both were in
love with the Middle Ages, Shorey with its theatre and Bill with its art.
More important than this common ground was Shorey's confidence in
Bill's ability as an artist. The actor believed that his friend had talent,
even genius, an attitude calculated to seal the bond cemented by
mutual interests and that curious mid-Atlantic encounter. The two had
planned to room together, but Bill's choice of 588 Huron Street was
too far from the Crest Theatre to suit Shorey. Lacking personal tele-
phones, they began to correspond. Then, as later, conversation cen-

tred on politics and religion, fuelled by Bill's private hope of converting his friend to Roman Catholicism and by Shorey's hope of making a conservative out of Bill.[18] As Shorey puts it, "We talked our own language and carried on a running debate for almost twenty years."[19]

In the fall of 1959, Shorey and Norma Renault, Isaacs' wife, were acting together in the Crest Theatre's production of *Under Milk Wood*. Shorey told Renault that he had a friend who painted like Hieronymus Bosch. At this point Bill may have already met Isaacs in his capacity as a framer rather than as a painter.[20] Renault offered to suggest to her husband that he drive to Willowdale, where Bill's paintings were stored, to see his work. The artist had spent part of the summer with his friends the Rueters, and had left his paintings stacked in their garage. Shorey recalls helping to set out a sizeable number of Bill's paintings in the Rueters' living-room: "A skeptical Av Isaacs entered the house, took one sweeping glance around, and said, 'My God.'"[21] Apparently Isaacs began almost immediately on negotiations for Bill's first solo exhibition, which took place the following spring. Bill later favored the version that Isaacs had been sufficiently struck by a couple of paintings Bill carried under his arm as samples of his ability as a framer to raise the possibility of a show.

Certainly the encounter with Isaacs was providential. There seems little doubt that without this particular dealer, Bill's fame would have grown much more slowly than it did. The two became friends, with Isaacs playing the role of elder brother as well as business partner. Bill trusted the dealer, and remained loyal to him throughout his career. There was a brief flurry of infidelity when Bill was thinking of seeking a Christian dealer with an interest in religious art. Dr. Evan Turner, Director of the Montréal Museum of Fine Arts, spoke against such a plan, advising Bill to paint in the marketplace rather than preach to the converted. Bill took the advice, and in years to come would stoutly resist occasional suggestions from family and friends that he could do better with another dealer or with no dealer at all.

The partnership, and the relation between artist and dealer, would remain enigmatic. There were those who thought the two had nothing in common, philosophically or artistically: "They simply used one another—and the arrangement worked."[22] Isaacs' tastes were avant-garde; his other artists were largely abstract painters. Through the sixties he was fond of joking that Kurelek, the most "literal" artist he had ever carried, insisted on adding explanatory texts to his realistic paintings. Isaacs had no interest in Christian art or "religious propaganda", the cause Bill had espoused in 1955. Conversely, Bill had ethical reservations or objections to some of Isaacs' other artists in the 1960s and '70s. Dealer and artist appear as an odd couple, yet the "marriage" lasted.

After graduating in political science and economics from the University of Toronto, Isaacs had opened a framing shop in 1951, and later a gallery and framing business on Bay Street called the Greenwich Art Gallery. Toronto had very few galleries at the time, and none of the others were showing the work of contemporary Canadians. Isaacs moved to his current location at 832 Yonge Street in 1961. Bill's first exhibition was at the older location, and his second at the gallery which has now become something of a Toronto landmark or institution. Gordon Rayner, a senior Canadian abstract painter, speaks of Isaacs' impact on the Toronto art scene: "'He was an innovator who took chances during the early days. He helped change the cultural face of Canada.' "[23] Isaacs is known as a nationalist with a sturdy respect for Canadian art; as adventurous in his tastes; and as a strong supporter of his artists. His loyalty helped many of them to survive the rough spots any artist encounters. His confidence in Bill would prove invaluable.

Perhaps Isaacs thrived because he combined an eye for the good with an instinct for the saleable: "'I find the best artists I can,' Isaacs says simply. 'In that respect I am a taste-maker. By bringing a new value to the scene, eventually people will accept the new art I have introduced. If I've guessed right, then we'll all make money.' "[24] He looks for "a certain mental toughness", art being (in his opinion) ten per cent talent and ninety per cent commitment. In 1959 he must have sensed that toughness, that commitment, in Bill.

Isaacs was also avant-garde in fostering the mingling of several arts. His gallery was the only place in Toronto in the late 1950s where poetry readings were held or "underground" (artist-made) films shown. One of his artists, Michael Snow, was also a jazz musician, so the arts (as Colombo put it) interacted: "To be part of Av's stable *made* an artist."[25]

Bill's first exhibition with Isaacs, from March 26 through April 7, 1960, was high drama, and not without its comic side. For the artist, it was the fulfilment of a dream, the first major step on the road towards his secular goal: success. The show consisted of some twenty paintings and drawings, including two magnificent self-portraits (1950, 1957); three *trompe-l'oeil*; still lifes; allegories; and drawings from his Mexican period. The works had been done between the late 1940s and the winter of 1959-60; several belonged to friends and relatives and were not for sale. The hospital period was represented by *Remorse*, which shows a male figure wracked with pain. Western scenes of a time and place remembered with deep emotion and depicted with meticulous detail, the type of Kurelek painting which would become so widely known and loved in years to come, were prefigured by *Farm Children's Games in Western Canada*, a large composition with an evident debt to Brueghel, and by *Saw-Sharpener*, from lumber-camp days. A moody, impressionistic work called *When I Have Come Back Home* shows a man with a suitcase trudging up a long farm lane. The emotion is palpable. *The Modern Tower of Babel* and *Behold Man Without God* warn of disaster to come unless mankind forsakes its violent, greedy ways. Techniques varied greatly. These paintings were indebted to traditions in Western art for some six hundred years, but none were currently fashionable in North America. As for the seeing eye, it was wholly Bill's own. Emotionally and intellectually, the paintings struck the viewer like a well-placed bomb.

The comedy lay in the human drama of the opening or *vernissage*. Those present could be divided into two groups or types, as compatible as oil and water. On the one hand there was the artist, his Ukrainian parents (looking pleased and no doubt surprised), and their friends. On the other were the habitués of Isaacs' popular opening nights, city sophisticates with dangling earrings, silver cigarette holders, lamé dresses, and the bohemian costumes affected at the time.[26] Colombo recalls the shock to eyes accustomed to abstract expressionism: "There were a lot of strange-looking people, not the usual art crowd. Bill looked terribly out of place at his own opening. He wouldn't hold a wine glass. The paintings stuck out like sore thumbs. Bill stuck out too. He had a reddish complexion and looked like a lumberjack; he looked as if he were in the wrong country, the wrong century, the wrong situation. It didn't look as if *he* had produced this work!" But he had. The essential comedy lay in the incongruous mix of this Daniel outfacing his lions. His work had just begun.

The first Kurelek exhibition drew the biggest crowd the four-year-old gallery had ever had. The second, two years later, featured paintings of farm and bush life, scenes that would prove perennially popular.[27] Works that would become famous included *Sunday Dinner Call in the Bush*, *Russian Thistles Migrating*, and *Gathering in the Garden Before Freeze-Up*. Prices ranged from $160 to $500, and paintings sold briskly. Many critics agreed that Kurelek's work was unique in contemporary Canadian painting.[28] Janice Tyrwhitt wrote perceptively of the "lurking terror" found in even apparently ordinary farm scenes:

> In Kurelek's pictures you feel a sense of doom, a certainty
> that something terrible *will* happen. Often a storm is com-
> ing, darkness is falling, men are hurrying through work
> that can't be finished in the short prairie day. Around and
> beyond them land and sky stretch vast, lonely and hostile.
> Landscapes are tilted to exaggerate distances. ... In this
> recent show the sense of foreboding was mellowed by
> nostalgia and tenderness for the land. ... The tension in

Kurelek's pictures springs from the imposition of a literal mind on a burning imagination.[29]

Between the two exhibitions, Kurelek's talent and Isaacs' promotional skill had led to a signal honor for the artist. In 1961 the Women's Committee of the Art Gallery of Ontario had invited Alfred Barr, Director of Collections at New York's Museum of Modern Art and perhaps the most prestigious figure in modern art at the time, to choose a Canadian painting for his collections as their gift. Expected to favor an abstract expressionist painting, the American director astonished Toronto's art world by choosing a representational Kurelek oil called *Hailstorm in Alberta*. Kurelek had never heard of Barr, was not (unlike the other artists) in the Gallery at the time, and did not know that his dealer had entered *Hailstorm* in the contest.

When contacted by telephone, Bill proposed to come down by streetcar and had to be pressured to take a taxi. Jeanne Parkin recalls the meeting of Barr with Kurelek: "He was so shy, he just kept looking at the floor. You couldn't have found a greater contrast: this very sophisticated, refined, elegant man from New York, and Bill's rumpled shock of hair and lumbering figure. He looked like a farmer. Yet Barr was also shy, a private man in many ways, modest and gentle. Both men were introspective. There was a bond, they understood one another."[30] Parkin believed that Barr, who had returned repeatedly to the painting before making his choice, had felt its psychological power. Elizabeth Kilbourn's description suggests the painting's emotional strengths: "Out of a pale Western sky, two small sudden black clouds pelt down hailstones each of which seems imbued with a fierce cosmic life of its own. ... The painting itself is organized with a classic simplicity and spareness but, as an image of chaos and doom in an age of doomsday diplomacy, is unbearably poignant."[31]

Meanwhile, Bill was spending most of his time painting the Passion pictures, while earning a living working for Isaacs. His very first job was painting the walls of the Bay Street gallery. From late 1959 on he was framing, "at first only a few hours, later a whole day, still later two days a week. ... And here was sure proof of how God provides, for I had only about $15 of my savings left when this upswing of fortune began." (A1 489)

The framing work, originally carried on in an unused warehouse near the waterfront, was later attached to the gallery proper. Foreman Emmett Maddix would become Bill's friend, while a Belfast Orangeman provided a lively forum for theological arguments. Maddix remembers separating the disputants. He felt that Bill was strange to the other framers, some of whom picked on him as an "oddball": "He looked like an immigrant. He was so quiet some of the framers thought he was semi-retarded. When he talked, it was about religion. And he was always writing, even when he was talking to you. Always sketching or writing."[32]

Swearing was common in the framing shop. Bill objected to it as sacrilegious. When he rebuked Maddix for swearing, the foreman decided that offence was the best defence. He told Bill that since he was working so much slower than the others, and since they were all paid by the hour, he was actually stealing from Av and his co-workers. The charge was backed up by accurate statistics:

Maddix: He looked at the figures, he made faces—typical!— and then he said he was sorry and he'd work a couple of days without pay. I said no, just work faster and it will average out.

P.M.: But this was simple work, sandpaper moldings, and Bill was very experienced. Was he hungry?

Maddix: He always brought a heavy lunch. No, I think he was nervous and preoccupied. On the very next day, he did five times as much. He said his mind wasn't clear and he hadn't realized he was working so slowly. He rarely spoke about swearing again. If I swore, he'd just give me a look. From then on, Bill became one of our fastest framers. Later, we realized the fine quality he was capable of. Bill was one of the top gilders in Canada. It's an art. By 1961 he was making specialized frames.

The story speaks volumes on Bill's inner state that first winter at home, and his fierce rectitude.

The artist enjoyed framing. He usually framed his own work, often in colorful Ukrainian designs and old barnwood. He would continue to frame for Isaacs until 1970, and to use Isaacs' facilities for framing his paintings, keeping track of the materials used and reimbursing his dealer. Maddix observed that he had seen Bill spend eight hours on framing a work he had painted in three.

During his first three years back in Canada Bill turned to the Catholic Information Centre for social activities and spiritual encouragement. Centrally located on Bathurst Street at Bloor Street, in the heart of the immigrant quarter, the Centre was the focus of Catholic Action. When Bill approached it in November of 1959, it was experiencing a period of expansion and creativity under its director and founder, Father Frank Stone.[33] Father Stone had institutionalized an idea that was novel for its time and place: the involvement of lay Catholics to assist priests

The Isaacs Gallery Workshop, 1972. Drawing, 28″ x 36″. Courtesy The Isaacs Gallery.

in the instruction and encouragement of converts. A few years later, after Vatican II, an emphasis on ecumenism would replace the emphasis on conversion that dominated the Centre in Bill's time.[34] Bill was a recent convert, "all starry-eyed in the faith" as he had described himself on several occasions. He found Father Stone's ideas perfectly compatible, and took to the Centre like a duck to water. In his first autobiography he speaks of his social life revolving around it for three years till "all the extra burdens of marriage" compelled him to leave

(A1 489-91). Given his remark to the Colombos, Bill must have had marriage on his mind and was using the CIC as he had used the Little Club in London, as an informal marriage bureau.

Bill went there regularly, two nights per week. He writes enthusiastically of the teaching work, organized on the military model of the Roman army, where a unit was called a *praesidium*. The Legion of Mary consisted of five such groups, the fifth one (Bill's) giving clerical and technical assistance to the other four:

> I had settled for that rather than actually teaching the
> Faith because memory of the College of Education's rejec-
> tion of me was still hot in my ears. Nevertheless, equally
> burning was the desire to communicate to my fellow
> human beings the wonderful thing—my Faith—that had
> so changed my life and in fact had saved it. Eventually the
> latter fire overcame the previous. I took a course on how
> to teach catechism. The instructor was Helen Cannon.
> (A1 490)

This course was also to be significant for Bill. For one thing, it showed him that he *could* teach, "granted of course that the pupils want to be taught" (A1 492): he became a co-instructor in Our Lady of the Snows Praesidium. For another, it initiated a lasting friendship with the older woman, a widow and a professional nurse, who had been his instructor. The friendship was consolidated after Mrs. Cannon attended Bill's first exhibition and was overcome by the power of his paintings. She would later write to Isaacs, describing the Kurelek paintings as "a magnificent imaginative interpretation of the realities of life" and urging the dealer to exhibit *Lord That I May See* and *Behold Man Without God* once again.[35]

Cannon also wrote to the artist, after the 1960 exhibition, to express her admiration for his work. This precipitated a weekly correspondence which continued until Bill married in the fall of 1962. Bi-weekly meetings at the CIC facilitated the exchange: "I took a letter on Tuesday, he'd bring an answer on Thursday. We shared our spiritual development. We had a friendship in Christ that was rare in human experience."[36] They talked, Cannon recalls, of the significance of Bill's art as a comment on the human condition; and of Tissot's two-volume life of Christ. They walked together: "He loved Nature, he'd always loved it but once he'd found the Creator then it had more meaning."

Prior to his marriage, Bill must have found in Helen Cannon the sympathetic listener he always required, the role filled for some years by Margaret Smith in England. Shorey, having married, was less available in 1960 and, being Protestant, was perhaps less compatible as a

Bill outside the Catholic Information Centre at Bathurst and Bloor streets, Toronto, 1961. Courtesy the Centre.

spiritual confidant. Bill's spiritual struggles continued long after his conversion. He spoke of this inner pain to very few people other than (presumably) his confessors at church. There is no mention of it in the autobiographies; his writing structures his formal conversion as the end, rather than the beginning, of spiritual struggles. This silence is curious. Did Bill think that a confession of this type would weaken his evangelistic message? Discourage new converts? Shatter the symmetry of his conversion tale?

Cannon remembers: "There were periods of darkness and pain, of brokenness in him. It's a *lifetime* work. He personified the great commandment, to love God and your neighbor, he *lived* that, and you can't do it without pain. Healing is a lifelong thing, not instantaneous. He touched the world's pain with Christ. Av [Isaacs] told me he'd seen men crying in front of Bill's paintings." Cannon believes that the artist's paintings of the Sacred Heart express his identification with Christ as the suffering servant of God's love. An extraordinary incident at Madonna House during the early sixties would corroborate this view that Bill's conversion was a process, the start of a continuing struggle. Pain was Bill's constant companion.

Bill's relation to the Centre highlights his current ideas and hopes. Conversion was one of his central concerns, then as later, although his attitude to non-Catholics would soften over the years: one suspects that by the late sixties he had come to accept his "separated brothers" as fellow-Christians destined for external salvation. He believed that dogmatic differences between the Orthodox Church and the Roman Church were negligible, and he continued to hope for their reunification. In an undated letter to Shorey, about 1961, he wrote: "Now with the people at the Centre their primary dedication is to the salvation of souls.... And we believe that salvation is more important than theatre because the state of the theatre is a temporary concern ... but the success or failure of the work of saving souls lasts for all eternity." The phrase "all eternity", with its redundant modifier, was a favorite with Bill. His lust for souls would appear admirable to some, and to others (including many Christians), it was one of the unattractive sides of his personality.

Shorey had been offended by a reference in Catholic literature to Baptists as heretics. Bill writes to distinguish "material" or inherited heresy from the "formal", wilful type: "If I had my way the word wouldn't be used at all. And in fact enlightened Catholics don't use it. ... We use the term 'separated brothers' to designate Protestants or simply non-Catholics."[37] Continuing, he describes Christian disunity as tragic, "because through it souls are lost for all eternity," and the Centre as a place that promotes tolerance and understanding among churches. The theatre project, he adds, was an example of this.

"The theatre project" was the December 1961 production at the Centre of *Christmas in the Marketplace* by Henri Ghéon, a French dramatist and adult convert to Catholicism. Initiated by Shorey, who played the lead, the production involved five actors and producer Michael Pearson. The players called themselves the Evergreen Stage Company. Some were Catholics, most were not; all were outsiders at the Centre.

The production had grown out of classes in voice and improvisation offered at the Centre earlier in 1961 by Shorey and Pearson. Bill was initially interested in the play's Christian message, but once rehearsals began, "he got heavily involved in designing and meddling."[38] Bill designed the costumes.

The "meddling" to which Shorey refers spilled over into various areas of the production and led to many disputes among the participants. There were problems with the availability of rehearsal space, with the delegation of promotional efforts, with adequate attendance of the performances by Centre members, to name a few.

The theatre affair showed some of the Centre volunteers in an unattractive light. Twenty years later, Shorey remembers the affair as a tempest in a teapot. Shorey wrote that the Company was well treated by the Centre, and the play reasonably successful. Not having seen Bill's report to Father Stone, Shorey failed to appreciate the emotional intensity of Bill's hope for converts.

After the play had finished and the Company departed, Bill wrote a long report to the Centre's director. He apologized for bringing the players into the Centre, and explained that he had done so in the hope of converting several of them. He had initially viewed the Centre's volunteers as ideal Christians, "the cream of the crop"; seeing them in action, he reasoned, would surely attract others to the fold. But the volunteers had not supported the actors or the production as Bill would have liked them to do.

He wrote of Shorey in particular as a man "with God-given talents and drive", talents which Bill thought would be of great value "if channeled into the service of the Mystical Body."[39] He described himself as "liaison and watchdog" between Centre and Company, one who might now be seen as a trouble-maker; at the end, after indicting the Centre's members for a lack of charity, Bill said that he had no relish for writing the letter, "or playing the role of Savonarola".

The comparison with the fiery reformer is rather apt. Bill closed like a monk submitting himself in obedience to his superior: henceforth he will avoid putting himself forward in the life of the Centre but will continue to serve it through his legionary duties. These letters to Shorey and Father Stone reveal the artist as a man of good will whose life was often complicated by naïveté. His lack of understanding of human nature could be startling.

Meanwhile, Bill was spending most of his days and many of his nights painting the Passion of Christ According to St. Matthew. His dream of illustrating the Passion verse by verse, the dream which had become the focus of his life in 1955 and '56, was becoming a reality. Since that time, he had done some eight hundred sketches and numerous paintings for the project. It seemed important to him, however, to believe that he had begun the series proper on New Year's Day, 1960, and that success had followed as God's response to his commitment:

> I had done a small separate series, The Temptation in the
> Desert, at the Rueters' place in summer as a trial run.
> Now, exactly on New Year's Day, I began the Passion
> paintings in earnest and promising myself to get one fin-
> ished every week for three years. As I've explained before
> there were no strings attached. This series was done for
> love, not money. Their prime purpose was to help spread
> the Gospel's story. I also promised myself if by chance
> there was a market for the pictures themselves some-
> day—I had not much hope because religious pictures are
> no longer in demand—then the series would not be
> broken up. Almost as soon as I did begin the "for love"
> project, cracks began to appear in the apparently hopeless
> wall before me. (A1 87-88)

First, I got part-time work at the picture-frame shop of Av Isaacs; next, a one-man show with him in March 1960. It was a total success. I had made the major breakthrough to public acceptance as an artist.[40]

The Passion paintings, one hundred and sixty in all, reflect the intensity of Bill's spiritual life at this period. Anyone wishing to understand his inner life should study them. His devotion to historical realism as he understood the concept made a "realistic" approach inevitable, while his 1959 trip to the Holy Land and his thorough acquaintance with James Tissot's pictorial interpretation of the same subject made the technique feasible. Some of the later works in the series were "looser", less detailed.[41] Despite the surface realism, the vision behind the works—passionate, personal and full of pain—was entirely Bill's own.

That vision had been forming since childhood. In the Foreword to the book which reproduces the series in its entirety, Bill writes: "The formation of the idea is itself a strange story and, seen through the eyes of faith, a wonderful one. The ambition to do some epic, monumental work actually came earlier, in the headier and more worldly days of my late boyhood. ... It was then that I conceived the idea of someday illustrating the whole of Canadian history."[42] In high school, under the influence of a Ukrainian nationalist priest, the planned epic was to be a history of the Ukraine. Both projects failed when his nationalism waned.

When sorrow, in Bill's phrase, had remarried him to God, the plan matured: "What better story in the whole wide world to illustrate than the word of God itself?" The closest approach Bill knew to the plan of illustrating the Gospel sentence by sentence had been Tissot's, late in the nineteenth century. The paintings, which had taken the French artist ten years of on-site research, depicted scenes from all four Gospels. It was providential that Father Lynch had given Tissot's two volumes to Bill in 1956. He found them invaluable for detailed reference material, and supplemented them by press photos of Israelis purchased in Tel Aviv in 1959. Some of the faces in the series resemble the peasant faces of Ukrainian-Canadian immigrants in his Western Canadian scenes.

Why Matthew? This Gospel was chosen, as the Foreword informs us, because it is the "most comprehensive" account of Christ's life, and the most detailed. Bill's passion for sharing his faith and the overriding evangelical purpose of the series suggest another reason. Matthew's Gospel ends with the ringing injunction to go out, making disciples of all nations, baptizing, teaching, "until the consummation of the world". It struck the apocalyptic note which lay deep in Bill's personality. Those closing words sum up so much of his last twenty years.

A selection from the Passion series was exhibited at the Catholic Information Centre in the early 1960s. The paintings were vividly remembered twenty years later by individuals who had found them surprising, original, and strong. Some of the paintings, such as the scourged Christ, might be considered frightening, but then, as one viewer noted, "so is the Gospel."[43]

Other works that were frightening, even grotesque, were being painted concurrently, as were farm scenes. Inspired by the New Testament description of the apostle Peter as the rock upon which Christ's Church is built, *The Rock* (1962) depicts an Eastern church perched on a rock in a sea of blood. The purple sky is filled with saints, arms extended, who dot the heavens like stars. Breaking foam and splashing drops are all red. The bloody sea is filled with monsters, their forms indebted to Bosch and their banners (like pennants) providing a short list of Bill's pet hates. Slogans include "apostasy", "puritanism", "modernism", "arrogance", "wealth", "simony", "schism", "ennui", "graft", "absenteeism", "heresy", "factions", "dearth of vocation", "racial intolerance", and "power". Power? Some of the slogans, such as "absenteeism", seem very much of our time, while others sound medieval. Some, such as "modernism", are in strange company, while others are curiously ambiguous ("puritanism", "wealth", "power"). Striking details include a crocodile-beast whose tail opens to reveal human heads; and the upper half of a face drowning in blood, whose terrified eyes look straight at the viewer. Didactic labels and tortured eyes: the imposition of a literal mind on a burning imagination indeed.

It had been Bill's custom, since his conversion, to seek periodic retreats. Father Stone knew of an order which he was sure would offer spiritual renewal to the lonely artist. In the winter of 1962-63 Bill found his way to Madonna House near Combermere, in the Madawaska Valley northwest of Ottawa. He was still nursing his disappointment over the theatre affair at the Centre, and his idealistic temperament craved a religious community he could admire without reserve. He found it in Madonna House and its charismatic director, Catherine de Hueck Doherty. In the years that followed, its dedicated members would become dear to his heart. Soon he would paint its worn, symbolic buildings as "the hope of the world". Although a decade would pass before Bill would buy property and a farmhouse near by, that first visit told him that something of great significance in his life had occurred.

Madonna House is a Catholic community of lay men and women, and priests; a community that lives by begging, and gives away much of what it begs. The lay apostolate was founded in 1947 by a Russian baroness with a vocation to serve the poor. Catherine and her first husband had come to Canada after the First World War as refugees from the 1917 Revolution. Her husband died in 1931, and during the Depression she opened Friendship House in Toronto to feed and help the poor. As a woman and a Russian, Catherine was doubly suspect in those conservative times. In 1938 she moved to New York's Harlem to work with the poor and to fight for racial justice. In 1943 Catherine married a prominent American journalist, an Irish Catholic who promised to share in Catherine's vocation. The United States was not ready for racial equality in the 1940s. When Catherine lost for the second time the confidence of her lay community in Chicago, she and her husband left the United States and headed north. In Combermere they were gradually joined by other seekers who took the traditional monastic vows of poverty, chastity, and obedience. After Eddie Doherty became a priest in the 1960s, he and Catherine lived as brother and sister.

Catherine has recorded some of her extraordinary experiences in more than a score of books. Works like *Fragments of My Life* and *Poustinia* help to explain how Bill responded to this unique woman. Several people have claimed to be his mentor, but the honor properly belongs to Catherine. But why would the artist be attracted to a Russian baroness whose background seems so different from his own?

Catherine was a woman acquainted with pain, a woman who had been taught at an early age, by devout parents, to relate that pain to Christ's. Like Bill, she had a sense of destiny, a conviction from childhood that God had special work for her to do. Like him, she found the established church self-indulgent. Although she revered its priests and obeyed its bishops, its affluence disturbed her and she felt deeply drawn towards the poor. Like Bill, she had been suicidal, and had been saved by a personal vision of Christ, whose face had appeared to her in the water below Brooklyn Bridge. She had experienced persecution and had been led, because of unfair criticism and other pain, through what she believed to be the stages of Christ's passion. Bill's experiences and convictions were strikingly parallel. In the community inspired by Catherine's Russian spirituality, with its identification with the poor and its understanding of all human suffering as part of the Mystical Body of Christ, Bill found his religious ideal.[44]

Madonna House now embraces numerous buildings and many acres. Food for the community, which numbers more than one hundred members and copes with thousands of visitors annually, is raised on their farm, St. Benedict's Acres. Now, as then, daily life is based on rigorous discipline, frequent prayer, and the sanctity of common work. The members, each with a large distinctive cross, wear second-hand clothing. They help their neighbors, whether near at

Catherine Doherty, founder and Director-General, Madonna House, Combermere. Of Bill she said, "We had something in common." Courtesy Catherine Doherty.

hand or in developing countries, through providing used clothing and other necessaries, and through an example of a lifestyle based on self-sufficiency and faith. Nothing is wasted, as Bill had noted with approval. Members live together as a family, concerned for the environment, living without compromise the gospel of peace and love. Bill had found much to admire, not least the unusual combination of Eastern and Western Christian traditions.[45]

Twenty years after the encounter, Catherine remembered her first meeting with the artist. Bill's opening words were, "I am Ukrainian." This was followed immediately with "And I'm a believer, but there's a lot wrong with the Church, I don't think the Church is what it should be." Catherine readily agreed that the Church was imperfect, since she and Bill were part of it "and we are sinful!" After this exchange, recalled with amusement, Catherine and Father Emile Brière continued:

Catherine: He entered into the hearts of Madonna House and everybody loved him. He wanted to be near me, I gave him some kind of security.

Fr. B.: He listened to Catherine like a disciple. He sat at her feet. Madonna House was his anchor, it gave him security in his faith.

Catherine: I don't *like* disciples. He was a *source* himself, he didn't need me. But he didn't realize that. His great virtue was humility. He had a great devotion to the

167

> Passion, and so did I, so we had something in com-
> mon. His relationship with us at Madonna House
> went on *without words* over many years.[46]

The Baroness received visitors in her log cabin near the main house. On her door hung two signs: "Peace", and "I am third". Her secretary explained that God and one's neighbor came first. Catherine was convalescing from an illness and remained in her bed. She was still beautiful at eighty, a woman with great presence yet without pretensions, an impressive figure.

On the occasion of his first visit to Madonna House, Bill was received by Father Brière, who already knew something of his reputation as a man with a message, a man of faith. Madonna House had recently opened their first *poustinia*, or hermitage: a small, unpainted farmhouse whose interior was dominated by a large, bare cross and a picture of the scourged Christ.[47] Father Brière never forgot the scene. In front of the picture of Christ, Bill fell to his knees, sobbing uncontrollably. He remained there for some time as if in a trance, saying nothing.[48] What was there to say? This was the lions' den, in truth.

Poustinia (literally "desert") is an ancient religious tradition which comes from Russia. By extension, the word denotes a vibrant openness of the heart and spirit in the individual who has chosen fasting and solitude in penance for the sins of the world. The *poustinik* is alone, yet not alone: the individual is freely available to those who seek his or her help in that solitude. Catherine had felt called to this expression of her vocation years earlier. After 1962, the concept and a number of lonely little cabins belonged to the lifestyle of her community.[49]

This was the *poustinia* which Bill painted in the foreground of a panoramic view of the community's central buildings beside the Madawaska River. Titled *Madonna House, Combermere, the hope of the world* (1965), the painting was the last in "Glory to Man in the Highest" (1966), a series of socio-religious satirical paintings which Bill described as a sweeping look at some of the world's major ills: imminent nuclear war, political tyranny, poverty and hunger, crime, and social discrimination. To avoid being merely negative, Bill alternated scenes depicting problems with ones suggesting solutions. The Madonna House apostolate was his "all embracing solution" for the world's woes, a place where the atmosphere of joy and brotherly love was immediately felt. He praised their frugality, noting that it pained him (after witnessing starvation in Mexico) to see crusts thrown away in his own house. He praised their practicality, their trades and crafts, and their spirituality, including traditions of fasting and *poustinia*. In the one in his painting he had shown himself (as he notes in a letter)

Madonna House, Combermere, the hope of the world, 1965. Oil, 27½" x 30½". Private collection.

praying in front of the large black cross: "I have painted the sky a cold overcast color as of a premature fall because it gives the mood of foreboding. Men will not read the signs of the times and are courting disaster. The planes in the sky are delivering a nuclear bombload."[50] The companion piece to this painting shows nuclear devastation and horror, but even the scene of "hope" contains a warning and a threat.

Catherine's doomsday vision was both similar and different. Unlike the artist, she does not threaten, nor do her writings ever suggest the contempt for this world which can be so disturbing in Bill's. She too sees catastrophe coming; indeed, *Fragments* ends on an apocalyptic note: "the church needs prayer, for this is the time of the shaking of the foundations of the world. ... Nothing else can stem the barbarism of a secular world busy worshipping itself and not caring about anything or anybody except its own satisfaction and gratification."[51] Had Catherine lacked that prophetic vision, Bill would probably not have found in her community "the hope of the world". Old Testament warnings and New Testament grace were intricately blended in his faith.

The artist had been seeking a bride for some half-dozen years. He wanted children, and had always been drawn to maternal women. The sight of a small red-haired child in England had prompted Bill to exclaim, "I would like to marry a woman with red hair!"[52] By 1962, he had found his redhead: Anglo-Canadian Jean Andrews, a woman of approximately Bill's own age, who was equally devoted to Catholic Action. They had met at the CIC, where Jean was part of Our Lady of the Wayside Praesidium, a group devoted to rehabilitating prostitutes and drug addicts. Bill admired this work as "a rather brave kind of Christian charity" (A2 169).

Bill had chosen a strong-willed woman, who may well have concealed her strength during courtship days, as many women instinctively do. Jean is pragmatic, outgoing, and, above all, maternal. In 1962 she was in her mid-thirties and wanted children. Perhaps Bill hoped to find a solution to his extreme introversion in Jean's extroverted personality, a social helpmeet to compensate for his own social inadequacies. (His later discovery that it is difficult or impossible for one person to serve another in this way must have been painful.) Doubtless a primary consideration for both parties at this stage of their lives was the creation of a family. A Catholic family.

The attractive nurse was agreeable, priests strongly encouraged the marriage plans, and the die was cast. Bill had not forgotten his parents' four criteria for success, and indeed he listed them tongue in cheek, just after describing his meeting with Jean. The successful man should wear a hat in winter and acquire a car, an apartment, and a wife. Bill was nearly there. Save for this joking reference, he is curiously silent as to his reasons for marrying.

On October 8, 1962, Bill married Jean Andrews, whom he had met at the Catholic Information Centre in Toronto. From his scrapbook.

His parents' feelings were ambivalent. They were delighted that their eldest son was now ready to marry, this being (in their view) an essential part of maturity; they regretted that Jean was not a Ukrainian-Canadian but they were pleased with his choice nevertheless. In the years to come, Bill and Jean and their children would always enjoy Ukrainian Christmas dinner with Dmytro and Mary.

"Centre Legionaries to wed" read the *CIC Ambassador* in October 1962. Jean and Bill were married on October 8 in the Church of Our Lady of Perpetual Help, at Mt. Pleasant Road and St. Clair Avenue. They received their guests at the Centre where they had met, in an auditorium decorated in Ukrainian style. John Kurelek was his brother's best man. Photographs show a beautiful bride and a proud and handsome groom—a radiantly happy couple. A week's honeymoon was spent in Québec City, Montréal, and New York, much of it in art galleries. More than a decade later, Bill would celebrate the event in paint in a touching scene entitled *Honeymooners in Québec City.*[53]

10

The Dark Prophet,
1957-77

"'When the Son of Man comes all will be as
it was in the days of Noah' ... this text
means that when one is warned to prepare
for disaster one is foolish to carry on
life as if it is not coming."
William Kurelek,
"The Last Days" Series, 1971.

IN THE YEAR OF THEIR MARRIAGE, BILL PAINTED A LARGE PORTRAIT OF HIS
bride with a plain, church-basement background.[1] Five years later he
reworked the backdrop and added an Orwellian title, *Mendelssohn in
Canadian Winter, 1977*. The seated figure now divides two scenes: a
happy one of small children with flowers and butterflies; and one of
stark misery where groups of refugees huddle round a campfire in
winter or trek through desolate, snowy plains. In the background a
soldier herds some survivors into a large van labelled "Utopia Express",
while distant families argue over whether or not to return to such
dubious refuge. Bill wrote that his prophetic work was set in Northern
Ontario "roundabout ten years hence":

> An anti-Christian "1984" type government (either of
> North American origin or by conquest from abroad) is
> offering food and comforts (note Utopia Express) in
> return for apostasy (symbolized by the man trampling on
> the crucifix) and submission to the tyrannical regime.
> Groups, families and friends break up. One family is
> determined to carry on to independence and have lit a
> bonfire for warmth as they rest and play a small tape
> recorder for morale. In the smoke they see a vision of
> their relatively happy and secure earlier life (symbolized

172

Mendelssohn in Canadian Winter, 1977, 1967.

Oil, 27" x 37".

Private collection.

> by my wife and three children on a walk in the ravine
> back of our street in Toronto). ... Main sources of inspira-
> tion for this painting are (1) *1984* (2) *A Man for All Sea-
> sons* (3) *Dr. Zhivago* (4) Mendelssohn's Violin Concerto
> [op. 64].[2]

The concerto, he notes, had been written at a happy time in Mendelssohn's life when his family was just beginning. The parallel with Bill's
own life is obvious: the children in the painting are his first three,
Catherine, Stephen, and Barbara. His happiness, however, is curiously
mixed with dark fears which he was convinced stemmed not from
personal anxiety but from prophetic intuition. The imminent danger
was not simply to himself and his family but to the entire North
American society. Throughout the 1960s and '70s, his attempts to
build two bomb shelters and his hundreds of "doomsday" paintings
can be understood only in the light of the burning religious faith that
underlay everything he did.

His growing family made space a pressing need. The Evelyn Avenue
apartment near High Park which had suited the newlyweds was soon
too small. In the spring of 1965, the Kureleks moved to The Beaches,
an attractive area of older houses in Toronto's east end near Lake
Ontario. The moderately sized house with its small garden is described
by Bill as "modest in comparison with some of the wealthier areas of
town". In the *Toronto* series, its back appears in *It's Hard for Us to
Realize*, and Balsam Avenue is featured in the charming city snowscape
which graces the book's front cover.

The basement would become Bill's prime preserve, his special
territory, despite frequent invasions by his children. Here he built
cupboards that were decorated with elaborate Ukrainian designs. An
open secret to Bill's callers, they concealed dozens of stored paintings.
Here he constructed his tiny artist's studio, a windowless bunker that
had begun life as a coal cellar. Here he painted and here, in his first and
simplest plan for a shelter capable of withstanding a nuclear attack, was
the beginning of the bomb shelter itself. By 1980, its massive door,
resembling the entrance to a bank vault, was the only visible remnant
of the aborted scheme.

Efforts to build a shelter in Toronto and in Combermere occupied
the artist during the last dozen years of his life. His own writings
clarify what the shelter meant to him and why the affair was no trifling
matter but a concern that casts light on the essential nature of his faith.

> To me wanting to build a blast shelter can be a sign of
> either neurotic fearfulness or of provident courage and
> belief in the value of human life. I believe or hope that I

belong to the latter. ... We have a duty to go on living since its God's will that the mystical Body be completed. ... The world cannot come to an end yet because of the Biblical prophecy that Christ must first be preached to all mankind. So far only 1/3 of mankind is Christian or has heard of Christ. ... The sign of the times I feel is that of St. Thomas More. ... I may or may not be a saint—only God can make me or anyone else into one. I know from experience that I am a physical and social coward. It is agony sometimes being misunderstood or sneered at but whatever I can do now to prepare to be the sort of person He can use for His purposes I must try to do so.[3]

If those efforts seem futile or misjudged we should remember the atmosphere of the early 1960s, when the Cuban missile crisis of 1962 led to a rash of private shelters in the Toronto area. The Ontario government commissioned a private bunker for its provincial leaders, and Toronto schools sent notices to parents to inform them of procedures to be followed in the case of a nuclear attack. Bill was not alone in wanting a shelter, but his reasons for wanting one may well have been unique.

He foresaw two major problems: money, and a city building permit. Being perennially short of money, Bill had established, almost from the beginning of his career as an artist, a system of barter by which he would pay with paintings for goods and services he needed. He therefore saw the solution to the two problems in terms of prospective customers with particular skills. He needed an engineer or an architect, followed by a builder, professionals who would be pleased to be paid for their work in this way. A simple shelter below the Balsam Avenue house would cost in the range of three thousand dollars: six paintings might do the job.

In 1967, a Winnipeg engineer who had seen and liked photographs of Bill's work in *Weekend Magazine* phoned to commission a painting. He subsequently met the artist in the studio space he was renting at the time in a vacant downtown building on Queen Street East. The engineer found him secretive, slow to trust and slow to confide, but was able to earn his confidence while doing some repairs to the Balsam Avenue house. Bill then sought help in developing the plans for a shelter, saying that the municipality had been "giving him the runaround", that his neighbors objected, and that his wife opposed the scheme.

The media got wind of Bill's plans in August 1967. The affair was news because Bill was by now famous, and because he was the first

Toronto citizen in five years to apply for a permit to build a nuclear-blast shelter. (Many shelters had been constructed illicitly.) Two Toronto papers ran articles on what was termed Bill's "pessimism". He told reporters that his decision to build a shelter was based on artist's intuition and a Christian faith disturbed by the continual moral decline of society. Nuclear war was "pretty well inevitable", but would not be the end of the world. It might, he added, be "the great shock" society needed; a post-nuclear world *might be a better place to live and raise a family*. The ecological naïveté expressed in the latter view was perhaps more excusable in 1967 than it would be in the 1980s. The engineer, who was sympathetic to the artist if not to the scheme, drafted plans and pushed the matter at City Hall. Thanks largely to his efforts, a permit was granted in 1968.[4]

Meanwhile, Bill was in search of his builder. He wrote to William Teron, whose grandparents had settled in the Gardenton area of southern Manitoba, offering paintings based on Teron's Ukrainian heritage in that province in exchange for a shelter. Teron countered with the suggestion that Bill paint some of the impressive modern buildings he had constructed in Toronto or Ottawa. The artist declined to record this aspect of the Ukrainian-Canadian saga which Teron termed "a nice story of Ukrainian success". Bill explained that he was interested in their rural roots, and in religion. Teron felt that criticism was implicit in the refusal: "modern" meant "materialistic". To Bill, affluence was suspect.

By 1969, the plans had become considerably more ambitious. Bill approached L. L. Odette, of Eastern Construction, with sketchy plans for a large underground structure, separated from his house and capable of holding thirty people. Again, payment would be in paintings. Odette had entered into the discussion as a favor to the friend who had directed Bill to him, but was unaccustomed to working on projects in the order of twenty-five thousand dollars. Years later, he remembered that Bill had wanted a big concrete box with an underground stairwell, a relatively luxurious shelter with puzzling features like television and air-conditioning. In pursuit of the builder's favor, Bill painted a large, detailed scene of an Eastern Construction building site at the corner of Toronto's Bay and Bloor streets in the summer of 1970. Odette attempted to discourage the artist, and eventually he declined the project.[5]

Most of Bill's friends were unsympathetic to the shelter scheme, while some were openly critical. A Christian, they argued, should not be so fearful of death. Few if any understood his personal reasoning. In August 1968, Bill set out to correct the misunderstandings by means of an exceptionally long written manifesto. The writing took the literal form of a letter to Kenneth Shorey, but Bill had always intended it for wide readership and he distributed copies to all the friends and relatives who questioned the wisdom of his bomb-shelter plans.[6]

The piece began with a historical analysis of his own progress as a painter. Eight years and some half-dozen solo exhibitions with The Isaacs Gallery had brought him fame. His rapid and unexpected success had convinced him that he was God's instrument, that God was calling him (as He had called the ancient Jewish prophets) to warn a stubborn, sinful generation that He would not be mocked. His comparisons ranged wildly from Hans Christian Andersen to the Virgin Mary. Was it pride, or genuine humility? The two extremes appear to meet. He had experienced a reversal of fortune quite as striking; *he* was the ugly duckling who had moved from being shy and unimportant to being successful beyond his wildest dream. Were he to deny his good fortune, he argues, he would be refusing to give God the praise He deserves.

Why, he asks, has God given him his unusual talent for a style with universal appeal? Why does a sense of foreboding seep from his happiest paintings? Why is he possessed by a premonition of approaching cataclysm? If this is attributed to personal anxiety, then why did God give him the father that He did? He is not, he reminds us, the first man to intuit and foretell disaster: examples here include Isaiah's prophecy of Babylon's destruction, and the story of Sodom and Gomorrah. Nuclear bombs are real, the destruction at Hiroshima is history! "So no one can doubt me if I paint one people dropping that kind of holocaust on other people." Most men sweep such thoughts away, Bill writes, but he chooses to face them openly. Had Dr. Carstairs known of Bill's post-hospital career as an artist, he might well have seen in him the "very man" the doctor had called for in an article on art and illness: an artist to alert mankind to the threat of nuclear annihilation. Bill reasons: "I am not even 100 percent sure that God means to use me as this instrument although as I've been pointing out in these pages, it certainly appears that way."

So much for premonitions. But why a shelter? The latter stemmed, as day follows night, from Bill's literal belief in biblical prophecies and from his faith in God's word. The apostles had written that the world would not end until the Gospel had been preached to every soul. Bill concluded that the end of the world "cannot come in the foreseeable future for the simple reason that Christ has not been preached to all mankind." Christians thus have a duty to survive. In the hideous aftermath of nuclear holocaust, there must be survivors to preach. Bill

Bill at work. Photograph by Michael Lambeth, courtesy of The Isaacs Gallery.

felt called to the task.

To several friends in the late sixties and early seventies, Bill expressed a resignation to God's will. If he was intended to have a shelter, he would be successful in locating a builder willing to be paid in paintings. He would accept the lack of such a builder as a sign that his shelter was not part of God's pian. He described the difficulties he had experienced over several years in the form of municipal red tape and exorbitant costs, difficulties that would quickly discourage the average citizen.

The latter part of the long letter to Shorey in 1968 reads like an expanded text to *Mendelssohn in Canadian Winter, 1977*. The reasoning is close, if chilling. Nuclear war is inevitable within the next ten or fifteen years: "A large part of the human race will die. With the modern, largely urban way of life destroyed or drastically crippled, there will follow a political tyranny of some kind, probably anti-Christian." To prepare for this inevitability, Bill believed that people should begin a course of physical and spiritual training. Habits bred in a Spartan, highly disciplined lifestyle would enable them to survive after the bomb had fallen:

> It is because I believe Christians have to go on living and persevere in their Faith through physical hardships and persecution that I am so concerned that my own children do not grow up physical and moral softies. Once the initial nuclear attacks are over, we will emerge from the shelter and will be compelled to migrate to the country-side or even into the northland forests. This will be the first test of my wife's, my children's, and even my physical endurance and cheerfulness in the face of plain old material shortages and discomforts. This is one reason (though not the only one) why I practice periodic fasts, why I try to do without sleep or with little, under various conditions. This is why I have taken up gardening, because once we do reach an uncontaminated area we will have to grow our own food. This is also why I believe our family vacations should now be camping rather than cottaging. This is when our Faith will first be tested, probably in the form of an offer from the authorities to provide us with the comforts we'd be used to in return for apostasy. The sign of our times I feel is emerging ever clearer, that of St. Thomas More. ... People in his country rationalized their surrender to corruption, just as today the boundaries of good and evil are being deliberately or willy-nilly blurred. ... We should deliberately learn to do without things we take for granted, e.g. stoves, insect repellants, a roof over one's head, regular sleep, vitamins and medicines, packaged foods. If you get down to the bottom of the matter, it seems to me that those who prepare for the coming catastrophe with the intention of carrying on after it's over, are actually less pessimistic than those who throw up their hands and say, interiorly, "what's the use!"

In this manifesto, Bill unconsciously depicts some of the psychic strains that may well have been imposed on his family by the late

1960s. His fears that his children were over-protected and/or over-indulged were not shared by his wife, who disagreed with his dooms-day convictions. Arguments over how the children would be brought up inevitably followed. In search of support for his views, Bill would sometimes consult more than one priest, and would reluctantly give in to Jean's policies only when two or three priests counselled him to do so. He seemed oblivious to the psychic strain imposed on his children by his expectation of imminent nuclear holocaust; oblivious, too, to the ironic parallels between his stern goals for his children and Dmytro's treatment of himself and his siblings.

The strains created by children cut both ways. The months following the birth of a first child are difficult ones for all parents. In 1963-64, Bill had found them particularly trying. For a man who had lived so frugally and earned so little since his student days, the financial responsibility must have been terrifying. His exhibitions seemed few and far between. The loss of quiet in the small apartment where he had been accustomed to working in peace had probably not been anticipated, despite the fact that the child was expected and wanted by both parents.

Bill became depressed. Perhaps his faith faltered briefly. He made one more ineffectual try at suicide. It was his first attempt since Netherne, and would be the last of such gestures, sad, wordless efforts at communication. Jean's brisk, no-nonsense reaction was like a bucket of cold water in his face. How *dare* he do such a thing? Didn't he realize he had a wife and child to support? *Don't you ever try that again*. Bill didn't. So much for psychiatry. Common-sense and self-interest appear to have been considerably more therapeutic in this case. Meanwhile, Bill's rapidly growing success as an artist was proving effective medicine.

The last point in Bill's schema was his optimism, so called. The artist saw himself as a realist acting out of "provident courage and belief in the value of human life". His analogies were drawn more from the Old Testament than from Revelation, and featured symbolic experiences (mythic or historic) which the Israelites had undergone as the Chosen People. Noah's flood was one such story, the Babylonian Captivity under Nebuchadnezzar was another. Phrases such as "a new golden age" and "a new heaven" recur in Bill's writings. When he had told reporters in 1967 that a post-nuclear world might be a better place in which to live and raise children, he was envisaging a chosen remnant, purged by suffering, cleansed of materialism, and reunited with God:

> I foresee a new golden age of Faith after intense suffering
> has purged us of our materialistic pride. The supernatural

will impinge more on the natural world once again as it did dramatically in the first centuries of the Christian era. But even if human history were to end soon, it beats me how anyone can see a Christian's philosophy as pessimistic. ... The Christian knows that death is but the door to everlasting life—united with the family of God, he will be forever perfectly happy. The lifespan of man on earth is but a brief testing period in preparation for that total fulfillment. What earthly goal could possibly be more joyful and optimistic?

Two years later, the Artist's Foreword to the catalogue for a Kurelek Retrospective at the Edmonton Art Gallery shows that his thoughts on the matter were unchanged: "For despite outward appearances, I *am* optimistic about the world's future—*after* we've passed through the Dark Night toward which the present materialism is tending." The possibility that post-nuclear chaos would make survivors more cruel and selfish is rarely entertained, despite the prophecy of a tyrannical regime, nor did Bill realistically envisage the devastating effects of radiation.

His acknowledgement of the film *Dr. Zhivago* as an influence is significant. It played an important part in his imagination. Pasternak's story takes place during the First World War and the 1917 Revolution; after surviving incredible suffering, an upper-class family experiences a brief idyll in a primitive cottage in Russia's frozen north. Many references in Bill's holocaust writings seem more relevant to the early decades of this century than to the latter ones.

For a few brief years Bill's proselytizing fervor had been poured into the Catholic Information Centre. After his marriage, it was channelled into his didactic paintings, the work he considered his serious and significant contribution, his "real" work, let the critics say what they would. This complex artist was many things, but certainly one of his protean forms was that of a missionary in paint.

Models for evangelical activity included the twentieth-century crusader Douglas Hyde. An ex-Communist and double agent, Hyde was also a double convert. He had been converted to Communism at the age of seventeen, and to Catholicism at the age of thirty-seven. After his second conversion Hyde devoted his life to converting key Communists, often risking his own life to do so. His novel technique was to allow himself to be imprisoned with the men he hoped to convert to Christianity. The incarceration was real, and so were the dangers. Hyde had vowed to make more converts in ten years after his conversion to Catholicism than he had made to Communism in the twenty preceding years. Daniel Maron calls Hyde a latter-day Don Quixote, a term equally applicable to Bill: "Hyde engages the Communist as a complete insider, sharing his grim prison situation and thoroughly indoctrinated in his Communism. Hyde then proceeds to work as an ideological double-agent, applying his basic formula of conversion: to show, in gradual stages, how Communism has betrayed this man's dedication and the ideals which brought him to Communism."[7]

Hyde's autobiography, *I Believe*, had great personal relevance to Bill. One of the 1968 letters to Shorey explaining the reasons for wanting a shelter begins, "I devour anything by my idol Douglas Hyde." Bill's post-holocaust scenario focused more on the hazards of apostasy under Communist pressure than on the hazards of radiation. One had eternal consequences; the other, temporal. Both Hyde and Kurelek were world-changers. Both, believing that Christian faith involved social responsibility, hated injustice. Orwell's *1984* and Communist friends in Bill's youth had taught him to see Communism as an alternative faith. While the focus of Hyde's attack was Communism, the focus of Bill's was the materialistic complacency that undermined the will of affluent Westerners to resist that "Godless" alternative. As New Testament parables point out, the concerns and possessions of this world can also be alternatives to God. In something he called "materialism", Bill found a focus for his fight.

Driven by a dream of service and sacrifice after the Bomb, he embarked on a series of didactic paintings. Beginning in 1963, his goal was to alternate pastoral or "secular" series with instructive ones. His dealer co-operated by tolerating what could not be discouraged.[8] Together with the texts Bill wrote to go with them, these works express his faith, and his fears for the future of his society. His attempts to build a shelter on Balsam Avenue appeared to have ended by the early 1970s and became, after the purchase of property at Combermere, a northern dream. His public attempts to warn a deaf and complacent society peaked at about the same period, with two series entitled "The Last Days" (1971) and "Toronto" (1972).

The introductions to Bill's first two didactic series were somewhat defensive. He observed that people were free to ignore his work, just as he was free to paint and exhibit it. He was painfully aware that people do not, as he put it, like being preached to. Yet he could not keep silent when he saw (in his analogy) his neighbor's house starting to burn. The sense of urgency which he felt had been shared by painters whom he called "the great propagandists, moralisers, illustrators": Bosch, Brueghel, Goya, Hogarth, Daumier, Rivera, and Rouault.

The latter's titles, curiously, moved Bill more than the paintings themselves. He disliked this Catholic painter's style but admired "the humility and compassion in his titles for the 'Miserere' etchings, because their length serves as a starting point for meditation on the subject-matter." (Bill would borrow the idea for the long poetic titles for his "Nature, Poor Stepdame" series.) The title of the first didactic series was tentative ("Experiments in Didactic Art"), but his individual titles were not: witness *The Day the Bomb Fell on Hamilton, Hell,* and *The Wages of Sin Is Death.* Earlier work such as *Behold Man Without God* continued to be exhibited in group shows.

The didactic paintings elicited mixed but frequently favorable reactions from the critics, some of whom were less enchanted with abstract art than the curators and dealers appeared to be. Robert Ayre admired Kurelek's seriousness and involvement with the human predicament; he found an abstract by Michael Snow trivial, even trashy, by comparison.[9] Paul Duval was generally less enthusiastic, yet praised Kurelek's humility, sincerity, and courage. He was particularly impressed by *Dinnertime on the Prairies*: "I cannot recall any Canadian religious painting to equal it for sheer dramatic impact." This extraordinary painting depicts Christ crucified amid a flat prairie landscape, nailed to a fence which is under construction.[10] The fence divides a dark ploughed field and a shining one of pale grain, creating an almost abstract impression. John Robert Colombo found the same painting "an almost perfect combination of the prairies and the religious image".

Colombo voiced the artistic community's concern that morality might limit or constrain the imagination. However, he praised the "tensions" in the paintings, and called Kurelek "one of the few artists in Canada whose subject matter is as distinctive as his style."[11] Elizabeth Kilbourn criticized *Heaven, Hell,* and *The Garden of Eden* as the failures of "a theological tourist in a never-never land", but had high praise for most of the works in the first didactic exhibition: "If this is didactic art, I would willingly expose myself to more even at the risk of conversion."[12]

The intimate connection between Bill's predilection for scenes of nuclear holocaust and his general Christian propaganda remained unnoticed by the critics. His second didactic show, which alternated pleasant and unpleasant scenes of moral good and evil, drew strong reactions, as it could hardly fail to do. In a generally favorable review, Kay Kritzwiser wrote: "Viewers need a strong stomach to stand unmoved before the horror of the annual Christmas bloat, and the terror of *The Have-Nots Will Come.* Kurelek's final preachment is painted in specific religious terms, but his own creed seems to sum up the moral underlying the series: 'When at last we are purged of our conceits and comforts, we can begin a new civilization.'"[13] The unusu-

Bill with his *Self-Portrait* (1957) at the Windsor Art Gallery in 1974. Photo by Gladys Cada, *Windsor Star.*

al desire for a civilization purged of all comfort went unremarked.

Harry Malcolmson, in a review that gained a certain notoriety, took strong exception to Bill's moral earnestness in general and to his concentration-camp scenes in particular. Malcolmson argued that Kurelek lacked first-hand knowledge of such horrors and should stick to what he knew, namely scenes of a rural boyhood and Ukrainian culture. Kurelek's propaganda had grown blunter; it was hardly satirical, Malcolmson insisted: "satire generally implies making a point by indirection. There is about as much indirection in Kurelek's sledgehammer attack as in the Ten Commandments. . . . This is not so much an art show as a fire and brimstone sermon exhorting us to right conduct."[14] What Malcolmson missed was that although Bill had never been in a concentration camp, he *had* personally experienced extreme humiliation and fear.

Malcolmson's attack moved Bill to an extraordinarily long personal reply.[15] He began by thanking the critic for "the first really serious adverse criticism" he had ever received on his art. It had thus served as a needed lesson in humility, and he was enclosing one of his lithographs as a token of appreciation. He considered it necessary to reply because Malcolmson represented an important group of people whom Bill wished to reach. *The Have-Nots Will Come* (a painting of a woman being led away by soldiers while her abandoned baby is about to be eaten by rats) was not intended primarily as an attack on Communism, as Malcolmson had stated: "I only use Communism as an example of some form of harsh justice that may catch up with our pampered way of life because we no longer have Christian awareness of being our brother's keeper."

William Blake's wife once observed that life with her husband was not an easy affair, and Jean Kurelek would have known what she meant. Here is the extraordinary spectacle of Bill painting such a scene while his wife was pregnant with their second child. His own frequent references (to Malcolmson, Shorey, *et al.*) to family arguments over child care were sparked by Bill's desire to see his children toughened up, from infancy on, in preparation for a coming holocaust. He firmly expected to see it before they had reached maturity. His deep-seated conviction of the oneness of mankind is as admirable as his occasional lack of commonsense is puzzling.

In urging a return to farm scenes of innocence and wonder, Malcolmson had struck a nerve, as Bill's letter reveals. If the world were happy and settled, he would be pleased to simply record such scenes: "But it is not—ours is a civilization in crisis." Not only have his frightening and prophetic paintings been with him from the beginning of his career in the 1920s, but bleakness oozes from even his apparently happy scenes. He perceives that a melancholic streak runs deep in his being; the perception bothers him, since Christianity celebrates a loving God and a Christian should be joyous. He took the problem to the spiritual directors of Madonna House:

> In fact I don't mind telling you this was one of the few
> times in my life when I broke down and wept from relief
> after unburdening myself. The answer they gave me was
> that there have to be a few individuals (there have always
> been as we see in the Bible) who have been allowed by
> God to live through certain trials so that they can be bet-
> ter instruments for revealing this particular facet of the
> truth. Even though Christ was full of love and compassion
> and gentle wisdom there is that certain part of His teach-
> ings that includes His prophecies of destruction, the reve-
> lations of Hell, His righteous indignation at hypocrisy and
> unbelief. ... Just as Christ's hard sayings were rejected and
> He was persecuted I should be prepared to accept
> hostility.

Bill's sense, here, of being called as a witness or prophet who can find no corner in which to hide from his God is powerful and very moving: far more so than in the 1968 manifesto to Shorey, which strays occasionally into pomposity and presents a harsh picture of a faith verging on fanaticism.

Bill's final point to Malcolmson deals with the charge that he has no personal knowledge of heaven and hell. He writes that he is not the first artist to venture into such territory. He defends the legitimacy of using personal experience as a source for artistic versions of spiritual states. As for concentration camps, he has seen films, studied documentary reports, and talked with former inmates. The latter have confirmed the accuracy of many of his representations. He has suffered in his youth, and can therefore imagine greater horrors. He fully intends to continue painting such works, saleable or not, because it is absolutely necessary to get them "out of his system".

Bill returned to the attack in two exhibitions entitled "The Burning Barn" and "The Last Days". In the former, sixteen paired works were devoted to making the point that human experience hinges upon good and evil and always will (as Bill notes in the Introduction) "while man remains man." Convinced that the world was on fire because the boundaries of good and evil were blurred and disregarded, Bill painted himself as a tiny John the Baptist lost in the landscape and minus an audience. Themes included Hunger and Plenty, Love and Hate. All were caught up in the impressive core painting, *Our World Today*, which depicts children playing, oblivious to the fact that their shelter has begun to burn: "The children in the barn represent each of man's main activities: home-making, construction, agriculture, amusement (the girl teasing the kitten), competitive sport and the space race (the boy on the rope) and our quest for sex kicks (the fellow masturbating in the corner)."

His public warnings peaked two years later in 1971, when thirty paintings illustrating the twenty-fourth chapter of the Gospel of St. Matthew were shown at Galerie Godard Lefort in Montréal. The Matthew chapter anticipates Christ's return and the world's last days. This apocalyptic vision of the end of the world had fascinated Bill for many years. He dealt with it verse by verse, interpreting the cataclysmic warnings in terms of the nuclear holocaust he had been expecting for some fifteen years, or through natural disasters such as flooding. Once again Bill stressed that the doomsday vision was an essential part of himself. Once again he pointed to the signs that reinforced his conviction: nuclear stockpiles, increasing violence, and the erosion of legitimate authority. Once again he evoked his predecessors, Goya, Bosch, and Bacon. Society, he wrote, was like the prodigal son taking leave of his father, God. He was not an Adventist, since he did not pretend to know when the millennium would come, but personal preparation was essential. Like Stanley Spencer, he was using his own time and place—a Manitoba farm—to express a New Testament vision.

It had become Bill's habit to isolate himself for weeks at a time in order to paint without interruption. Several cheap hotels in Montréal had served this purpose more than once. The series "The Last Days" had been painted during a two-week retreat at Ste. Marguerite du Lac

Masson, in a cottage belonging to Maria and Michael Logush of Mont-réal. They had met the artist the previous year in connection with a Kurelek presentation to the Montréal Museum of Fine Arts from the Ukrainian Auxiliary Committee, a gift sparked by Mrs. Logush. In the Foreword to the series, Bill had observed that Laurentian solitude had provided an ideal setting for his highly disciplined routine of seventeen-hour days devoted to prayer, meditation, and painting. Throughout the period he had fasted on orange juice and vitamin pills, and attended daily Mass.

The Logush family were somewhat awed by their guest, who had stayed with them briefly in 1970 and whom they had driven to their cottage in the Laurentian hills north of Montréal in April 1971. Bill's reluctance to sign his paintings ("it was God's hand directing his, he said") seemed to them an act of extraordinary humility. His conviction that we were becoming spiritually blind in the midst of abundance they found unforgettable, along with his deep love of nature. It is strange to think of Bill working amid exceptional natural beauty and peace, using these surroundings as the setting for the fears his faith had shaped. His text for *Nuclear Age Madonna* states: "In the painting nuclear fallout has increased the lushness of vegetation, but unborn babies affected by radiation are later born deformed. Moreover the mother is still suffering from a nuclear heat flash and her hair has suddenly fallen out."[16]

After the summer of 1971, a great deal of Bill's attention was taken up by paintings that were intended for book publication in series form. They tended, of necessity, to deal with happier themes. At the same time, thanks to an improving financial situation, the purchase of a northern property was becoming a possibility. It was an old dream fed by many longings, one of which remained constant. In the hinterland, he could build a blast shelter unhampered by local permits and bylaws. Bill had asked Louis Stoeckle, a friend at Madonna House who worked on the community's farm, to help him locate a property to buy in the area. Stoeckle felt a deep bond with Bill's penchant for silence: "I perceived in this man a sense of reality with a capital R. I sensed in him something I had in common with him then, a mistrust of the spoken word, a preference for human interchange on the intuitive level. My relationship with him was largely non-verbal. He was like a peasant, with his mistrust of words. I had spent four years with Indians in the Yukon and I understood people who didn't use words. I respected the space he was coming from."[17]

On an April day in 1974, the two set out to check the listings Stoeckle had collected. It was a day of silence. Bill had indicated neither the approximate amount of money he could spend nor the

Bill's cartoon sketch of his wife's cousin, Michael Clayton, drawn quickly on a restaurant placemat, July 1975. Courtesy Michael Clayton.

features he was seeking. His single proviso was that the property should be no further than thirty-five miles from Madonna House. Stoeckle recalls:

> We spent the whole day, from early morning to sunset, searching. Bill was very vague. He wanted a place to paint in seclusion, a summer place for his kids, an escape from the city. In the Bancroft area Bill almost bought an enormous wooden structure with more than twenty rooms, a former railway hotel. He liked its rustic appearance, you could see he was tempted, but it was a firetrap. After looking at each property he would simply say, "Let's look a little more." Finally we arrived back in Combermere, around twilight, at the last place on my list. I didn't think Bill had that much money and besides, the farm had been stripped of its topsoil. Pecoskie told him about the stripping, and other features, but Bill didn't seem to be listening. He seemed to see something of his own. He didn't walk over the land. He went into the farmhouse and sat down. He didn't look around, he didn't go upstairs. He took out his chequebook and wrote a cheque.

The Adolphe Pecoskie farmhouse, with eighty-five acres of land, had been listed at $32,000. Topsoil had been left on the single acre round the house. Its owner was surprised that Bill made no attempt to bargain, and further surprised by the speed of the deal: "He didn't spend five minutes looking at the house! My wife kept saying, Are you *sure*, when your wife hasn't seen it?" A mortgage was taken out, but the entire sum was paid off before its first payment came due on July 1 of the same year.[18]

The Combermere area was already important to Bill, and would become more so in the last three years of his life. He must have noticed the granite hills near the house. They would become the locus for his second and final attempt at a shelter, aided by his brother-in-law, Geza Takacs. Geza and Bill's sister Sandy knew that he considered it a duty to prepare for a conclusion he believed inevitable, but they knew nothing of the artist's desire to witness to God among the survivors of a holocaust.

Takacs had had experience with shelters. As a draughtsman he had worked with an architect on plans for a forty-person shelter for military brass in 1966. He had also experienced war and revolution in Hungary in 1956, yet he disagreed with Bill's plan: "I thought it was ridiculous, but I didn't tell him so. We talked of the feasibility of a shelter cut into the hill. Some bulldozing of a road to it was done. Sandy was in charge of food plans, but they were never carried out."[19] Bill's brother John remembers the beginning of a cavern carved out of the hillside.[20] Some of the bills for the work arrived after Bill's death by cancer. Among God's attributes, surely the taste for irony has not received the attention it deserves.

11

"Nature, Poor Stepdame"

THROUGHOUT HIS LIFE, BILL'S FEELINGS FOR THE NATURAL WORLD RAN DEEP. He had grown up on Canada's wide-open prairie land, and had discovered its wonders at an early age, as the dedication to *Prairie Boy's Summer* reveals. He had frequently been moved to semi-mystical states of ecstasy by the play of wind and light on a natural landscape. After his conversion, however, conflicting ideas about Nature in relation to God left the artist with ambivalent feelings about the relative importance of landscape painting. Theological convictions, along with memories in which pain and pleasure were almost inseparable, complicated Bill's reaction to nature and may help to explain why people and human actions were always central to his work.

Within months of his marriage, Bill had begun what would become a pattern in the remaining fifteen years of his life: namely, trips westward, principally to Manitoba and Alberta, to paint the areas where he had lived as a child and which would become the basis for his most popular paintings. The earliest of many such trips is recorded in a letter to Shorey in February of 1963: "I am flying to Winnipeg for five days to make on the spot sketches and photos of the farm where I was brought up." Half a year later he made a week-long trip to Stonewall by car, and writes that as he photographs the area he begins to see, increasingly, "the possibilities of the district as a source of painting inspiration". What seems to us, with hindsight, an inevitable subject for the artist was actually discovered and forged in the early years of his association with Av Isaacs.

Inspiration during this particular week became eighteen finished paintings and two hundred and seventy-five photographs for future use. Eleven years later the photos were still inspiring paintings, as Bill notes in his text for *The Painter*: "I photographed the skies all afternoon as well as making a series of watercolours of them until it was completely dark and the moon came out, at which time I was working

190

Av Isaacs at the Kurelek farm in Vinemount, Ontario, in the early 1960s. From Bill's scrapbook.

by the car ceiling light. I still get a shiver of awe sometimes when I look at that series of photos in my album."[1] He calls that entire afternoon and evening on the bog in 1963 an ecstatic experience.

The trips were recorded in meticulous detail in travel diaries or in letters to his wife, his dealer, or his friend Ken. Early in the course of their association, Isaacs had given Bill the idea that there would doubtless be, in good time, a biography. Bill's sense of destiny, and his driving need to find lasting meaning in his personal experience, did the rest. "God had arranged my life so that experiences would one day be recorded," he wrote in 1967.[2] Letters or diaries had their allotted place in his day's work, no matter how long the day or how tired the artist might be. Some diaries contain phrases like "you Easterners"; some ended with "Goodbye Reader", others with "Goodnight my wife and children" (although the children in question were infants at the time). Bill's syntax was far from normative and his spelling frequently abominable, yet his letters call up his experiences with great vividness. To Isaacs Bill writes:

> I decided to spend the night out on the farm so as to
> relive and recall the dark hours of the farm late evening
> and the night itself. This I could best do by parking the
> car in the middle of the bog land to the east of our farm
> and catnapping all night. ... I drove down hay wagon trails
> until I found a road to Poplar Spring. This is a large spring

in the middle of the bog at the very end of the bog ditch and we children used to make "pilgrimages" to it many years ago. I used to be fascinated by the deep blue green waters. When the surface is still the bottom looks like a fantastic underwater world. And it still is. . . .

It was a bit scary being so far away from everything. . . . But it was thrilling too. The vastness of the prairies with occasional clumps of poplar bushes really gives me a feel-ing of communion. Nobody else seems to understand why I'm fascinated by the place not even the local people. Only I it seems can express it though others may feel it inarticulately. . . .

It was chilly, uncomfortable and bleak night but worth it rather than heading for the warm bed in Winnipeg. The last hour before daybreak I entertained myself playing the mouthorgan. I didn't want to put on the car radio because that would bring urban civilization into the picture. . . . The best way to get to know a countryside is to get out into it and don't shield yourself from it. In this case it was reliving the communion in order to refresh memory.[3]

The word "communion" recurs, in the sense of religious awe. The artist often appreciated nature both for its own sake and as a means of recalling childhood memories.

By the following summer, Bill's ability to turn the Stonewall scenery into art had moved into high gear. In June 1964, he drove to the area in his little red Volkswagen with friend and cousin William Budjak, now nearly blind. The tiny car served the two for travelling, sleeping, and dining. It was also his studio. The rugged camping trip included being stuck in the bog for two days during a rainstorm. Bill was alone at the time and, as usual, made the best of a bad situation. He writes that such mishaps are valuable to an artist as they help to keep him "close to real life and in my case to the land".

The resulting twenty paintings supplied an exhibition the following year and, as the 1963 trip had done, a lifetime of ideas for work. It is puzzling to find Bill writing, in the Foreword to the "Manitoba Bog Paintings" exhibition at Galerie Agnès Lefort in March 1965, that this was the first time he had painted directly from nature: "All my previous paintings of farm life were done from memory." Perhaps the show contained works from September 1963 as well as June 1964, although Bill refers specifically to the 1964 trip. His writing abounds in chrono-logical errors, but their source may be as much in Bill's disbelief in the importance of such data as in a damaged memory. He was always a storyteller, not a historian. He was also very tired on many of the occasions when he would make time for writing.

Bill's diary for the 1964 trip touches on a theme which becomes central in the Foreword to the Bog Paintings. How is he to fuse his religious message with his "nature pictures"? The problem was partly solved by giving religious or didactic titles to idyllic and bucolic scenes. The passage of sheep across the road in front of his car suggests "We like sheep have gone astray"; Bill needed only to exaggerate the confusion of the sheep. An evening sky becomes "Can you not read the signs of the times?" and would be used much later in the *Fields* series.

The diaries are delightfully revealing of Bill's habits and attitudes. Talkativeness in friends or relatives was resented ("they are using up valuable time!") but their offers of food were usually accepted. Bill "consents" to have tea and cookies, or a meal. Prayers were made no matter how late the hour, sometimes by the car's headlights. A stray church provided an opportunity to give thanks for safe travel. Turquoise paint spilled on socks and shoes, or margarine squashed on the food supplies, deserved only a brief mention. Bill was a superb survivor, and perhaps if anyone was physically and psychologically fitted for surviving a nuclear holocaust he was. He was also ingenious in adapting things to the needs of the moment: "Working in the car as usual I draped a tea towel over the front window to shut out strong light falling on the palette."

His sense of humor bested the irritation of an interruption by a neighboring farm woman carrying four of her own paintings for Bill to evaluate: "This was no doubt the first 2 man show in the history of THE BOG." A toad in a deserted pioneer farmhouse was christened Thomas and a small frog, Freddie. Houseflies, however, found no mercy: "I'm a fanatical racist where those varmints are concerned and though it was probably their remote remote ancestors that tortured me and made my horses nervy when I was a farm boy I have never forgiven them and squash them without mercy." Curious cows were christened country bumpkins.

The bog, or Poplar Spring, continued to draw him like a magnet, not least because of its isolation: "I'm parked out on the bog, after just finishing a sketch for a painting tomorrow. The stillness out here is frightening and yet fascinating. Sights of civilization are far in the distance and they bring on waves of loneliness and yet I know I can't turn tail and flee to human company. I must paint that peculiar sense of isolation."[4] He hoped to capture the spring's weird colors and shapes which reminded him of Coleridge's lines "Where Alph the sacred river ran/Through caverns measureless to man/Down to a sunless sea." He feared that his skills were insufficient to paint the intricacies of the bog. He also feared that it might soon be drained and ploughed under.

The romantic nature of these challenging camping trips continued to suit Bill's needs and aspirations, many of which were evidence of the continued influence of Joyce and Van Gogh. He drove his little car as if it were a Land Rover: "I feel the thrill of being an explorer. With my trusty Volks I drive down gulleys through over hayfields with the hay sweeping my undercarriage and on top of ditch embankments. When stopped by fences I go round them." Certainly that car, like his grandfather's McLaughlin-Buick, had stood a lot. Mired in the mud by a rainstorm, Bill found his depression soon turned to elation when he was able to produce two paintings in as many hours each: "I really am blessed. With the talent God gave me I turn even misfortune to advantage." He managed to reach a neighbor's farm on foot ("Boy this is he-man country") but chose to spend a second night in the car rather than sleep at the farm. Getting drinking water became an exhilarating expedition, enlivened by marsh birds. The spring continued to fascinate ("I love this place—so wild, lonely and strong") even though his car remained trapped in the mud. But when he found two long, thin boards in a garbage dump his excitement knew no bounds. The boards, and Bill's flamboyant driving, did the trick: "Finally, like Robert Bruce and his spider I gave one extra last try I moved and kept going.... I said a short fervent prayer, put the car into second and gave her the gun." Twenty paintings were the product of these eight adventurous days on the bog.

The magical lure of the bog is a theme in the early autobiography. Bill wrote that it spoke to him because it was lonely, as he often was "and sometimes still am". It was also associated with freedom, since his boyhood Sunday afternoons had often been spent there when he and his friends were freed from farm duties:

> For many years we did not even know what was on the
> other side of the bog or how many miles it was before
> human habitation could be seen again. On clear dark
> nights we'd see a glow of lights on the horizon off centre
> to the right and were told that that was Selkirk, Manitoba.
> But to the great left of centre it remained dark for always.
> (A1 67)

The note of high adventure sounds again in the record of a 1967 trip back to the Stonewall farm. Perhaps it was the sense of the adventure of daily life and of the seasons that made many of his paintings speak to such a wide cross-section of ordinary people:

> I suppose it would need a poet to get across the thrill of
> the spring thaw in the West as we knew it; watching the

giant snowbanks we'd become intimately acquainted with by playing on them during the long winter months shrink and dwindle day by day. Not even country people we knew could be articulate about the vast chorus of frogs in the evening on the bogland to the east, or the swish of wild ducks' wings heard overhead before dawn while we did our morning chores. Going out to see flood waters running over sections of the farm at no other time flooded would not be a city boy's idea of high adventure. But to me it was.[5]

Prairie Boy's Summer is dedicated to the sister who shared the surprise and wonder of prairie seasons and who felt, with Bill, a sense of "awe and love" for their Creator. Some called the wonders Nature: "We two call it: God." Yet the texts for these idyllic scenes are constantly observing, *sotto voce*, that Nature is cruel and her seasons hard taskmasters. The latter are feared as well as loved. Milking means wrists that ache so badly they prevent sleep; cutting grain is hot, dry work that leaves harvesters "so dead tired they fell into bed without even washing off the field dust." Within the context of *A Northern Nativity*, the idyllic note sounds again: "'Only a Creator who is beauty itself can create beauty—only those who are made in His image can appreciate that beauty.'"[6]

The editorial preface to *Fields* (1976) catches the very mixed emotions Bill felt in this regard. His relation to nature was shaped partly by his family and partly by the economic hardships of the thirties: "Fatigue, monotony, aching muscles, thirst for ten years of summers on the slow time scale of boyhood." The fields were prison and playground, and nature was both provider and tyrant: a temperamental tyrant "who according to mood could stage storms, fire, drought—occasionally a welcome, if frightening, relief from monotony." The book's editor saw the tension in even the quietest of Kurelek paintings as stemming from these mixed memories of pleasure and pain.

The dozen paintings that make up *Fields* are prophetic rather than idyllic. Like the doomsday works with their mushroom-shaped clouds and threatening texts, they call the viewer to repent and return to Nature's Master. Here the texts are simply proverbs, Ukrainian or English, or brief quotations from the New Testament. Proverbs and quotations provide title and text. The tonic note, and the only non-quotation, is "Nature: beautiful but heartless (Artist's observation)".

In "Old age is not joy", the eye is drawn past playing children to an old man limping down the road. Nature as flesh is an unreliable ally. "Nature: beautiful but heartless" features a bloated carcass, a feast for crows. A grass fire set by an arsonist and a field thick with weeds are used to suggest the spiritual enemy of New Testament parables, while "Here today, and tomorrow fed into the oven" is the sombre text for a sunny harvest scene. The series climaxes with a rosy evening sky scanned for the next day's weather by two farmers: "But how is it you cannot read the signs of the times?" Doomsday again, but here is the subtlety that Malcolmson found lacking in the 1966 exhibition of didactic work. The painting, or its prototype, dates from the first trips back to the Stonewall farm in the early sixties.

Among the very few scenes in *Fields* that celebrate Nature's beauty rather than her heartlessness is "Everyone that is born of the breath of the Spirit". It shows the artist, eyes closed and hands uplifted, in the middle of a sunny, wind-swept field. The first autobiography records an experience that doubtless provided the germ of this painting. Bill calls it "a whopper" of an impression, one that showed his Wordsworthian sensitivity to nature (A1 447). He was seeing the Irish countryside near Dublin by bus on a shoestring budget. As a high wind whipped the long grasses and the surface of ponds, Bill felt a rising euphoria. In a valley where the bus stopped near monastery ruins, the vegetation moved wildly. Bill writes:

> I was in ecstasy. I even recall doing a dance on a pathway out of sight of the other tourists. It's a state of soul that demands physical involvement too. I just had to climb the mountain and I did, through the lush vegetation crawling with snails and dripping moist from the blanket of fog that now and then dragged itself across the top of the valley. Even as the spell wore off with the dying of the wind in the evening, the lavender hills took up the quiet refrain. I was able to join in the Irish sing-along our guide conducted on the way home. Only having to give the guide a good fat tip like the other tourists did, marred a memorable day. (A1 448)

Had Bill (or his biographer) ended at "quiet refrain", our impression of him would be different. It seems wise to remember that even nature mystics have other needs and interests and irritating foibles.

The farm and nature paintings sold well, and their dark side often passed unnoticed. In 1970, Bill shaped a series of sixteen farm scenes around a poem by the English mystic Francis Thompson. "The Hound of Heaven" (1893), the autobiographical narrative of a fugitive from God's redemptive love, had long been a favorite with Bill. The cosmic Lover is depicted as a hound, relentlessly pursuing the Beloved. In the series' Foreword, Bill writes that no other poem expresses so completely "this personal life lesson" which he is always trying to portray in paintings. That lesson is caught in the Thompson line that provides the series' title: "Nature, poor stepdame, cannot slake my drouth".

Poor stepdame? Quite simply, the creature is not the real parent, the Creator. The Foreword plays on the "beautiful but heartless" theme of *Fields*, yet here as elsewhere the artist is ambivalent. The series (he writes) stems from verses inspired by Thompson's worship of nature in his youth, which parallels Bill's own boyhood closeness to nature on the Manitoba farm: "So it is the moods of nature—in different seasons, different times of the day, different states of mind in which I myself met her—that I range over in these sixteen large works." Prairie land is marked by size and simplicity. The paintings, accordingly, focus on the basic elements of soil, sky, cloud, wind, grass, poplar bush, snow, and sun, but they also include rare beauties such as northern lights, rainbows, and fireflies.

Christianity has always embraced the linked concepts of immanence and transcendence, God in our midst and God over and above us. In the conservative mood of British theology in the 1950s, before Vatican II, the stress was on transcendence. The closeness to nature which Bill had felt in youth and explored in high school through the work of Romantic poets such as Wordsworth became suspect as pantheism. His Foreword notes his years of gradual disillusionment with "mere earthly hopes", and the cruelty of nature as false mother or pretender: "Nature gives us not a drop of comfort, can do nothing, will do nothing. ... Living beings are trapped by her pitiless laws ... [her] deafness to man's predicament."

Many of the texts continue this theme. Nature does not comfort a frightened boy, for she is nothing but "a set of natural laws". She is silent and unsympathetic, as Bill realized in Netherne Hospital during his midnight experience of utter abandonment: "that was the beginning of the end of my long flight to creatures. The pursuing Hound has finally halted, as He stands back of the cabbage patch waiting for me to come over to Him."[7]

Had Bill seen God as immanent in nature he might have found his landscape paintings more significant. Luckily, their saleability drove him to paint them, thus allowing him to satisfy his emotional need to do so with only a modicum of guilt. He called his farm paintings "pot-boilers", as distinct from the religious and didactic paintings which he considered his serious work, and which he sometimes claimed would have occupied him exclusively had he no financial need. On the other hand, the popular farm scenes caught the public's eye and served to draw attention to the didactic paintings.

Joan Murray, the curator responsible for the posthumous retrospective entitled "Kurelek's Vision of Canada", writes that the artist almost never painted landscape as such, "but during his lifetime he painted the length and breadth of the country and Canada's physical presence informs almost everything he did."[8] Western artists Ivan Eyre and Dennis Burton were great admirers of Kurelek's prairie landscapes. Murray finds that he brings to these paintings both his sense of doom and his redemptive rapture.

Bill's polemical Foreword to *The Last of the Arctic* describes his painting trip to Pangnirtung in the Northwest Territories in October 1975. The Foreword is a fighting tract in defence of missionary activity in the North and of Bill's view that nature by itself is nothing but a set of physical laws: "It is not a person. It cannot plan or design anything. But it *is* a person, an infinitely wise and powerful Designer and Provider who created Nature."[9] Man may and does function as saboteur in the Garden, yet Bill has little sympathy for ecological crusades: "I believe that our white man's guilt feelings are wasted if we are to channel all our energy into ecological work while turning a blind eye to the bad example of our increasingly corrupt southern society" (p. 15). Despite his shame at the behavior of many members of his society, Bill remains convinced that Christian southerners have the "right" philosophy and that Inuit spiritual beliefs are simply wrong. Inuit are *pagans*: the Victorian word is not used but the concept, with its negative judgment, is clearly there (*LA* 30, 62).

The biblical creation story was interpreted by Bill very literally. In the divine commandment to subdue the earth (Genesis 1:28), he found the title for a painting of the Sudbury area whose text expounds his belief that pollution is legitimate if it creates jobs for family men. The text locates the painting in time and place and continues:

> I loved that bleak area round Sudbury where the vegetation is killed by sulphur fumes because it reminded me of the Wilderness of Judea where Christ was tempted by the Devil during his 40 days fast. I heard that some International Nickel executive was hurt because he jumped to the conclusion that the theme of the painting was that his company pollutes the atmosphere. Actually this is not at all what I was saying. As a believing Christian I see man's exploitation of the minerals of the earth as perfectly legitimate and a fulfillment of God's first commandment when he made the first human pair and told them to be fruitful and multiply and subdue the earth and make it theirs. Therefore mining insofar as it provides employment for family men who raise up more children and the metals that are shipped round the world to be made into earth subduing machines is a desirable occupation. Ecology

(Above) *Old Water Pail*, one of Bill's many still-life paintings, c. 1970. Mixed media. Private collection.

Bill addressing students at the Windsor Art Gallery, 1974. Photo by Gladys Cada, *Windsor Star*.

should of course be taken into account but if it is not profitable or possible then mining takes first place. This theme I've dwelt on several times and still do.[10]

Not profitable? Obviously industry finds it cheaper to pollute than to operate with a decent regard for a clean, safe environment. Acid rain was not part of our vocabulary in the sixties, and chemical disasters such as the Love Canal were almost unheard of. One wonders how Bill would have reacted twenty years later to widespread stories of various pollutants killing and maiming humans as well as other species.

Bill's nature paintings were commonly grouped as "farm" or "bush". He would also term them "nostalgia" paintings. For his lumberjack scenes he drew on his two experiences, in 1947 and 1951. His first exposure to Canada's northern lakes and forests, in the logging camp near Neys, Ontario, had made a deep impression on him. In a Foreword to an exhibition of "Ontario and Québec Bush Camp Memories" (1973/74), he calls that summer of 1947 "a glorious romantic adventure" despite the back-breaking work: "Looking back on it all now, I realize how lucky I was in terms of my work as *a painter of Canadiana*, to have had that bush experience" (emphasis added). Exciting incidents that Bill would paint included dynamiting log jams and driving logs down river. Those with similar experiences have testified that these paintings are both accurate in detail and evocative of atmosphere.

His attitude to the camps near La Tuque and Cochrane in 1951 was similar. Memory had softened the flies, heat, cold, and fatigue. What remained were memories of a way of life that had changed relatively little for hundreds of years but that was soon to be revolutionized by modern technology. His own brother John's invention of a mechanical tree harvester would be in the forefront of those changes. Bill painted *The Koehring Waterous Tree Harvester* as the last of his twenty-seven scenes. The others all stemmed from his personal experience of the old ways, which were, he strongly suspected, "more romantic, more human, more socially satisfying".

Lumberjack, the book in which these paintings are collected, ends with Bill's satisfaction at having been part of "that good life" before it passed into history. Like Bill's other publications in the 1970s, the book's Foreword exemplifies the paradoxical relation to nature that marked the last twenty years of his life. On the one hand he was a poet, a nature mystic reacting with delight to magical beauties in the northern bush: "I shall never forget them: the wraiths of mist rising from our lily-padded lake in the morning; the laughter of the loon echoing over the water in the moonlight; rainy days when the hillside covered with dark green forest stretched up into the clouds." On the other hand he did not shrink from despoiling that beauty through lumbering operations, since (in his view) man is divinely commanded to subdue the earth and make it his own. Bill saw in the lakes and forests a heritage so vast that it would always be there, unspoiled. He did not see that the world is growing smaller.

Two series painted near the end of his life confirm Bill's feeling for the vastness of Canada, and for nature as a source of joy. *Kurelek's Canada* (1975) consists of thirty scenes (three per province) to celebrate his native land. In the Foreword, Bill writes that the book's theme is Joy, and that he deliberately chose rural settings because "it is usually close to Nature that the simplest, most elemental pleasures are found." The qualifier is close behind, as usual: true happiness is found in union with God, the source of all joys. Yet the land continued to call to him, just as it did in his youth in Stonewall, where "the great free flat bogland" drew the boy whenever he could be spared from chores. The paintings take the reader, province by province, from Canada's east coast to her west, where the mountains of British Columbia become a melodic metaphor of joyous worship: *Divine Symphony of Forest Rock and Snow*. In the last two scenes, a ship and the Pacific Ocean symbolize life's dreaming, searching journey.

The paradox of isolation and community is prominent in this series, and in Bill's life in general. He writes of the sea's expansiveness finding its echo in the prairie land. In such a setting, human company is welcome and even distant signs of neighbors bring joy: "the simple elemental pleasure of recognizing an acquaintance's boat across the water at dawn . . . is somewhat akin to the warm glow a prairie farmer gets from seeing a far-off neighbour's farmhouse lights come on in the evenings." *Kurelek's Canada* celebrates social joy as much as the beauty of the land. The lonely artist who would much rather paint than socialize became one of the great painters of human fellowship. Working in isolation, he painted social bonds.

The title for a series Bill called "Big Lonely" comes from a slang term for Canada used by hoboes, a term that catches the enormity of a land that "dwarfs and dominates life".[11] Calling himself a loner since boyhood, Bill identified with the tramps who roam the land. He too had "hoboed" across the country. His Foreword stresses that Canadian territory, unlike that of Europe, has not been tamed or dominated by man. Much of it still retains the haunting loneliness which is caught in a ship's foghorn or a freight train's whistle. *Night Hunters* is cited as an example of "a disaster theme in which nature not only menaces, but has the power to actually destroy or injure."[12] The viewer's eye goes first to the predatory cat, but a deeper threat seems to lurk in the vast land and dark sky. Typically, the passage ends with a reversal: the artist has no wish to labor the threatening aspect of nature but intends his series to be enjoyed as pure poetry.

Bill lived in the middle of one of Canada's largest cities, yet remained rural by attitude and inclination. His east-end neighborhood bordered on Lake Ontario. A ten-minute walk would bring him to the beach, and a shorter one to a deeply wooded ravine. Much of the local atmosphere was that of a small Ontario town. In Bill's mind, the future lay in Canada's wilderness to the north, where survivors of a nuclear holocaust could flee, like some kind of post-modern Robinson Crusoes. Urban life was sullied by its links to modernism and materialism, the conditions the artist deplored. For Bill, the beauty and mystery of nature had been captured archetypally in the bogland east of his family's Manitoba farm. He never lost that feeling of closeness to the land, the elements, and the seasons, but after his conversion it became, according to mood, a heartless pretender or an image of its maker. His joyful communion, in the closing words of *Kurelek's Canada*, was paradoxically within himself and at the same time beyond all boundaries: "It is in God."

By early 1964, Bill's steps were firmly set in the direction in which they would continue for life. He had rediscovered the haunts of his youth and, in them, an endless source of inspiration for his work. His exhibited paintings already embraced religious, ethical, social, philosophic, and lyric themes. The "two streams" of which he often spoke, nature and religion, had already met and fused in his work. One portion of his past, however, remained largely untapped: his ethnicity. The mid-sixties would see the mining of this rich vein.

12

The Odyssey Toward
Ethnic Awareness

"My grandparents cut their farm from the
bush, and my childhood recollections of an
old culture in a new land have profoundly
influenced all my work."
William Kurelek, "The Ukrainian Pioneers"
1980

DURING HIS YEARS IN LONDON, BILL HAD SPOKEN OCCASIONALLY OF HIS
Ukrainian background. He had asked Edward Adamson to call him
Vasyl. He had once taken David and Marianne John to a Ukrainian
Orthodox church service. For the most part, however, his sense of himself as a Ukrainian-Canadian had gone underground during these seven
years abroad. This was due in no small part to the kindness of the British
people he met, to his gratitude for free hospitalization, and to his guilt
for the anti-British, pro-German sympathies of the Kurelek family
during the Second World War. Dmytro's difficulties had sometimes
been compounded by the general prejudice against non-Anglo-Saxon
immigrants. There was even a Ku Klux Klan movement in Western
Canada in the 1930s. Bill writes that his father was pro-German simply
because he was anti-establishment; after the war, the family had been
dismayed to realize their mistake.

Neither Bill's first years back in Toronto nor his marriage to an
Anglo-Canadian woman had done anything to revive his own sense of
himself as a Ukrainian Canadian. Indeed, the universalism of his new-
found church militated against such a view. After joining the Catholic
Church, Bill prided hmself on being (in his phrase) a World Citizen. In
the mid-sixties, it remained for the Ukrainian-Canadian community to
discover Bill, and for Bill to rediscover that part of himself. In a talk
presented at the University of Toronto in 1973 at a Canadian Ethnic
Studies Association Conference, Bill traced what he called "the story of

one man's odyssey towards ethnic awareness".[1] By this date, unlike ten years earlier, he could see his ethnicity as a significant part of his artistic consciousness—and indeed inseparable from it.

His lecture is an admittedly rambling tale, beginning with a memory from his first days in primary school. Bill found it painful to discover that Ukrainian was not to be spoken in the schoolroom. His first-grade class was also the place where he had found that he could draw, and that drawing attracted the attention and admiration for which he was starved. Anglo-Saxon prejudices against East European immigrants and Bill's developing antagonism towards his father combined to make his Ukrainian culture appear undesirable—a source of embarrassment, even of inferiority. His future, he believed, lay elsewhere.

Bill's first contact with a group that respected and actually idealized things Ukrainian came during his high school years in Winnipeg. Just across the street from the little house at 834 Burrows Avenue lay the Orthodox Cathedral of St. Mary the Protectress: "there I fell under the influence of the teacher, Father Mayevsky, a dedicated Ukrainian Nationalist.... I identified with him as 'a father figure' head on heels.... I was at last clear in my mind (or so I thought) that I was a Ukrainian not a Canadian. I dreamed dreams of doing great things for the cause of Ukrainian liberation and I idealized its countryside, its people and its culture."[2]

Ethnicity and art were soon connected, as they seemed to have been in primary school. The Orthodox priest noticed Bill's artistic talent, gave him artwork to do for the church, and even spoke to Dmytro in defence of his son's artistic vocation. The priest's intercession prompted Dmytro's grudging recognition that art might earn prestige and money. This concession, of course, did not mean that Dmytro favored such a career for his son. An idea, however, had been planted, and Bill was grateful. His first patron was Ukrainian. There were night classes at the cathedral in the Ukrainian language, history, and culture. Bill had discovered a new love, and was undergoing his first conversion experience: "I soon realized that the fire had passed from him to me" (A1 151). His admiration for Father Mayevsky was boundless, but short-lived.

Father Mayevsky's influence was replaced by the gospel according to Joyce and Van Gogh. Bill later condemned them as "atheists", but in 1948-49 they bred potent rebellion in the impressionable and romantic young university student. He ascribed three results to their influence. His Ukrainian fervor waned, since Father Mayevsky represented organized religion, which Bill had ceased to respect. His search for Self meant the rejection of parents seen as domineering, and, with them, his own Ukrainian roots. Finally, college friends whom Bill called

"Leftist rebels against Society" moved to fill the political vacuum thus created. Even the large painting (1951-52) illustrating Gogol's Cossack novel *Taras Bulba* is described in 1973 as one that celebrated "the solid virtues of working people such as peasants" rather than his Ukrainian heritage, the more obvious theme.

The next step in the odyssey was Bill's conversion to Christianity. This may seem an unlikely explanation for his becoming an ethnic artist, but to Bill the logic was irrefutable: "To me being a genuinely religious person is inextricably tied in with being an ethnic artist." By this, Bill meant that he had found in the biblical command to honor one's father and mother the way to harness farm paintings to religious ends. He conceived of his fourth show at The Isaacs Gallery in September 1964 as an act of honoring and thus forgiving the father under whom he had suffered and to whom he intended to return good for ill. "An Immigrant Farms in Canada" was highly popular with the public. Bill was becoming adept at killing several birds with one stone.

The exhibition in honor of Dmytro Kurelek brought Bill into contact with members of the Ukrainian-Canadian community. It was just beginning to find a voice as a group, as well as a significant place in Canadian society. At and after that show there were Ukrainian buyers of his work. Their patronage touched Bill deeply, and became a two-way street which influenced what he painted. In the 1973 talk, he explained that patronage was important to him because he ascribed to the view of art held in the Middle Ages: art is not esoteric and sacrosanct, but a craft and a commodity. The artist-craftsman painted what he had been commissioned to paint or what was saleable. It was his livelihood: "since I have now a large portion of Ukrainian buyers and they often buy Ukrainian themes, I automatically find myself producing ethnic art. It's as simple as that."

It was, of course, not as simple as that, since this explanation makes no allowance for the religious propaganda or the socio-didactic works which Bill felt compelled to paint and which were far less saleable than his ethnic or farm scenes. Consistency was never one of Bill's virtues. His buyer's theory also conceals the psychological importance to him of praise, since purchase of one's creations is an indisputable form of admiration. The ethnic series of the mid-seventies would eventually be abandoned because they did not earn Bill sufficient money and attention.

His talk listed the events that had followed the 1964 exhibition in honor of his father, events he saw as milestones in the development of his ethnic consciousness. Most of these events are famous stages in a remarkable career. They included a 1968 show to honor his mother ("The Ukrainian Pioneer Woman in Canada"); the purchase of his entire Passion series by a Ukrainian couple who built a gallery for its permanent exhibition; his first trip to the Ukraine and to his father's village of Borivtsi; and his plans to paint a Ukrainian-Canadian epic, a mural to hang in Ottawa as a permanent witness to the hardships and the courage of Canadian pioneers.

Bill's writing and speeches were always personal, and often surprising. He concluded this one with a lengthy reflection on his marriage to a Canadian of British origin, a relationship that typified in many ways the process of assimilation various ethnic groups in Canada were undergoing. He said that Jean had assured him during their courtship that she would learn the Ukrainian language; Bill had assumed that this indicated a sufficiently strong motivation on her part to assimilate the rest of the culture. Jean's promise, however, proved rash and the attempt was abandoned after a few months. Bill seemed surprised, but soon resigned himself to the prospect that his children would learn neither the language nor the culture. He quotes his father on the old saw that the mother's culture dominates, because children are physically closest to the mother. It does not seem to have occurred to Bill that the mother of even one small child, let alone four, has little time for studying a difficult foreign language with an unfamiliar alphabet. He undertook the task himself, but teaching his children Ukrainian speech and culture took time that had to be taken from painting. He eventually abandoned the practice as too time-consuming. Nevertheless, he makes much of this disappointment, of the fact that one-quarter to one-third of his cultural background was doomed to remain "strange, foreign, non-shared".

From many sources it seems clear that Bill wanted children and loved them, but that his passion for painting left him relatively little time to spend with them. On successive weeks each shared a few hours alone with his or her father, but since there were soon four young Kureleks, that schedule meant that each one might enjoy Bill's undivided attention only once a month; even then, the time might do double duty for visiting someone Bill needed to see. As Dmytro had been, he remained oblivious to the often disturbing effect of some of his convictions and goals on young minds. There must certainly have been times when Bill's children knew that he loved them, but other times when their perception of that love was blocked and their wills were rebelliously set against that of their father.

The 1973 talk, with its complaint that his children were not sharing his culture, also illustrates Bill's tendency to resignation in certain situations: to resignation, followed by the finding of something *good* in the pain. It was his deepest belief that God allowed pain so that good could come out of it.

(Left) Bill's caption reads: "Wife Jean and Katrina with crib (i.e. crêche) I am making", Christmas 1963.

Bill with his family, c. 1968. Courtesy Olga and John Tomyk.

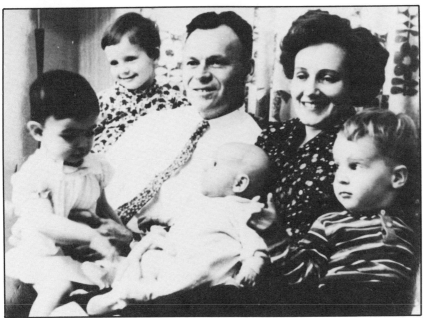

Balked within his own household, he found himself compelled to return to his heritage by a painful route: "disappointment and loneliness were to be catalysts for keener awareness." He found that Ukrainians began to come to his home, to buy and to socialize. The Kureleks were invited more and more to Ukrainian cultural and social events — concerts, dinners, films, displays: "and the more I tasted that culture

207

Jean with Barbara and Tommy on the lawn of their house, Toronto, late 1960s. From Bill's scrapbook.

the more I came to love it. ... I was getting closer to my heritage, further from my wife and children for the simple reason that they showed hardly a glimmer of interest in that heritage." Bill spoke of heartaches in this connection, as his heritage became increasingly important to him over the passage of a decade.

And where was the good in this pain? By becoming more keenly aware of the differences in cultures, he felt himself better able to represent them in paintings. When Bill made this statement in 1973 he was on the verge of beginning a series of paintings and books that would celebrate some of the major cultural groups in the Canadian mosaic. The differences, he added, also helped him to appreciate how lucky they all were to live in Canada, where heritage can sometimes be shared and always freely expressed.

The series designed to honor Bill's father in the fall of 1964 was composed of twenty paintings grouped under four headings: leaving the Ukraine and farming in Alberta, Manitoba, and southern Ontario. It drew largely on the artist's memories, of which his father's stories formed part. Bill had approached travel agencies, implement companies, and Alberta relatives for data. He had framed the pictures himself, using weathered lumber from his father's farm; and had set what he called "explanations" beside the pictures in The Isaacs Gallery, beginning a personal tradition of providing such commentary to his work. Bill believed that his father's experience had been typical of many immigrants, and wished the paintings to hang in chronological order.

Dmytro with one of his grandchildren at the Vinemount farm, mid-1960s.

Viewed in this way, they told a story, a pioneer saga.

The incidents he traced will be familiar to readers of *Someone With Me*. Since the paintings included masterworks like *Hauling Grain in Winter*, *Easter Vigil*, and *Depression Diet*, the near-sellout was not surprising. One critic's reaction was. Barrie Hale wrote sneeringly that the exhibition represented "money and success and all that sort of thing", and went on to review another show.[3]

The young Dmytro whose back is shown in *Leaving the Old Country* looks exactly like his oldest son, although if Bill knew just how much he resembled his father in stubborn determination and pride, he never acknowledged it. One scene, *Ukrainian Orthodox Easter Vigil*, is strongly evocative of the culture Bill had experienced at his parents' home. A night scene, it shows an onion-domed rural church from the outside. Men are warming themselves at bonfires in front of the church, whose open door reveals the massed worshippers standing in the all-night vigil. Wagons are parked and baskets await the morning blessing of the *paska*. One wagon, just arriving, holds a boy of six who suggests another self-portrait. The greenish-black earth and darkly green sky cast an eerie look over the whole, lit by the fires and the open door. As Bill observed many times, his parents were not religious but the major Ukrainian festivals such as Easter and Christmas were kept in their home: "the Kurelek family stuck to celebrating the Ukrainian Christmas on the 7th of January and even considered [it] a worthwhile sacrifice to lose a perfect attendance record at school if the 7th fell on a weekday."[4]

His parents' loss of religious faith continued to be a thorn in his side.

They were of course included in the roster of people for whom the artist prayed daily. It is unfortunate that his further efforts at their conversion often took the form of a kind of public shaming or bullying through paintings with matching texts. In the 1960s, both of the series designed to "honor" his parents ended with clear-cut denunciations of their "materialism" and a stern pronouncement on the fate that awaited those who would not change their ways. Understanding the subtleties of human nature was not one of Bill's strengths, and his unwavering faith in the religious dogmas he had acquired in the 1950s could drive him to behavior that others might consider cruel. When Bill weighed an earthly life and human feelings in the scale against "all eternity", there was, quite simply, no contest. And his personal wounds went deep.

The series on his father ended with an oil entitled *In the Autumn of Life*. The scene depicts his father's Ontario farm and his extended family, children, and grandchildren gathered on the front lawn to have their photograph taken. In 1964, Bill's original text was more general in its attack on society at large, and less specific with regard to his father. By 1966, in "Notes on Symbolism" made for the Winnipeg Exhibition, Bill had sharpened his denunciation of the man who was being "honored" by the twenty paintings of which this formed the climax. He writes:

> (1) Atomic cloud bursting over Hamilton, 14 miles from my father's farm, illustrated in this painting, is like a premonition of the disaster that will befall our materialistic society because it is so bent on pursuit of security and prestige, it ignores God. What I'm trying to say is that my

Bill with his aunt, Helen Shulhan, during his nostalgic trip back to Alberta to see the Whitford farm and his Huculak relations in the spring of 1965. Courtesy Mrs. Shulhan.

VII
*The Apparition of Our Lady
to Bernadette at Lourdes*, 1955-56.
Gouache, 29″ x 20½″.
Private collection.
(see page 125)

VIII
Children's Games in Western Canada, 1953.
Mixed media, 24″ x 30″.
Private collection.
(see page 86)

father's life, hard as it may have been, is not a happy ending story, even though it may appear to be on the surface,
judging by the large healthy family he has raised and the
extent of his possessions. He will still have to meet "the
day of Judgment". And Christ, whom he has ignored all
his life, and maybe even helped crucify with his sins, is
like a "skeleton" in his closet. It's an unpleasant scene,
that he may try to keep off his property, but it's still there
nevertheless.
(2) The dogs in the picture are "supernatural" ones referring to the enemies of Christ talked of in one of the
Psalms of David.[5]

Individual members of the Kurelek family, in this work, are tiny but
recognizable, and one is satirized rather meanly. The figure of Christ,
crucified on a dead tree, adds a surreal touch in the left foreground. It
is perhaps no more extraordinary than the text in a series supposedly
designed as a tribute to his father.

A short documentary film by the National Film Board of Canada was
a spin-off from this show. John Sims, a young Ukrainian-Canadian
writer and song composer, saw and was moved by the exhibition. He
interviewed Dmytro and sought backers for a film, which was finally
produced in time for Canada's Centennial celebration in 1967. Bill was
delighted. Calling it a little masterpiece, he revelled in the idea that in
this way he had brought his father's story to people throughout Canada
and even in the major cities of the Ukraine.[6]

Talk of Canada's Centennial was in the air. In 1965 Bill was
approached by three members of the executive of the Toronto branch
of UWAC, the Ukrainian Women's Association of Canada. Anna Balan,
Olga Hamara, and Stella Olynyk were framing a proposal to the
members for a Centennial project. The three women hoped to persuade the committee to commission Bill to paint the role of Ukrainian
pioneer women in the development of Western Canada. Initially, they
proposed to buy only five paintings. Bill was grateful for the idea and
began to plan a twenty-work series, promising the committee first
choice.

Meanwhile, the women were struggling to convince their fellow
members of the worthiness of their plan. It would be their first venture
as a group into the world of painting. Balan recalls a very emotional
plenary meeting on the subject. Many of the members wanted their
Centennial project to be the construction of a museum to hold artifacts, such as embroidered pillows and blouses which Ukrainian
women had done so beautifully for centuries. These crafts were "their
aesthetic pleasure", Balan explained.[7]

Bill was particularly impressed by the Ukrainian Pioneer Museum near Shandro, Alberta. He slept here during one visit. From Bill's scrapbook.

Some wanted a written rather than a pictorial history of women's work. There were other problems. UWAC was connected to the Orthodox Church, which Bill had left to become a Roman Catholic. Moreover, his portrayal of their past was far from acceptable to many of UWAC's members. Most were mature women who had grown up on farms in the West and now considered themselves urban sophisticates. Bill's vision of them as Ukrainian-Canadian farmers with heavy peasant faces and shabby clothes was far too close for comfort. Others found his rendering grotesque. When Bill's paintings were later available for the group to make their selection, one woman noticed that he had painted a hole in a curtain. Surely, she argued, this was not the way in which their people should be presented. Balan generously interpreted such feelings as insecurity which sought perfection. She writes:

> Kurelek's simple style was offensive... especially in his
> portrayal of people. Quite often his women, children
> looked grotesque, dour and very unappealing. ... He
> expressed the hardship, the drudgery of homesteading—a
> condition many members remembered well—but I think
> were not ready to have portrayed so strongly. After all
> these women were comfortable middle class people,
> whose children were professionals, well educated. I
> believe the past was too close to them, they were usually
> born on the homestead, managed to achieve material suc-
> cess and didn't want to be reminded of the struggle. You
> will find that their children reacted differently. And lastly,
> we do not have a history of fine arts in our pioneer com-
> munity. To many, art was handicraft—the Easter egg tradi-

tion, embroidery, weaving, etc., so the idea of an art project was very daring and innovative. Since they were
unsure of it, they were cautious.[8]

Anna, the prime mover behind the project, saw Bill frequently in
1965-67 as he worked on this project. Under his direction, she framed
and arranged in albums vast quantities of the photographs he had
acquired out west. In December 1966, the UWAC executive chose six
large scenes from the nearly completed series, and six small oval ones.[9]
These would be shown by UWAC in 1967, and at The Isaacs Gallery in
January 1968 along with the balance of the series. They would finally
be given to the association's museum in Saskatoon. Bill's Foreword to
the "Ukrainian Woman Pioneer in Canada" series credited these
women with moral support and encouragement as his research and
painting progressed.

After the household upheaval of moving to the Beaches in the spring
of 1965, Bill had recuperated for several weeks by painting at his
father's Vinemount farm and had then completed work on his second
satiric series, "Glory to Man in the Highest". By late 1965, he was
planning a three-week trip to the Willingdon-Andrew area of Alberta
where his mother's people had begun life in Canada. It would be his
first trip back to the scene of his birth and early childhood, one that
proved a triumphal tour. Bill played to the hilt the role of the Son
Returning Home, and was happy to find himself a local hero. His
lengthy diary for the trip by train and bus records his pleasure in
rediscovering old haunts, his relatives, and the lively evidence of his
people's history. To his friends at The Isaacs Gallery and workshop,
"William Da Vinci Kurelek" wrote cheerily that he was very busy
"collecting an encyclopedia" of information on early Ukrainian
settlers, painting the countryside, and enjoying great Western
hospitality.[10]

His work began in Saskatoon, with two local museums. Saskatchewan impressed the artist because he had never seen it before, despite
his claim to be a prairie painter, and because it provided his first sight of
grain elevators, which he dubbed "a very handy shape and colour" for
artists and photographers.[11] The Institute Mohyla proved extremely
disappointing. It was small, and unfinished. Its specialty, Ukrainian
handicrafts, interested Bill less than early handmade utensils. He found
the Western Development Museum, which still occupies a plane han-
gar on the outskirts of the city, more relevant to his needs. He had
come across it by chance and revelled in its collection of old farm
machinery, household furnishings, and bake ovens.

In Shandro, near the town of Andrew, where Bill was staying with his
Uncle Peter and Aunt Rose Huculak, a third museum provided him

with "precious" insights and a wealth of detail. Wasyl Zazula and his wife Anastasia had spearheaded a working group which had begun to construct a Historic Village and Pioneer Museum in 1959. With the aid of the local Ukrainian community, they had started (Zazula remembers) by organizing old-timers; "we started from matches" his wife adds, using a Ukrainian proverb to mean "from nothing". By 1966, a three-acre lot held four buildings, including a log house with a thatched straw roof, an early school, and an Orthodox church.[12]

The Zazulas had yet to reconstruct the *boorday*, which Bill would paint, but they were able to explain the construction of this primitive Ukrainian house to him in detail. They had known the artist's parents, and were surprised that one of his generation could speak Ukrainian. For his part, Bill was surprised by the bitter cold, after Peter's truck got stuck and Bill helped to shovel it free: "Then I had to admit it *was* fierce. Gives me some idea of what my father had to face on his many sleigh trips hauling logs, grain, visiting town etc. And what the earliest pioneers faced when living in sod huts." It is interesting that Bill thought only of his father on this occasion, although his mother had faced the same weather doing a "man's" work, and although the artist's current project was to be in her honor.

During this visit, Bill was typically attracted to the oldest structures. He would photograph them surreptitiously, not wanting to embarrass their owners. The Hawrelek house belonging to Rose's father was greatly admired, and described in detail. Steep, ladder-like steps led up to the bedroom, and down to the cellar lined with preserves and root vegetables: "I love the old style cellar," Bill exclaimed. As he travelled from home to home he collected information, tales, and old photographs.[13] Rose could even remember clay floors at her grandmother's house, floors "made clean and sweet-smelling every Saturday with a thin mixture of cow dung and clay applied with a broom." Bill's preference for old things seems to reflect a feeling that old ways were less materialistic than new ones and thus morally superior.

After a few days Bill left Rose and Peter and moved to the home of his Uncle William Huculak and Aunt Arla. Their farm's fascination lay in the fact that it was the site of his parents' second house and of his own life from ages two to seven. Dmytro and Mary's old house is now a small barn or shed. Bill photographed it from every angle, shooting three rolls of film around the barnyard. His sense of the significance of his life made him marvel at the sites where it had all begun:

> While they were away I used the flash camera inside our
> old home which is now a chicken coop and storage room.
> I had to force myself to believe that those vital years 1 to

6 of my life with its strong and dim memories really took place within those cramped 5 walls [*sic*]. Life is so strange. In the chimney column the chickens now lay their eggs. In that corner stood John's and my crib where I had those fearsome hallucinations. Father and Mother seemed so far away in my insecurity then and yet looking at the dimensions of that room probably about fifteen feet long there was actually no more than *2 or 3* feet between their beds and mine.

The quarter section where he had been born, some three and one-half miles away, elicited similar excitement: "I took three photos of that field for right there in that field I came into this world! Its hard to believe." He longed to paint the area.

The nearby town of Whitford struck Bill as a ghost town, with only a store, a filling station, and "more ghost stores with their peculiar cowboy town false fronts". Another Huculak uncle, George, occupied the large frame farmhouse built by Vasyl Huculak in 1913. Bill writes that his grandfather's house, which once seemed like a palace, had "now gone to rack and ruin."

Some fifty or sixty members of the Huculak clan gathered at the home of Rose and Peter to celebrate Bill's visit. The occasion moved him to reflect: "This is beautiful and healthy country. I could do a lot of painting here. I think I shall be coming back. I have a lot to thank God for even though I am a failure in some things in life. I am also blessed with talent and success in work and income." He leaves his reader to speculate on the areas of failure, but he asks the assembled company to give praise or thanks for his work to God rather than to himself. He repeatedly dated his success from his first exhibition with Isaacs in the spring of 1960. Throughout the visit, Bill managed to produce two paintings a day despite a heavy schedule of visiting and taking notes.

By far the most Ukrainian period of Bill's existence, prior to his last decade in Toronto, had been the Alberta years spent in the little enclave where his people had lived *en bloc* and had temporarily recreated in Canada much of their former life in the old country. In those two highly intense weeks, Bill had recovered much of that heritage. Now, his head filled with images of women in Bukovynian costume, women drawing water and clearing the bush, he set out to capture that life in paint.

If we discount a Cossack tryptych placed at the beginning of the series, the paintings span three-quarters of a century, beginning in 1890. Unlike the series to honor his father, this series did not compose an individual biography of his mother's life but was more general.

Number Eight, entitled *Mama*, consisted of fourteen oval panels showing a small boy's impressions of his farm mother's roles: "She is usually working. Sometimes she is tormentor, sometimes tender, but always there—the pillar of home and farmyard."[14] By praising his mother's virtues, Bill wrote, he had completed his observance of the third commandment and thus given the series a religious dimension. And by ending on what he called a prophetic note, he had reinforced its religious witness.

Bill seemed oblivious to the fact that what he termed religious and prophetic was in fact a denunciation of a large part of his mother's efforts and hopes for her children. Like the 1964 series in honor of his father, this one ended with a text which implicitly repudiated much of his praise. Once again, Bill's heart and head had agreed to differ. His text for Number 20, *Material Success*, runs as follows:

> This is the fourth and last house in the series as suggested by my father illustrating the material advancement of Ukrainians settling in Canada. This time however the scene is from the inside looking out on the previous two houses across the road where a wedding reception is just beginning. The people in the house are related to the wedding couple for there is a good deal of interrelationship in all Ukrainian district such as I was born in in Alberta. They are getting dressed and preparing food consisting of traditional dishes still popular as ever to take to the feast. The person facing the audience is granny (baba) the only original pioneer still living and resting satisfied now to see her children, even her great-grandchildren about her. In one lifetime she remembers as a small girl the family trudging into their homestead where there was no civilization whatever just untouched bush, bears, mosquitoes and wild grass. Now the fields are lush and productive, symbolic of this land of plenty. All the latest gadgets and furniture fill the house. The older children are educated in universities and useful trades. The babies and youngsters are healthy, fattened by vitamin conscious parents. And they still retain some of their cultural heritage.
>
> So what now? The same eternal questions pursue man no matter how many thousands of miles he wanders to put in new roots. What does it profit a man if he gain the whole world yet suffer the loss of his soul? Only the children seem to notice the portentious cloud on the

horizon and communications media turned down and
forgotten for the moment broadcast too late the nemesis
of mere materialism.[15]

The theme of this text prefigures the longer one that accompanies
Harvest of Our Mere Humanism Years, in his book *O Toronto* (1973).
In the "Ukrainian Woman Pioneer in Canada" series, a similar note is
struck at the end of Number 7, *Farmer's Wife Feeding Her Baby in
Hayfield*, where Bill concludes, "would that the motivation for her
industry had been that of the ideal wife of the Book of Proverbs." To
the eye of a modern woman, there is something unconsciously comic
in both the Kurelek text and the rousing chapter that concludes the
Old Testament's definition of ideal womanhood. Bill describes the
pioneer woman working in the fields with the men, nursing her baby
there, and hurrying home "to get up a meal for the menfolk". While the
woman is doing a double job, the farmer "takes a short break", survey-
ing another field and estimating the harvest. The writer of Proverbs
describes a pious superwoman who appears to work forty hours a day.
She buys property from her egg money, weaves her materials, makes
the family's clothing, grows their food, and so on. In life, the lady would
be exhausted; in Scripture, she is "clothed in dignity and power".[16]
Ukrainian culture has always been strongly patriarchal; Bill's very male
eye was perhaps a Ukrainian heritage of which he was unaware.[17]
Mercifully, the texts had very little circulation, and the paintings were
praise indeed for the pioneer women who helped to build this
country.

After 1966, as Bill observed, Ukrainian buyers and friends began to
draw him into the life of their community. He told John and Mary
Stefura of Sudbury that they were his first Ukrainian patrons. In 1967,
Mrs. Stefura helped to arrange an exhibition and sale for the work of
five Ukrainian artists in Sudbury; some ten or twelve Kurelek paintings
were included, although none of them sold. Ukrainian friends and
patrons in Toronto included Gloria and Stanley Frolick, I. Walter
Bardyn, Borden and Ann Cirka, Henry and Stella Slaby, Anna Balan, and
a host of others.[18]

Ethnicity was in the air, as well as the Centennial. The search for
roots was becoming fashionable. Toronto, which had been a WASP
stronghold until the Second World War, was becoming multicultural.
By the mid-sixties, the word "mosaic" had entered the vocabulary of
Canadian sociologists, and was catching the public imagination. Fed-
eral and provincial funding was becoming available to various ethnic
groups bent on preserving and publicizing their heritage. As the
Ukrainian community became proudly self-conscious, Bill was caught

217

Farm Scene Outside Toronto, 1970. Oil on masonite, 31″ x 41″. The Montreal Museum of Fine Arts, Gift of the Ukrainian Cultural Committee. Note the human arms and the crown of thorns in the trash heap (detail). By these symbols Kurelek signified the rejection of Christ by our society.

up in its spirit. "Ukrainian Is Beautiful" might never have become a slogan, but the idea was catching on.[19] As his fame spread in the 1970s, the pressure on Bill to represent the Ukrainian community increased, a situation that may well have appeared threatening to his wife.

UWAC had a lively Montréal branch whose members were also discovering Bill during the Centennial. Maria Logush first saw and admired his work in the Ukrainian Pavilion at Expo 67. She was instrumental in the formation of the Ukrainian Auxiliary Committee of the Montréal Museum of Fine Arts in 1969. The group's first important project was the donation of a Kurelek painting, *Farm Scene Outside Toronto*. Like their Toronto sisters, the members were initially sceptical because of Bill's unflattering depiction of Ukrainians in Canada ("that's not us, it's some stone people") and because of the ruthless integrity of many of his farm scenes. Many of the women had actually experienced the hardships he was painting and were not eager to recall them.[20]

The visionary scene shows a prosperous farm perched on a hill beneath a threatening sky. Its focus lies in the left foreground, where a pile of junk by a farm gate includes two outstretched, blood-stained arms and a crown of thorns. Bill consented to attend the gala presentation to the Museum, on the condition that he could show the one hundred and sixty slides of his Passion series in the afternoon.[21] Mrs. Logush continued to follow his career with interest. She made the family cottage available to the artist as a painting retreat in the spring of 1971, and was responsible for further Kurelek exhibitions in the 1970s, including one in the fall of 1972 consisting of seventy-nine drawings of Ukrainian utensils and artifacts.[22] Other prominent Ukrainian admirers and patrons in Montréal included Dr. and Mrs. E. Klemchuk.

Among paintings on Ukrainian themes seen in the Montréal area is a small masterpiece entitled *A Little Lick* (1970).[23] It depicts a woman making *warennyky* or *pyrohy*, working on scarred oilcloth with a wooden knife; a small girl watches, rapt, while her little brother licks the edges of the pastry turnovers. Drops of perspiration stand out on the mother's face. The background contains an old wooden chest, its open lid barely discernible in the gloom, and above it a framed portrait of the nineteenth-century poet and patriot Taras Shevchenko. The handling of composition, color, chiaroscuro, and theme is expertly done. As Bill acknowledged in 1973, the Ukrainian influence on his work could be very fruitful.

Bill's steadily increasing circle of Ukrainian contacts and friends in the late sixties served to educate him further in things Ukrainian. When he stayed for two weeks in 1967 with Dr. Konstatin Peryma and his wife Aka in their home near Troy, Ohio, the doctor read aloud in Ukrainian while Bill painted. Peryma read folktales and stories by Vasyl Stefanyk, whose writing (Bill observed) has been compared with Kurelek's art by the Ukrainian art critic Stebelski. Bill greatly enjoyed the tales because Stefanyk uses a simple Bukovynian dialect similar to Dmytro's, and deals with a simple people, rather like Maxim Gorki.[24] Bill found it soothing to hear Ukrainian ("my father's Ukrainian at that") and to enjoy the doctor's respect for his hard work and creativity. Bill credits this experience with having a maturing effect upon him: the implication is that another part of the vast wound he sustained regarding his father had been healed. "It sure was nice," he adds, "to talk Ukrainian for two weeks."[25]

Nice or not, Bill grudged the Perymas their cup of conversation out of his intensive work schedule: "The studio separate from the house was unheated in winter so I had to muck in with the family in an upstairs bedroom and they wanted and expected me to socialize. . . . I set my sights on three 'potboilers' per day . . . and had to put my foot down with the Perymas even to the point of being rude or asocial."

Bill had told his Toronto audience in 1973 that his ethnicity and his religious faith were inseparable. This had been unexpectedly demonstrated in connection with the Passion series. Gloria Ochitwa of Port Credit, Ontario, a free-lance art consultant, had seen a few of the St. Matthew paintings in a local Toronto church. She was moved by their power ("they stayed in my mind very strongly") and was eventually responsible for the entire series being shown in the Art Gallery of St. Vladimir Institute, the new cultural centre for Canadian-born Ukrainians in Toronto. Art reviewer Kay Kritzwiser described the tempera-on-masonite paintings as having a relentless force; St. Matthew's final prophecy of the consummation of the world is "all purple fire and Kurelek at his brimstone best".[26] It was a first showing for the series in its entirety, and the first formal exhibition in the new institute, February 26, 1970. Press coverage was excellent, and attendance high. The exhibition crackled with excitement.[27] Ola and Mykola Kolankiwsky were among those who saw it, and they were smitten.

The Kolankiwskys had come to Canada from the Western Ukraine, via Paris, in 1955. They were lovers of art, and collectors. In Toronto, they opened first one gallery, then two more; all were named after the initials of the Ukrainian-language magazine *We and the World*, which Mykola Kolankiwsky edited and published. The W and W Gallery Yonge was near The Isaacs Gallery, and a friendship soon sprang up between Bill and the Kolankiwskys on the basis of their common heritage. Kolankiwsky writes that Bill had already shown them a few paintings from the Passion series in the early sixties: "Afterwards, he used to enjoy, at our expense, relating the story of how we turned him down."[28] At that time, the Kolankiwskys had no resources to promote an unknown Ukrainian artist. They would eventually redeem themselves by the purchase of the entire series in 1970.

Bill would always remember that meeting and decision:

> There was a knock on the door that evening. My wife was
> peeved somewhat for it was right at suppertime. I let the
> Kolankiwskys in. They were obviously excited. They said
> that they had come right over to see me for they had been
> so impressed by the Passion series that they wanted to
> buy it in its entirety and house it in the Art Gallery and
> Museum they were planning to build in Niagara Falls. I
> was flabbergasted. . . . I had practically no hope of selling
> the paintings. It was enough that I had made slides and

Interior of part of the Niagara Falls Art Gallery and Museum where Kurelek's 160 St. Matthew Passion paintings are displayed. Note the Black Madonna which fits perfectly in the space left. Courtesy Mrs. Ola Kolankiwsky.

that the right to reproduce them for missionary use had been assumed by a monastery in New Jersey. ... It was a real act of faith on their part both from a spiritual and economic point of view.[29]

The sale was shortly closed, and by the summer of 1971 the gallery was open to visitors. Bill was only forty-four. To have a gallery devoted largely to his work at this young age was success indeed.

How had the matter been managed with such speed? For years the Kolankiwskys had dreamed of having a gallery to feature the work of a single artist, impressionist painter Mykola Krychevsky. Plans for the building were under way by the late sixties. At St. Vladimir, the dream was suddenly reshaped.

Today the Niagara Falls Art Gallery stands at 8058 Oakwood Drive near the McLeod Road exit from the Queen Elizabeth Way. Stern and beautiful, the red-brick structure was designed by Montréal architect Radoslav Zuk. The main area is circular, like a windowless tower, with two of its five levels below ground. The directors, the Kolankiwskys, live on the top floor, and the Kurelek paintings occupy the fourth.

The hanging of the one hundred and sixty works proved to be high drama. Working against time for the summer opening, the Kolankiwskys hung the paintings in their proper sequence close together on the main floor without pre-measurement. Not only did they fit exactly, with no space left over, but the painting depicting the central point in the Passion narrative ("And they crucified him") happened to be positioned in the room's natural centre, beside a niche which seemed destined to hold the Black Madonna, an eighteenth-century icon from the Ukraine. When Bill arrived and saw the perfect fit he exclaimed, "This is a miracle!"[30]

Within weeks of the Kolankiwskys' decision to buy the Passion series, and before the deal had been closed, Bill elected to accompany them on a three-week trip to the Ukraine. The Kolankiwskys were organizing a tour for Canadian and American artists in Kiev, Lvov, Kharkov, Odessa, Zaporizhzha, and Poltava. They were surprised and delighted when Bill decided to go.[31] He had obtained a private patron who would pay his way in return for two paintings.

He felt guilty about leaving Jean with the children during his increasingly frequent trips, but his guilt is curious, considering that his household help was minimal at the best of times. On this occasion he wrote to her from the Ukraine to say, "although its a beautiful and interesting country I shouldnt have been here when youre back there looking after the house and children."[32]

Bill was wary of guided tours in general and of Intourist authorities in particular. His fears were fully justified. In the long diary that provides a day-by-day account of this trip, Bill writes that guided tours are *forced*: a prison and a bore. Occasionally, the group was expected to admire a Soviet triumph such as a vast power station and dam on the Dnieper: "you know how mechanical or electrical things bore me." More frequently, they were shown churches converted to museums, and expected to eat large meals. Bill enjoyed brief visits to art galleries in the major cities of the Soviet Ukraine, and lived for the day when he might be allowed to visit his father's village of Borivtsi.

His hopes vacillated. To Shorey, he wrote that getting into local villages was a long and tedious affair, usually futile; his group leader, however, had connections in official Soviet circles that might help: "My sponsor believes I'm as yet apolitical enough to be allowed into my father's village specially since I seem to have gained some reputation as a Ukrainian artist even over there."[33] Seven Kurelek cousins were awaiting his arrival. During the first days in the Soviet Ukraine, it seemed likely that permission for the private visit would be denied, but luck was with Bill. Permission for a one-day trip was finally granted.

Bill describes his visit to Borivtsi in superlatives. It was the highlight of the trip, one of the biggest days of his life, an agony and an ecstasy. Two Intourist guides accompanied him on the long drive to the village by the private taxi for which he had paid. In heavy rain, the trip took five hours each way over a narrow road filled with potholes. Asphalt turned to gravel, then to deeply rutted mud. The guides were upset at the lack of a tourist-type restaurant, while Bill was upset by the prospect of political conversations (he intended to abstain) or the possibility of somehow incriminating the villagers. As they approached Borivtsi, he was fascinated to find that the vast rolling fields of wind-swept black earth resembled Alberta. This was not the grey, sheltered country of his imagination. People wore quilted coats, or sheepskin jackets. The photos garnered from Alberta relatives were coming to life.

Dmytro had provided him with a hand-drawn map which proved surprisingly accurate and serviceable, despite the passing of nearly fifty years. Their arrival in Borivtsi startled and delighted the villagers. Deeply moved, Bill reacted to them all as to long-lost family:

> Everyone was the same, unkempt, dirty but excitable
> and as lovable as children. From then on, things were just
> a jumble of greetings, recollections, being pulled this way
> and that. ... It was like I'd dropped out of heaven. ... They
> had heard of me on the radio. Some even mentioned Nina
> Krushchev remark on me during her visit to the States. ...
> We went over to THE HOUSE where father was born and
> lived. ... The people were so likeable and simple, I knew I
> was with my roots. This is the real Ukraine.[34]

The homes were dark and dirty, but Bill was excited by their style and by the furnishings, many of which resembled ones he had seen in museums in Saskatchewan and Alberta: "the cheap calendar icons, the little windows, the loaf of bread on the bed, the pail of slops." He and his guides were treated to an outdoor feast, buffet style. Mercifully, the rain had stopped when they arrived in the village. There was a name-sake, one William Kurelek, aged three or four: "He had such a Ukrain-ian Boy face." Plied with anecdotes, tales, and proverbs, Bill concluded that the people were "innocent as children, yet crafty as philosophers". He was finally dragged away by the impatient chauffeur and two guides. Rain started again as they reached the highway. Had it con-tinued throughout the day, they could not have reached the village.

Bill had had four hours in Borivtsi, under supervision, and had left it with the determination to return. It would be seven years before this dream was fulfilled, in a dark and tragic way. During the 1970 tour, he was asked repeatedly if he felt Canadian or Ukrainian. After Borivtsi, he would always reply that he didn't know, but now knew how to find out:

> Let the authorities let me come back to spend six weeks
> painting the real (to me) Ukrainian people in their day to
> day life, not the townspeople, not the intelligentsia. ... Let

me live with these people, dress as they dress, eat their food, sleep on the *peech*. Let me wander freely from village to village in Bukovina ... as Van Gogh did in Holland and France. This is the real Ukraine and if it speaks louder to me than the farmlands and life of the farm people in Canada, then I will know that I am Ukrainian and not Canadian. ... I know my proposal is impossible.[35]

The impossible takes longer. He would eventually be granted three weeks, at a time when he was exhausted by illness. He began by applying to the Soviet Embassy in Ottawa in 1970 for a six-week visa for 1971; thereafter he suffered the disappointments of delay, year after year.

His trip diary illumines his very personal concept of what subjects were suitable for his work. His art sprang from emotional depths connected with his early life on the farm, his ethnic heritage, and the deeply felt ideas and beliefs of his religious faith. In the Ukraine in 1970, he wrote with loving enthusiasm of steep thatched roofs, of chickens on a rail beside a row of people, a strutting white gobbler, old wagons, a cat "decorating" a roof end: these were "delightful, paintable subjects". The shabby dark interiors in the village were "all so paintable and alive". The life of the peasants, he wrote, spoke to him as an artist as it did to Van Gogh, a favorite comparison. He was drawn to the old ways, always: ways seen as more human, more satisfying, more spiritual, and therefore "paintable".

While in the Ukraine, Bill had managed to get five paintings done by using every spare moment and by working at night. The trip was also a partial inspiration for a series of six large paintings done the following year after the opening of the Kolankiwskys' gallery. Bill was planning to donate a six-part mural for a gallery wall, a pictorial narrative to celebrate the part played by Ukrainian pioneers in the development of the Canadian West. The directors encouraged him to paint on individual panels so that the work could be moved should it become necessary. In 1980, after Bill's death, the series would appear in book form. The paintings would eventually be sold to the Government of Canada in 1983 and hang in the Railway Committee Room of the House of Commons. The editor's Introduction gives the details of its construction in the fall of 1971, and the artist's text witnesses to the significant part played by his Ukrainian heritage in his art: "My grandparents cut their farm from the bush, and my childhood recollections of an old culture in a new land have profoundly influenced all my work."[36] After seeing that old culture in its original setting, the transplanted version meant even more to Bill. His mural was a labor of love. The book delighted readers in 1980, and still charms:

The Ukrainian Pioneer is an intriguing book into which
one enters—or burrows—slowly, almost circuitously.
Slight at first sight, it reveals itself only gradually and
echoes in the mind after being closed.

It consists largely of colour photographs of a six-
panelled painting. ... One double-page spread of all six
panels is followed by photos of the individual paintings
and a series of close-ups. The effect of this technique,
coupled with the power of Kurelek's painting and his love
of detail, is to give the viewer the feeling of entering the
paintings, of being there.

The paintings depict the poverty and oppression of a
Ukrainian village; the sea voyage to Canada; first confrontation with bush and forest; summer and winter farm
scenes; and harvest, dominated by a golden sea stretching
to infinity and a farmer, waist-high in wheat, who contemplates a handful of grain. Biblical parables and allusions
are never far from Kurelek's work.[37]

Among the most fascinating paintings to emerge from Bill's contact
with the Ukrainian community is his set of seventy-two drawings
illustrating Ivan Franko's folktale *Fox Mykyta*. Its genesis and gestation
form a curious story from 1974 to 1978, when Bohdan Melnyk's
translation of Franko's best-known work was published with the
Kurelek illustrations. Melnyk, a Ukrainian-born writer and translator,
particularly admired the nineteenth-century Ukrainian patriot. After
seeing *The Maze*, the film based on Bill's life, on television, Melnyk
wrote to Bill to request illustrations for his translation. He described
Franko as the giant of Ukrainian literature, and his humorous animal
story as one that dealt with universal human problems in allegoric
form. Melnyk noted that Bill had recently praised the Toronto folk
festival "Caravan" as an example of the Canadian way of assimilation by
mosaic, not melting-pot. In line with Bill's own emphasis on the
sharing of cultural traditions, Melnyk proposed that Franko's classic
should become "part and parcel of our common Canadian culture".[38]

Bill knew nothing of Franko, but gallantly wrote that it would be an
honor to illustrate such a Ukrainian classic—should time permit; he
was so pressured by commitments for the balance of the year that
there was no possibility of beginning such a project before 1975.
Subsequent correspondence revealed legal difficulties between Melnyk and his previous publisher. Bill had a horror of such squabbles. By
the end of December he had decided to work on the drawings during
his two-week trip to Lourdes in February of 1975. He would carry the
verse translation with him to France. As for the money, Bill told Melnyk

not to worry about royalty arrangements. God had blessed him with prosperity beyond his wildest dreams, and any money which the book might generate for him was earmarked for relief to impoverished Ukrainians in Brazil.

Bill kept his word, completing seventy-three drawings in black ink while at Lourdes: six per chapter, with an extra one for Melnyk to show to prospective publishers. He was dubious about the book's being accepted for children because of its violence. He had had (he wrote Melnyk) "paintings and stories for books much less cruel than Fox the Sly rejected on the grounds it won't sell." The small drawings were approximately five inches square. Photographs of them were being forwarded.

Melnyk was delighted, until events took a strange turn. The drawings were to be exhibited by the Kolankiwskys at a Kurelek Festival in their gallery that July. In the spring, Mykola Kolankiwsky included part of Bill's interpretive Foreword to *Fox Mykyta* in *We and the World*, the Ukrainian-language magazine that he edited and published. Franko's translated text had made Bill uneasy at the time and distinctly critical upon reflection. Did Franko (he asks Melynk) expect us to *admire* his hero? The rascally fox was cynical, cruel, and unscrupulous. You could hardly call him *Christian*, Bill wrote, and his behavior was no more acceptable than that of the "violent, licentious worldly heroes" foisted upon us by the commercial media.

He considered Franko's own behavior equally suspect. It had begun to dawn on Bill that the Ukrainian patriot was actually anticlerical. His fox used clerical disguises for selfish ends. Bill acknowledged that Melnyk had told him of the corruption of the Ukrainian church in Franko's time, and of clerical abuse of authority. However, Bill refused to be party to an attack on the priesthood, which he called "a sacred thing designed by God for our salvation through the sacraments it dispenses". Franko had made peace with the Church on his deathbed, but Bill felt this was hardly enough to compensate for the "jungle philosophy" of his tale.

The heavy, moralistic Foreword is typical of one of Bill's least attractive sides. He could be remarkably obtuse at times. Despite his comparison of *Fox Mykyta* with *Gulliver's Travels*, and despite his reference to the book's political overtones, Bill misses the story's moral point. In the folk tradition of the lovable rogue, Fox lives by his courage and his wits. His actions suggest that God helps those who help themselves in this "beautiful, cruel world". Since greed, hypocrisy, opportunism are often self-defeating, Fox astutely plays upon these moral flaws. The drawings sparkle with the energy, humor, and hard-won wisdom of both Franko and Kurelek. It seems extraordinary that

Bohdan Melnyk, translator of *Fox Mykyta*, illustrated by Bill, and published in 1978 after his death. Courtesy Mr. B. Melnyk.

part of Bill could respond to the tale on a creative level while another part of his mind was busy preparing a grand denunciation.

Franko's comedy, like those of Shakespeare, draws the community together at the end in a spirit of reconciliation. King Lion praises the fox for defending his rights, offers to let bygones be bygones, and condemns hatred. The fox also expresses a wish to forget old quarrels and hatreds. Bill seemed oblivious to the spirit of Franko's closing, and Melnyk had good reason to be upset with his Foreword. It was hardly calculated to help sell the book, and the translator considered it grossly untrue with regard to Franko. Melnyk and his wife were stymied by Bill's respect for unscrupulous priests, Franko's target. Since the Melnyks believed in Bill's personal rectitude, they concluded that he held to a medieval way of thinking.

Bill had not anticipated Melnyk's dismay at the Foreword, nor did the artist expect his diatribe to offend Ukrainian-Canadians in general. The project hung fire for two years, while the translator hoped that the artist would change his mind and permit his illustrations to be used without the damning Foreword. At one point the Shevchenko Foundation in Winnipeg was interested in the manuscript and Melnyk's hopes began to revive. He suggested that Bill might like to illustrate his translation of Franko's *Moses*. Once again, he stressed that they should share this great writer with the non-Ukrainian world. By 1976, Bill seemed ready to waive his insistence on the inclusion of the Foreword.

With his death, the project took off. Melnyk came to an agreement with the artist's widow and with May Cutler of Tundra Books, Bill's primary publisher. Unfortunately for the translator, who loved his creation like a child, May Cutler did not believe in verse narrative for modern children, and insisted that Melnyk rewrite the story in prose.[39] A few of his rhymed couplets survive as chapter headings: "When tolerance and reason reign/Then life for all is sweet again". Critics greeted the book enthusiastically, blissfully unaware that Kurelek's relation to Franko's text had been anything other than "fun-filled" (a favorite critical tag).[40] Typical comments were: "Kurelek responded with gusto to the wicked wit of Ivan Franko's classic retelling of the Reynard the Fox tales";[41] "a charmer". The clever fox was called "the con artist everyone wants to be conned by".[42] The book was chosen as a "Best of the Best" by the International Youth Library. Its publication, in November of 1978, was marked by an exhibition of the drawings at The Isaacs Gallery.

A briefer project, in 1972-73, led to Bill's illustrating the history of a Ukrainian-Canadian family from Stuartburn in southeastern Manitoba. Theodosy Wachna had led thirty Ukrainian families there in 1897, establishing one of the oldest Ukrainian settlements in Canada. Bill accepted the family commission and went to the area in the fall of 1972. By that time the bush had reclaimed much of the settlers' work. Bill found the skeletal remains of a thatched house with a haunted, abandoned feeling: "It was as if the mournful wind blowing through the uprooted weeds were the ghosts of departed pioneers sighing for the old times."[43] He saw the oldest Orthodox church in Canada and was touched by "its honest cheapness (all the ikons were only calendar religious pictures surrounded by plastic flowers)". His illustrations for the Wachna family history include two paintings which grace the cover and a number of black-and-white drawings of community life and implements.

In the mid-seventies, the heightened sense of ethnicity that had been growing in Bill for a decade issued in a series of paintings on some of the various groups that compose the Canadian mosaic: the Jews, the Inuit, the French, the Irish, and the Poles. The first was done with a view to repaying a debt to his dealer and his earliest patrons: "I wasn't thinking of doing it in terms of the various groups," Bill told Abraham Arnold in 1977.[44] He had met Arnold, who became his collaborator on *Jewish Life in Canada*, at the Toronto conference on ethnicity in 1973.

That public talk had served as the catalyst for Bill's hard look at the role his Ukrainian roots had played in his career, and would play in years to come. Four years later, he told Arnold that his wife's Irish background had triggered the Irish series, and that Québec separatism had led to the French-Canadian one, through his desire to promote peace and understanding between people. Talking with Arnold, Bill revealed his deep need for attention and admiration, needs established through the deprivations of his early years: "The Irish and the French-Canadians which I did last year I feel were flops in the sense of the reaction. There was no feedback, there was no enthusiasm, there was no follow-up like the Jewish." By follow-up, Bill meant primarily publication in book form. He was also strongly disappointed to find that the latter two exhibitions attracted relatively little media attention, and was cut to the quick by a single critic's verdict that he was not the right person to have illustrated W. O. Mitchell's prairie novel *Who Has Seen the Wind* (1976), because he (allegedly) had no gift for interpreting the Anglo-Saxon community.

It is clear from the March 1977 talk with Arnold that Bill intended to head in a different direction *unless* his series on Canadian ethnic groups led to publications and favorable attention in the media: "I'm not going to just waste my time by trying to do something I'm not suited for." Arnold's attempt to convince the artist that his judgement was premature fell on deaf ears.

To Anna Balan, Bill's ethnic paintings confirmed the ethnic diversity of our society as a concrete Canadian reality: "Initially and essentially they assured Kurelek financial security, allowed him to support his numerous charities, and gave him the artistic freedom to paint what he truly wanted."[45] Bill's own thoughts, in 1973, were similar. Know yourself, he advised, and know your race, with its weakness and its strength. No group was perfect, none should be idealized, nor should anyone feel ashamed of his cultural background. Most importantly, our multicultural society should be seen in the context of the whole family of man: "put God first and ones nationality or ethnic origin second." This creed was written on his bones and flowing in his veins: *God first*.

229

13

Promoters and Friends: The Circle Widens

BY THE LATE SIXTIES, BILL WAS ESTABLISHED AS A LEADING CANADIAN ARTIST, thanks in part to the promotion of his work by one of the country's leading dealers. In the last eight or nine years of his life, his reputation would spread rapidly through films, publications, and travel. A film on Kurelek made by educational psychologist James Maas in the United States received wide circulation in North America and Britain. Meanwhile, Bill's own perspective was widening as his travels took him to Canada's Arctic and around the world.

A reciprocal loyalty between Bill and his dealer is one of the central facts of the artist's career. The relationship puzzled a great many people because the two men seemed so dissimilar. Both came from the Winnipeg area, but one was rural and religious in a deeply traditional way while the other was the essence of modernity and sophistication.

Avrom Isaacs was only slightly older than Bill, but must have seemed older because of his experience in the art world which Bill, in 1959, was determined to enter. The dealer believes that Bill saw him as a father-figure, especially in the 1960s; consequently, the artist struggled to maintain his independence and equality in the relationship.[1] Since Bill had acquired an ideal father in 1955 through his faith, I suspect that the dealer was more an elder brother than a foster-parent to the artist. Whatever the metaphor used, there was a benevolent strength in Isaacs to which Bill responded. Obviously, there were tensions, difficulties, arguments, as there are in any close relationship, but goodwill and mutual trust predominated. Referring to their regular correspondence, Isaacs wrote to Bill in 1967: "I very much enjoy receiving your notes even if they are sometimes caused by differences of opinion."[2]

Gratitude to Isaacs and to his Jewish customers had sparked Bill's series of paintings on Jewish life in Canada.[3] This appreciation was voiced very frequently, to the dealer himself and to others. "I am always grateful to you for 'making' me as an artist," Bill wrote in 1966.[4] Strong words. In a letter to Shorey, he credited his immediate fame to Isaacs' effective promotion, while giving God thanks for whatever lasting genius he might have. He consistently dated his breakthrough to success from his first exhibition at The Isaacs Gallery in 1960, and never forgot that the dealer at that time had taken a chance on a totally unknown artist. Since then, he wrote, the dealer had continued to sell, promote, and exhibit his work very effectively: "I don't mind repeating too that you are the most understanding and generous employer I've ever had."[5] The artist's Foreword to *The Passion of Christ* describes his dealer as the person who had done most for him after Margaret Smith, the occupational therapist at the Maudsley Hospital: "It was he who first recognized the merit of my work and took the risk of exhibiting it. And he has been promoting it ever since."[6]

Since childhood, Bill had found silence a defence and a means of avoiding confrontations. Indeed, he much preferred written to verbal communication in general. "I have always written: when I made a proposal of marriage, when I finally complained to my father about his treatment of me, when I have differences with my dealer or boss, even with my wife" (May 22, 1977). Hence a sizeable correspondence between Bill and Isaacs came into existence, despite the frequency of their actual encounters. Whenever information had to be exchanged, Bill would write to Isaacs, who took the cue from his artist and replied in kind. Bill also wrote during his numerous painting trips outside Toronto. A bulky correspondence on a rather extraordinary range of topics survives. These include family concerns as seen through the eyes of the financial provider.

On Bill's side, the correspondence was often emotional and theoret-

Av Isaacs, Bill's dealer.
Photo by L. Pavlychenko,
courtesy The Isaacs
Gallery.

ical as well as practical; on Isaacs', good-humored, patient, and pragmatic. Both complained periodically that the system had problems, but for nearly two decades it worked. Isaacs' letters began "My dear Bill" or "Dear Willy"; Bill's, "Dear Av". He once signed himself "Your gadfly". Letters that dealt with difficult matters Bill jokingly called "love letters".[7] Both men indulged their sense of humor from time to time. When Bill wrote from Montréal describing his fasting and noting that his total daily restaurant bill was twenty cents for a glass of milk, Isaacs sent him that sum to cover a day's food, adding "don't ever say that your dealer is not a big spender."[8]

Isaacs was always the sole agent for Kurelek's work in Canada; exhibitions at other galleries were arranged through him. Rather remarkably, business arrangements between Isaacs and Kurelek remained unwritten. Their verbal contract was scrupulously observed on both sides. Bill was minutely exact in business dealings which concerned his conscience, to the point of repaying to his employer the difference between the wholesale and retail price of ink on one occasion when he was forced to buy a bottle in order to get on with his framing work for the gallery.[9] He was careful to see that the dealer got forty per cent on every private sale, with the exception of those sold directly to close friends and relatives. The definition of a close friend could be sticky, but Bill felt grateful that Isaacs had left him this degree of freedom at a time when the dealer might easily have opted for total control.[10]

Tensions remained. Indeed few, if any, of Bill's relationships were tension-free, given his difficult childhood, his super-sensitive personality, and his hyperactive conscience. Bill was keen to sell privately, since he desperately needed income over and above the regular monthly allowance sent by the gallery.

The Isaacs Gallery paid to Kurelek a monthly stipend from his own credit account. This totalled $500 a month through the mid-sixties, $600 in the late sixties, $1,000 in the early seventies, and $2,000 in the mid-seventies. The cheque was frequently one or even two weeks late, and a reminder might be necessary. This situation embarrassed Kurelek and frequently precipitated a flood of detailed financial explanations by way of apology.[11]

Private sales provided a pleasant opportunity to socialize, and a source of ready cash outside the Gallery's slow and (to Bill) unwieldy system of accounting. On his side, Isaacs granted Bill's right to make direct sales but continued to harbor the suspicion that private customers were exploiting the artist and wasting his valuable time.[12] The tensions implicit in these positions continued throughout the eighteen years of this singular friendship and business association.[13]

Isaacs' letters included advice, offered in a friendly, low-key manner. There was the frequent proviso that decisions were "of course" Bill's. The dealer habitually advised the artist to take life easier and to work at a slower pace: "I have always personally marvelled at how hard you worked. As far as I'm concerned you could lie on a sandy beach for two years doing nothing, and my only thought would be that you deserved every second of it."[14] From the late sixties on, Isaacs frequently expressed his concern that Bill was painting too quickly, spreading himself too thin. He might as well have tried, like Canute, to hold back the tide. Bill continued to work fifteen- and eighteen-hour days. The dealer advised Bill to use nothing but the best-quality paper, and permanent ink: on one occasion, his signature was followed by "The Society for the Preservation of William Kurelek as a Cultural Fountain".[15] Minimum prices were also a concern. Isaacs considered himself the official guardian of every aspect of the artist's public career; he felt it his responsibility, in short, to see that the artist and his paintings were properly treated.[16]

Bill's habit of making copies of his work (whether for profit, convenience, or customer satisfaction) remained a thorn in his dealer's side. Over the years, Isaacs tried without success to discourage the practice. He then urged that the size of subsequent versions should vary, and that there should be some noticeable differences in composition or subject matter: "I think the word 'copy' should be removed from our vocabulary. I prefer to see these paintings as a continuum in a series."[17] Bill did vary the details on occasion, but in general Isaacs' cautions against copying his own work fell on deaf ears. Copies of his favorite paintings were highly saleable, and the extra income they provided was badly needed.

Bill suffered from a chronic shortage of money to meet the needs of his growing family. His frenetic work habits were due in part to his attempt to maintain a middle-class standard of living without debt. In 1966, for example, his income totalled approximately twelve thousand dollars; of this only one-quarter had been taxed at the source, namely his salary as a framer and finisher for The Isaacs Gallery.[18] The need for money to pay his income tax caused a crisis each spring, one usually solved by painting faster. The trip to Ohio in February of 1967, for example, had been undertaken in order to paint a series for the Galerie Agnès Lefort in Montréal, an exhibition undertaken with a view to raising a lump sum of money for Revenue Canada.

In numerous letters to Isaacs, Bill details the saga of his financial crises, with a touching sincerity and humility, and a genuine concern for the dealer's problems, too. Charities added considerably to Bill's expenses, but he had no intention of curtailing them. The letters are brave, sad, and unintentionally comic:

> Once again the $500 is gone—poof—just like that. I know
> you have told me you're not interested in my financial
> affairs and the only reason I'm quoting you the sums
> above is to prove to you I am not merely being money
> mad. Also I am supporting various people in under-
> developed countries—Korea, Hong Kong, Vietnam, India,
> South America, etc. ... It's no use saying that I should look
> after my own needs first and then what's left over give to
> these other people. The fact remains they are hungry and
> cold NOW and need help *now*.[19]

The notion of this frugal artist as money-mad must have raised a smile on the dealer's face. Bill concluded that he *must* sell privately, for extra income. He would stop the practice, he assured Isaacs, when he was in the clear, perhaps the next year. That day, of course, never came.

Isaacs' brother Nathan became the artist's accountant in the late 1960s, providing another ear for Bill's financial woes. The dealer's failure to appreciate the difference to Bill of cash in hand versus credit in a gallery account was a source of continual frustration. Bill feared and hated debt, preferring to "do without" wherever possible rather than buy on credit. Cash flow remained a problem. To his accountant, he wrote of the short-term loss of an individual sale, where the cheque had been made payable to the Gallery through a misunderstanding:

> I had been counting on that $250.00 to pay for the paving
> of our driveway because my wife has been asking 3 years
> already to have it done to stop our kids and the neigh-
> bours digging potholes in it. Av showed me the cheque
> but I didn't really get it because it went into my account.
> Its comparable to pouring a bucket of drinking water into
> a cistern just as I was specially thirsty. I know that $250
> ($150. really after 40% is deducted) will eventually come
> to me via the $600 [monthly allowance] cheques but
> meantime I have no driveway. Do you see what I mean? ...
> I hate concerning myself about money and I don't want to
> be thought of as materialistic or money grasping. After all
> its the false god I condemn in my paintings and I really do
> want to practice what I preach.[20]

Bill realized that much of his reluctance to discuss money matters in person stemmed from childhood and his relation to his father. He told the accountant that he continued to see a psychiatrist once a month, in an attempt to root out his remaining phobias. These included a fear of using the telephone, because his father had been the only one to use it in their home: "I associated it with maturity and he continually berated me for immaturity." The letters reveal the distance Bill had come and the distance he had still to go. Within a few years he would be confidently addressing students in an auditorium at Cornell, and an audience of physicians in the lecture hall of the very psychiatric hospital where he had been a patient.

One of the interesting themes in the Kurelek/Isaacs correspondence concerns the handling of religious and didactic paintings. Isaacs never exhibited the Passion series, but he did promote and show many of Bill's "message" paintings. As early as 1964, he wrote to the artist to praise four works that formed the start of Bill's second major didactic series:

> I was so excited by what I saw. . . . You are combining all
> your gifts, intensities, profound beliefs, etc. Your feelings
> for the land, your religious beliefs (broadly speaking). . . . I
> don't know if the show will sell and I don't care. I will be
> proud to exhibit it (but I think it will sell). I know that
> life has not been easy for you, and probably because it has
> not, your creative gifts have been heightened. . . . Your
> thinking has matured a great deal since the [first] didactic
> show, which means that I agree with you now a great deal
> more.[21]

Despite this encouragement, Bill was upset by negative criticism of his second didactic exhibition, and lumped Isaacs together with the "intelligentsia" who opposed it. Bill wrote that he was unable to stop doing such paintings since they represented the most important things he had to say and since they were also a kind of therapy or release for him. He had, however, decided to stop selling such work through a commercial gallery. Expecting Isaacs to support it would be neither reasonable nor fair. He thanked his dealer for being a philanthropist, adding that St. Peter would open the door of heaven for him when no one was looking and bar it to some church-goers he knew.[22]

Isaacs replied that such a decision was entirely up to Bill. The artist was clearly ambivalent, and indeed the decision not to show message paintings in commercial galleries was short-lived. Bill continued to hope that some day he might find a patron to support what he saw as his serious paintings, and possibly a building that would be devoted to them, like Stanley Spencer's Burghclere Chapel in England.[23] He also thought that these paintings might be donated to institutions, or given to people in return for the promise of their support for one or two foster-children abroad. What *was* clear (he wrote) was that he could not stop painting such works. He was already bursting with new ideas. In retrospect, the decision seems to have been a temporary reaction to Harry Malcolmson's review in March 1966, which Bill described as the first seriously adverse criticism he had ever received. After 1966, his shows at The Isaacs Gallery usually contained a mixture of different types of paintings. Ironically, Isaacs served as advocate and broker in arranging for the series "The Last Days" in Montréal at the Galerie Godard Lefort in 1971.[24]

Gradually, the silent witness in paint began to find vocal expression on public platforms. Much to his own surprise, Bill was becoming a public speaker. The motivation to conquer his shyness was always, in his view, to witness to his faith: "It was the yearning to share the good news of the Gospel that drove me into actual public speaking" (A1 512). He never credited his increased social confidence to his growing success as an artist, although the relationship between the two seems evident. Nor did he ever publicly acknowledge his psychological need for success to show to his father.

Looking back over the twenty years prior to the publication of his first autobiography, Bill saw the beginnings of his later social ease as one result of his conversion. First there had been Margaret, then the Little Club, where Catholic acquaintances were friendly and welcoming. With faith, Bill also acquired the *desire* to relate to his fellows, in order to witness to Christ; "charisma" could be used to advance the Kingdom. He writes of realizing "the great need to become, as St. Paul puts it, 'all things to all men' in a real secular world" (A1 509), adding that his parents had recommended the right thing but for the wrong reason.[25] He was convinced that serving Mass daily had helped his sociability, although for much of the 1960s he was unable to even look at the other worshippers (A1 511). There were times when Bill saw God as his personal promoter: "... He so arranged that in my case there was an actual demand for my talks. He made me a minor celebrity overnight despite myself." (A1 512)

Certainly opportunities to speak publicly were becoming more frequent. By the late 1960s, Bill was finding himself in the limelight, and loving it, despite his nervousness. The Maas story is part of that growth. The two men proved useful to one another, and became friends. Through Dr. James Maas, Bill would participate in an award-winning documentary film on his life, and the publication of his autobiography, a goal he had long sought. Maas made it possible for him to comment on his slides to an audience of some twelve hundred students in a university concert hall, an accomplishment of which a shy person could be justly proud. For a man attempting to be all things to all men in the service of Christ, it was a step of some magnitude. He spoke of his childhood and hospitalization; of his Hound of Heaven series (i.e. "Nature, Poor Stepdame", 1970), and of the appalling scenes he had witnessed in India the previous year. His syntax was broken, his thought occasionally incoherent. No one could call his talk a lecture. But Bill spoke to that enormous audience and his voice, Maas recalls, was strong.[26]

Dr. James Maas of Cornell University, who arranged to have Bill's autobiography published and to have the film *The Maze* made of Bill's life. Courtesy Dr. J. Maas.

Dr. Maas of Cornell University is a professor of psychology, with a special interest in undergraduate education. In the late 1960s, he had signed a contract with Houghton Mifflin to produce a series of films and other teaching materials for introductory psychology courses. His search for these materials led him to London's Maudsley Hospital and its collection of psychiatric art. It was there that he found the Kurelek painting *The Maze* and, he felt sure, the substance of his first film. Maas was excited by the painting's vivid depiction of emotional problems and its exposure of a creative mind.[27] He phoned Bill for his permission, and then flew from London to Toronto for preliminary talks with the artist. Bill was pleased to have the opportunity to tell his story for the benefit of others. He wrote enthusiastically to Dr. Davies that Dr. Carstairs had recently convinced him that social attitudes to mental illness had altered so much that he should feel no hesitation in telling his story publicly. Such witness, indeed, "might actually help some other gifted persons suffering nervous or mental trouble to pull through."[28]

After talking with the artist, Maas and his crew flew back to London to film statements from Dr. Morris Carstairs, Dr. Davies, Margaret Smith, and Father Lynch. In October, they returned to Ontario to film Bill in his home and his parents on their farm, on Thanksgiving Day, 1969. The filming of various Kurelek paintings completed the shooting.

The edited film was shown to Bill and Jean in 1970, while the financial backers held their breath. Maas had given Bill full editorial control. Would he accept the film? And how would he react to seeing the people who had played such a sensitive role in his life fifteen years earlier? Maas vividly remembered the private screening: "After the film was over Bill said nothing for a good five minutes. The producers, sitting at the back, were getting very nervous. Finally we got up, steeling our courage, and slowly walked to the front. He said it was very accurate, a fine job. He was quite taken by it, and a huge sigh of relief went up from the back of the auditorium."[29]

Billed as "a film at the frontiers of psychological enquiry" and subtitled "The Story of William Kurelek", *The Maze*, released later that year, is a thirty-minute documentary on the artist's breakdown in the early 1950s, and his subsequent recovery and family relationships. The

Bill being photographed in his house for the film *The Maze*, 1969.

The proud father with Tommy (far left) on the front lawn, 1970.

Dmytro, Mary, and Bill at family gathering in the early 1970s. Courtesy Mrs. Helen Shulhan.

film won second place in the American Film Festival Awards in 1972, first place in the International Culture and Psychiatry Film Festival, and was shown three times on America's national television channel, PBS. Maas speaks of Kurelek sharing his intimate experiences with the viewer in an open context so that both artist and audience are left to find their own answers as to cause and cure.

Dominated by Bill himself, the film conveys the same viewpoint as that of *Someone With Me*. Bill is very much the star of his story, which he says he would like to tell like a fireside chat. He speaks of his childhood, of his father's feeling that he was not sufficiently "manly", and of his own very mixed feelings for and against him: "I was terrified of my father but I admired him."[30] The Kurelek parents appear as impressive figures, particularly the artist's mother, racked with regret for having somehow failed her sensitive son. She speaks of lacking the money to take better care of her children; of having to hoe the garden and care for toddlers simultaneously. No one could fail to conclude from this film that Mary's love for her son was real and deep. Dmytro, made of sterner stuff, insists that his children were well cared for and educated. He expresses pride in his son's success as an artist, yet stubbornly insists that he would have made more money as a doctor or a lawyer. For his part, Bill claims to renounce his former bitterness against his father and to see his suffering as ordained by God, to enable him to paint Christ's sufferings realistically. After the electroconvulsive therapy treatments, Bill had found faith and a "proper" father in God. The film ends with his mention of a coming holocaust, a shot of a Kurelek painting of a destroyed city, and the saying of grace at Bill's table: "May God provide for the needs of others."

In the film, Bill remarks that he found it difficult to cuddle his children until Tommy, the fourth and last. Physical contact, which was lacking in his own childhood, had never come easily, although his sister Sandy remembers with pleasure the rough-housing that his youngest siblings had enjoyed with their big brother on his return from England in 1956.

Maas remembers Bill as a reclusive figure, a man who refused to look him in the face, yet who was not at all hesitant to tell his life story. Bill's memory, full of remarkable details, seemed photographic. Maas suspects that some of the difficulties encountered by the artist in his early life were biogenetic; in other words, Bill's biological make-up had predisposed him to be extraordinarily sensitive and possibly anxious, tendencies aggravated by an environment hostile to his type.[31]

Maas had been pleased when Bill came to Cornell in the fall of 1969 to address a seminar; and he was surprised by his agreeing to address some twelve hundred students in the concert hall the following year. Bill received a standing ovation for his slide show and commentary, a situation which (in Maas's observation) "whetted his appetite for more." The students liked the artist *and* his paintings. They invaded the university's art gallery in droves for the first Kurelek exhibition in 1971. Bill was there, selling his own Christmas cards for charity and signing books and cards, much to the students' delight. They responded to his openness, his sensitivity and directness, whether or not they agreed with his religious views. Some, Maas believes, identified with his experience of suffering and healing, and were encouraged. Reactions by the local art critics were much less favorable. Some Kurelek paintings were dismissed as maudlin, mawkish, and boring, while the show as a whole was judged "uneven".[32]

To Maas, Bill owed the publication of his autobiography, which he always called his conversion story.[33] As a result of student interest in the film and in Bill's personal appearances at Cornell, Maas asked the artist for a written account of his life. The psychologist was ignorant of the fact that Bill already had over five hundred pages in a drawer, much of it dating from the 1950s. Length was never discussed between them. Maas had in mind an essay of some fifteen pages which could be printed by the Center for Improvement of Undergraduate Education for his students' use. He was overwhelmed some months later by the arrival of a thick manuscript, roughly typed and illustrated with graphite drawings. The psychologist turned to Houghton Mifflin, who refused the manuscript. Maas suggested to Bill that the "proofs of the existence of God" section might be shortened; Bill refused, saying that no one was forced to read those pages. Eventually, feeling indebted to him, Maas made the decision to publish the entire unedited manuscript by a photographic process through the Center.

Bill received the first copies of *Someone With Me* in the fall of 1973, and wrote at once to say that they had given him "real and deep pleasure". He found some hundred errors in copying or typing, but concluded that the book was "beautifully legible" and that the drawings were particularly pleasing.[34]

The confidence that Bill displayed at Cornell, and his growing desire to reach larger audiences, had been nurtured by a trip around the world to study poverty in 1969. It was not his first exposure to the Third World; that had been in 1951 in Mexico. It *was* his first time in Africa and India, and his first transatlantic flight. Looking down, he thought of the first European explorers, five hundred years earlier, venturing fearfully across the same sea. For someone as sensitive as Bill, this sudden exposure to human degradation and misery was bound to be traumatic. The memories were to stay with him for the rest of his life, and increase the many pressures on him. Henceforth, his mission would be twofold: the salvation of souls, and the relief of poverty. The two were linked, since he believed that Christian faith and culture would somehow carry with them the principles of hygiene, hard work, and efficiency.

Why India? Anna Balan had suggested to Bill that the Canadian Indian would be a worthy subject for painting. His letters show that he was aware of North American Indians as a disadvantaged subculture. Canada Council travel grants, however, would support only trips abroad. In August 1968, Bill wrote to the Council to explain that he wished to visit a missionary friend (Father Murray Abraham) near Darjeeling who operated a boys' school on principles of self-help. The trip would make possible a series of paintings and a film on the subject of Canadian aid to underdeveloped countries. These would, he hoped, increase public awareness of the importance of foreign aid.

His first letter to the Council spoke of the need for "2 or 3, 2 week flying trips to India spread over the year", since he felt he could not leave his growing family for longer periods. He also hoped for a subsidy to support his family during his absence. There was no mention of any particular difficulties at home, beyond the fact that Bill and Jean now had four children under six years of age, which indicates something of the stresses in the Kurelek household.

Council reaction was discreet. Bill was advised that, given the expense of airfare, his case would be greatly strengthened by a request for a single trip. He took the hint and reorganized his program, domestic difficulties notwithstanding. On discovering the advantages of a round-the-world ticket, he added Africa and Hong Kong to his plans. The final itinerary included a week in Africa, three and one-half weeks in India, and nine days in Hong Kong, where he had a foster-child. He wrote that his projected drawings would resemble Goya's series of

241

etchings "The Horrors of War", but would include "a note of hope". He would later call the trip a pilgrimage.

Bill's research methods on this arduous field trip were heavily dependent on photography. Something between one-third and one-half of the Council's grant of nearly five thousand dollars went into cameras, film, and the cost of filming his drawings. He carried two relatively sophisticated cameras and sometimes advanced using both at once, like a Western gunslinger. Speed could be important in situations where his welcome as a foreigner was uncertain, although most of his subjects did not object. He photographed from the windows of hotel rooms, and from taxis and speeding trains. Confronting the destitute took courage. He was sensitive to their feelings, yet felt that certain "rights" went with his mission. The telephoto lens ("marvellous gadget") was one solution to this problem.

His beloved sister Nancy lived with her husband and family in Durban, Natal, in South Africa. Apartheid troubled Bill's liberal conscience. Nancy, and Kenneth Shorey, had given him arguments in support of the system of segregation. Bill's letters from Durban and Nairobi reveal a sensitive, humane, and well-intentioned man of considerable political naïveté: "I see no obvious signs of a police state and no evidence of the white man lording it over the black man."[35] With Nancy, he diligently visited black reserves, farmsteads, and a Catholic hospital, concluding that "like our North American Indian, the black is bewildered and demoralized."[36] He considered apartheid to be not unlike the Canadian response to Indian and Inuit problems.

His visit to Nairobi enabled him to compare blacks living under self-rule with those living under apartheid. He found that blacks in the slums of Nairobi carried themselves with the pride of an independent people.[37] Curiously, he identified with native African houses because of his East European heritage, calling them "a near spitten image of Ukrainian straw thatched homes". Not only the roof but the process of coating the earthen floor with a mixture of cow manure and clay seemed to be very similar to that used by his peasant forebears.

The poverty Bill had come to observe and record hit him in Calcutta, with no holds barred. He described many of his impressions in regular letters home to Jean. At the airport, a thundering mass of porters fought for his single suitcase: "They were like a pack of wild beasts—poor, poor people." He was not prepared for the teeming traffic or for the sidewalks of the city: "Its fantastic and 'out of the world'. I might as well be on the moon were it not that the moon is dead and this place is the opposite—a seething mass of humanity desperately clinging to life. The only thing I can compare it to is things I used to see in my boyhood — a horrible image, a dead chicken crawling with maggots, a mass of ticking maggots worming in and out amongst each other."[38]

IX
Easter Vigil, 1963.
Mixed media, 23½″ x 39½″.
Private collection.

(see page 209)

X
Mama, 1966-67.
Mixed media, composite, 45″ x 65″.
Private collection.
(see page 215)

For the balance of his time in India, Bill would be haunted by his memories of the beggars to whom he had given, not given, or not given enough. Christ was in each, as he believed and was reminded by "Pacem in Terris", a poem by Father Abraham he intended to illustrate. The sanctuary of his hotel room was ephemeral: "I actually feel trapped like a big fat rat in this hotel room. It's like a bit of back-home floating like a balloon above a bed of crushed glass." From the window he studied the dying and the barely living on the sidewalks below. He cried, long and helplessly.

Chastened by Calcutta, Bill took a first-class carriage to the mission school near Darjeeling. (Later, he would venture into third-class trains, and buses.) Father Abraham was unfortunately absent during his five days at St. Alphonsus, where students were learning practical farming in a bright, clean atmosphere: "No doubt about it, real Christianity would do wonders for this country.... I saw the boys carrying rocks to earn their tuition and to learn the virture of hard work. I'm doing a picture of that."[39] Bill had taken only ballpoint pens and paper to the mission at Kurseong. He was surprised to find his production rate well below average: "Ink drawing I see now takes a lot more work than brush painting.... I still think Father A's poem lends itself to the bleak colors of drawing on tinted paper. The second part where he condemns our affluent Christmas may do in gaudy colors."[40]

Bill's long letters to Jean, the India Diary, reveal a warm, compassionate, and courageous man with tremendous self-discipline. He was surprised by his own powers of endurance.[41] Some of his experiences are unintentionally amusing, such as the saga of his pants. He took only one pair on the long trip. The seams kept splitting, and were mended by Bill in washrooms and, once, by an Indian hostess. Their owner wore a dhoti during this last operation.

His religious faith was of course an integral part of his way of seeing India. He judged Indians to be a naturally happy people used to hardships: "All they need is employment—more heigiene and of course our faith."[42] The theory with which he had set out, that the conversion of India to Christianity would solve that country's "backwardness and misery", was confirmed to his own satisfaction.[43] He was upset by the sight of a wealthy seminary donated to the church in India by Cardinal Spellman. Bill found its spacious gardens and marbled entrance a "distressing sight ... misguided Christianity".[44] He would have preferred to see prefab or quonset huts on small plots, with the rest given to build houses for local squatters. Beauty, when it surprised him with delight, was always a reminder of the Creator. A chameleon's ability to blend with the floor was termed a marvellous example of God's design.

In Hong Kong, Bill spent two days seeing the city and his foster-child, and one week in isolation, working in a windowless room in the cheapest hotel he could find. It suited him. Undistracted, he could project himself back into India, aided by the mass of black-and-white photographs he had had developed. He revelled in the privacy.

And his conclusions? To his wife he wrote that he was no expert after only six weeks. His views, however, were firm. He was "no more convinced than before that birth control is the answer," despite the overcrowding seen in Calcutta.[45] He wrote that government interference was stifling initiative; that official corruption and inefficiency could not be cured overnight; that technical progress was inevitable and adherence to tribal customs would not help the African. His proposed film, illustrating Father Murray Abraham's poem, "Pacem in Terris", would offer no solutions. Like the poem, it would be a plea for each individual's compassion. He hoped it would move North Americans to help the dispossessed.

Certainly the experience had moved Bill. Many of the sights would haunt him for life. Possibly his desire to help foreign students in Toronto, as he later did, began at this time. He had always been frugal; after India he became obsessive in his abhorrence of waste. Kenneth Shorey recalls dining with the Kureleks in the winter of 1969-70: "Jean K., the children and I were asked to pass our plates down to Bill after we'd finished eating. . . . I had the impression this was a daily ritual, not something done simply for my benefit. Bill methodically scraped the scraps from each plate onto his own, adding leftover potatoes from a common dish and whatever was left on the roast beef. The mound thus created on his plate was larger than the original meal, and Bill consumed the entire thing, potato skins and all."[46]

His preoccupation with world hunger may have created strains on his children's emotions, and no doubt a certain amount of guilt in them. It is doubtful that Bill would have been aware of such subtleties. Third World hunger was far too vivid in his memory and imagination. A Kurelek neighbor recalled that his children had orders to save any bread crusts they might be discarding and to put them in a paper bag for their father.

Bill's drawings, illustrating Father Abraham's poem, were made into a film of the same name: *Pacem in Terris*. The priest's haunting descriptions of human squalor are contrasted with what he calls basic human rights: to life, food, shelter, clothing, work. In the years that followed, Bill showed the film on every possible occasion: in his own house, in churches and halls. Many of his paintings throughout the seventies continued its themes, such as the attack on the North American Christmas as extravagant and self-indulgent. He painted pictures of cows, and sold them for the price of an actual cow in Kurseong; when they were sold, the money went to support the work of his friend Father Theophilus in India. He made and sold Christmas cards for specific Indian projects such as a leper clinic in Calcutta. To the Canada Council, Bill reported that the tour had been extremely helpful but by no means pleasant. The diary suggests that this is an understatement of some magnitude. Yet the trip had proved to be a growing experience for the artist.

The Commonwealth Exhibition in London also shows the incredible improvement in Bill's public-speaking ability and general confidence. In 1972, in connection with an exhibition of his work at the Art Gallery of the prestigious Commonwealth Institute on Kensington High Street, Bill was a guest lecturer at the Maudsley Hospital, where he had been a patient twenty years earlier—surely a unique achievement.

Some paintings for the exhibition were shipped from Canada; many were lent by their British owners. One new one, of the Kurelek family happily picnicking, constituted Bill's gift to the Maudsley for his free treatment (he had also given them *The Maze*). There was only one sale, an ink drawing entitled *The Deformed Destitute of India*, but the paintings as a whole roused considerable interest and were viewed by 8,650 visitors to the Gallery.[47] After the exhibition closed, the paintings were shipped to the Royal Edinburgh Hospital for a showing arranged by Dr. Carstairs. Bill called it a homecoming to the country where he had first begun to paint in earnest and where the turning-point in his life had taken place.

To the friends and relatives with whom the Kureleks stayed during their time in England, Jean confided that Bill "might be a saint, but was very difficult to live with." His artistic ego, his obsessive work habits, and his expectations of nuclear holocaust must have made marital life difficult.

Bill's caption to this family photograph reads: "pulling Cathy and Steve around the family house on a sleigh I made for them for Christmas. They donated the money for their Christmas presents to hungry children in Africa" (c. 1966).

14

The Mass Marketing of Kurelek

BY THE EARLY 1970S, KURELEK WAS MODERATELY PROSPEROUS, RELATIVELY well known, and highly respected as a Canadian artist. His success had followed some fifteen years of unremitting struggle to build a reputation and to earn his living as an artist. Another man might have felt that he could finally relax. Not Bill. He was about to enter the busiest years of his life, a frenetic period of ceaseless production and incredible accomplishment. He was no longer framing, a change in his activities that would gradually alter his relationship with his dealer.

In the last four years of his life he underwent a meteoric rise to fame and prominence. Between 1973 and 1976 he published eleven books with six different publishers. Two of them, May Cutler and Christopher Ondaatje, played significant roles in his life. Throughout those four years, Bill was painting faster than ever. He was producing limited-edition photo-prints, some in print runs of nearly one thousand. He was making documentary films and showing films by and about himself to overflow audiences and standing ovations across the country.[1] During these years, Kurelek became a household name, while his books and photo reproductions flooded the market. Few artists achieve such prominence in their lifetime, if ever. What was going on?

One of Bill's new business associates was a tall, thin man who exudes charm and self-confidence. Christopher Ondaatje prides himself on having achieved the mass marketing of the artist in the mid-seventies. Suddenly there were Kurelek books and photo-prints everywhere. Ondaatje recalls: "The whole thing worked in a circle. The books fanned the fire for his paintings and prints, and vice versa. I didn't replace Av, but I opened the mass marketing of Kurelek.... There was a new window, the mass appeal of William Kurelek. I started it, and he wanted it."[2]

He wanted it. While Tundra Books would become Kurelek's primary publisher, with seven books to Ondaatje's two, there remains a fair degree of accuracy in Ondaatje's claim. The idea of prints was his suggestion. We are, however, left with a conundrum. Why did Bill want to be mass-marketed?

The answers, which can be only tentative, lie deep within the artist's aspirations and character. Ondaatje believed that as early as 1975 Bill suspected he was dying: "He said he had no time to pull lithographs. The photo-print method was *his* idea, *I* wanted lithographs."[3] Since Bill had also worked at an extraordinary pace in the 1960s, this theory must remain inconclusive. Ondaatje also noted in Bill a sense of destiny, of being marked by Fate to accomplish great things. Feeling the same way about himself, the publisher sympathized: "We talked of this."

Clearly, by the early 1970s Bill wanted money, more for his works of charity than for himself. Just as clearly, he wanted increased exposure, following a logic he had established ten years earlier: an audience that had been gained initially through pleasant paintings and books he hoped would remain to hear his serious pleas on behalf of God and man. His old need to evangelize was moving into high gear. The psychological mechanisms behind Bill's conscious goals can only be guessed. Ondaatje observed that he blossomed. His confidence soared. For the boy who had been branded a failure, the crowning vindication was sweet indeed.

Bill in the basement of his Balsam Avenue home. The walls behind him are decorated with Ukrainian motifs. Photo by Daniel M. Newman, courtesy Art Gallery of Windsor.

The woman who made most of his publications possible is, like his dealer, an impressive figure in her own right. May Ebbitt Cutler, President and Editor-in-Chief of Tundra Books in Montréal, had begun publishing in a small way in the late sixties. Among her first titles were a series of pamphlets on the arts at Expo 67, and her own story of an Indian woman she had known. She scored in 1971 with several award-winning children's books, including *Mary of Mile 18* and *A Child in Prison Camp*. As the granddaughter of rural Irish immigrants, Cutler could empathize with Bill and understand a background to which she herself felt very close.[4]

Cutler has an eye for quality. For winners. And she is a fighter. Praising her style and feisty courage, William French described the publisher as a woman who is "unafraid to tweak the nose of anyone who puts obstacles in her way".[5] French varied his metaphor by borrowing from karate, an analogy that recurs when reading some of her correspondence in defence of her own and her writers' interests. She regards children's books as artistic creations, not merely stories with illustrations; as works no less important than books for adults. In the seventies, they became her specialty.

With hindsight, the partnership of Cutler and Kurelek seems inevitable. Cutler had been following the progress of Bill's paintings for several years and suspected that some of his series would make excellent books. The two were introduced by Mira Godard at the Montréal exhibition of the series "The Last Days" in June 1971. During that first meeting, Cutler asked Bill if he would do a children's book for her. He

May Ebbitt Cutler, publisher of Tundra Books, who published most of Kurelek's books. Courtesy Tundra Books.

replied that he had always wanted to do a children's book. Throughout the first year or two of their acquaintance, Cutler was impressed by the strength of the painter's desire to publish.[6]

The book that would become *A Prairie Boy's Winter* took shape rapidly in the correspondence that followed hard on that meeting. Cutler suggested a winter setting, since winter books were unusual and people, particularly outside Canada, found them exotic.[7] She also urged him to keep it autobiographical, and to focus on a single character with whom a child reader could identify. By late July, Bill had planned the twenty scenes and was working on the sketches in the snatches of time available to him during a family holiday. The paintings themselves were done in five weeks, in August and early September. Cutler remembers her surprise at the result. She felt that by suggesting the book, she had played God:

> A few months later, very soon (I was astonished), he phoned me: "I finished the book." It seemed only a few weeks! So I went to Toronto to his basement. An extraordinary moment. I never felt so much like God in my whole life. It was spooky. They were dazzling. It was like, Let there be light, and there was light. Give me a book, and there's the book, twenty paintings lined up.[8]

Cutler's face lit up at the memory, and her hands and voice conveyed her pleasure.

It was the start of a fruitful partnership. Bill was generous in praise of his chief publisher: "It was she who discovered me as a possible author just as Avrom Isaacs of Toronto discovered me as a painter. Both introduced me to success I'd not even dreamt of."[9] To Robert Fulford, Cutler later wrote that she was the first person ever to ask Kurelek to do a book: "Now everybody wants Kurelek to do books."[10]

The publication of *A Prairie Boy's Winter* took patience, and faith, since it proved enormously expensive to reproduce the paintings with good color accuracy and detail. Cutler negotiated joint publication with Houghton Mifflin in the United States to help cut expenses. After a year's delay, caused by various financial problems, *A Prairie Boy's Winter* was published with striking success in 1973. One out of many publishing difficulties had been the cost of insuring the paintings en route to the American publisher. Cutler considers this story her favorite, her classic tale of Bill Kurelek. When the artist learned of the high cost of insurance, he wrote serenely to advise his publisher to disregard it altogether. Why bother? If the works were lost or damaged, he would "simply make new ones", painting as many as three a day if need be.[11]

Houghton Mifflin shared Cutler's enthusiasm. The Montréal publisher's intuitions about *A Prairie Boy's Winter* ("I feel it's going to be a knock-out!") proved correct. The book was launched in late September to coincide with the exhibition and sale of ten of the twenty paintings at the Marlborough Godard Gallery. This was followed by the sale of the other ten works at The Isaacs Gallery. In Montréal, the works sold out in the first half-hour; some disappointed patrons flew down to Isaacs' opening to try to obtain one of the series. Just before the press interviews for the Montréal opening, Bill had provided Cutler with another classic Kurelek tale. This one struck terror into the listener: "He shyly confided that he had a confession to make, 'That book is not honest.' I was nearly dying. I said, What do you mean? Bill said, 'I gave all the children bright clothes, but we had navy blue, brown or dark grey.' My heart fell back into place and I told him, I think that that is artistic licence."[12]

The autobiography had come out from Cornell a few weeks earlier, and his next book, on Toronto, was due out shortly.[13] Bill spoke depreciatingly of the first, but was unable to hide his pleasure in it: "Although its only a university handbook its illustrated by myself and looks like a real book and I guess you know the satisfaction of first time getting oneself in print in a whole book."[14] The latter was the offshoot of an exhibition at The Isaacs Gallery the previous year of twenty-one paintings, one for each of the main districts of his city. In the artist's Foreword to the exhibition, Bill observed that he was known as a portrayer of "past farm life" or as a missionary in paint; however, he had come to love Toronto, and was therefore attempting to portray a new subject, "the soul of a city". Among the Toronto paintings, six were didactic works. They included the now-famous anti-abortion scene, *Our My Lai, the Massacre of Highland Creek*.[15] The abortion issue would escalate in the 1970s, with Bill of course supporting the Right to Life side of the dispute.

Tundra Books followed the success of *A Prairie Boy's Winter* with *Lumberjack* (1974), *A Prairie Boy's Summer* (1975), *Fields* (1976), and *A Northern Nativity* (1976). Relations between Cutler and Kurelek were always friendly.[16]

Bill now had a publisher, whose contracts called for exclusive control of his books for children. He had had a dealer since 1960, and was loyal to him. Where did Ondaatje come in? The publisher of Pagurian Press is quick to emphasize that Bill's growing needs for money and publicity in the early seventies were not being met.

Bill's relationship with Ondaatje is puzzling because of the striking difference between the two men. The fashionably dressed dealer, like the gallery he owns and directs, is the epitome of elegance. We talked in his office there in 1982, in an atmosphere of polished wood, burnished brass, and fine china. The mental image of Kurelek with Ondaatje is jarringly incongruous. The publisher projects an aura of worldly power. Both the man and his wealth were foreign to Bill. Ondaatje believes that he fascinated him. Was the artist attracted to the wealth and power he had always eschewed?

Ondaatje suggests that the two felt a bond as immigrants, and says that they talked together of starving. The publisher was an immigrant with a difference, one whose career had realized the success of which many merely dreamed. He came from a wealthy Ceylonese family whose holdings had been lost in the socialist government's confiscation of assets. Penniless, Ondaatje arrived in Canada in 1955 at the age of twenty-one and became a salesman for several publishing and financial companies.

By the late sixties, his own press was flourishing, using other publishers to put together and distribute its books. The name, Pagurian, is indicative of Ondaatje's flair and methods: a pagurian is a hermit-crab that makes its home in larger molluscs' shells. Publishers such as General and Macmillan were accommodating hosts to Pagurian Press in those years.[17] Between 1967 and 1977, Ondaatje published some six hundred books. Meanwhile, he had become a partner in the new brokerage house of Loewen, Ondaatje and McCutcheon, which was incorporated on January 1, 1970. With the establishment of a gallery and the rapid growth of his art collection, Ondaatje was acquiring local

Christopher Ondaatje of the Pagurian Corporation. Courtesy of The Financial Post.

media labels like "the aesthetic entrepreneur" and "the unsung connoisseur".

Some observers saw Ondaatje as a man who could sell anything to anybody. He saw his own forte in controlling and profiting from cash flow.[18] His fierce independence, confidence, and audacity attracted Bill, who must have been flattered by the attention and admiration of such a man. In Kurelek, Ondaatje found a superb painter; a genius. He also felt he had found an artist whose work could be promoted on a vast scale. Accordingly he sank time as well as money into their relationship. Through much of the early seventies, Ondaatje sat in Bill's basement studio and talked with him for hours while he painted. The publisher found him a "frustrated" man, hungry for talk about art and other projects close to his heart.[19]

Bill's projects with Ondaatje and Pagurian Press between 1971 and 1976 can be grouped under three headings. There were the early photo-prints (*Toronto Stock Exchange, Breakaway, Map of Canada, Map of Toronto*); two books; and the later photo-prints—a sporting series with twelve scenes, and four prints from each of the two books.[20]

Ondaatje's preferred method was to buy the paintings along with copyright, the right to publish facsimiles. He called it "a triangle thing": commission, buy, and mass-produce. By controlling every phase, he anticipated large profits. Bill was attracted by Ondaatje's ability to move quickly; by the apparent simplicity of the financial arrangements, from his point of view; and by the large lump sums he stood to gain at the beginning of each project. Standard royalties were a trickle when he wanted a flood. Cash flow might be the publisher's genius, but it had always been the artist's headache, not to say nightmare.

The Kurelek painting of Toronto's Stock Exchange is both realistic and whimsical. Personal touches include a clock approaching twelve and an unobtrusive crown of thorns lying neglected against a wall: two sermons in miniature. Ondaatje is there in a white shirt and tie, talking to a man who resembles Bill, head bent for writing or sketching. The *Map of Toronto* print carries a short Kurelek text, a eulogy to the city he had made his own.[21] Beneath an actual map, a gala scene of Nathan Phillips Square in winter catches the vitality and excitement that Bill found in Toronto in the 1970s. Ondaatje describes the two maps, done at his suggestion, as "fun projects".

In November of 1974, the biennial Kurelek exhibition at The Isaacs Gallery was a series of thirty paintings of Canada, three for each province. Bill had been collecting ideas for characteristic scenes for some time, and had long been irritated to find himself labelled a gloomy Christian. The series "The Happy Canadian" was intended to set the record straight. In the Foreword to the book (eventually published as *Kurelek's Canada*), the artist notes with heavy irony that even a hypercritical public should find "pure, unadulterated joy" in these scenes. Typically, he adds that individual joys will fade and die like wildflowers; permanent joy lies in union with God, the source of all joys. By widening his subject, he hopes to reach more people with his messages. He observes that the paintings came first, the book idea followed.[22]

Correspondence establishes that the idea for a book came early in 1974. The idea for the series was Bill's, but his publisher contributed the inspired title. Bill found the title immodest, and fought unsuccessfully for "Kurelek, the Happy Canadian". "I wanted the emphasis shifted from me to the Christian philosophy which enables me at last to appreciate this country and citizenship in it." Kurelek would eventually add a clause to the contract for *Kurelek's Canada*, as follows: "Should the publisher change the religious intent of the author's script in the course of editing or otherwise this contract shall be null and void."[23]

The Arctic book was Ondaatje's idea. He wanted a record of a pre-technological society before it disappeared forever. Because Bill had already been to the Arctic to paint landscapes around Cape Dorset on Baffin Island, he was reluctant to go again, but the cash offer was irresistible. Ondaatje remembers putting the suggestion to Bill in his basement, and waiting through what seemed an interminable silence for an answer. After agreeing to do the project, Bill toyed with the idea of doing the paintings without going north. He had his memories from 1968; he had photographs and books. He eventually decided on a mini-tour to Pangnirtung for a week.[24] The work could be finished at his farm in Combermere. He usually fasted on painting trips, but he planned to eat one meal a day in the north, to give him energy for the outdoor work. When he missed his flight at Dorval, he calmly settled into his favorite Montréal hotel to do some preliminary sketches.

The artist's Foreword to *The Last of the Arctic* links the project to his ethnic series, and defends his religious thesis. Bill's nostalgic preference for the old in things Ukrainian did not extend to Inuit ways; wherever they conflicted with Christian ideas, he viewed them simply as wrong. Despite his condemnation of the bad example set by "our increasingly corrupt southern society", he was convinced that Inuit salvation could come only from that society's Christianity. The dedication reflects Kurelek's convictions: "To the white men, missionaries, traders, government officials, and others who courageously faced cold and privation to give of themselves beyond the call of duty out of love for the Inuit." Beautifully produced, the book was a bestseller in Canada in 1975.

Four prints from each of the Pagurian books were eventually made into photo-prints, in limited editions signed and numbered by the artist. These were followed by twelve prints on popular American sports, such as (oddly) golf, football, and sailing. As business dealings with Ondaatje multiplied in the early seventies, their existence could no longer be kept from Isaacs, as they had been initially. The dealer believes that Bill wanted to do something separate as a gesture of independence, "something on his own".[25] Bill's contract with Isaacs did not extend to prints or publications. On moneys earned from the sale of paintings to Pagurian, Bill had given his dealer his usual percentage. Eventually, Bill sought Isaacs' help in business dealings with Pagurian Press, and Isaacs supervised the later contracts: "I don't trust my own judgment," Bill wrote to Ondaatje in 1976, confirming this arrangement. Correspondence suggests that the relationship had cooled by that time.

The tangled thickets of Bill's business affairs provoke amazement and smiles. If Bill is termed "scrupulous", the reference is to his ethical intentions: "There was not a scintilla of personal aggrandizement in his dealings," recalls a man who worked for Pagurian in 1975 and dealt with the artist.[26] In practical financial matters Bill was careless in the extreme. Cutler emphasizes his lack of business sense and general financial naïveté: "He loved simple commissions for flat sums."[27]

Bill knew little or nothing of the world of royalties, permissions, and galley proofs, and had no desire to learn. He wrote vaguely of "the copywright fee or whatever its called" and, with unconscious humor, of the "gallow press" (galley proof). His idea of solving a difficulty in the phrasing of a sentence was to send his publisher a diagram. In one instance the diagram served to explain how fuel is siphoned. Bill suggested that Cutler file it for future reference and forward it to the copy-editor at the American co-publisher, Houghton Mifflin.[28]

Bill simply wanted money for his projects and peace for his work. He would walk away from anything faintly contentious, even if it meant a loss to himself. When Kurelek found a shortfall in the number of prints given to him to sign for Pagurian, he made the correction out of the number assigned to himself: "Incidentally there were only 546 maps so I figured if you promised me 10 for my own use out of 554 then I'm only able to take 2 maps which is what I did take."[29]

In a detailed letter to Ondaatje early in 1976, Bill attempted to clarify his general attitude to business matters and his long-standing relationship with Av Isaacs. He was not prepared to fight with either man. To Ondaatje he wrote in January: "I can use business worries like a hole in the head. ... I will simply withdraw if our relationship continues to force a confrontation with Isaacs."[30] His dealer's questions and comments concerning arrangements for the Arctic book were making Bill very uneasy. He hated being caught in the middle. He told Ondaatje that he had dealt with him because he needed the advance for the paintings; that the publisher had done well from the deal; and that Isaacs was "still the best and most deserving dealer", one whom Bill had no intention of leaving.[31] He was not, he added, a businessman. No one could argue the point.

The artist's final dealings with Pagurian were a mixture of black comedy and tragic irony. The publisher had suggested a series for a book to be called *Kurelek's America* with fifty paintings, one for each American state. Pagurian would purchase the entire series outright. Ondaatje was also pressing the idea of a sporting-print series. Bill was resisting both in the spring of 1976, observing that he was making enough money and "wasn't all that interested in America."[32]

Fate then dealt Bill a curious card: the house adjacent to his own came up for sale. Bill had wanted for years to help students from underdeveloped countries by giving them free room and board. Understandably, Jean had been uncooperative, not to say firm. He now saw his dream within reach. All he needed was eighty thousand dollars, cash. Bill offered Ondaatje fifty-one paintings for a *Kurelek's America* in return for that sum; or, alternatively, smaller paintings to a total of eighty for *Kurelek's America* and one other book project.

In the weeks that followed, Bill believed that Pagurian would accept his conditions. Accordingly, he gave his word to his neighbor that he would buy the house. The July purchase date for the house arrived and the Pagurian contract did not. Bill saw no honorable way to proceed save to buy the house, using a bank loan for fifty thousand dollars. His old dream of a student hostel had become a nightmare. He writes of having always dreaded debt; of having fallen into a pit; of God helping those who help themselves. He refused a contract for the sporting-print series in October, only to accept it later that year, presumably in response to a better offer. He would be signing some of the finished prints with his dying strength.

Meanwhile, his books from Tundra Books had been winning awards as "Best Illustrated Children's Books" in both Canada and the United States. By late 1973, Houghton Mifflin had undertaken to publish American editions of *A Prairie Boy's Summer* and *Lumberjack*. Cutler wrote that their timing was uncertain, since Kurelek was very busy, "very much in demand".[33] She urged Bill to rewrite the text for *Lumberjack*, adding human interest and an individual focus. Cutler's titles (Bill had chosen "William's Winter" and "The Student Lumberjack"), along with her superb editing and reshaping of rough Kurelek texts, formed no small part of the books' success. Declining credit,

Cutler said that she had merely played midwife to the publications.[34]

Bill's basic gratitude alternated with feelings of irritation that his texts were being changed. His ambivalence was one factor in his choosing to publish with Pagurian. Lacking sensitivity towards language, Bill tended to ignore improvements to his basic text ("my not-so-brilliant text") while focussing on details of particular significance to himself. The dedication to *A Prairie Boy's Winter* had become a sore point. Back in 1971, in response to Cutler's request for a dedication Bill had written that one to his wife and children would not be "true". They belonged to a different culture and simply did not see the value of endurance and effort.[35] The passage makes painful reading: Bill seemed so alone. Since he believed that a dedication should be to someone who understands, he considered that the only suitable party would be God. He chose not to have a dedication at all. Later, he opted for a dedicatory prayer, which Cutler rejected without consultation.

After the publication of *A Prairie Boy's Winter*, Bill was hurt to find Cutler's simple dedication ("For everyone who ever spent a winter on the prairies—and for all the others who wonder what it was like") ascribed to himself. "Even some small prayer-like dedication," he told Cutler, "would be better than nothing in the secular subjects I do. 'Oh Toronto' was the ideal balance as far as I'm concerned. But of course that book lacked the technical perfection and love that you put into your publication."[36] He returned to his favorite theme: that without God's mercy and love he would not be producing either paintings or books.

One result of this exchange would be the religious dedication to *A Prairie Boy's Summer*. With all his publishers, Bill insisted that the religious content of his work be left untouched.[37] To Cutler, perhaps inspired by her insistence on quality, he downplayed his need for money prior to the summer of 1976, when the purchase of his neighbor's house led to financial panic. In 1974 Bill could afford to write cheerily that finances were not an issue: "Please don't worry about advances or anything like that as far as *I* am concerned—the important thing to me is to get my foothold in publishing widened."[38]

In January of 1974, Bill flew to Saskatoon on a painting retreat. The twenty scenes for *A Prairie Boy's Summer* were painted there in the Albany Hotel in the dead of winter. They took a week. Bill was on his usual schedule of seventeen hours of work per day, fasting. He took time off only for daily Mass, and two cups of coffee. He wrote to Cutler that the paintings were turning out well: "It helps to work uninterrupted." A few days later he wrote again to report that they were finished: "It was 37 below yesterday and with the wind that made it 78 below zero. ... However temperatures have nothing to do with my creativity. I work on a schedule and dig down inside myself."[39] The text for *Summer* had taken the better part of a day, which was slow for Bill. In response to his mention of a planned February exhibition of eighty-five pioneer artifact drawings in Ottawa, his publisher exclaimed, with good reason, "My goodness, you have so many things going on I just can't keep up."

Through the spring and summer of 1974, Bill's activities included revising the text of *Summer*, researching *Jewish Life in Canada*, and painting thirty scenes for "The Happy Canadian".[40] He was settling happily into his new farm near Combermere and finding the northern property an excellent place to paint. "It's almost too isolated here and undisturbed," he wrote to Cutler, "and so beautiful I love it more every day."[41] Set in a clearing on a hill, the land provided a panoramic view of a sky which reminded Bill of the prairies. He had been awed by the *aurora borealis* as a child; now, at Combermere, he could see those fantastic night skies once again.

A relationship had begun with W. O. Mitchell late in 1973. The novelist was working in Toronto that winter as Writer-in-Residence at the university. He had seen the paintings for *A Prairie Boy's Winter* and been impressed. Soon after, he received a call from a man who identified himself as "a painter" who needed help with his writing. Mitchell would subsequently do some editing on *A Prairie Boy's Summer*, including the all-important dedication, while urging Bill to settle down to the major work of rewriting *Someone With Me*.[42] He warned the painter that the job would require one or two years' work. Mitchell found Bill "strangely innocent about the craft and the work involved in another art". Any student of the painter's life would agree. In his last years Bill did spend time on the autobiography. Unfortunately he continued to believe that it required cosmetic rather than major surgery, and to harbor the suspicion that every editor was hostile to his religious message. The manuscript would eventually be taken out of his hands by fate, to be edited posthumously.

Bill's naïve hope of learning to write like Mitchell was never realized, but their friendship led to a beautiful edition of *Who Has Seen the Wind*. To illustrate Mitchell's classic prairie novel (1947), Bill created eight paintings and thirty-two black-and-white sketches, one for each chapter. Sparkling with humor and vitality, artwork and text are wonderfully complementary. A delighted Mitchell calls it "one of the most beautiful marriages between two arts" that he has ever seen. He recalls that Bill believed the two men were very similar: "We're both rural prairies and we're both religious."[43] Feeling that his religious humanism was very different from Bill's Catholicism, Mitchell countered the idea, with little success. His novel had apparently convinced the painter that he would "do" in the area of religion, a reaction that suggests a broadening of Bill's religious attitudes in the last years of his life.

The genesis of the art edition of *Who Has Seen the Wind* came with Bill's confession that the novel had moved him to do several paintings. Mitchell put the idea to his publisher, and Isaacs supervised the contract.

During their sessions together Bill never looked at Mitchell directly. The novelist believes that their relationship was somehow blocked, that he puzzled Bill. The artist found it surprising that someone would help him without expecting a painting as payment: "that was when I realized that Kurelek didn't think he was lovable." Mitchell wrestled with the word "suspicious", rejecting it as being perhaps harsh and unfair but returning to it in the end to describe Bill's attitude to himself and to others who were kind to him. Ironically, Bill had observed this same cast of mind in his father and had disliked it. Mitchell found that Bill tended to think in terms of adversary relationships. The novelist's strongest impression of the artist would be of Bill's suspicion of the motives of those who helped him.[44]

Published by Macmillan in the fall of 1976, the handsome gift edition drew enthusiastic reviews—with one exception. One critic believed that Bill showed an insufficient understanding of Anglo-Saxons in the book. That one remark rankled. Even at the height of his fame and popularity, there was a small boy in Kurelek who found any criticism painful.

In the fall of 1974, Bill was embarking on what would eventually become his fifth book with Tundra Books. Should his Nativity book be set in the prairies, he asked Cutler, or in Canada as a whole? The publisher had suggested the book after seeing some Kurelek Nativity scenes with contemporary Canadian settings. She now advised that two entirely different books were lurking in these alternatives. She conceived of the Canada book as being simply the manger scene in different locations, ones that Bill had experienced personally: "a lumbercamp, a railway siding, a barn, a cheap hotel, and so on ... [with] Mary holding the baby Jesus after his birth, and whatever creatures may happen to be around whether they are tramps, bums, lumberjacks, farm animals or what have you."[45] She thought that a possible second book, showing the entire Nativity story in contemporary terms, would be more difficult, since it would involve finding modern equivalents for the many New Testament characters in the drama. Bill was pleased at the prospect of two volumes, and promptly decided to work first on the one that could be done more easily and quickly.[46]

That summer, Bill had written that things were getting hectic. He had just experienced his "most marathon painting session ever", in

March 27, 1975

The Editor in chief
MacMillan Publ. Company

Dear Sirs :

I don't know if you remember me. I was the artist whom Bill Mitchell arranged to have illustrate "Who has Seen the Wind" for a republication of that classic by your company. I've heard nothing from him to date if you accepted the illustration or infact if you are going ahead with the publication.

What I'm really writing about however is that during the meal we had at the Westbury with Bill you told me you'd publish my autobiography if I rewrote it. Well I have now. So I need to know if in fact you're still thinking of doing it. Or if I should approach another publisher who's also expressed interest in it. By the end of this year I will have had 7 books published. But of those 7 the autobiography I feel most attached to. Please answer soon if you can.

Sincerely
Bill Kurelek

This letter to the Macmillan Company of Canada regarding the publication of W. O. Mitchell's classic novel *Who Has Seen the Wind* (1947) in a new illustrated hardcover edition is typical of Bill's correspondence.

Edmonton: "I shut myself up for forty-eight hours painting with just brief catnaps for rest."[47] He had fallen asleep at the airport and nearly missed his plane. That fall, he was working on "The Happy Canadian" and on a film by the same name while creating, at Isaacs' suggestion, four lithographs for Olivetti Underwood: "I'm bungling aplenty, never having done anything like that," he wrote to Cutler, while admitting to burning the candle "at three ends these days". Cutler reacted with characteristic forthrightness and genuine concern for Bill's health: "For *God's* sake—and I am *not* blaspheming—if not for your own, slow down! Why don't you take some time to look at the work of your favorite artist—should I spell it with a capital A? An artist needs replenishment of the spirit in more ways than one."[48] To this heartfelt plea Bill paid, of course, no attention at all. He had work to be done, and he would do it if it killed him.

By January 1975, Bill was ready to tackle another project that had been waiting in the wings. With two books in progress at Tundra, he asked Cutler to show him Montréal in a one-day tour she had promised him earlier. The editor had offered to provide an "unorthodox" tour that she was sure Bill would love.[49] The artist was hoping to repeat the success he had had with *O Toronto*. In a taxi hired for the day, the two toured the city in search of the ethnic diversity, human interest, and moral lessons Bill always sought. Cutler remembers two incidents in particular. In a McGill medical building where animals are kept for experimentation, they took the elevator to the top floor to discover it was full of sheep: "Bill thought it was hilarious. A penthouse view of the city next to sheep. Penthouse sheep." The scene, reproduced from memory, was bought by the university. The old Bleury Mission was of particular interest to Bill, who returned there alone later to photograph and sketch: "The lost and the lonely he identified with."[50] The "Montréal" series was exhibited and sold by Mira Godard but never became a book, much to Bill's disappointment.[51]

The same year also saw the completion of the drawings for *Fox Mykyta*, the paintings for *Jewish Life in Canada*, and *Fields*. With plans for a series on Polish Canadians, Bill had begun to visit picturesque farmsteads belonging to Polish settlers in the Combermere area. He had no intention of slowing down, but would listen to his publisher when it suited him. He wrote to Cutler to thank her for pointing out the self-pitying element in the *Prairie* books: "I'll make a point of avoiding it in future books. Its an element I objected to in Shevchenkos poetry (he's the Ukrainian Shakespear) and I blush to realize I was doing the same."[52] His next letter observed that he was "in high gear production". This was an understatement.

The text for *A Northern Nativity* did not come easily. Cutler was insistent that the book not repeat *Kurelek's Canada*. Geography, as she reminded the artist, was not the focus: "It is essentially a *religious* book whose theme is simply that Jesus comes to all men who are humble and open *wherever* they are."[53] She asked for a clear and powerful text: "no heavy-handed moralizing please."[54] Cutler does not describe herself as a religious person, yet her editing of *A Northern Nativity* definitely clarified and heightened its religious message. Bill, who had never forgotten the dedication to *A Prairie Boy's Winter*, was far from grateful. In the give and take of that summer's correspondence, he acknowledged that her edited version was "beautifully poetic" but complained that it now seemed more Cutler than Kurelek.[55] He worked to restore what he called "a Kurelek flavour".

The resulting book is as beautiful as Cutler was determined it should be. It mirrors Bill's experience, his faith, his humanity, and his religious genius. Settings range freely from a fish-drying hut near Port-aux-Basques to bush camps, construction sites, cattle country, a Salvation Army hostel, and the farmhouse belonging to Madonna House, Combermere. It closes with *Flight Into a Far Country*, in which the Holy Family prepare to flee in a Mennonite buggy along a snowy northern road. Scenes are presented as the dreams of a twelve-year-old boy, sparked by the questions: "If it happened there, why not here? If it happened then, why not now?" The character William is sorry to see the Holy Family leaving, yet is "no readier than the people in his dreams to receive them if it meant giving up his dream of independence."[56]

With the publication of *A Northern Nativity*, the Cutler/Kurelek correspondence becomes sparser, loses its intensity, and begins to wind down. As fate would have it, his next two Tundra publications would be posthumous. Cutler had hoped that Bill would illustrate a book of Ukrainian nursery rhymes. After the purchase of his neighbor's house for a student hostel, however, the artist was obsessed with financial worries. In the fall of 1976 he was refusing all projects except those that would generate large and immediate sums of money, ten thousand dollars or more. His one exception was an offer to Cutler for a book to be called *A Prairie Girl's Summer*, inspired by his sister Nancy.[57]

Relations with Isaacs during these years of publications and prints had their ups and downs, but the long period of good faith between the two men had created a bond that held firm. Very naturally, Isaacs was hurt to learn of the secret deals between Bill and Ondaatje, and told Bill so.[58] The dealer continued to refrain from suggesting topics for paintings; that was not, he firmly believed, his role.[59] He also continued to offer business advice, while insisting on Bill's independence in such matters. Usually the artist took his advice, sometimes after painful periods of learning by experience. "What really bugs me," Isaacs wrote in 1976, "is that if we disagree it becomes very painful for you. If two people are going to relate, sooner or later they are going to have to disagree."[60]

After 1970, Bill used Isaacs' facilities for his own framing but no longer worked for his dealer as a framer. Both men noticed a subsequent improvement in their relationship. Isaacs found that Bill seemed much more open. And Bill observed that he had a more "man to man" attitude to the dealer after he had ceased to be his employee.[61] Bill knew that he lacked business experience, and thought he should learn; in actual fact he was never willing to put time into such activities. He was aware that he projected an image of helplessness which encouraged people to try to manage him. He told Isaacs that he was sturdier than he looked, and willing to make his own mistakes. As for his new business ventures, he wished to expand "further and faster for financial and 'propaganda' reasons".[62] Expansion included exhibitions, publications, lectures, and films.

The dealer appreciated the publicity and popularity connected with Bill's publications, but remained cautious. He warned Bill that the books had convinced many buyers that Kurelek's only kind of painting was of children playing; these collectors would have to be shown that the artist had "much more breadth" than that. Like Cutler, Isaacs worried about the speed at which Bill was working in these frantic years. He knew the painter's extraordinary capacity for work, but felt that he needed time to evolve his own ways: too many commitments might push him in directions alien to his spirit.[63] Bill's pace, however, was about to increase.

Sandwiched into 1975 were the main research and all the painting of *Jewish Life in Canada*. Bill's collaborator, historian Abraham Arnold, was currently the executive secretary of the Winnipeg-based Jewish Historical Society of Western Canada. He had learned of the Kurelek project through a mutual friend, Abe Schwartz. The proposed book was to focus on the years between 1880 and 1920. Arnold had met the artist in 1973, at the Toronto conference where Bill spoke on the development of his ethnic consciousness. By the summer of 1974 they were in touch by mail, and Arnold was sending selected photographs. On a stormy weekend in January, Bill flew to Winnipeg for two intensive days of research and briefing. Arnold and his wife, Bertha, opened the Society's archival resources to Bill, providing him with hundreds of photographs.[64] The writer also provided an entrée into Jewish society, food, friends, and customs.

Their fruitful collaboration led to a beautiful book and an unusual friendship. A reviewer called them Canada's "Odd Couple": "One is a shy, sensitive, introverted and devout Ukrainian Catholic; the other is a brash, energetic, outgoing, and committed Jew. They're so different—both in background and character—that when they come together it's like a meeting of two complete strangers across two different centuries."[65]

Odder still might be the fact that the actual paintings, sixteen in all, were done in Lourdes, accompanied (as usual) by prayer and fasting. Bill considered it perfectly appropriate, "since that is where hundreds of miraculous cures attributed to the intercession of Mary, a Jewish maiden, have taken place."[66] His Introduction noted that the project, initiated out of gratitude to his dealer and patrons, was also to help pay the debt that he felt Christians owed to Jews because of the atrocities committed by a supposedly Christian country, Nazi Germany. In Canada, the artist concluded, we can at least show respect for and interest in other people's traditions.

Ironically, while the Jewish book was in progress, the relationship between Bill and the Arnolds was strained by the publication of *The Passion of Christ*. Bertha Arnold considered that Jews in this series had been vilified by an insensitive man with no understanding of them: "It's an anti-Semitic tract."[67] Abe reacted more mildly, out of a firm conviction that Bill never intended to insult the Jews. He agreed, however, that Bill's emphasis on Semitic features in the Passion series was unfortunate, and that the artist was naïve. Bill's lack of understanding of community organizations, also noted by Arnold, helps to explain why the artist remained oblivious to the active work that Arnold put into promoting their book. Ignorant of the need for such effort, Bill was later puzzled when his French and Irish series failed to generate equal enthusiasm and publicity.

By 1976, Bill aspired to illustrate the pioneer story of each of the main ethnic groups of Canada. He had painted Ukrainians, Inuit, Jews, and, in the summer, the Irish. Now he would do the French. Typically, he sought an "unspoiled" area of Québec where some of the old ways survived. Commercial revivals, for tourists, were to be avoided at all costs. When a dealer wrote from Québec to suggest a show, Bill replied that his letter was "providential", and offered a series on a French-Canadian village. He explained that he sought the reaction of a real French-Canadian audience, as distinct from the mixed nationalities of the Montréal area. He asked Michel de Kerdour to show him an unspoiled area, and to provide an interpreter/guide.[68]

In September, he spent five days in Charlevoix County, east of Québec City, guided by a local painter of Irish and French ancestry. James Halpin had known nothing of Kurelek prior to that meeting. Obviously Kurelek's reputation had not reached that part of Canada.

Bill's preliminary work on any of his ethnic series involved a great deal of research — and the use of a good camera. Here Bill collects ideas for his Jewish Canadians series. Courtesy Mr. Michael Clayton.

Genial and generous, Halpin undertook the task as a gesture of friendship to a fellow painter. Initially, Bill thought that Halpin had been paid. Finding he had not been, Bill was surprised and uneasy. Like W. O. Mitchell, Halpin found Bill suspicious of his motives: "he was very suspicious, he couldn't believe I'd done all this for nothing."[69]

Two trips to the airport were needed to collect Bill, who had arrived by an early plane, sequestered himself in a corner, lost track of time, and finished a painting. Halpin suggested Charlevoix County or the Île d'Orléans. The six villages of the Charlevoix region captured Bill's heart at once. "I'm staying here," he told Halpin, "forget the island." They settled at Les Éboulements. Bill slept at the local inn, where his bedroom light was seen burning till one and two each morning. Thirty minutes after dinner he would leave his host in order to work. Halpin remembers Bill asking more than once to be excused if he seemed "ruthless": "I have so little time." The innkeepers found him unsociable, "*sauvage*".

Topics for the paintings were heavily influenced by Vladimir Horik, a Ukrainian painter who lives and works near St. Hilarion. Halpin introduced the two, and Bill was invited to stay with his fellow artist. Horik suggested that Bill consider painting a Mass; children waiting for the school bus; the story he told of a moose in a nearby village; a roofing bee; chicken-plucking; a sawmill; and the hydro wires. Bill absorbed Horik's tales, then made the subjects wholly his own. To Horik Bill was a workaholic, and he suspected that he already knew he had cancer. Normally, Slavs are quick to laugh at small things; in Bill there was "a lot of determination but no joy".[70] He was, Horik thought, a very lonely man.

Bill sought the old ways, the roots, of the living generation. He had a good eye for the genuinely typical, a distaste for the quaint or the picturesque. A panoramic view of mountains and water at Cap aux Corbeaux, beloved of landscape painters for generations, excited Bill not at all. He painted people, working people: a blacksmith, bakers, farmers, and his friendly guide. All would eventually receive invitations to the exhibition, sent personally by Bill. His Foreword records his regret that the old ways were being "swamped by materialistic culture influences ... from the South."

One evidence of this was the entertainment in the Auberge on his last night in Les Éboulements. A local accordion player began the festivities, but was soon superseded by rock music from the juke box: "I can accept that a Québecois would change from a cartwheel to a

Bill with Vladimir Horik in St. Hilarion, Quebec, in September 1976. The Ukrainian-Canadian painter gave Bill many useful suggestions for the Charlevoix County series. Courtesy Mr. J. Halpin.

diesel engine to power his sawmill. But to see him changing his mode of expression and his spiritual values for something cheaper—that hurts." Beside an old spinning-wheel he painted beer cans and plastic curtains, signs (as he wrote in the painting's text) of "our tawdry modern consumer civilization".

For Bill, even the diesel engine had sinister implications. The one message-painting in this series, entitled *Satan's Web*, features hydro wires, snowmobiles, and a little wayside shrine. Two local priests strongly disagreed with its text. Bill wrote:

> As a Catholic I cannot but be saddened at the waning of the Church in Québec, ... its loss of authority on moral matters. ... Temporal power and temporal concerns (symbolized by the power line) and pursuit of physical pleasure (symbolized by the snowmobile towing skiers) now hold sway. Because so many have rejected taking up their daily cross in favour of worldly ease they no longer discern evil as it takes over. Satan's Web therefore I have represented by overwhelming the composition with hydro and fence wires. ... When I talk of evil and the devil, whose face incidentally I see in the shape of the power pylon, I am regarded by many as medieval and reactionary. When I depict nuclear holocaust as a sign of retribution (its coming I represent in this painting by the jet in the sky), I am called a pessimist.

Clearly, Bill's preoccupation with a coming disaster had not gone away. Horik's intuitions seem sound.

Father Leo Letarte met and talked with the artist in Québec City. From Bill's appearance at the exhibition, his shabby suit and humble demeanor, the priest had judged him to be a saintly man. Bill had been scandalized to find the priest without his Roman collar, a reaction Father Leo ascribed to the zeal of a convert. As for the text of *Satan's Web*, the priest believed that Bill's judgment was quick and superficial; faith was not neglected in modern Québec, and hydro pylons represented man's genius as well as God's gift.[71]

Father Guy Bruneau's reaction to Bill was similar. Bill had talked with him at the exhibition, and had given him a copy of the book on Christ's Passion. The priest, himself a painter, was saddened to see Bill focus on the powers of evil rather than on the powers of renewal in the Holy Spirit: the Passion book emphasized the aggressiveness of the torturers far more than the joy and hope of the Resurrection. Had Bill chosen the Gospel of John, rather than that of Matthew, he would have had more scope for joy. As for the text to *Satan's Web*, Bill had not been

Bill sketching the church in St. Hilarion in his custom-
ary stance. Asked if the pose was uncomfortable, he
replied that he had no time to set up an easel and other
equipment. Courtesy Mr. J. Halpin.

fair to modern Québec. He had exaggerated the dark side of trends and ignored the very real faith of those people who might not attend church regularly. Father Bruneau implied that Bill's spiritual standards were materialistic, setting the letter (church attendance) above the spirit which Christ had praised: "I admired the man, and suffered from *his* suffering. I wanted to share my religious joy with him."[72] More than one co-religionist had felt the same way. But Bill had been given his own joy, his own cross, and he was true to them.

The texts to the twenty Charlevoix paintings, and Halpin's memories, suggest that Bill derived considerable satisfaction from the trip. Many of the paintings sparkle with vitality, such as the breathtaking *Première Neige aux Éboulements*, or the darkly beautiful *Smelt Fishing at St. Irene*. Bill's own favorite was *Old Village Blacksmith*; it demonstrates his lifelong pleasure in chiaroscuro and cluttered interiors.[73] His new Polaroid camera helped with details. Bill sketched standing, with a large board propped on one knee. Asked if this tired him, he replied that he had no time to set up easels or carry equipment. No time, in other words, to be tired. Halpin preferred Kurelek's drawings to his paintings, but found in the latter a freshness and spontaneity reminiscent of Brueghel.

In the midst of these hectic years, Bill made time for a project that brought him no money and very little publicity. Like some Canadian Michelangelo, he covered a massive church wall in Saskatoon with a striking mural of Christ Feeding the Five Thousand. It was his first such work.[74]

The Basilian Fathers of St. Thomas More College on the campus of the University of Saskatchewan were preparing to celebrate the fortieth anniversary of their institution in 1976. A Kurelek mural on the end chapel wall of More College seemed the perfect project, and plans proceeded by mail between the artist and the Fathers, starting in the spring of 1975. Bill was enthusiastic, and his generosity made the commission possible.[75] The wall behind the altar, thirty-eight feet at the base, was refinished to prevent the paint from peeling on account of dampness. The mural was to be Bill's largest work, and the first time that he had painted from scaffolding. The actual painting was done in ten days, in January 1976, while Bill fasted on coffee, vitamin pills, and a daily orange.

One major problem was the existence of an earlier mural on the same wall, painted in 1956 by Lionel Thomas in pale colors and semi-abstract style. The Thomas mural sat squarely at the centre bottom of the area that Bill proposed to paint. He solved the difficulty in two ingenious ways. Decorative elements from the earlier work were incorporated into the larger design; two of Bill's three principal

Bill with one of the works from the Quebec series (1976) showing a moose that has wandered into a village. Courtesy Mr. J. Halpin.

figures are pointing into the Thomas mural as if explaining that its abstractions are symbolic of the Kingdom of which Christ speaks in the Saskatchewan wheat field above.[76]

The idea of the multiplication of the loaves and fishes, set in a field of prairie grain, was suggested to Bill by Father Alphonse de Valk as a variation on the Last Supper. The painter might like to add the two famous Catholic churchmen Sir Thomas More and Cardinal Newman, along with hunters, Indians, Métis, Oblate missionaries, Grey Nuns, and settlers in their individual costumes: "You might even want to put a Basilian Father in!"[77] All of these suggestions bore fruit in the finished work. Bill requested and received research help, including photographs of the clothing of the peoples who had formed the province.

One suggestion, however, was stoutly resisted. Father de Valk had proposed that a figure of God the Father, seated on a throne, should fill the apex of the triangular wall. Bill, however, chose to depict the Godhead by the sun, the Trinity by a triangle, and divine love by a heart. He had been troubled, he told the priest, by anthropormorphic concepts of God during his time of religious seeking in the 1950s. The brilliant prairie sun was suggested by Father Kevin Kirley.[78]

Much of the composition took shape as Bill worked with his usual intensity. He felt that the sun seemed to call for white birds, the souls of

Detail of the base of the Kurelek mural in St. Thomas
More Chapel, Saskatoon, painted in ten days in January
1976 by Bill and an assistant. Bill had to incorporate an
earlier, more stylized mural by Lionel Thomas in 1956
into his overall design. Courtesy Rev. W. H. O'Brien,
C.S.B.

the faithful. The twelve apostles became their contemporary succes-
sors, the Basilians at the College. The artist's on-the-spot decision to
make them recognizably the local Fathers was extremely popular, and
allowed him to exercise his sense of humor. Bill was supplied with
photographs of faculty members, students, and staff. As the news
leaked out, Father de Valk was continually approached by people at the
College who, for one reason or another, were afraid that they might be
omitted and who greatly wished to be included. Since there were
more than twelve, some were included in the approaching crowds.[79]

The original inhabitants of the prairie and the European colonizers
are represented by the crowd on the left; the group on the right

270

represents the mass migration of the late nineteenth and early twentieth centuries after the surveys had been done. A gathering storm symbolizes the artist's personal premonition that society is headed for catastrophe. The crowd—God's plenty—includes Dutch, Hutterites, Swedes, Irish, Jews, Russians, East Indians, Ukrainians, and a Cockney carrying the Canadian flag. Harvesters in the foreground represent the artist's parents. Bill had used Stonewall as a model for the field.

The stern side of Bill's faith was not confined to the thunderstorm. To represent man in rebellion against God he painted fists emerging from deep fissures: without freedom, love is meaningless, and freedom means the possibility of refusing God. Unlike his judgmental paintings of the 1960s, however, which depict Bill's father as the one refusing grace, the Saskatoon mural shows the artist himself as the stubborn rebel. The difference is significant. Bill wrote: "I've shown this 'turning away' on the right side of the mural by the labourer (who represents myself in my student and labourer years) and by the capitalist; and on the left side by an original Métis and White entrepreneur of the prairies. These figures are chosen at random. It's not for me to judge

271

who the lost really are." To the Basilians, he said that the fate of those who reject Christ is not stressed today, but that Christ did not mince words. Painted legends carry Orwellian texts such as "Pornography is Truth", "Relevance is Goodness".

The problem of working at the great heights the job required had worried Bill. Painters, following his instructions, had covered the upper half of the wall in "baby blue", and left their scaffolding in place. Bill had climbed up the first day and, by his own admission, lost his nerve. The highest platform had no railing. A Fine Arts student and volunteer assistant came to his rescue. Awed by Bill and his reputation, Geralyn "Gerry" Jansen was happy to help. Her willingness to climb to the apex convinced Bill that she was fearless of heights. With the artist hanging onto the ladder and coaching his apprentice, Geralyn painted the sun with its triangle, heart, and rays.

It was not done easily. Geralyn remembers: "I went right up on the scaffold like a fool, not realizing that there wasn't any railing. He mentions that I was not afraid of heights...I'm scared stiff when it comes to heights, but for an opportunity to work with a man like that, a little bit of time up on a scaffold is something I can handle. We put a triangle in the sun, and a heart. I had a bit of a problem spraying the rays and had to do it over a couple of times."[80] Her use of "we" is rather touching.

Symbolically, the mural centres in a stiff and formal Christ. Far more striking in visual terms are the large, dramatic figures of Cardinal Newman and St. Thomas More, and the rows of students in the foreground who are listening to them. Warm and vital, these plain people give life to the historic tableau above them. Parts of the foreground are handled in *trompe-l'oeil* technique. A bearded man has turned to look at the viewers of the mural. A figure of Geralyn leans on the symbolic border taking notes, her elbow shadowing its painted ledge.

Like Bill, Geralyn had grown up on a farm. Her personal qualities of sympathy, integrity, and religious faith made them compatible. The artist was very pleased with his assistant, who found their silences companionable rather than stiff: "He was a very easy man to work for." At times Bill would question her about her family's farm: about fences, gophers, or machinery. He expounded on his belief that artists should educate themselves, and/or apprentice to a master. He had little faith in classes. He showed her other paintings he was working on: prairie scenes, and a *trompe-l'oeil*. She was impressed by his ability to capture the feeling of a prairie spring, and touched when he gave her one of his books, inscribed "from one farm child to another".

Listening to Geralyn talk, one suspects that the artist also enjoyed her company. Perhaps he drew emotional strength from her presence during those long, fasting days of intense creativity. Geralyn remem-

Fine-arts student Geralyn ("Gerry") Jansen was Bill's
assistant for the giant mural. In gratitude for her help,
Bill painted her into the right foreground, sketching,
her arm resting, *trompe-l'oeil* fashion, on the painted
ledge. Courtesy Geralyn Jansen Hall.

bers his enthusiasm, his genuine interest in her answers to his questions, his boyishness: "He had bright eyes. There was an eagerness
there."

The Basilian Fathers were delighted with the results of the anniversary project "beyond their stoutest expectations".[81] The two Fathers
who had been especially close to the project and to the artist during his
two weeks in residence with them, Fathers de Valk and Kirley, had
both kept diaries of those weeks recording Bill's remarks and reactions. Father Kirley was touched by Bill's apparent reluctance to
believe that art was a powerful medium for preaching, and at his
pleasure when the priest spoke of having been influenced himself by
the Florentine frescoes of Fra Angelico.[82]

The secrecy that had surrounded the project ended abruptly with
the artist's departure on January 26. Bill flew home with the Indian
crafts the Fathers had purchased for his children, and resumed his
hectic pace in Toronto, turning out in rapid succession twenty Nativity
scenes, series on the Irish and the French, and the illustrations for *Who
Has Seen the Wind*. As he told the Basilian Fathers, there were
thousands of paintings waiting to be born. No time to lose.

15

The Crusader

BILL'S CRUSADING ZEAL IN HIS FINAL YEARS WENT FAR BEYOND EVANGELIZING in the narrow sense. He worked passionately to reshape the world nearer to his heart's desire and to the Gospel as he understood it. In the sixties he had fought apostasy, agnosticism, atheism, materialism, and greed through his art and his writings. In the seventies he discovered a new target: sexual permissiveness. The 1960s had seen a revolution in attitudes towards sexuality in the Western world. By the early seventies, many conservative moralists were mounting a strong counter-attack against abortion, homosexuality, and pre-marital sex. Perhaps Bill's own willingness to oppose the currently fashionable sexual leniency reflected his growing consciousness of himself as a crusader.

Bill's most famous blow against abortion had been struck in 1972 with *Our My Lai, the Massacre of Highland Creek*, a painting which equates the slaughter of innocent and helpless civilians in Vietnam with the killing of human fetuses. In the same series, the portion of Toronto's lower Yonge Street devoted to commercial sex is transformed as an allegory of the fate of couples having illicit sexual relations. The crowds who fill the broad avenue are ripe for harvesting by a jaunty devil driving his tractor down "The Strip":

> The term "strip" is used in farming and lumbering to designate a small parcel of a crop to be harvested by one man. ... The wandering crowds congregating on the sidewalks of Yonge Street in the evenings appear allegorically like the crop talked of in the Bible. They are ready for harvesting, but alas, in this case, by the wrong person. The devil's work is a breeze in our times because he is universally regarded as a fairy tale. He is like the farmer who drives his tractor, cocksure of his bumper crop, his foot placed flamboyantly on the fender flaunting his mastery of the situation.

> I should add that each time I do a painting on this sub-
> ject I also have to make a point of denying that I am a
> prude. I know that sex is a marvellous creation of God's
> and so it is good. It is the misuse and the exploitation of
> sex that is wrong.[1]

Throughout the long association with Isaacs, Bill had objected to his work being hung near sexually suggestive paintings, either in Toronto or in other galleries across Canada: "At times I do feel a little like DANIAL in the lions den when I see my works among those atheistic or pornographic ones on the same walls."[2] When he was unsuccessful in battles of this type he took comfort in the idea that at least the public would have "a choice of who they'll side with". Perhaps his growing family added a note of urgency. There were four children, born between 1963 and 1967: Catherine, Stephen, Barbara, and Tommy. Soon they would be teenagers, vulnerable to the sexually liberal ideas that now filled the media.

By late 1975, the problem was very much on his mind, and brought to a head by an article in the Toronto *Globe and Mail's Weekend Magazine*. In "The Noisy Revolution—Sex", John Aitken argued that individual freedom should take precedence over traditional restrictions which were, in his opinion, no longer necessary and which led to cruelty and hypocrisy.[3] Aitken's casual acceptance of pornography ("skin magazines for all possible persuasions") reminded Bill that such magazines were sold at several neighborhood stores in the village of Combermere. Since acquiring the farm property in the spring of 1974, the Kurelek family had begun to spend their Christmases there.

On Christmas Day, 1975, Bill wrote a long letter to the owner of Valley Market, Combermere, whom he had seen in church that morn-ing. Was he seriously dependent, Bill inquired, on the sale of magazines such as *Playboy* and *Penthouse*? Had he considered Christ's remarks, that even thinking lustfully was sinful and that anyone leading one of His children astray would be better off drowned? Bill's final point expressed his regret that licit sex had no better encouragement than these magazines. He made no distinction between erotica and porno-graphy, if the latter is defined as material designed to exploit and degrade women. His male-centred view was entirely preoccupied with the distinction between marital and pre-marital sex:

> I myself regret we Christian couples have no formally
> recognized erotic literature to help us in our sex lives. On
> the surface at least it seems to be alright for married
> couples to buy and read these magazines for stimulation.
> But when one gets into it deeper I see no way out of the

dilemma as yet. Because if we do buy Playboy, for example, then we are helping its publishers to stay in business
and their business is not concerned with morals but with
making money. The Church cant produce alternative
reading material for its married people because the young
and the unmarried would get hold of them. So it seems
we have no choice except each married couple excite
each other in their own homemade fashion as it has
always been in the past. What is your own view on this
point?[4]

Somewhat nonplussed, the owner made no reply but stopped carrying
the magazines in question. Several Kurelek traits are evident in Bill's
letter: idealism, stubborn courage, a readiness to fight for his beliefs,
and a naïve, quixotic streak that could be unconsciously comic at
times.

Sexual ethics preoccupied Bill that winter. Aitken's article had made
him angry, and he leapt at the chance to reply in print. His refutation
touched off a storm of letters to himself and to the magazine. Articles
Editor Jacqui Bishop told the artist that the response had been
"incredible".

In fifteen hundred words, Bill argued that permissive philosophy of
this type contradicted both natural and divine law. He defended the
gender roles that have dominated Western urban society until the
middle of this century as "natural law". Nature, as defined by Bill,
would have the last word in arguments with those who sought to
circumvent her: "It is that same greed for pleasure and ease that has
built those enormous industrial complexes which produce more food,
clothing, cars, fridges et cetera, than we really need and which pollute
our water and poison our air."[5] The attack on materialism was old; the
concern for the environment, new.

He attacked homosexuality for not leading to procreation and for
being unnatural: "It's not right." Abortion was compared to the ancient
Roman practice of inducing vomiting to permit further eating: "The
modern equivalent is to feast on the pleasure of sex (in or out of
marriage) and in the vomiting process butcher a completely defence-
less living being." Such practices, he argued, would inevitably extend
to euthanasia for the aged, the retarded, "and finally anyone at all who
stands in the way of getting maximum pleasure out of life." He foresaw
the loss of age-old virtues such as abstention, self-discipline, loyalty,
perseverance, and self-sacrifice. In closing, he anticipated sexual
delight in an afterlife with God.

His condemnation of even marital sex in excess, and his emphasis on virtues such as abstention and self-discipline, add up to a Spartan creed and not a little confusion. How much is too much? As for sexual delight in heaven in reunion with God, the notion is a novel one in traditional Christian theology.[6]

The response to Bill's essay became a flood. So many replies were received that Bill resorted to a form letter to thank his supporters. He was surprised and delighted; he had expected to be a voice crying in the wilderness. He urged his correspondents to write to the magazine, which might then consider publishing further articles by himself in the same vein. It was a yoke which was clearly anticipated with pleasure, apologies notwithstanding: "I as usual wont have the time or the expertize. But if my writings do help then I'll have to sacrifice time from my work because it seems the written word reaches more people than paintings do."[7] The uncertainty voiced in January to Father Kirley in Saskatoon sounds again: are paintings an effective medium for preaching? Significantly, the article in *Weekend Magazine* identified Kurelek as "artist and writer", a self-description almost certainly supplied by the painter.

Letters to the Editor were comically contradictory. Personal fan mail included assurances that he had produced the finest article ever seen in a secular magazine, a work of wisdom written so that even a child could understand it. The same correspondent urged him to continue his opposition to "women's lib". Some called Kurelek's ideas foolishly idealistic and narrow-minded, calculated to instil guilt, anxiety, and frustration. His "legalistic moralism" was compared with the morality of William Blake and found wanting. Blake was described as seeking sensual enjoyment through imagination, forgiveness, and love, whereas Kurelek wrote "in a mood of judgment rather than love". The writer found Blake's ideas more human and sane. Others, however, wrote to thank the artist for an article which they likened to a breath of fresh, pure air blowing into the stagnant wastes of current immorality.[8] For the man at the centre of the controversy this was heady stuff.

One of the critical debates that rage perennially round Bill's work concerns its didactic aspects. At the start of his career, Kurelek stated that he intended to devote his life to propaganda for Catholicism. His writings sometimes slight the importance of art and the modern emphasis on aesthetics. He argues that people (or, more specifically, human souls) are more important than art, yet claims that his strong belief in the value of art kept him from worrying about whether or not he was producing it. Art, as he put it, was "quite capable of taking care of itself" (A1 502).

In "Kurelek: Artist or Propagandist?" Professor Donald DeMarco weighs the alternatives and concludes that artistic purity has not been compromised. Like aesthetic philosopher Etienne Gilson, DeMarco believes that abstract art is rooted in representational art, and that all true works of art are essentially religious. He points to the primacy given in Kurelek's work to compositional, sensuous, and aesthetic values. He rejects as naïve a simplistic dichotomy between aesthetics and propaganda: art flows from the artist's whole being and expresses that totality. Kurelek's art reflects his world and his understanding of it. Art and vision are inseparable.

DeMarco discovered Kurelek's work in 1974 at the gallery in Niagara Falls. A shared interest in the Right to Life movement soon brought together the professor of aesthetics and the artist. DeMarco's Epilogue to *The Passion of Christ* (1975) addresses the question "Is Genius Abnormal?" Kurelek had been a patient in a psychiatric hospital, and his personality was highly unconventional. In our commercialized culture, DeMarco argues, normalcy has become synonymous with mediocrity. The truly real, in human terms, is often evaded, while the exceptional is dismissed as abnormal. The popular judgment of Mozart is typical: "Kurelek is an artist who, like Mozart, brings light from another world. He is unusual inasmuch as he has willed that light to penetrate his heart where suffering mixes the divine with the human and genius understands them as one; but he is not abnormal.... Kurelek suffered his way into normalcy and the eminently human quality of his paintings amply attests to that normalcy."[9] His long hours of painting may thus be seen as an expression of his love. His paintings were his prayers.

Much of Bill's crusading energy in the 1970s was pouring into his fight against abortions as a solution for unwanted pregnancies, which were becoming alarmingly frequent. One incident in his continuing battle occurred in 1976, in connection with a close friend of some ten years' standing. Writer Gloria Frolick had grown up in a Ukrainian community in Alberta, very near to the first Kurelek homestead. She had known Bill in Toronto since the mid-sixties, when his shyness made him seem "like a Ukrianian boy of fourteen". They had talked at length of their rural backgrounds, and Gloria had supplied Bill with some eighty detailed sketches of childhood memories as subject matter for his work. Twenty-four of these inspired a series of farm and landscape scenes. Gloria had also produced a manuscript, a novella, which Bill intended to illustrate and which he carried with him to Saskatoon.

Attempts at abortion, many of them bungled, were not uncommon in Canada in the first two-thirds of this century. Gloria knew of three women whose lives had been lost through attempted abortions. Her manuscript, "The Chicken Man", was a poetic fiction written out of the deeply felt experiences of her childhood. The story concerned the death of a prairie farmer whose wife had died from an abortion many years before. When she gave Bill her story, Gloria may not have known that by the mid-seventies he had become closely identified with the Right to Life movement.

In scattered hours away from his work on the giant mural, and in the few days after its completion while Bill stayed on in More College, he finished fifteen paintings to illustrate Frolick's novella. He was particularly pleased with *Death of the Chicken Man*, his painting intended for the cover. He described it to Gloria as "a surrealist public-eye catcher that I never thought I had in me".[10] There was, however, a problem.

After consultation with Father Kirley, Bill wrote to tell Gloria that he feared her book might be co-opted as ammunition by the people who favored liberalization of the abortion laws. If she wished to use his work to illustrate her fiction, she would have to change the text, turning the abortion into a miscarriage performed by an unqualified midwife. In reaching this decision, Bill had hesitated only once, briefly disturbed by the knowledge that the original version was based on actual happenings. Was it *honest* to distort this reality? The conviction that abortion was murder and must therefore always be wrong soon settled the matter in his mind.[11] The manuscript was changed accordingly.

Throughout the 1970s, enthusiastic reviews of his books and personal fan mail commending his stand on several public issues further impressed the painter with the power of the written word. As his wife observes in a Foreword to the 1980 edition of the autobiography, Bill was spending so much time writing in 1977 that she inquired if he was thinking of changing his career: "To my surprise, he replied 'I don't know yet.'" It is difficult to take the remark seriously. It does indicate, however, that writing was consuming more of Bill's time in his last years and that he recognized its usefulness as a propaganda vehicle.

One suspects that it also fed his ego. Praise for his paintings was no longer novel, but praise for his writing obviously meant a great deal. To the children of a sixth-grade class in Windsor, Ontario, Bill wrote as follows:

> How do I like being author and writer? I do like it but I
> can tell you I'm really surprised that I turned out to be a
> writer too. God has been generous to me beyond my
> wildest dreams. I knew that He had given me the talent to
> draw and paint since I was 7 years old but as for the abil-
> ity to write it only came out when Tundra Books asked
> me to write notes to explain the paintings reproduced in
> *A Prairie Boys Summer*.

279

Did William catch the ball? Sorry I cant tell you because
I dont know myself. William represents me when a boy.
... I put it in the form of a question because I was trying
to express Williams own acute self doubts about his
success.[12]

Were those doubts ever really satisfied, or was the need for reassurance infinite?

His autobiography had always been of central importance to him. The original writing had been therapeutic, and perhaps it continued to serve that function through its many revisions over the years. By the early 1970s, a pattern had established itself. Bill would seek editorial advice from a writer whom he hoped to find sympathetic; the writer would recommend that the manuscript be radically shortened and that the "proofs of the existence of God" be deleted or placed at the end; Bill would then withdraw. He sought approval, not correction. In his heart, he was convinced that his manuscript needed only minor changes.

Through the seventies, Barry Callaghan was closely associated with the autobiography and with plans for its revision. Bill sought his help on the project, and allowed him to edit a narrative portion from the early years on the farm. It appeared in 1972 in Callaghan's new journal, *Exile*, along with eight color reproductions of Kurelek paintings.

Callaghan found that the artist was startled by the idea of major revisions and deletions. As with most novices, Bill felt protective towards his writing: every word was sacred. To this natural tendency was added the force of a stubborn personality and the fear that editors would remove or weaken his evangelical message. W. O. Mitchell met with exactly the same reaction in 1974.

Bill's "conversion story" was a focus for the tensions in his life. He desperately wanted to tell the truth about that life and to make it an exemplum in the medieval sense, but the old wounds made *success* imperative. Callaghan put it this way: "He wanted that book to read well, to be published, be persuasive. I could feel it almost like a lust in him. He wanted his story Out There. But he didn't want to yield to any judgment of his prose. I had to operate with great care, almost apologetically.... He really wanted a blessing, not criticism.... He couldn't write to save his soul!"[13]

Their uneasy relationship continued for years, with frustrations on both sides. Bill hoped to bring Callaghan back into the Catholic Church. Callaghan continued to hope for a radically revised, carefully edited version of the autobiography. He considered the first edition merely a writer's first draft, and interpreted Bill's refusal to revise his words as an expression of vanity. Perhaps his criticism had made more of an impression than Callaghan realized, judging by Bill's letter to his wife's cousin in 1975: "I agree the chapters on theology and philosophy in my autobiography are heavy going but they are the whole reason for the books existence in the first place so the obvious solution is to get a professional writer to rewrite them to make them snappy. This I will be doing shortly as the book has to be republished."[14] Snappy? Snappy theology? And was the theology really the book's entire *raison d'être*? Why did it *have* to be republished?

January 1974. Bill in his tiny studio in the basement of the Kureleks' Balsam Avenue house. Photo by Daniel M. Newman, courtesy Art Gallery of Windsor.

The basement of the Kurelek house was the scene of brisk activity in the 1970s. At one end was Bill's studio, a tiny cell approximately eight feet long by four feet wide, which had begun life as a coal cellar. It had been deepened and given a heavy, fireproof door, a narrow double bunk, a small table, and a strong artificial light. In the early 1980s, a life-sized crown of thorns made by the artist still lay propped against one wall.

Visitors were commonly appalled by the airless studio. Some thought it masochistic. American painter and print-maker Jacques Hnizdovsky writes:

> It was virtually a tiny closet, without daylight and without ventilation, filled with odor from the heavy fumes. I was shocked by the condition in which he was working long hours and which may even have contributed to his untimely death. ... He could have afforded a good studio, yet worked in a closet as if to punish himself for something. I remember urging him for the sake of health to at least install a ventilator. As I was told later, he did it.[15]

Bill at work; his beloved spray paints are in the foreground.

Kenneth Shorey shares the suspicion that Bill was masochistic. In *Someone With Me*, Bill had written of wanting to be all things to all men, in order (like St. Paul) to preach Christ crucified (A1 509). Shorey suspects that Bill identified with St. Paul "because Paul was anxious to suffer more than Jesus had suffered. ... Perhaps (subconsciously) he knew he was courting cancer by breathing the paint fumes."[16]

One of his assistants suffered from headaches after working in the studio in 1973. Agnes Krumins was advised by a physician to work henceforth only in ventilated areas, but her warnings to Bill went unheeded. Information concerning the hazards of art materials was not widespread in the 1970s, and physicians at St. Michael's Hospital agreed, after Bill's death, that there was no "firm" evidence as to the cause of his carcinoma.

In the decade that followed his death, evidence of the connection between spray paints and a higher incidence of cancer has been mounting.[17] Symptoms of toxic poisoning include headaches, chest pains, coughing, dizziness, nausea—symptoms that Bill experienced in his last two years. By 1975 he was beginning to make an effort to change some of his work habits. Photographs show him spraying paintings outside, on the driveway and in the garden. He also conceived of a protective covering, like a diver's suit, and planned to have it made.[18]

By 1975 Bill had been warned by his own physician to avoid using spray paints. For Pagurian's Inuit series that fall, he used only acrylics. Neither the method nor the result satisfied the painter, who told his chief assistant that he intended to paint the way he liked even if it injured his health. "He liked the effect of the sprays with mixed media,"

Sylvia Chan recalled. "He used sprays, oils, ballpoint pens, colored pencils, magic markers, and an artist's knife."

While Bill was painting in the studio, one of his assistants would usually be working in the large adjacent room, whose cupboards were covered in Ukrainian designs. The scene might be further enlivened by his young sons shooting a hockey puck around the paintings. Assistants were important to Bill in the 1970s, not only to prepare his boards with gesso but also to paint background areas, especially the detailed grasses and stones which are one of his trademarks. When copies were required, his helpers would outline the scene from the original with a special tracing method Bill had devised.[19]

The twin practices of copying his own work and allowing apprentices to paint parts of the backgrounds of the paintings had become essential to Bill in the 1970s. Isaacs disapproved, but the artist believed that he had history on his side. He told Sylvia that Renaissance masters had had helpers like herself who had painted parts of their canvases. This same assistant, who worked with Bill from September 1973 until his death, unintentionally supplied him with further fuel for this debate. Returning from a visit to Hong Kong she brought a book on twentieth-century Chinese landscape painters as a gift for her employer. Much to Bill's delight, the book stated that modern Chinese artists employed apprentices to help with their paintings. Prior to this reinforcement, Bill had asked Sylvia to do something other than painting when customers came into the new basement: "Later he didn't care, he didn't tell me to stop when people came in."[20]

Copying his own paintings had been part of Bill's life as an artist since the early 1960s. Certainly it was part of his means of financial survival, for himself and for his many charities. Barry Callaghan considered the practice meanly commercial and ethically dishonest, since many customers believed they were buying unique works. Callaghan tried to persuade Bill that changing a detail made no real difference; believing that it did so was merely the defence of an extraordinarily legalistic mind, "the manoeuvring of the justified sinner".[21] Hnizdovsky was one of the few people in the art world who accepted the practice of copying. He noted that El Greco was a great self-copyist, as well as a great painter.

Bill's chief assistants found him inspiring, and held him in awe.[22] Krumins calls him a very giving person who tried to make people happy by his paintings: "It was his enthusiasm for his work that was inspiring. He seemed to be enjoying it so much." He was patient with his young helpers, never condescending. He encouraged them with their own painting, framed their work for them, and encouraged them to make painting a career.

Like Agnes, Sylvia admired Bill deeply. In 1973 she was an art student, an immigrant from Hong Kong. Bill had put a notice on the bulletin board of the Ontario College of Art, advertising for someone to run errands, buy supplies, and answer the phone. Ironically, Sylvia was almost refused on her first response—for being female. She was finally granted an interview, and then a chance to prove her worth. *Try me*, she had urged. Bill smiled. They were both quiet people. Soon she would be working on parts of his paintings and would become, in Jean's words, "invaluable to him". One of the projects aborted by his death was a series of paintings on Chinese proverbs, illustrated with Canadian settings. The idea had been sparked by the friendship between master and apprentice, and Bill intended it as an expression of his gratitude for Sylvia's help.

She found him humble and hard-working. His personality impressed her even more than his painting. For four years she saw him living simply and dealing with everyone in the same way, with kindness and patience. Children would come into the basement, his own and others. Once a strange boy of about ten came to interview the artist for a school project. Bill answered all his questions patiently. Was it not, Sylvia asked later, a waste of his time? Bill replied that in his own youth he had written to famous artists and received no reply; he did not want others to be depressed by rejection as he had once been. When his own children asked for something, Sylvia observed that he often stopped his work to help them.

In his youth, Bill had sought in vain for a master to whom he could apprentice himself. Now he was the master, with apprentice artists of his own. In the text for *First Snow, From the South* in the Charlevoix series, he wrote that he would regard it as a great honor to paint even a single pebble in one of Brueghel's masterpieces: "At that time it wasn't considered a sacrilege for apprentices to assist their masters in the actual production of one of their originals."

Sylvia had begun with odd jobs and progressed to gesso: three coats per board. Within a year she was painting grass, leaves, wheat, bushes, pebbles, rocks, bricks, the texture of a road, perhaps a fence, or a roof. The artist would paint a sample patch of the detailed area, then leave his assistant to continue in the same manner. She was an apt pupil, and his confidence in her grew rapidly. Bill drew the design on the gessoed board, and painted the sky, the figures, the final touches. Like Bill, Sylvia worked long hours and did other work as a rest from painting: "He'd work anywhere, any time. He never wasted a second! I never saw him not working, except when he was playing the accordion." During those years Bill was teaching himself to play, and he practised for one hour each day.

The gentle, loving man encountered by his assistants seems another Kurelek from the crusader, the man on the white horse who rode out to do battle with pornography and indulgence. Perhaps the two met in the Kurelek who never stopped working and who valued self-discipline and self-sacrifice so highly. There is a wistfulness in his remark to Shorey that he wished he had the time to see a film; or to Anna Balan, in the spring of 1976, that he finds it "increasingly hard to cope with the wear and tear".

The man's complexity is perhaps best caught in his letters, which are legion. To Gordon Rayner, a fellow artist at The Isaacs Gallery, he wrote to express his pleasure at Rayner's new work: "Our philosophies and styles of painting are so different [but] I really love this show. In the past individual canvases of yours spoke to me even though I've never had much use or understanding of abstract art. In this show they all speak to me. There is a lovely moving kind of poetic sensibility in them."[23] For a man who had never liked abstract art, the response is surprising and suggests a continuing growth in artistic sensibility in his fifth decade.

To an official at Canadian National he wrote with a strange proposal which was very much on his mind during the building of the CN Tower in downtown Toronto in the mid-seventies:

> The idea is to have a very short prayer inscribed on a
> small copper plate said by two figures also inscribed on
> the plate in very simple lines. ... Your tower fascinates me
> even though I recognize the vanity of mere bigness. ...
> One of the signs of bigness on our part is to recognize
> ourselves for what we really are: small yet capable of
> greatness in Him who strengthens us. Therefore I visual-
> ize this businessman and construction worker joining
> hands and saying this prayer of manly humility: O
> Supreme Builder of the Universe help us not to make the
> mistake of the builders of the first tower which you
> confounded.[24]

He offered to make the plate and to pay for its installation at the top of the tower, where no one but God would see it. His father, as Bill understood him, had wanted manliness; his heavenly father wanted humility. Bill was attempting to please both.

Many who knew the artist saw or suspected a change in him in his last years. Balan expresses what others confirm. In the 1960s she found him rigid, dogmatic, consumed by a faith that taught him that his civilization deserved to be destroyed by fire. At that time he had appeared to her as a Canadian Savonarola: "There was I felt a lack of love—his church or faith did not give him peace of mind. Gradually I noticed him changing. Towards the end of his life, I think Bill came to terms with himself, with his faith and with the world. He finally had the wisdom to understand that he could not change everything and therefore concentrated on the things he could."[25] The medieval monk was never really banished, but in his final years the lion had learned to lie down with the lamb.

16

Strange Prophecy

THE FINAL COUNTDOWN FOR BILL BEGAN IN SEPTEMBER 1977. BY THEN HE had only two months to live. No one knew that, although he must have been in considerable pain that summer. Certain remarks to friends would be interpreted much later as hints. At the start of September, he was able to function, to pass as a healthy man; by the end of the month he was barely able to stand without assistance and had entered St. Michael's Hospital.

All summer Bill had been planning his second trip to the Ukraine, a trip for which he had waited seven years and which had now become possible. The Soviet Embassy had finally granted a visa for an extended stay in Borivtsi, his father's village. Bill had been applying for it ever since he had been allowed four precious hours there as part of his trip with the group led by the Kolankiwskys in 1970.

Bill had been hoping to spend six weeks in the Ukraine. He would have only three (September 3-25). He wished to prepare for a huge series of murals depicting the history of Ukrainian pioneer settlement in Canada. He called it a project close to his heart, a painter's dream, and intended to execute it in Ottawa, on the walls of a government building. The text for a painting called *Hunger Strike in Ottawa for V. Moroz* (1974) outlines the plan. By doing this painting and thus contributing to a protest against a Soviet violation of human rights, Bill feared that he was sacrificing his dream. The Soviets might no longer consider him apolitical and would never grant the visa. In the painting's text he had written of needing six weeks to research in two Ukrainian villages, his father's and that of "William" (Vasyl) Stephanyk, a writer famous for depicting the motives and moods of Ukrainian peasants forced to emigrate to the New World. In Borivtsi, in a few brief hours in 1970, he had sensed his roots; now he longed to return to paint them. He was not, he added, a Ukrainian nationalist, although he was proud of his ancestry. He considered himself a Canadian "first and foremost".

Stanley and Gloria Frolick remembered his excitement in late August at the prospect of getting on with his dream.[1] Bill was already planning a second and final trip to the Ukraine in 1978 for his "village research project". Financing had been arranged through the generous help of a Ukrainian-Canadian association and a private patron.[2] Bill suspected that the Soviets might be willing to offer help in return for favorable propaganda. Since he was strongly anti-communist, he had no wish to be indebted. He hoped to board in a village house but foresaw problems: "The Kieve officials want to put me in the nicest house in the village so I'll get the best impression of their regime. ... I would have preferred to stay with my cousins (their houses are considered too poor)."[3]

To May Cutler, Bill wrote with unconscious irony that he was "as good as gone to the land of the dead for all September"; his work in the Ukraine meant that he could take on no other commitments for that time. Moreover, his health was worrisome: "I hope I survive the Ukraine trip healthwise. I been ill with something for the past half year. Nobody seems to know what's wrong. I'll try the Mayo clinic after I return. But the comrades over there put on high pressure hospitality to impress special guests and my father's family just won't take 'no' to their offers of food and drink. It took 8 years [*sic*] to get that special visa. That's why I'm going in even if it kills me."[4]

To his wife, Bill varied the remark, saying that he would go even if he had to be carried on a stretcher. He had not felt well for six months and had been quite sick since early August.[5] No doubt he attempted to conceal the extent to which the illness was exhausting him. After the long years of waiting, he naturally feared that if he refused the opportunity that September he might never have another chance. As he told several friends, it was the chance of a lifetime.

Bill had always kept in touch with his sister Nancy, who had been living in Africa for some years. To her he sent a franker assessment of his health problems and a guess as to possible causes:

> I've not been feeling well for a year or two now. It began in my chest and has worked its way down to my stomach now. It may be the poisons I've absorbed from spray paints or else its psychological. The doctors haven't been able to trace it to any specific organ. Jean is getting a Madonna House prayer group to try a cure for me tonight by laying on of hands. God's usual answer for me when I try to escape suffering is "NO" so although I firmly believe I can be cured by miracle the answer will probably be NO again. I'll tell you in the remaining space.
>
> No, nothing happened. God bless, your brother Will.[6]

A letter to Father de Valk of Saskatoon, written twenty months earlier, shows that Bill had developed serious chest pains as early as 1975, and that he suspected fumes from his oil sprays and lacquers as a cause. He therefore intended to use acrylic paints for the mural: "It could have fatally poisoned me and I'm not sure how far I've damaged myself."[7]

Bill's iron will would carry him through September and to the land of his dreams. He set out wearing the mask of normalcy. He returned barely able to stand, yet he carried with him almost one hundred fine drawings and five paintings![8] He had fulfilled exactly the schedule set for himself before leaving home.[9]

Kolankiwsky records an incident from the trip:

> Someone who assisted Kurelek during his stay in Borivtsi afterwards told me a story which so aptly illustrated the artist's attitude to his Ukrainian heritage. One day when Kurelek was alone, painting in the fields, a small child came running into the house crying "Uncle is ill, he is lying on the ground!" ... He found him on the path with his face turned to the freshly ploughed furrows. Touching his arm he enquired about his health. Kurelek answered "I'm alright—I'm only searching for my roots."[10]

The paintings done in the Ukraine that September reveal Bill's gift for satire. His dislike of communist regimes is wittily encoded; had it been overt, officials would very probably not have allowed the works to leave the Ukraine. The government had asked Kurelek to record recent achievements and advances as well as the old ways they knew he loved. Accordingly, Bill painted *Geese Hissing at the New Asphalt Road in Village of Borivtsi*. The brief and ugly stretch of black asphalt through the village centre begins nowhere and leads nowhere. Since the villagers' opinions were better kept to themselves, the geese express the distaste felt by both species.

His painting of a primitive bread-making machine shows a grotesque contraption, humanoid yet worm-like, with a red hand. The form and colors of the old Ukrainian flag, currently forbidden by the Soviets, are worked in by means of yellow wall tiles and blue supporting pillars. Bags of flour are stacked by the pillars, while people are conspicuously absent. *The Mechanized Baba Feeds Nine Villages* mocks the concept of technological advance by the repulsive, antiquated appearance of the machine.

Many of the drawings from the Ukraine had been done with a felt pen. The Kolankiwskys remember that Bill called these drawings *wymucheni*, "tormented", because of the difficulties which attended their creation. The day after his return, Bill was apologizing to his friends for being unable to stand as he showed them the new work.[11] He was pale, and coughed frequently. The Kolankiwskys found him very weak, and feared the worst.[12]

His brother John also saw Bill in late September. He could not stand unaided but said nothing more than "John, I'm not well." He seemed surprised, almost incredulous, to find himself betrayed by his body. Stamina and will-power were no longer sufficient: "He said that he had thought he was rather invincible, that it wouldn't happen to him. And he *must* have thought that he was invincible, the way he punished his body with fasting and long hours."[13]

John thought Bill's reference to his health referred to incapacity rather than death, as the talk at this date was of diagnosis, treatment, and cure.

On September 30, Bill entered St. Michael's Hospital. He anticipated a stay of fifteen days, for tests concerning "a long standing illness".[14] Henceforth only the closest of family and friends would be permitted to visit. None the less he was still hoping to extend the St. Matthew Gospel project to 800 works to cover the entire Gospel; Kolankiwsky intended to publish them himself in a series of books. Soon Jean knew that her husband had cancer, with little or no chance of survival; later, Isaacs knew. No one told Bill that he had tumors until his very last days. No one discussed death with him. That October may well have been the loneliest month of his life.

Much later, people would remember Bill's Shelter Manifesto to Shorey in the summer of 1968. In trying to explain his reasons for building a bomb shelter and his hope to survive the blast, Bill stoutly affirmed that he was not afraid of death but would be happy to return to his Creator. He had given the matter a great deal of thought and concluded that cancer was the kind of death that he would choose in peacetime. Such a death would have three advantages: it would give him plenty of time to make his peace with God; it would allow him to offer the physical pain "in atonement" for his sins and those of others; and it would allow him to demonstrate the joy and courage with which a Christian should face death. In short, it would be a *useful* death, like those of the martyrs in past ages. Martyrdom, he told Shorey, was his "secret longing". He feared that his courage might fail, but trusted that God would provide the necessary strength.

Martyrdom may have looked attractive ten years earlier, but in the fall of 1977 Bill very much wanted to live. That was evident to all who saw him. So much remained to be done. Mute witness to his state of mind is found in what may well have been his last painting, dating from early October.[15] It depicts three figures, two self-portraits and Death, personified in the medieval manner as a black-robed skeleton. The white background suggests the tiles of a clinical room. Across the base of the short, wide scene is a prostrate Kurelek in a hospital bed. Above his head is a second Kurelek, this one a little fighting cock of a man in black pants and white shirt, fists raised and clenched against Death. The skeletal figure shrinks back as if intimidated, hands crossed to ward off the blows of the valiant little man. This rather extraordinary work is titled (in Ukrainian script across its face) *Death Fears Him Who Resists Her*. The oversized right hand of the prostrate figure is prominently placed on the abdomen—the gifted hand, over the critical area. The body is inert but the eyes are wide open, the will strong. The face resembles both Bill and his father. They were stubborn men. Fighters. There was anger in Bill that fall; and there was disbelief.

Death Fears Him Who Resists Her, mixed media, 13″ x 6¼″. Private collection, photo by Wolf Studio. This may be Bill's last painting.

The odds for the last fight were overwhelmingly against him. How soon might he have known? His doctor suspects that he would have guessed the outcome early in October, from the lack of hope displayed by those around him. The withdrawal of family and even physicians from the terminally ill is well documented; negative body language and even avoidance by people close to the patient have led to the development of palliative-care units.[16] The doctor who admitted Bill said that any physician would feel defeated before he started with the symptoms Kurelek displayed during his first week in hospital.[17]

For more than a year Bill had been experiencing abdominal pain, increasing fatigue, depression, general weakness, and shortness of breath. By the time he was admitted, the enlargement of his liver could be felt from the outside. His skin was jaundiced. Abnormally high levels of calcium were producing drowsiness and periods of confusion. Towards the end of the month an operation revealed that the carcinoma had spread throughout the liver, bile duct, pancreas, stomach, and lungs. Bill's condition was untreatable.

Some of the doctors found their patient introverted, withdrawn, rather frightened. Fear is a common reaction to hospitalization and the loss of liberty. Anger is also common in the early stages of coming to terms with death. Bill showed no desire to talk of himself or his health problems. He never asked for a prognosis. Occasionally he would talk in Ukrainian to the physician who shared his heritage. He sketched with decreasing frequency as the days went by. He read. As his strength permitted, he signed his name to Pagurian sporting prints, over and over and over.

For a man like Bill, his body's betrayal must have been a terrible blow. His old friend Father James McConica speculates on just what this humiliation might have meant to the artist: "When he knew he was dying, he felt that the disease had got him where he was most proud.... He had confidence in his physical strength and energy, and how appropriate this was in a way that the disease which was taking him would be one that would sap his energy.... He was very proud of his strength and he saw this then as another form of pride that had to be dealt with, before he was ready to meet with his Lord."[18]

To relatives and friends, Bill did not speak in pious phrases. His talk was not of meeting his Lord but of old times, old friends in Stonewall and Winnipeg. Jean found it disconcerting; John felt their bond confirmed. Bill remembered high school names not mentioned for thirty-five years. The family recall that he talked of the past continually. Near the end he told John, "I don't want to be any trouble, get them to put me into a neat box and send me out west."[19]

Many friends felt that his final weeks were made even more painful by an unpleasant diet, and by the hospital tests which continued to the last day of his life. Forbidden to bring food, the Kolankiwskys came in late October bearing roses, cologne, and slides of the Polish-Canadian paintings exhibited in Warsaw that same month. Their news of the possibility of the series showing in Kiev in 1978 pleased Bill, who urged them to press the necessary Soviet officials. His mind was clear. He was thin, with a stomach grossly distended by abdominal fluid; he joked that he was like a child with malnutrition. When they urged him to pray for a miraculous cure, he replied, "It's easy for you to talk." A nurse brought pills and painkillers, and he threw them in the wastebasket. He spoke of being tormented by terrifying dreams.

Bill underwent exploratory surgery on October 28. There were malignant tumors in his liver, pancreas, gall bladder—"everywhere". The surgeon, Dr. D. W. Jirsch, remembers talking with his patient a few days later:

> I asked him, Bill, are you having any pain? I call people by
> their first name, especially when they're sick, they need all

the friends they can get. And he said, In my body or in my soul? No one else had ever said that to me, and it was almost as if my question were amusing to him. I thought it was a very positive reaction on his part and indicated that he still had a sense of humor. So I said, Bill, I meant in your body, it's all *I* can deal with. He said, My body's fine, thank you. He looked peaceful, he was playing with me, even though he knew he was going to die. He was very peaceful and serene in his last days.[20]

On November 3, having received the last rites of the Church, Bill died.

17

Shifting Portraits

THERE WERE TWO FUNERAL CEREMONIES, NOVEMBER 6 AND 7, THE FIRST FOR family and close friends. Some one hundred mourners more than filled a local funeral parlor. Kurelek lay in an open coffin, wearing a Ukrainian shirt beneath a tailored jacket. Ukrainian music was sung by a church choir led by his brother-in-law, Nat Olynyk. On the following day, a memorial Mass was held at midday in the church where Kurelek had painted a Resurrection mural earlier that same year. Corpus Christi was filled to overflowing. The spectacle was dramatic and impressive. The country was mourning one of its heroes. Incense rose as censers swung. Robed in white, symbol of the Resurrection, a dozen priests filled the sanctuary. Almost all were Irish Catholics. Toronto's Ukrainian community was surprised and disappointed to find not a single Ukrainian priest, Catholic or Orthodox, sharing in the ceremony. The elements that Kurelek had held together in his life had separated, with his death, like oil and water.

Jean wore a Ukrainian blouse to the funerals. She said that her husband was with God. She was smiling and serene.

The interment followed. A long line of cars drove through heavy rain to Resthaven Cemetery on Kingston Road at Brimley, in Scarborough. Discouraged by the downpour, some mourners remained in their cars. Huddled beneath umbrellas, the others scattered quickly after the brief graveside service. The coffin remained on the grass, to be lowered later. Still later, a brass plaque was added, which read, "William Kurelek. Living with Christ."

The eulogy in Corpus Christi was given by Father James McConica, who had known the artist since the late 1950s. Dr. McConica spoke of Kurelek as rooted in his family, his people, and his God. He called his faith heroic, inspired, even consuming: "In a life that was in every way extraordinary, it may be oddly fitting that the end should come when he was still so vital and secure in his strength. We will remember him always at the height of his powers." That faith, he continued, is inscribed in the enduring legacy of the paintings:

> It is also inscribed in the hearts of all whose lives he touched. ... It can be read in powerful images in this very Church, in the three panels he painted over the altar of the Blessed Sacrament: the loneliness and seeming defeat of death, the power of the Resurrection, and the final victory of life and hope. At the apex is his vision of the overwhelming power of Christ's resurrection. ... It was his last major work to be completed; and it is his message to us today. ... Proclaiming [the Resurrection] was the constant theme of his work, even when it was not outwardly religious. His love of ordinary people, his vital sense of life, his blunt, plain style, as unadorned as was the man himself, made him perhaps the first truly national painter Canada has seen. ... The thing that mattered most to him was the life of the ordinary man and woman. And they stream through his canvasses. ... They are God's gathering in what the artist in his autobiography called "this tragic, puzzling, yet wonderful world". I believe he lived his life so urgently because he wanted to arouse the consciences of men to the needs of this vast human family of God— needs of the body and needs of the spirit.[1]

After the memorial Mass, McConica felt an extraordinary sense of peace, and the conviction that Kurelek's life was completely fulfilled.

Mrs. Mary Kurelek, Bill's mother, with Prime Minister Pierre Trudeau, at the official opening of the Kurelek Ukrainian Pioneer series in the House of Commons, Ottawa, February 1983. Courtesy Kurelek family.

There was no shortage of public eulogies, and they were glowing. The press called Kurelek "the people's painter", a man with a vision, an artist of extraordinary achievement and of intense significance to Canada and the world. Father Kevin Kirley termed him a quiet man, shy and boyish, with a penetrating glance, "a man who had known suffering, physical and mental anguish, but who had expunged all bitterness from his heart." Kurelek was described as a strong, courageous man who was also a seeker, "still very much a pilgrim with us all".[2]

Eulogies, by definition, are one-sided; not necessarily dishonest, simply partial. Anyone wishing to canonize the artist must wrestle with a second Kurelek, a dark and puzzling figure. If bitterness was truly expunged from his heart, it was routed only in the last few weeks of his life. His final state of mind will always remain a mystery. But how can we reconcile his public protestations of forgiveness with his equally public denunciations of his father's ill-treatment of him? For nearly half a lifetime those protestations played a major role in Kurelek's inner and outer life. His religion taught him that what mattered was the will, not the emotions. He forced his will to forgive while his emotions fought a rearguard action. By Kurelek's own account, his father had taught his family to harbor grudges. Having sown the wind, Dmytro would reap the whirlwind.

Artist Jacques Hnizdovsky perceived two opposing forces in his friend's psyche, "extreme goodness and cruelty". He failed to understand how a man as sensitive and intelligent as Kurelek could remain blind to the fact that his mother had obviously been forced to leave her young children in order to work in the barns and the fields. Surely, Hnizdovsky writes, Kurelek could have seen that his parents loved him and wished him well: "Deep in his soul Kurelek knew this and this is why he again and again returns to the same problem as if to confess his own injustice towards his parents."[3] Hnizdovsky had been impressed by the senior Kureleks: "Without question Kurelek's mother would stand as an embodiment of pure love; right after her I would put his father."

Kurelek had begun life with the central paradox of loving and hating his father. Like all who strive to be saints or martyrs, the artist struggled always with feelings of love and hate, forgiveness and vengeance, humility and pride, masochism and joy. His need for self-justification was very strong. Barry Callaghan found him a stubborn, vain, and generous man, "a troublesome mixture" of humility and fierce pride: "He had an excuse for everything. He could be narrow and prejudiced. He was always a contradiction to me."[4]

In Callaghan's eyes, Kurelek was harsh, judgmental, and unforgiving. He judged himself and he judged others, as his father had done before: "He blamed his father for his own temperament. Sometimes he mistook his own harshness for his father's. Some of the wounds he suffered were self-imposed, but he blamed his father for them, not understanding that he wounded and judged himself." Callaghan saw Bill as insecure, lacking in confidence yet fiercely determined to *be someone*. The autobiography seemed to be something absolutely necessary to him to satisfy a sense of destiny and to heal his pain. Eric Freifeld's view is very similar. Freifeld believes that during his decade away from Canada, Kurelek changed very little; he was vain and self-centred: "There was always a central narcissism."

Sincere self-delusion has been called the privilege of genius and the secret of success. Was Kurelek aware of these contradictions within himself? At some level of consciousness he must have been. In his painting of Judas in torment, where a hand covers one eye, the face suggests his own. What were his frequent public protestations of success but the reassurance needed by one who lacked self-confidence yet desperately *needed* to succeed? His "doomsday" pronouncements swung wildly between modesty and pride. To his patron and friend Dr. Wachna he had written that he lived in a "classy" neighborhood inhabited by doctors and engineers, the type of men admired by his father. He was bitterly disappointed by his father's failure to attend the banquet in his honor given in 1968 by the Ukrainian Business and Professional Men's Association; these men, he told Shorey on the day of the banquet, were "the very class of people, wealthy, influential professionals that it had been my father's ambition I should become." The pride is obvious, yet nearly everyone who knew the man was impressed by the humility that marked his daily words and actions.

He was called generous, even by those most critical of him. His charities were legion, his small acts of kindness beyond count. His debts of gratitude to Margaret Smith and Av Isaacs were paid many times over, yet his parents' efforts on his behalf were slighted or ignored, brushed off as acts of mere duty. His parents, he wrote in 1972, were "obligated" to help him. The context clearly implied that such necessary actions were hardly praiseworthy, unlike the freely given help of strangers.[5] The twin series of works in the mid-sixties in honor of his father and mother both end in denunciations of them, as we have seen, although the Forewords stress that Kurelek is fulfilling the biblical injunction to honor one's parents.

For his part, Dmytro seems to have publicly acknowledged his son's success by the 1970s. He was impressed by the letter from the Queen, thanking Kurelek for the gift of a painting; and he was somewhat awed by the prices the paintings commanded. In general, the relationship was much improved. The father was shattered by his son's untimely death, and grieved deeply. He said it was "unjust" that his son should die before him. Tragically, the block in their communication had never been healed. In hospital, the son had longed to tell of his recent trip to the Ukraine, while the father longed for just such news, but something had stood in the way: "They both wanted the same thing but couldn't communicate," Kurelek's sister observed.[6] The remark covered a lifetime.

The death, like the life, was a scene of contradictions. The surgeon remembers his final days as peaceful and serene. But on the evening of November 3, a strange scene took place in Kurelek's hospital room. His wife described it to me in 1981. He cried out. Holding his wife's hand, he struggled to rise from his bed and to break loose from his oxygen mask. Shouting "Jean! Jean!" he tore off the connection. There were elements of violence and confusion in the death that followed almost immediately.

In the end, we come back to Dr. McConica's intuition: this was a life completely fulfilled. He may well have been right. Kurelek drove himself cruelly, but for most of his adult life he did what he wanted to do: paint. And gloried in the doing. He was not happy unless he was working and the work that mattered most was painting. In Catholicism he had discovered a reason for his pain, even for his anxieties, one that satisfied him fully. His joy was very real. He had found, in his own words, success beyond his wildest dreams. How many of us can say the same?

In the summer of 1983, on a cliff overlooking the St. Lawrence, I watched three hang-gliders soaring like giant dragonflies over the great river. I had gone on Kurelek research to Québec City, and to a Christian Brothers farm near St. Nicolas on the south shore. On the drive back with James Halpin and Father Leo Letarte, we were arrested by the spectacle of the hang-gliders in flight and stopped to watch. The priest said that it must be a fantastic feeling, like a drug high: "Bill must have felt the same thing, sometimes, of being carried beyond himself."

It was a sunny, windy day. We parked and walked past an old stone farmhouse to the cliffs. There was a sheer drop of two hundred and fifty feet to the river. The tide was half out, the water turquoise and purple and blue. The green fields were dotted with vetch, mustard, daisies, and orange tiger-lilies. Darting swallows seemed to imitate the human flyers. A red and orange glider swooped low over our heads at the speed of a car on a freeway. Suspended horizontally, the flyer held onto metal handlebars while his legs were held in a harness at the knees. I gasped at the colors, the nearness, the sheer audacity of the man. The thought came to me: Bill must have felt like that.

Two boys were helping another flyer prepare for take-off. Methodically he unpacked the parts from a dufflebag and assembled them. A black-and-yellow glider, like a great bat, took shape. The man would hang below a metal triangle, the trapeze. The wings were thirty-three feet wide. I asked if he felt free when he flew, and he said Yes, but it was hard to explain. I asked if he was afraid, especially on take-off. He replied in French, We have confidence in our wings. He said he could fly in all seasons but he liked winter best, when he could hear the ice forming in the river. The cold made it more challenging. Then he steadied himself at the edge of the cliff, facing out, the boys holding the wing tips. At the next gust of wind he jumped forward. He was flying. It seemed unreal. I could sympathize with Halpin, who disapproved: "If they dropped, they'd kill themselves. You'd have to be crazy to do that."

But the priest's imagination had been caught; he saw the danger as part of the game. "You have to, Jimmy, St. Paul said it. It's not crazy, you accept without understanding. Like the freedom of the Cross."

The wind was in our faces, the air alive with swallows. The river moved in its steady path to the sea. I thought of Kierkegaard's phrase "the leap of faith". I thought of those who found Kurelek's life strange, radical, incomprehensible. I was looking at challenge accepted; at daring, mystery, and joy. It was time to leave.

Appendix:
Kurelek and Huculak
Family History

ON THE ARTIST'S MOTHER'S SIDE, RECORDED FAMILY HISTORY BEGINS WITH her grandparents, Simeon Huculak (1867-1926) and his wife Kateryna, *née* Balanko. They had ten children, five sons and five daughters: six born in the Ukraine and four more in Canada. Their first child, Vasyl (1881-1946), married Maria Fedorak; and the first child of Vasyl and Maria, also called Maria, became the artist's mother. Vasyl was born when his father Simeon was only fourteen, according to family records.

In 1899, the Huculak family left their village of Borivtsi in Bukovyna, Ukraine, and emigrated to Canada with six children: Vasyl, Maria, Vasylyna, Anna, Ivan (John), and Peter. Four more children were born in the Shandro area, namely Alex, Magdelyna (Mabel), Christine, and Michael. The family arrived in Halifax, May 9, 1899, on the ship *Brasilia*, and proceeded by Canadian Pacific Railway to Edmonton, and by wagon to Vostok.

Maria Fedorak (1887-1963) was born in Borivtsi to Mykyta Fedorak and his wife Anna, *née* Strembitsky. Maria was the first of their eight children. In 1899 the Fedorak family and all eight children came to Canada on the same ship as Maria's future husband, travelled on the same train, and continued to the same village. Fedorak children included Maria (Huculak), Wasylyna (Yakimchuk), Kateryna (Dowhanuk), William, Magdelyna (Cherveniuk), and Sanda (Hancharuk).

The Fedorak family lived with the John Hunchak family in Vostok for a few months, then took up their homestead SW30-58-15, two miles south of the North Saskatchewan River at Kahwin. Vasyl Huculak lived for a short time on his family's homestead, then filed on an adjoining quarter for himself, SE16-57-15.W.4. Both families doubtless survived briefly in the *boorday* dugouts which Kurelek would later paint.

In February 1904, Vasyl and Maria were married in the Russo-Greek Orthodox church in Vostok, and began farming Vasyl's land. Vasyl became a naturalized Canadian citizen in 1906. Vasyl and Maria had eleven children, seven sons and four daughters. Most received high school education, and two went on to university. All but John, the oldest son (1908-78), survived into the 1980s. The children of Vasyl and Maria Huculak, born between 1906 and 1930, are: Mary, John, Peter, Steven, Samuel, Kate, Alice, Daniel, William, George, and Helen.

Their oldest daughter, Mary Huculak (b. August 11, 1906), married Dmytro Kurelek in June 1925. They had seven children: William, the artist (March 3, 1927-November 3, 1977); John (November 4, 1928); Vasylyna or "Win" (January 21, 1930); Nancy (June 22, 1936); Alexandra (November 30, 1944); Paul (September 3, 1946); and Iris (September 2, 1948).

The Kurelek family history has been taken from a tape made by Georg Kurelek, Dmytro's younger brother, who followed Dmytro to Canada in 1937. Georg and his wife Maria lived for six or nine months with Dmytro and Mary at Stonewall. They quarrelled, separated, and lost touch with one another, hence Georg's confusion as to the number of children born to Dmytro and Mary, and the very negative personal opinion of his brother expressed at the end of the tape. Georg refers to his sister as both "Maritsa" and "Maria": the former is a variant on "Maria" common in the southwestern Ukraine. The tape, in Ukrainian, has been translated by Yaroslaw Kit of Manotick. A transcription follows:

> The elders from our village told us that the first Kurelek was Vasyl. He was a Cossack who left that occupation and built himself a house in the valley surrounded by small trees, where our village Borivtsi was just beginning to come into existence. At that time the Turks were still raiding the village, so Vasyl made a tunnel, an escape hole in his house, that led into the valley covered with bushes. There is a saying that he was very strong physically, and when the Turks raided near his house he killed many, but if he could not overcome them he would escape through his secret passage into the valley. He would cover the hole and no one could find it.
>
> He had only one son, Ivan; Ivan had only one son, Philip; Philip had one son, Dmytro. Dmytro was my father. He had two sisters younger than he, Maritsa and Kateryna. Maritsa married Budjak and had four children, two sons and two daughters. Kateryna married Mulyk in the next village, Kysyliv, and had only one son and three daughters. Those were my first brothers and sisters [i.e. cousins]. My mother Agaphia was the daughter of Mykola (or Nicola)

Huculak. Mykola had only one daughter, the oldest, and five sons: Theodore, Georg, Sandor, Gregory, Vasyl. Those were my uncles on my mother's side. Theodore had three sons; Georg had two sons and two daughters; Sandor had one son, and two daughters from a third wife. ...

In our family there were three brothers and two sisters [i.e. children of Dmytro and Agaphia]: the oldest Maritsa, then Ivan, Kateryna, Dmytro, and myself the youngest, Georg. Maritsa married Georg [Potza ?—tape is unclear] and had three sons and two daughters: Ivan, Ilana, Dmytro, Vaselyna, Vasyl. Vasyl was my age. We grew together, because Sister Maritsa lived only two houses away. We never parted, from our youngest days. We were like twins: at school, as shepherds in the field, and as young men looking for brides at dances, we were always together. We went into the army together and were sent to the same town, Bucharest. Only in 1937 my Canada [i.e. emigration to Canada] separated us forever, because Vasyl died in 1944 in the War.

Ivan, our oldest brother, married Anastasia, daughter of Sandor Unchuk, and had three sons, Sandor, Vasyl, Dmytro. Kateryna married Mykola Krovchuk and had two daughters, Maria and Anastasia. Dmytro I think had three sons and three daughters, the oldest Vasyl [William, the artist], then Ivan, then Vasylyna, and the others whose names I don't know, because of his meanness and deceptive nature. Because of his base nature I had no real understanding, no meeting of minds with him in Canada. ...

The balance of the tape traces the family of Maria Shevchuk, Georg's wife.

NOTES

Chapter One—Kurelek: The Man and the Myth

1. W. K., *O Toronto*, Introduction by James Bacque (Toronto: General Publishing, 1973).

2. Kurelek's parents had belonged to the Russian Orthodox Church and had baptized him into this faith in infancy. Schism between the Orthodox and the Roman Catholics pained him deeply. In January 1976, he told a priest that he had just heard, in church that morning, that the Orthodox Church was hoping to reunite with Rome: "When I heard it I wept," Kurelek told Father de Valk, adding that the news had made it one of the happiest days of his life.

3. Biographer Leon Edel speaks of "the inner myth we all create in order to live": see "The Figure Under the Carpet," *Telling Lives*, ed. Marc Pachter (Washington, D.C.: New Republic Books, 1979). Cf. Phyllis Grosskurth, "Search and Psyche: The Writing of Biography," *English Studies in Canada*, vol. XI, no. 2 (June 1985), p. 151: "In each of the biographies in which I have been involved, the subject has written an autobiography—and it has always served as a misguided set of directions. Each of us creates self-mythologies." Cf. George Woodcock, "Editorial Memory," *City and Country Home*, vol. 4, no. 3 (May 1985), p. 14: "Computer memory records. Human memory incessantly creates. We remember the past as it never was. ... Proust taught that as soon as an experience is past, memory begins to modify it. ... Memory is an act of imagination as much as an act of recording. ... If the autobiographer has any scrap of literary feeling, [the autobiography] is manifestly not 'true', partly because material has to be selected to save the reader from being swamped ... partly because we all create myths about ourselves and shape our recollections to fit. ...."

4. The artist's sister Win, Mrs. N. Olynyk, noted that their youngest siblings, who went to school in rural Ontario in the early 1950s, suffered greatly from discrimination in a school where they were the only non-Anglo-Saxons. She added that most immigrants are strongly motivated towards success for themselves and their children, and that the racial discrimination they suffered in Canada and elsewhere only increased their desire to show that they could equal or overtake their tormentors in professional and social accomplishments. The flood of immigrants to Canada in the 1950s and '60s changed this situation and established a multicultural society in which many groups could feel at home, an ethnic diversity which Kurelek would eventually paint.

5. Father Michael Barida (Toronto, August 20, 1983) shares the author's conviction.

6. See William Spengemann, *The Forms of Autobiography: Episodes in the History of a Literary Genre* (New Haven and London: Yale University Press, 1980).

7. Catalogue, William Kurelek Retrospective, Edmonton Art Gallery, September 1970.

8. In response to an inquiry concerning the purchase of a painting in the 1970s, Kurelek wrote to ask if the would-be purchaser was "well-heeled". A favorite verbal construction involved the use of "-wise" as a suffix: "correspondence-wise", "religiouswise", "prosperitywise", "a bargain square inch wise". His language was peppered with rural expressions ("a spitten likeness") and the occasional neologism: a poplar bush is called "scrumpy"; a historical fiction, *Sons of the Soil*, is "too ramantsy" to consider illustrating.

9. Cf. letter by Donald DeMarco to P.M., August 9, 1985: "He seemed more interested in observing people and storing impressions than in involving himself in face to face relationships. He was always gracious and thoughtful, but private and withdrawn. He seemed to be genuinely humble, although there also seemed to be a hint of a lack of confidence. I think he allowed people he loved or admired to inspire him so that he could express his feeling, not back to those individuals necessarily, but through painting to the world at large. In this sense he reflected an heroic loneliness."

10. Henry Slaby, Kurelek's accountant in the 1970s, asked the artist why he worked so hard: "He said he felt an inner urge—something *pushed* him to produce, and he felt fulfilment in it" (Slaby talking with P.M., Toronto, August 16, 1983). Cf. Father Michael Barida talking with P.M., August 19, 1983: "In the early seventies, I warned him that he should take better care of himself, and he said—it took me aback!—'There's a time for sleep and a time for work. When I'm dead I'll sleep, but now I must work!' "

Chapter Two—The Family Story: Kureleks and Huculaks

1. Data on Huculak family history is taken from interviews and from the following books: *Ukrainians in Alberta*, ed. Isidore Goresky (Edmonton: Ukrainian News Publisher, 1975), pp. 346-51; from *Dreams and Destinies: Andrew and District* (Andrew, Alberta: Alberta Historical Society, 1980), pp. 372-76; and from various family members. Kurelek genealogy comes from a tape made by Georg Kurelek, Dmytro's brother and the artist's uncle (see Appendix). Homy details connected with immigration, such as the limitation of baggage to fifty pounds, the typical objects taken, the appearance of the colonist cars on the route between Québec and Winnipeg, etc., may be found in Mary Paximadis, *Look Who's Coming: The Wachna Story*, Illustrations by William Kurelek (Oshawa, Ontario: Maracle Press, 1976).

2. See Sylvia Fraser, "A Ukrainian Immigrant in Canada," *Star Weekly Magazine*, October 17, 1964, pp. 18-23.

3. William Kurelek, *The Ukrainian Pioneer* (Niagara Falls: Niagara Falls Art Gallery Kurelek Collection, 1980), pp. 20-36.

4. Interview with Michael Shulhan, Edmonton, May 16, 1982, and with other members of the Huculak family. A lively dispute followed as to whether the roasts in question were beef or pork: pork was the pre-war staple; beef became common only after the Second World War.

5. Mrs. Alice Krawchuk, Mary's sister, talking with P.M., Edmonton, May 16, 1982.

6. Mrs. Mary Kurelek, talking with P.M., Edmonton, May 16, 1982.

7. In an interview with the Huculak family, May 16, 1982, Mary's brother Steve recalled seeing Dmytro kissing Mary in the barn in 1924. Mary defended herself with the wonderful line: "When I was milking, I was milking."

8. Not until the Second World War did agricultural prices solve Dmytro's pressing financial problems. In 1982, during a family discussion in Edmonton, Mary's exclamation spoke volumes: "You can't live without money!"

9. The Huculak family in Alberta seemed unaware of the fact that Mary's mother-in-law, whom she had never seen, was also a Huculak, perhaps a distant cousin. Huculak is a common name in Bukovyna.

10. Cf. the wedding scene depicted on the cover of William Kurelek, *The Polish Canadians* (Montréal: Tundra Books, 1981). See also Sylvia Fraser, "A Ukrainian Immigrant in Canada," *Star Weekly Magazine*, October 17, 1964, p. 21, where Dmytro Kurelek recalls: "We had a big Greek Orthodox wedding. Everyone danced and sang, and since many folks had migrated from my own village, they knew my parents. I was very happy."

11. Family accounts differ. Mary believes that the first quarter section was a clear gift, but had no explanation for the switch to a different quarter. Peter recalls that when Dmytro was dissatisfied, Vasyl purchased a new quarter section from a mortgage company for $4000. Dmytro received 150 acres; the remaining ten belonged to an old couple who lived on it and whose ten acres were to revert to the quarter on their death.

12. Peter and Rose Huculak talking with P.M., Andrew, Alberta, May 10, 1982: "Dmytro liked to twist stories, to add spice. He'd embroider family history as well as folk tales."

13. Bumper crops in 1922 and 1923 had enabled Vasyl to tour Europe and to visit Borivtsi within a year of Dmytro's arrival. Whether Vasyl travelled in 1922 and arranged in person to sponsor Kurelek and to pay his passage, or whether he went in 1924 or 1925 after Dmytro had begun to work for him is unclear. Sources differ. Kost Shevchuk worked for Vasyl Huculak in the 1920s, and was interviewed in Willingdon Hospital in 1982. Shevchuk remembers that Vasyl returned from Borivtsi in the fall and Dmytro arrived the following spring. Shevchuk thought that Dmytro had arrived in 1925, yet later spoke of working with him on the Huculak farm in 1924. *Ukrainians in Canada* mentions Vasyl's European trip but omits the year. Whether the trip was before or after Dmytro's emigration, it is clear that the Shandro settlers were in close touch with their native village. Feelings might be ambivalent, as Vasyl's father Simeon apparently opposed his trip and his wife Maria had no wish to accompany him to the Ukraine.

14. Peter Huculak and other members of the Huculak family, talking with P.M., Edmonton, May 11, 1982.

15. Mrs. Helen Shulhan (*née* Huculak), talking with P.M., May 10, 1982: "My father was very strict, yet you could tell he loved us. He'd take me for rides in the car, a great treat, and buy me ice cream. He'd always take me with him on errands. He had a strap, the strap for his straight razor, for punishing his sons."

16. Mrs. Mary Kurelek, talking with P.M., May 16, 1982, Edmonton.

17. William Huculak was three years older, and Georg three months older, than their nephew William Kurelek; Helen was born in 1930.

18. Letter by W.K. to J.K., September 16, 1957, and A1 25.

19. Dmytro Kurelek, talking with P.M., Vinemount, Ontario, October 18, 1981.

20. After the Kureleks left for Manitoba, the land was re-purchased by Vasyl and eventually given to Mary's brother William. The two-room Kurelek house survives today as a chicken shed on William Huculak's farm.

21. See Sylvia Fraser, "A Ukrainian Immigrant in Canada," p. 21, where Dmytro varied the year of purchase and the size of acreage in Stonewall, calling it a 480-acre farm. His mention of 1932 as a purchase year may represent the year of his *decision* to move.

Chapter Three—Stonewall: The Crucial Years, 1934-46

1. Mrs. N. Olynyk, talking with P.M., Oakville, July 8, 1981: "She kept digging and digging at him, till something broke in him and he attacked her with the piece of wood he was carving. He just exploded and couldn't take it any longer. Will made life easier for us." Cf. A2 69.

2. John Giesbrecht, "Recollections of My Associations With William Kurelek," unpublished memoir, 1983.

3. Ibid. Orally, Giesbrecht observed that William had confessed to a total lack of books in his household at the time.

4. Cf. letter by Ethel M. Houghton to W.K., February 16, 1968: "But I well remember a shy little boy who loved to draw. *And I remember the deep sense of guilt I felt at being of no help to you except to allow the drawing to go on at any and all times*, regardless of what else was in progress" (emphasis added). What unusual needs did Mrs. Houghton discern in the boy, needs she felt unable to meet?

5. Giesbrecht, April 1983.

6. J.K., talking with P.M., Brantford, July 8, 1981.

7. Peter Lesko, talking with P.M., May 18, 1982, Edmonton.

8. Carl Inman, talking with P.M., Edmonton, May 18, 1982. Cf. William Budjak, talking with P.M., Smithville, Ontario, June 18, 1983: "Bullying was common in country schools. *Any* strange kid was picked on, and Ukrainians were picked on as 'Bohunks'. Kids are cruel. Once they got to know you it was better. Even a year later, it wasn't so bad."

9. Joseph Gay, talking with P.M., Edmonton, May 19, 1982.

10. Mrs. Lois Crozier, talking with P.M., Fort Saskatchewan, May 10, 1982. In her Kurelek painting, *Fox and Geese*, the individual faces of the children playing tag can be recognized and identified as Bill's schoolmates.

11. Ibid. Cf. Mr. Fred Tomyk, talking with P.M., Regina, May 7, 1982, who considered the Kurelek parents "normal" in their strictness.

12. Mrs. Patricia Barnicko (*née* Koroluk), talking with P.M., May 6, 1982.

13. W.K.'s sister, Mrs. Iris Gauthier, talking with P.M., Redwater, Alberta, May 19, 1982.

14. W.K.'s sister, Mrs. Alexandra Takacs, talking with P.M., Toronto, August 14, 1983.

15. Mrs. Jean McNulty (*née* Budjak), talking with P.M., Smithville, Ontario, June 18, 1983.

16. Sisters Mrs. Effie Dutchak (*née* Koroluk) and Mrs. Patricia Barnicko, talking with P.M., Winnipeg, May 6, 1982.

17. J.K. and Mary Kurelek, talking with P.M., Vinemount, Ontario, October 18, 1981.

18. W.K., "From 'Another Person With Me,'" *Exile*, vol. I, no. 2 (1972), p. 68. Further page references are in the text as *Ex*.

19. Mrs. Effie Dutchak, talking with P.M., May 5, 1982.

20. Dmytro Kurelek, talking with P.M., Vinemount, October 18, 1981: "So I was afraid to go there. I said, don't do that, you're wasting your time, you'll fail school. He was quiet, and trying always to do what I wanted. So he tried to hide it from me. Half a year later, I found he was still doing it."

21. See W.K., A2 66: "Some of my sacrificial masochistic imagery may also have derived from a children's radio serial called 'Talking Drums'."

22. Cf. A1 82: "My wife analyzes this as repressed violent feelings towards my tormentors."

23. The Huculak family, including Mary Kurelek, talking with P.M., Edmonton, May 11, 1982.

24. Kurelek family, talking with P.M., Vinemount, October 18, 1981.

25. Mrs. Patricia Barnicko, talking with P.M., May 6, 1982.

26. Mary Kurelek, talking with P.M., May 11, 1982.

27. Cf. Old Testament tales of Jacob and Esau, or Joseph and his brothers.

28. See Sylvia Fraser, "A Ukrainian Immigrant in Canada," *Star Weekly Magazine*, October 17, 1964, p. 22.

29. Mrs. Mary Kurelek, talking with P.M., Edmonton, May 11, 1982.

30. Mrs. Jean McNulty and William Budjak, talking with P.M., June 18, 1983.

31. Cf. A2 63-64: "Had Father not been able to vent his pent-up anger on the animals, I myself would have got much worse than tongue-lashings"; "spankings were so few I can actually count on one hand the number I received from Father."

32. J.K., talking with P.M., Brantford, July 8, 1981.

33. Mrs. N. Olynyk, talking with P.M., Oakville, July 8, 1981. Cf. Mrs. Effie Dutchak, May 5, 1982: "Ukrainians were not well accepted, or felt they weren't; in those days there *was* a difference if you weren't Anglo-Saxon."

34. Mrs. Iris Gauthier, talking with P.M., May 19, 1982.

35. Mrs. A. Takacs, talking with P.M., August 14, 1983.

36. Mrs. Stella (Dutka) Ewanchuk, talking with P.M., Winnipeg, May 5, 1982.

37. Grade nine was taken by correspondence, the work being done in Victoria School under the supervision of the teacher.

38. Dr. Joseph Katz, talking with P.M., Vancouver, July 1, 1983.

39. Fellow student Nadia Niechoda (Vancouver, May 31, 1983) remembered Bill and John Kurelek's appearance at Isaac Newton in 1943: "They stood out as farm kids. They were timid, quiet. Most city kids were more outgoing."

40. Ibid.

41. Students whose parents lived outside the school area and were thus not ratepayers paid a sizeable school fee. The purchase of the Burrows Avenue house indicates Dmytro's financial acumen.

42. Classmate Fred Kuzina, May 3, 1982.

43. See *The Newtonian* (1944-45), p. 19: "*William Kurelek*: Einstein himself has nothing on our Bill. Claims the theory of relativity is wrong and that he must remedy it. (Oh well, he's got the rest of his life to do it.)" See also p. 31: "*John 'Beaver' Kurelek*: the little farm boy and scholar. *William 'Samson' Kurelek*: the brother of 'Beaver' and also another book-burner." Cf. classmate Norman Duvell, talking with P.M., Winnipeg, May 4, 1982: "He was a real bear for work."

44. Norman Duvell, talking with P.M., May 4, 1982: "He worked endlessly, studying till 4 a.m. I'd be surprised if he *didn't* have eye trouble. He couldn't sit in his room, the light was so bad. He'd be painfully printing away, claiming he could print as fast as he could write." Electricity reached the Kurelek farm only in the mid-1940s, hence Bill was accustomed to relatively dim light.

45. Ibid. Duvell painted a sympathetic portrait of Mary as a good woman who worked endlessly, "kept her mouth shut and worked." She had a sense of humor and would joke with the boys. She could never, in Duvell's opinion, have protected Bill from Dmytro, as she was desperately overworked "trying to keep body and soul together".

46. See interviews with Father E. Holloway, Dr. J. Maas, and Dr. D. Davies, 1981-83.

Chapter Four—The Lonely Road to Creativity, 1946-52

1. Kurelek's aunt, Mrs. Rose Huculak, remembers suggesting a change of tie to the artist before his 1970 Edmonton Exhibition. Smiling, Kurelek replied, "Does it matter?" He wore the tie he had on.

2. William Kurelek, *Lumberjack*, Author's Foreword (Montréal: Tundra Books, 1974). Kurelek, always careless of dates, sets the year as 1946 and his age at nineteen, while noting that it followed his first year at university. Official transcripts of his schooling indicate that the year was 1947. The artist was twenty, but doubtless felt younger.

3. Cf. Ms 2, p. 138: "To my utter disgust all the arguments I prepared for just such an occasion were overwhelmed by the breaking forth of emotions that had been extremely tensed for the past few weeks. . . . I explained in a few faltering words that the spirit of independence in a son springs forth as a result of overcriticism by the father—a fact that I had learned from the two units of psychology that I was taking up that year."

4. Author's Foreword, *Lumberjack*.

5. Ibid.

6. Architect John Champagne, talking with P.M., Ottawa, December 5, 1982. (Cf. Eric Freifeld, talking with P.M., June 22, 1982: Freifeld recalled that Kurelek thought highly of the writings of C. S. Lewis and kept urging his friends to read them.)

7. Ibid.: "He latched onto a few people. I sensed dependency and was worried. I didn't want the responsibility."

8. William Kurelek, *O Toronto*, Introduction by James Bacque (Don Mills, Ontario: General Publishing, 1973), p. 4.

9. Freifeld, June 22, 1982.

10. Ibid.

11. Ibid.

12. Group interview with the artist's mother and four of her Huculak relatives, Edmonton, May 1982.

13. The surname given in A2 is a pseudonym.

14. Cf. W.K. to his sister Win, July 12, 1950: "This letter . . . is more in the nature of a confession or explanation to anyone who would stop and listen. I choose you this time, Winnie. . . . I have broken off all correspondence with friends notably Zenon with whom I was intimate to an extreme. I was led to do this by an increasing suspicion that for many years I have been playing a role in a farce. I was building up my life into a beautiful pattern and decorating it with tinsel in order to have the outside world gawk at it in admiration. In plain words I have been much too conscious of being or becoming a somebody instead of just being content with being myself. The realization of this fact comes on me at intervals and makes me loathe my inward rottenness. I want to then shake off all the trappings of insincerity by daring to tell the truth about myself. First several weeks ago I got the impulse to break off all correspondence with you all at home because I realized that my letters had become as it were the channels by which I released the floods of self glorification onto the few people who were bound in some way or other to be aware of me." Cf. letter by W.K. to K.S., April 9, 1960, where Kurelek comments on a letter he has received from a friend: "I found it sickening in effusiveness but I'm rather inclined to pity her because the style of it reminds me very much of my early writings when I was terribly unhappy interiorly. . . ."

15. See A1 275; cf. A1 270, 179.

16. See A2 139, where a long excerpt from Dmytro's letter is quoted.

17. Letter by W.K. to Georgine Ferguson, February 22, 1952. Cf. A2 137, where the weekly sum is given as $20.

18. Ibid. (Cf. A2 138: "Train loads of European immigrants were pouring into Canada then and I drew them all.")

19. Ibid.

Chapter Five—A Bold Venture: London, 1952-53

1. See Ms 2 50, where Kurelek writes: "At times I am overwhelmed by boredom. I would like to see the world and I want adventure. I hate being tied down to one spot. I have tasted the vagabond spirit and I find it very much to my liking. It is my strong belief that my life has been stunted and that my thoughts travel in a rut because I have lived an isolated, repetitious life." The vagabondia to which he refers was his summer in the bush in 1947.

2. Dr. D. L. Davies talking with P.M., London, April 22, 1981.

3. Ibid. See also Edward Adamson, "Art for Mental Health," *The Social Context of Art*, ed. Jean Creedy (London: Tavistock, 1970), pp. 148-49.

4. See letter by Golf Rieser to staff psychiatrist Dr. Slater, July 10, 1952. See Rieser's obituary (*The Times*, April 1953, p. 12) for an assessment of his career and reputation.

5. Letter by Dr. D. L. Davies to Stanley Spencer, August 7, 1952.

6. Letter by Stanley Spencer to Miss Forstner at the Maudsley, September 12, 1952.

7. See W.K., *Tramlines*, n.d., no signature, in a gouache on masonite. The technique resembles thin oil. Cf. A1 303. Kurelek later called it his first English "masterpiece", in a letter to Edward Adamson (December 20, 1971).

8. Letter by Dr. G. M. Carstairs to H. F. Hutchinson, Publicity Officer, London Transport Executive, December 28, 1953.

9. Letter by W.K. to Dr. G. M. Carstairs, May 3, 1954.

10. C. F. Bonnett talking with P.M., London, May 3, 1983.

11. Dr. Bruno Cormier talking with P.M., Montréal, November 30, 1982.

12. Ibid. See also W.K.'s note to Cormier, September 11, 1952.

13. Mixed media in graphite, ink, gouache, 25" x 36" on hand-pieced paper. Private collection.

14. Margaret Smith talking with P.M., Tisbury, Wilts., April 28, 1981.

15. Dr. Morris Carstairs talking with P.M., London, May 10, 1981.

16. Smith, April 28, 1981.

17. Copies of Kurelek's texts, along with the original works (*Nightmare* and *The Maze*) are kept at the Archives, Bethlem Hospital, London. For some years *The Maze* hung in the office of Maudsley's House Governor, L. H. W. Paine, who was impressed with its inventiveness and draughtsmanship (L. H. W. Paine talking with P.M., April 22, 1981).

18. Carstairs, May 10, 1981.

19. Dr. D. L. Davies identified the faces for P.M., April 22, 1981.

20. Letter by Dr. D. L. Davies to Dr. R. F. Freudenberg, October 2, 1953.

Chapter Six—Sliding Down: Netherne Hospital, 1953-54

1. Chief Nursing Officer Noel Duffy talking with P.M., Netherne Hospital, May 4, 1984.

2. See Preface, John E. C. Timlin, *Selections from the Edward Adamson Collection* (Toronto: Art Gallery of Ontario, 1984).

3. Edward Adamson, *Art as Healing*, Foreword by Anthony Stevens (London: Coventure, 1984).

4. Ibid., p. 1.

5. Miss Vera Jenkins, psychiatric social worker, talking with P.M., May 8, 1981. Thirty years after seeing them, she found the Kurelek paintings were still vivid in her mind.

6. *Hospital Ward* is now part of the collection of the Royal College of Physicians and Surgeons of Canada.

7. Mixed media with an orange wash. Private collection.

8. Letter by W.K. to Dr. G. M. Carstairs, November 6, 1953.

9. The date varies slightly in the autobiographies: cf. A1 332-34 and A2 27-28. Since there is no mention of this experience in the Kurelek letter of November 6 to Dr. Carstairs, it would seem to have occurred at a later date.

10. Letter by W.K. to Dr. G. M. Carstairs, May 3, 1954.

11. See Caitlin Kelly, "Pioneer in art therapy expels demons," *Globe and Mail*, March 24, 1984, p. 13.

12. Margaret Smith talking with P.M., April 28, 1981.

13. W.K., *Behold Man Without God*, collection of The Art Gallery of Ontario.

14. In 1969 Kurelek insisted that this scene be edited out of the film *The Maze*, according to Dr. James Maas, Cornell University, July 12, 1983.

15. See A2 29: "I never leave a painting unfinished if I can help it, but that little corner is unfinished to this day. I like to think it was an omen of some kind."

16. John Timlin, "'An apple for the teacher,'"*Art As Healing*, Adamson, p. 64.

17. Edward Adamson, videotape, Art Gallery of Ontario, March 1984, accompanying an exhibition of works from the Adamson Collection of Psychiatric Art.

18. "Art as Therapy," radio program with Adamson and Dr. Vivian Rakoff, CBC-FM Stereo Morning, May 12, 1984.

19. See letters by W.K. to Dr. G. M. Carstairs, May 3, 1954, and by Margaret Smith to Dr. H. E. S. Marshall, August 22, 1954. Edward Adamson recalled that when Kurelek first came to Netherne he painted all day and practically all night (April 23, 1981).

20. Vera Jenkins, May 8, 1981. Kurelek erroneously writes that he gave *I Spit on Life* to Dr. Yates (A2 31); cf. A1 341, where the "going-away gift" is to society at large. Dr. Yates died in 1967.

21. Duffy, May 4, 1984; he added that current frequency of administering ECT is perhaps five treatments per week.

22. Dr. Isaac Marks talking with P.M., Maudsley Hospital, May 10, 1983.

23. In the 1980s, Carstairs, Smith, and Adamson all remarked on Kurelek's narcissism during his hospital period, and all observed that such introversion or self-preoccupation was typical of emotionally disturbed people of this type.

24. Letter by W.K. to Dr. Evan Turner, Director, Montréal Museum of Fine Arts, June 21, 1964.

Notes

Chapter Seven—Moving Up: England, 1955-56

1. Letter by W.K. to David John, October 30, 1955.
2. Margaret Smith talking with P.M., Tisbury, April 28, 1981.
3. See Harold Osborne, ed., *The Oxford Companion to Art* (Oxford: Oxford University Press, 1970); Kimberley Reynolds with Richard Seddon, *Illustrated Dictionary of Art Terms* (London: Ebury Press, 1981); and Reginald G. Haggar, *A Dictionary of Art Terms* (New York: Hawthorn Books, 1962).
4. Letter by W.K. to David John, October 30, 1955. John recalls that Kurelek's *trompe-l'oeil* were sold to an American collector and dealer at the Arthur Jeffress Gallery in London, priced by the artist at five pounds because they took a week to paint and it cost Kurelek that amount to live during the time required to do the painting. Whereas the reasoning sounds familiar (cf. the pricing of *Tramlines* by the hours required to paint times the hourly wage of a laborer on the road-gang), the budget details differ slightly from those recalled by Kurelek in his auto-biography or in conversations with friends (David John talking with P.M., Woodley, Berks., April 22, 1983).
5. John, April 22, 1983: "He was offended and scandalized by many practising Catholics. He was scrupulous!"
6. Ibid. In the 1950s, John saw Kurelek as an illustrator rather than an artist.
7. Ibid.
8. Ibid.
9. Marianne Hellwig talking with P.M., Woodley, April 22, 1983.
10. Letter by W.K. to David John, October 30, 1955.
11. Letter by W.K. to David John, January 1, 1956.
12. Ibid.
13. Ibid.
14. Hellwig, April 22, 1983.
15. Letter by W.K. to David John, January 1, 1956.
16. Ibid.
17. Cf. letter by W.K. to J.K., August 1957: "I believe it was my trip to Lourdes and my subsequent realization that miracles are real and the supernatural does exist that made it easier for me to accept that part of the Gospels which I could not at first."
18. Letter by W.K. to David John, October 30, 1955; Kurelek wonders if he is guilty of pride, but quickly dismisses the possibility.
19. Smith, April 28, 1983.
20. Letter by W.K. to David John, January 1, 1956.
21. Ibid.
22. Kurelek's text to the painting, in Bethlem Hospital, London.
23. Letter by W.K. to J.K., October 23, 1957. Years later (talking with P.M., July 8, 1981), John would remember his brother's letters as being noticeably more cheerful in 1956 than at the time he left for England in 1952.
24. Mrs. Alexandra (Kurelek) Takacs talking with P.M., Toronto, August 14, 1983.
25. A1 372. Cf. Dr. D. L. Davies, April 22, 1981: "Look at the life he led, with lumberjacks for example. He was tough with himself. Another kind of person would have sat around and expected help. He wasn't like that. He always chose something hard and exacting, something that needed tremendous endurance. He chose the hard way."

26. Letter by W.K. to a sibling, 1956-57: "I came back from Lourdes refreshed by the holiday but still confused by doubts big and small. And that was the way you saw me last summer. I felt it dishonest to be firm in talking religion to anyone if I wasn't sure myself. I did broach the subject with you and Nat and Nancy and Father and the kids too so that I could get some idea where you all stood on it. What's more you have all for a long time regarded me as an unusual member of the family and that makes my conversion less trustworthy in your eyes. 'Oh, another of his funny ideas' you might say, and I can't say I blame you. I found that you all tolerated it—up to a point—you weren't sure it was wise at the time to take away from me 'that something to hold on to'."

Chapter Eight—The Grand Design: England, 1956-59

1. Letter by W.K. to Stanley Beecham, May 7, 1957.
2. Father T. J. Lynch talking with P.M., Eastbourne, May 7, 1983.
3. The Kurelek crucifix remains over the altar of the Church of St. Simon and St. Jude, displayed on a plain white wall.
4. Letter by W.K. to J.K., August 1957.
5. Father Edward Holloway talking with P.M., Esher, Surrey, May 7, 1981. Holloway believes that all great mystics have this combination of rationalism and mysticism.
6. Edward Holloway, *Catholicism: A New Synthesis* (Wallington, Surrey: Faith Keyway Publications, 1970, 1976), p. 2.
7. Ibid., p. 18.
8. See Jeremiah, Chapters 1, 4, 5, 6, 7, 11, and *passim*.
9. Kurelek was also encouraged by Newman's distinction "a thousand difficulties do not make a doubt." See letter to his brother John, August 1957.
10. Certificate of baptism, Parish of St. Simon and St. Jude, February 11, 1957.
11. Kurelek's belief in Pollak's superiority (A2 158) is shared by Stanley Westlake, a senior craftsman at Pollak's from the 1950s to the 1980s.
12. Stanley Westlake talking with P.M., Stanmore, Middlesex, May 8, 1983.
13. Letters by W.K. to S. Beecham, December 19, 1957, and September 20, 1957.
14. Stanley Beecham talking with P.M., Maple, Ontario, April 1, 1982.
15. Kurelek was called a "master gilder" by Av Isaacs and Stan Beecham. Hans Roeder, who considers that mastery in the craft requires many years of practice, termed him merely "competent".
16. Letter by W.K. to S. Beecham, September 20, 1957.
17. Letter by W.K. to J.K., October 23, 1957. Cf. letter by W.K. to J.K., April 23, 1958: "The last two big jobs I did were designing and painting the tops of three coffee tables in the Chinese style, and painting two Venetian statues. ... Everything I learn will turn out useful I'm sure."
18. Hans Roeder talking with P.M., May 4, 1983. Kurelek's command of German, in Roeder's estimation, was very rough. Cf. A2 160: "My old habits of grudge-bearing had worn grooves so deep in my soul that I responded to abuse and supercilious treatment automatically in the old unforgiving way."
19. Letter by W.K. to S. Beecham, September 20, 1957.
20. Letter by W.K. to S. Beecham, December 19, 1957.

21. Ibid.

22. Roeder, May 4, 1983.

23. Westlake, May 8, 1983.

24. Beecham, April 1, 1982.

25. The Warwick Street Church was burned in the Gordon riots in June 1780 and rebuilt the same year. Known locally as the Bavarian Chapel, it is the only remaining Catholic Embassy Chapel that survives from penal times.

26. See also A2 162-63, and A1 440-42, 452, where Kurelek interprets his new freedom to drink in moderation as the result of his increased security; this, in turn, stemmed from the fact that he no longer felt compelled to masturbate, a habit that had dogged him from his early teens and had filled him with guilt.

27. See R. A. Record of Exhibits under "*Kurelek*: Catalogue items 632 (1956), 709 (1957), and 672 (1958)".

28. Private collector and friend talking with P.M.; name withheld by request.

29. Letter by W.K. to J.K., April 23, 1958.

30. Letter by W.K. to J.K., October 10, 1958.

31. Letter by W.K. to David John and Marianne Hellwig, October 11, 1958.

32. Letter by W.K. to S. Beecham, October 11, 1958.

33. Letter by W.K. to J.K., December 26, 1958.

34. Mrs. Anita John talking with P.M., April 30, 1984.

35. W. D. Stagg talking with P.M., Hammersmith and West London College, April 1983. Cf. letter by W.K. to J.K., August 1957: "I had a look in a microscope over a year ago at a slide of coral shell formation taken from the bottom of the Caribbean. The forms were so beautiful I felt like weeping. What is that beauty there for? For the fishes to see? How to account for man's ability to create beauty ... ?"

36. Letter by W.K. to J.K., December 26, 1958.

37. Letter by W.K. to a patron (name withheld by request), April 5, 1959.

38. Letter by W.K. to "Dear Everybody", undated (February 1959).

39. Ibid.

40. Letter by W.K. to John and Helen Kurelek, March 1, 1959.

41. Ibid.

42. See letter by W.K. to J.K., August 1957; and notes for Chapter Ten below.

43. Letter by W.K. to John and Helen Kurelek, March 1, 1959.

44. Letter by W.K. to J.K., May 4, 1959.

45. Letter by W.K. to a patron (name withheld by request), April 27, 1959.

46. Letter by W.K. to J.K., May 4, 1959.

47. W.K., *Sunday Observer*, April 26, 1959, p. 4.

48. Letter by W.K. to J.K., April 23, 1958.

49. Letter by W.K. to J.K., May 18, 1958.

Chapter Nine—In the Lions' Den: Toronto, 1959-62

1. Letter by K.S. to P.M., November 13, 1984. Shorey continued: "He looked young and we talked as equals, though he was not as articulate *in person* as I was. His physical mannerisms were not those of an older person, and his clothes were no better than mine. If he ever wore anything like a suit, it looked like Good-

will. Aboard the *Ivernia* he looked like a Soviet spy who hadn't yet figured out what North Americans were wearing that year. ... Bill's eyes were sad." See also K.S. to P.M., March 23, 1982.

2. Letter by K.S. to P.M., November 18, 1984.

3. Letter by K.S. to P.M., November 13, 1984.

4. Ibid.

5. Eric Freifeld talking with P.M., Toronto, June 22, 1982. It is possible that with the long lapse in time Freifeld may have confused "one a day" with "one a week", the schedule Kurelek maintained from January 1, 1960, to the end of 1962.

6. Freifeld, June 23, 1982.

7. Letter by John Robert Colombo to P.M., November 25, 1981.

8. John Robert Colombo talking with P.M., Toronto, February 28, 1982. Kenneth Shorey also sees Kurelek as masochistic: "Bill identified with St. Paul because Paul was anxious to suffer more than Jesus had suffered" (letter by K.S. to P.M., June 12, 1985).

9. Ruth Colombo talking with P.M., February 28, 1982.

10. Colombo's journal, copy to P.M., January 1, 1982.

11. Peter and Vivian Kuzina talking with P.M., Winnipeg, May 6, 1982.

12. Phil Lanthier, "The Artist as Piers Plowman," *Matrix* (Fall, 1975), p. 3; and interview, Montréal, October 21, 1983.

13. Letter by Brendan Foley to P.M., April 8, 1984.

14. Lanthier, "The Artist as Piers Plowman," p. 3.

15. Lanthier, October 21, 1983.

16. James Lanthier talking with P.M., Toronto, December 3, 1983.

17. Mrs. Jane Lanthier talking with P.M., Toronto, December 3 and 7, 1983.

18. See letters by W.K. to K.S., September 15 and October 21, 1959. See also A1 484, where Kurelek describes Shorey's passion for classical music and conservative values, and acknowledges the latter's influence on his ideas over the years.

19. Letter by K.S. to P.M., March 23, 1982.

20. The exact date of Kurelek's first meeting with Isaacs has not been established. Journalistic accounts tend to quote one another and to be influenced by hearsay. Kurelek himself is notoriously unreliable on dates, while Isaacs remembers the strong impressions made on him both by Bill's frames and by his paintings but not the dates when he first saw them. Records of Isaacs' first payments to Kurelek for framing have not been located.

21. Letter by K.S. to P.M., March 23, 1982. See also A1 488, in which Kurelek writes that Isaacs came "to the Rueters to see all my work that fall and mentioned March as an exhibition possibility." To A. Arnold, April 26, 1978, Isaacs confirmed that he offered Kurelek a show after seeing a large selection of his work at a friend's house. His interest had been first caught by a few paintings carried by the artist to The Isaacs Gallery (taped interview).

Kurelek would later write that the offer of a show followed his start on the Passion series in January 1960, but Isaacs had already committed himself to a March show by November 1959: see letter by Isaacs to The Canada Council, December 18, 1959.

22. Letter by K.S. to P.M., March 23, 1982.

23. Geoffrey Simmins, "Av Isaacs," *City and Country Home* (September 1984), p. 58. The Gallery was called the Greenwich Art Gallery from 1955, when it opened, till 1960, when the name was changed to The Isaacs Gallery: see letter by A.I. to P.M., January 18, 1985.

24. Ibid., p. 61.

25. Colombo, February 28, 1982.

26. Kay Kritzwiser talking with P.M., Toronto, July 31, 1984: "It was a hippie crowd, the beat generation. They wore clothes from the forties, Indian headbands, miniskirts, long skirts: everything." Mrs. G. Montague, Toronto, described the guests' clothing as bohemian and the atmosphere gala.

Early in 1960 the local Hadassah organization had offered to sponsor a Canadian artist's exhibition. Isaacs suggested Kurelek's. This resulted in what the delighted artist always called two openings for his first show, one for Jewish patrons and one for the general public and the press.

27. "Memories of Farm and Bush Life," The Isaacs Gallery, February 22-March 14, 1962.

28. Elizabeth Kilbourn, "William Kurelek," *Canadian Art* (March/April 1962).

29. Janice Tyrwhitt, "William Kurelek: The Power of Obsession," *Saturday Night* (May 26, 1962), pp. 30-31.

30. Jeanne Parkin talking with P.M., Toronto, December 6, 1983.

31. Kilbourn, *Canadian Art* (March/April 1962).

32. Emmett Maddix talking with P.M., Toronto, March 5, 1982, August 16, 1983, and December 6, 1983.

33. Father Francis W. Stone, CSP, Director, Paulist Fathers (Canada), had begun the Toronto branch of the Catholic Information Centre in 1938. Out of forty-five centres in North America, it was unique in its use of the laity; by 1963, more than two hundred volunteers were assisting three Paulist priests in an ecumenical apostolate.

34. Edward Bader, a Paulist priest until 1972 and Director of the Toronto CIC between 1966 and 1972, describes it in Kurelek's time as "a convert centre" which was bringing two hundred converts a year into the Church. Many co-instructors were themselves adult converts, like Kurelek, and there were many marriages among them. Bader described Kurelek as a good teacher, with a burning intensity about his belief "that made it difficult to joke with him" (Toronto, December 10, 1982).

35. Letter by Helen Cannon to A.I., June 21, 1961.

36. Helen Cannon talking with P.M., Toronto, June 24, 1982. Unfortunately, the Kurelek/Cannon correspondence has been destroyed.

37. Letter by W.K. to K.S., June 15 (1961). Cf. Carol Sinclair talking with P.M., Toronto, December 10, 1982: "Vatican II changed the atmosphere, made it clear that Protestants *could* be saved."

38. Letter by K.S. to P.M., January 10, 1983.

39. Letter by W.K. to Father F. Stone, undated (January 1961).

40. William Kurelek, *The Passion of Christ According to St. Matthew* (Niagara Falls: The Niagara Falls Art Gallery and Museum, 1975), Foreword, p. 11.

41. See ibid., pp. 14-15: "There are 160 paintings. ... Almost all of them are gouache water colour. ... I tried to make each picture as true to history and setting as possible. However, in a few instances where there is a reference to a prophecy or teaching, I have taken the liberty of projecting to places and times other than ancient Israel. The format of the paintings is standard: 20" x 22", a size designed specifically for television screens. Because I envisaged the series as one day being produced on film, there is also a deliberate camera-conscious arrangement of image. ... The earlier scenes are worked in greater precision of detail because, being unemployed at that stage, I had more time on my hands. Later, when I had to

devote more time to picture-framing and producing other paintings for exhibit or otherwise, the style becomes looser and sometimes more primitive."

See also J. James Tissot, *The Life of Our Lord Jesus Christ: Three Hundred and Sixty-Five Compositions from the Four Gospels, With Notes and Explanatory Drawings*, trans. Mrs. Arthur Bell (London: Sampson Low, Marston, [1897]). Tissot's Introduction emphasizes his devotion to "reality" and truth while noting that this method includes intuition.

42. Kurelek, *The Passion of Christ*, p. 7.

43. Bonnie Brennan talking with P.M., Ottawa, January 19, 1985: "It was a little like comic-book art as opposed to Rembrandt's style. It was modern, and very real, more real than the great masters because it was fresh. It helped me *hear* the Gospel again." Cf. Helen Coxe talking with P.M., December 13, 1982: "They were very striking, very unusual paintings. They impressed and intrigued me."

44. Beverly Maciag talking with P.M., Madonna House, August 12, 1982: "He had such a vision of our life, I was always kind of embarrassed around him: his vision of our calling was higher than mine. I suppose prophets are like that. You felt he was calling you to live the way he saw Madonna House in his vision."

45. See Catherine de Hueck Doherty, *Fragments of My Life* (Notre Dame, Indiana: Ave Maria Press, 1979); and *Poustinia*. See also S.R., "An escape from the material world," *Maclean's* (January 10, 1983), p. 36. Madonna House, Combermere, was granted canonical approval as a "Pious Union" in August 1978 by the Bishop of Pembroke. Official approval had been slow in coming because of the community's unusual structure, consisting of lay men and women living together under vows of chastity.

46. Catherine de Hueck Doherty and Father Emile Brière talking with P.M., Madonna House, October 20, 1981.

47. The first *poustinia* was opened at Madonna House, Combermere, on October 11, 1962. Its bare, life-sized cross represented a tradition established by Charles de Foucauld. With no figure on the cross, the penitent could imagine himself upon it. Sometimes a red heart was placed at the centre of the cross. Catherine found de Foucauld's ideas similar to her own and demonstrated that spiritual kinship by using his style of cross in her *poustinia*.

48. Father Emile Brière talking with P.M., Madonna House, in October 1981: "We walked into the kitchen and he saw a picture of Christ at a pillar, having been scourged. He walked over to it, crumpled in front of it, and sobbed and sobbed." Cf. Luke 20:9-19: "Everyone who falls on that stone will be broken to pieces"; the broken heart which the apostle foresees is the spiritual death (another biblical metaphor) from which new life comes.

49. See Doherty, *Fragments of My Life*, p. 204: "I wrote *Poustinia* to call people to the desert of prayer where they can face themselves and experience a change of heart. In the *poustinia, kenosis* (the Greek word for 'empty') takes place, a stripping of oneself, a burying of the 'I.'"

50. Letter by W.K., December 15, 1966. Recipient's name withheld by request.

51. Doherty, *Fragments of My Life*, p. 203.

52. David John and Marianne Hellwig talking with P.M., Woodley, April 22, 1983.

53. W.K., *Kurelek's Canada* (Toronto: Pagurian Press, 1975), pp. 61-63.

Chapter Ten—The Dark Prophet, 1957-77

1.See *Jean Andrews, Vice-President of Our Lady of the Wayside Praesidium* (1962, 1967).

2. Kurelek text for *Mendelssohn in Canadian Winter, 1977*. Some months earlier, Kurelek expressed similar ideas in a diary-letter begun in Ohio in early March 1967, on his way home from a painting session at the home of Dr. K. Peryma. The diary would continue into July. Kurelek is obviously preoccupied by his vision of Doom, and writes that it has been much in his thoughts for the previous four years. The diary's words echo phrases and entire sentences which later appeared in the August 1968 manifesto to Shorey:

> This catastrophe I feel approaching is going to fall on us all because we have forgotten God's laws or if not forgotten don't take them seriously. . . . I feel the compulsion to express in my art so I must put it down in this diary. It keeps recurring to me. This vision—very briefly it goes something like this. The political status quo in the world will deteriorate more and more partly because of population pressures, mostly because of increased immorality and materialism (you see it happening day by day in the papers both sides of the Iron Curtain) and then there will be an explosion a bit bigger than limited military action can contain. It will probably be in the next 10 years maybe 15 and it may not even be on the old Communist-Capitalist division lines, but perhaps on have and have-not lines on or racial lines. And then there will be nuclear war, the works. With modern ways of living and government destroyed or drastically cut there will follow a political tyranny of some kind, probably anti-Christian. This is the main reason I'm so concerned that my children be not brought up to be physical and moral softies. . . . I certainly believe we have a moral responsibility to try and survive, that is why I am soon going to build a shelter. I notice by the way, in Dayton, Ohio the other day that the Art Institute has survival arrangements. . . . Once the attack is over we will have to leave the city and make a go of living in the country or even in the bush. . . . This part of the vision has been with me for 3 or 4 years now since I did the little painting *Flight in Winter* and gradually the *Portrait of My Wife* which seems to be so unpopular for exhibition is taking shape in my mind as a dramatic illustration of that crucial test. It will be repainted and given a provocative title. Probably something like *Mendelssohn in Canadian Winter, 1977*. . . . It seems to me I was allowed by God to live through all those hardships I did live through so that I would be a fit instrument for His purposes. The very remarkable development of my artistic career and the sometimes uncanny arrangement of people and places in it seems to suggest that this may seem aweful spiritual pride. But I hope it is, really, a . . . true humility such as our Lady's, who though only a simple Jewish maid to outward appearances said, "He who is mighty has done great things to me." Being misunderstood by family even my wife and brothers and sisters and my friends and acquaintances seems to be the goad to keep me from getting too [word missing]
>
> To me wanting to build a blast shelter can be a sign. . . . The world cannot come to an end yet because of the Biblical prophecy that Christ must first be preached to all mankind. So far only 1/3 of mankind is Christian or has heard of Christ. . . . The sign of the times I feel is that of St. Thomas More. . . . I may or may not be a saint—only God can make me or anyone else into one. I know from experience that I am a physical and social

coward. It is agony sometimes being misunderstood or sneered at but whatever I can do now to prepare to be the sort of person He can use for His purposes I must try to do so. (Ohio Diary, 1967)

3. Ibid.

4. The engineer (name withheld by request) talking with P.M., Winnipeg, May 4, 1982. See also a letter by W.K. to K.S., December 16, 1967, where Kurelek describes a series of attempts to build a shelter. He began with a plan for one beneath his back garden. It would have been sufficiently large to accommodate immediate neighbors but was blocked by neighborhood protest. A second plan, for one beneath his house, was rejected by City Hall as impractical structurally: "They just can't believe that I have the will to work hard enough to build it myself piece by piece as the pioneers used to. . . . The illegal alternative is to build something small in secret. . . . The question is accordingly do I have the moral right to disobey a city law which I am personally convinced is completely out of date?"

5. L. L. Odette talking with P.M., Toronto, December 6, 1983. The Kurelek painting is unique in its city subject, yet typical in conveying the human significance of the scene. Like *Tramlines* (London, 1953), the structure is cruciform.

6. Letters by W.K. to K.S., undated (August 1968), and November 11 (1968). Shorey's replies establish month and year.

7. Daniel Maron, "Douglas Hyde Goes to Jail," *The Sign* (May 1963), p. 47.

8. The principal didactic exhibitions of Kurelek paintings are "Experiments in Didactic Art" (May 1963, The Isaacs Gallery); "Glory to Man in the Highest" (March 1966, Isaacs); "The Burning Barn" (March 1969, Hart House Gallery); and "The Last Days" (June 1971, Galerie Godard Lefort). However, the vast majority of his exhibitions included one or more didactic works.

9. Robert Ayre, "Humanity and Trash in Gallery XII," *Star Weekly* (April 13, 1963).

10. Paul Duval, "Humble, sincere, talented, religious tracts in paint," Toronto *Telegram* (May 25, 1963). See also Joan Murray, *Kurelek's Vision of Canada* (Oshawa: Robert McLaughlin Gallery, 1982), p. 24, for a reproduction of *Dinnertime on the Prairies* and Kurelek's text, where he states that our sins crucify Christ as much today as in ancient Palestine: the farmer and his sons, who have gone home for their noonday meal, have had angry words or lustful thoughts.

11. John Robert Colombo, "William Kurelek at The Isaacs Gallery, Toronto," *Arts Canada*, vol. 20 (September/October 1963), p. 270.

12. Elizabeth Kilbourn, "Dogma and Experience," *Toronto Star* (May 18, 1963).

13. Kay Kritzwiser, "Quiet Assessor in a Tartan Shirt," *Globe and Mail* (March 15, 1966).

14. Harry Malcolmson, "Art and Artists," Toronto *Telegram* (March 12, 1966), p. 66.

15. Letter by W.K. to H. Malcolmson, April 1966 (approx. 3000 words).

16. Kurelek text for *Nuclear Age Madonna*, No. 14, "The Last Days" series, quoted in Virginia Nixon, "Kurelek's message is sharp and clear," Montréal *Gazette* (June 19, 1971). Maria Logush talked with P.M., February 15, 1983. See also "Le Génie de Kurelek," Radio Québec television documentary, 1983.

17. Louis Stoeckle, talking with P.M., May 7, 1982.

18. Adolphe Pecoskie talking with P.M., Combermere, August 13, 1982.

19. Geza and Sandy Takacs talking with P.M., Toronto, August 1983.

20. John and Helen Kurelek talking with P.M., Brantford, August 15, 1983.

Notes

Chapter Eleven—"Nature, Poor Stepdame"

1. William Kurelek, *Kurelek's Canada* (Toronto: McGraw-Hill Ryerson, 1975), p. 91. See also Joan Murray, *Kurelek's Vision of Canada* (Oshawa: Robert McLaughlin Gallery, 1982), p. 48. See also letter by W.K. to K.S., October 30, 1963.

2. W.K., Manitoba Diary, July 17, 1967.

3. Letter by W.K. to A.I., September 2, 1963.

4. W.K., (Stonewall) Diary, June 9, 1964.

5. W.K., Manitoba Diary, July 17, 1967. Cf. W.K., Minnedosa Diary, April 24-28 (circa 1965), where spring break-up is termed "the most exciting time of year for me as a boy next to threshing time". Nature is an antagonist he enjoys confronting: "I still had to fight like Van Gogh did with the wind the French call Mistral. Horse hair and pieces of chaff settled into my sky soon as I sprayed it." High adventure includes an interruption by an officer of the RCMP: "Artists really are an unknown strange being out here. It reminds me so much of Van Gogh's persecution at Arles. The mountie almost interrupted a vital stage of the third drawing in fact I'd dropped the second soon as I saw this magnificent sun and cloud effect like God's glory streaming down."

6. W.K., *A Northern Nativity: Christmas Dreams of a Prairie Boy* (Montréal: Tundra Books, 1976), no. 6.

7. See texts to *Drop Yon Blue Bosom-Veil of Sky* and *All Things Betray Thee Who Betrayest Me* in the "Nature, Poor Stepdame" series, 1970, The Isaacs Gallery.

8. Murray, "Kurelek's Landscapes," *Kurelek's Vision of Canada*, p. 11.

9. William Kurelek, *The Last of the Arctic* (Toronto: Pagurian Press, 1976), p. 14.

10. William Kurelek, text to *Subdue the Earth* in William C. Forsey, *The Ontario Community Collects: A Survey of Canadian Painting from 1776 to the Present* (Toronto: Art Gallery of Ontario, 1975), p. 110.

11. W.K., Foreword to "Big Lonely" series, exhibited May 1977. Mira Godard Gallery, Montréal.

12. Ibid. Part of the Foreword is cited in Murray, *Kurelek's Vision of Canada*, p. 66.

Chapter Twelve—The Odyssey Toward Ethnic Awareness

1. See W.K., "Development of Ethnic Consciousness in a Canadian Artist," *Ethnic Studies Conference, Toronto, 1973. Identities: The Impact of Ethnicity on Canadian Society*, ed. W. Isajiw, Vol. 5 (Toronto: Peter Martin, 1977), pp. 46-56.

2. Ibid.

3. Barrie Hale, "Kurelek is the Man," Toronto *Telegram*, September 26, 1964, p. 25. See also Sylvia Fraser, "A Ukrainian Immigrant in Canada," *Star Weekly* (October 17, 1964), pp. 18-33, for ten colored photographs of paintings in this series.

4. W.K., "Development of Ethnic Consciousness in a Canadian Artist," 1973.

5. W.K., "Notes on Symbolism" (1966), in Murray, *Kurelek's Vision of Canada*, p. 27.

6. W.K., "Development of Ethnic Consciousness in a Canadian Artist," 1973.

7. Anna Balan talking with P.M., Toronto, December 13, 1982.

8. Letter by Anna Balan to P.M., July 15, 1982: Balan adds, "I would like to make it perfectly clear that this is a *personal* opinion."

9. Minutes of UWAC Executive Meeting, January 2, 1967. Purchase price for twelve works totalled approximately $3,500.

10. Card by W.K. to The Isaacs Gallery, February 1, 1966.

11. Letter by W.K. to Jean K., Vegreville, January 27, 1966. Further quotations are from this letter-diary, January 24-February 6, 1966.

12. Village and Museum are located near Shandro on Highway 857, ten kilometres north of Willingdon. Headed by Zazula, the Shandro Association had incorporated itself in 1960 and grown steadily. By 1980 it had some fifteen buildings and was attracting tourists from Canada and abroad. Kurelek returned to study it several times in the 1970s. Mr. and Mrs. W. Zazula talked with P.M., Shandro, Alberta, May 12, 1982.

13. One old family album contained a photograph which Kurelek found particularly moving. It showed his father with his arms around his mother in their courting days: "Because they had never been openly demonstrative this was the only time I'd ever seen visible sign of affection between them."

14. W.K., text to painting No. 8, "The Ukrainian Woman Pioneer in Canada" series (1967).

15. Ibid., Text No. 20. Cf. Andrea Chambers, "All About Bette," *People Weekly*, May 6, 1985, p. 40: "To publicly malign a mother ... is a chilling act. To do so during her lifetime, some would say, is cruel and self-destructive." Chambers is reviewing a savage book on Bette Davis written by her daughter, who calls her attack an act of love and a search for reconciliation with her mother.

16. Book of Proverbs, Chapter 31 and *passim*.

17. The Kurelek text to *The First House*, fourth painting in the series "The Ukrainian Woman Pioneer in Canada," notes that since the men might be absent for twelve months at a time, women did "men's" work in the summer when "manpower" was most needed for clearing and tilling the land, in order to satisfy homesteading regulations and obtain title to the land as well as to raise food. Kurelek apparently saw no conflict between this data and his text for *In the Beginning*, the first painting in the "Glory to Man in the Highest" series (1965-66), where he lays out a rigid stereotyping of work according to gender: in the "right" order of things, women should work in the home while man is "the provider".

18. John and Mary Stefura talking with P.M., March 20, 1982. After an initial purchase, Kurelek and the Stefuras had become friends; in the late sixties, they offered Kurelek the use of their cottage near Sudbury for a holiday with his family. Kurelek (who had defended industrial pollution in his painting *Subdue the Earth*, 1966) refused, citing pollution in the area as his excuse.

See also letter by W.K. to Stanley Frolick, May 10, 1973: "You were among my top half-dozen Ukrainian promoters." And letter by Stanley Frolick to W.K., May 15, 1973: "In this context of my personal philosophy or sense of duty [concerning the promotion of the Ukrainian-Canadian community], I admire you not only for your talent, but more importantly for me, because you are an artist of *Ukrainian* origin. This is also what has motivated me to promote you and your works as much as I am able to do. This is why our business and professional club of which I was the President, was one of the first Ukrainian organizations in Toronto to have a festive evening to pay tribute to you. ... Because we all bask in the glory reflected from you. When one of us achieves success and prominence, the rest grow also in stature."

19. T-shirts and posters with slogans like "Kiss Me, I'm Ukrainian", "Molson's Ukrainian", and "Campbell's Borsch" were initially bought by non-Ukrainian teenagers in the Canadian West. Later they were accepted by Ukrainian teens. In the urban centres of Eastern Canada, where there had always been less prejudice against Ukrainians, they were accepted more readily. Anna Balan talking with P.M., December 13, 1982.

20. Maria and Michael Logush talking with P.M., February 15, 1983.

21. Ukrainian Day, October 29, 1970, at the Montréal Museum of Fine Arts, was a formal affair attended by notables such as Sean Murphy, the Museum's president, Senator Paul Yuzyk, and Montréal's Mayor Jean Drapeau. Leo Rosshandler had chosen the painting, which had been purchased by the Ukrainian Auxiliary Committee of the Museum for $1,050. The evening program featured the music of Ukrainian composer George Fiala, performed by pianist Ireneus Zuk and violinist Eugene Husaruk. Fiala would later compose a five-part symphonic suite in honor of Kurelek (1985).

22. See UCYMA (Ukrainian Catholic Young Men's Association) Exhibit, Montréal, November 26, 1972; and an exhibit of Ukrainian Graphic Artists at the Université de Montréal in 1973, which included work by Kurelek.

23. Private collection, mixed media, 18″ x 24″. See Kurelek Calendar, Tundra Books, 1983.

24. W.K., Ohio Diary, 1967. See also Vasyl Stefanyk, *The Stone Cross*, translators Joseph Wiznuk and C. H. Andrusychen (Toronto: McClelland and Stewart, 1971). The comparison between Stefanyk's writing technique and Kurelek's genre painting is very apt.

25. Cf. Maria Logush talking with P.M., February 15, 1983: "He was not perfect in Ukrainian; he spoke the language of his folks, a pidgin Ukrainian like peasants speak, and wrote the same way. It was *not* the language of an educated Ukrainian." The Kolankiwskys found his Ukrainian adequate, sometimes "homespun". Anna Balan remembers Kurelek making many grammatical errors: "His sentence structure suggested thinking in English and writing in Ukrainian. His choice of words showed a small vocabulary. Still, he could be understood well" (to P.M., July 15, 1982).

26. Kay Kritzwiser, "A Solemn Gospel in Tempera," *Globe and Mail*, February 26, 1970.

27. Art Director Gloria Ochitwa talking with P.M., June 20, 1982: "It put St. Vladimir's Art Gallery on the map." Kurelek subsequently donated *Generosity*, from a series on the seven virtues, to the Institute in gratitude.

28. Mykola Kolankiwsky, Introduction to William Kurelek, *The Ukrainian Pioneer* (Niagara Falls Art Gallery, 1980), p. 6; and *Niagara Falls Art Gallery Kurelek Collection* (1983), p. 4.

29. W.K., Foreword, *The Passion of Christ According to St. Matthew* (Niagara Falls Art Gallery and Museum, 1975), p. 13. The series of 160 paintings sold for $32,000.

30. Olha and Mykola Kolankiwsky talking with P.M., Niagara Falls Art Gallery and Museum, June 1981. The icon depicts the Madonna holding a small crucifix instead of the infant Jesus. Critics record the gallery opening as July 10, 1971 (see e.g. Kay Kritzwiser, "Niagara Falls Art," *Globe and Mail*, July 10, 1971), while the Director has written that it opened on June 19, 1971.

31. See Kolankiwsky, Introduction, *The Ukrainian Pioneer*, p. 6. See also letter by W.K. to K.S., May 15, 1970, which establishes the dates of the trip as May

15-June 5, 1970. A Kurelek painting, *The Spirit of Shevchenko in Canada*, was presented to the Museum in Kiev.

32. See W.K., Diary of a Ukrainian Trip, May 17, 1970. In another letter he expresses his guilt at having done no work between supper the previous evening and the time of writing: 8 a.m. Kurelek's austere routine while travelling in the Soviet Ukraine included partial fasting. He averaged one and sometimes two meals per day, offering up the fast "for the Ukraine".

33. See letters by W.K. to K.S., January 9 and May 15, 1970.

34. W.K., Diary of a Ukrainian Trip, May 23, 1970.

35. Later in the diary, Kurelek returns to his fear that permission would never be granted: "It would be sheer madness for the authorities to let me find out the whole truth of the people's attitude to the collectives and to show the whole truth in my paintings in the outside world."

36. W.K., *The Ukrainian Pioneer*, p. 63. See also W.K., text to painting, *Hunger Strike in Ottawa for V. Moroz* (1974): "I am not a Ukrainian nationalist although I am proud of my Ukrainian ancestry. And I have no interest in Ukrainian politics. I consider myself a Canadian first and foremost."

37. Patricia Morley, "Odyssey to hell and back," *Ottawa Journal*, May 3, 1980. After Kurelek's first trip to the Ukraine, and even after he had completed the six-panel work on the Ukrainian pioneers, it remained his overriding ambition to paint a huge series of murals on the theme of Ukrainian settlement in Canada: see letter by Stanley W. Frolick, to P.M., May 10, 1985.

38. Letter by Bohdan Melnyk to W.K., July 22, 1974. Subsequent references are from the Melnyk-Kurelek correspondence (1974-77) and from Melnyk talking with P.M., St. Catharines, June 18, 1983.

39. Letter from May Cutler to Bohdan Melnyk, January 31, 1978.

40. Cf. May Cutler talking with P.M., November 22, 1982: "He found out Franko was an atheist, tied in with naturalist writers like Zola. Franko was a patriot but anti-church, so this upset Bill. ... It wasn't until after it was published that I discovered Bill's disapproval. It's a political satire and a *roman à clef*."

41. Jacquie Hunt, "Kurelek's last book most captivating," Ottawa *Citizen*, December 19, 1978, p. 45. See also letter by May Cutler to Glenn Edward Witmer, September 26, 1978: "In French, only Lafontaine's FABLES compare in popularity. ... Among Ukrainian children it is as well known as Mother Goose is to English children, but it is also so cherished by adults that many know the whole poem by heart, a total of 3,642 lines. To Ukrainians, LYS MYKYTA represents the independence and effectiveness of the individual."

42. *Canada Today/d'aujourd'hui*, vol. X, no. 1 (1979).

43. Letter by W.K. to Jean K., September 17-20 (1972). See also Mary Paximadis, *Look Who's Coming: The Wachna Story*, Illustrations by William Kurelek (Oshawa: Maracle Press, 1976); and letter by W.K. to Dr. Elias Wachna, February 13, 1972: "Ironically too, Isaacs promotion of my work has done a lot more for the Ukrainian awareness in this country than has many other businesses of professional Ukrainians."

44. W.K. talking with Abraham Arnold, March 30, 1977.

45. Anna Balan, unpublished ms.

Chapter Thirteen—Promoters and Friends: The Circle Widens

1. A.I. talking with P.M., December 5, 1983. Cf. A.I. to W.K., June 9, 1976: "I have realized for some time that for some reason you see me as some sort of father figure or in other words someone whose disapproval you were particularly sensitive to. I am not. I am just a guy who is trying to work with you and who may be wrong some of the time just as you are wrong. The main thing that you had better realize is that aside from monetary possibility of gain I genuinely have your best interests as an artist at heart."

2. Letter by A.I. to W.K., December 11, 1967.

3. See W.K. and Abraham Arnold, *Jewish Life in Canada* (Edmonton: Hurtig, 1976), Introduction by Kurelek, p. 7: "This series ... was meant to express my thanks to the Jewish community for their important part in my success as an artist. It was Avrom Isaacs, a Jew, who first discovered me and took the risk of exhibiting my work. After ten years of my trying in vain on my own for recognition he gave me that necessary break. ... Jewish art collectors were my first patrons." Cf. letter by W.K. to A.I., December 16, 1964: "I admire your people for their courage, history, scholarliness, culture and religion. I was impressed by their achievements in Israel." Kurelek wrote that he had more Jews among his patrons than any other ethnic group.

4. Letter by W.K. to A.I., undated (April 1966). See also letter by W.K. to K.S., January 25, 1966: "I am always conscious that my reputation is in good part due to Av Isaacs' effective promotion which as you know with modern communications media can make or break a man overnight. What genuine lasting genius is in me well its a gift of God's and He should be glorified and thanked." Cf. letter by W.K. to Nathan Isaacs, December 26, 1968: "Av is entitled to his commission even in the case where the buyer hasnt even heard of the Isaacs Gallery because he built up the value of my work with his promotion of it." In the same letter Kurelek stresses "the part Av played in guiding me to fame and prosperity". See also letter by W.K. to Ross Silversides, April 30, 1973: "Mr. Isaacs discovered me and made me when no one else had faith in my possibilities."

5. Letter by W.K. to A.I., April 1966. Cf. May Cutler talking with P.M., November 29, 1982: "Av is affable, easy, good-natured, relaxed: the kind of personality Bill needed."

6. W.K., *The Passion of Christ*, p. 12.

7. Letter by W.K. to A.I., April 1966.

8. Letter by A.I. to W.K., January 14, 1971.

9. See note by W.K. to The Isaacs Gallery, February 25, 1966.

10. See letter by W.K. to A.I., December 1, 1967: "You could easily have taken advantage of me just then and have me agree to *complete* control. Over the years since then I see it would have been an intolerable straight jacket. It is quite a chore as it is explaining and defending your right to a commission. And sometimes embarrassing too. ... As you can see all kinds of temptations are being put before me time after time and I'm having to study my business conscience regularly. Galleries approach me too to deal for me or to wean me away from the Isaacs gallery. ... It makes me mad these people who should know better wanting to capitalize on the spade work you did. ..." Kurelek sold to friends at one-third of the Gallery price.

11. See Kurelek correspondence, *passim*.

12. Letter by A.I. to W.K., December 11, 1967: "How many of these people are buying partially for investment purposes and not for pure motives."

13. Cf. letter of A.I. to W.K., undated: "I think only well of you so that if we ever have any problems please think of them as being only due to poor communication between us."

14. Letter by A.I. to W.K., December 11, 1967.

15. Letter by A.I. to W.K., December 10, 1976.

16. See letter by A.I. to W.K., December 11, 1967.

17. Letter by A.I. to W.K., January 25, 1977. See also letter by W.K. to A.I., January 17, 1972, in which Kurelek writes that he has copied *Behold Man Without God* (a major work from the 1950s) in order to have it available for shows without "the bother" of borrowing the original. In his autobiography, Kurelek complains that art today is regarded as "super-sacred" instead of as a craft; because he holds this attitude he has "no hesitation of doing copies or similar pictures of his work" (A1 504).

18. See letter by A.I. to the Dept. of Citizenship and Immigration, November 24, 1966. Isaacs was reporting details of Kurelek's income because the artist had offered to stand as sponsor to help a West Indian immigrant to enter Canada.

19. Letter by W.K. to A.I., October 14, 1966.

20. Letter by W.K. to Nathan Isaacs, December 26, 1968.

21. Letter by A.I. to W.K., December 16, 1964. Isaacs was perhaps more supportive of Kurelek's religious paintings than the artist realized or acknowledged. As early as December 18, 1959, the dealer had written to the Canada Council in support of a Kurelek application for an award; Isaacs praised the artist's religious paintings and his attempts "to recapture in his work the medieval dedication of art to the service of faith".

22. See letter by W.K. to A.I., April 1966.

23. See letter by W.K. to A.I., May 1966: "I might acquire a gallery of my own specifically for these unsaleable works to hang in."

24. See letter by W.K. to A.I., October 13, 1969: "I cant forever have only 'pot-boiler painting' exhibits in that city. The Montréal audience is too big and too important for me to miss out on trying there also to get my message across. ... I thought therefore that you'd have a better chance of presenting my case for a religious show at her gallery than I." The reference is to Mira Godard, of the Galerie Godard Lefort, where Kurelek shows were held in 1969, 1971, 1973, and 1976. The Gallery had changed its name to Marlborough Godard by 1973. The first two Kurelek exhibitions in Montréal were at Galerie Agnès Lefort (1965, 1967). Isaacs preferred to show Kurelek only biennially; Kurelek was eager to show more frequently and was therefore pleased when Godard approached him through Isaacs in 1963 (A1 515).

25. See 1 Corinthians 9:22 and 23, where St. Paul speaks of how he conducts himself: "I have become everything in turn to men of every sort, so that in one way or another I may save some. All this I do for the sake of the Gospel. ..."

26. James Maas holds a tape of Kurelek's talk at Cornell, 1970.

27. See Foreword by James Maas, William Kurelek, *Someone With Me* (Cornell University: Center for Improvement of Undergraduate Education, 1973), p. iv. Cf. James Maas talking with P.M., Cornell, July 12, 1983; and "This Is My Story," a taped public broadcast, undated, after Kurelek's death.

28. Letter by W.K. to Dr. David L. Davies, May 22, 1969.

29. Maas, July 12, 1983. Kurelek later specified that one scene be cut from the film: a shot of a farmer beating a horse, part of Kurelek's painting *I Spit on Life.*

30. *The Maze*, directed by Robert Young and David Gruben, produced by Irwin Young, Robert Young, and Stanley D. Plotnick. A Houghton Mifflin Production in Association with Du Art Film Laboratories, 1970. Sound by Dr. James B. Maas. His part in the film helped Maas to win the 1973 APA Award for Distinguished Teaching, with a special citation for having produced effective audio-visual material for educational use. The public version (30 min.) is edited down from the original 60-minute version retained by Du Art Film.

31. Maas, July 12, 1983.

32. See Jack Sherman, "Art Review," *Ithaca Journal*, November 9, 1971, p. 14: "the five or six really good pictures redeem all the rest" (of 30 works). *Behold Man Without God* was praised, but masterworks such as *Thunder Driven* and *All Things Betray Thee Who Betrayest Me* were ignored.

33. See letter by W.K. to May Cutler, September 21, 1973.

34. See letter by W.K. to J. Maas, September 11, 1973. The errors are closer in number to one thousand than one hundred. The edited posthumous edition (1980) contains no drawings.

35. Letter by W.K. to Jean K., June 21, 1969.

36. Letter by W.K. to Jean K., July 30, 1969.

37. Letter by W.K. to Jean K., June 22, 1969.

38. Letter by W.K. to Jean K., June 25, 1969.

39. Letter by W.K. to Jean K., June 27, 1969.

40. Letter by W.K. to Jean K., July 3, 1969.

41. Letter by W.K. to Jean K., June 26, 1969.

42. Letter by W.K. to Jean K., July 3, 1969. After observing fights among beggars, he wrote that Indians "are not a noble, suffering people, ... they are as much sinners as we are" (July 14, 1969).

43. Letter by W.K. to Jean K., July 12, 1969.

44. Letter by W.K. to Jean K., July 7, 1969. Kurelek's reaction to the Vatican in 1959 had been very similar; he rarely criticized the Church, but he believed that displays of wealth had no legitimate place in Christianity.

45. Letter by W.K. to Jean K., July 30-31, 1969.

46. Letter by K.S. to P.M., April 10, 1985.

47. See letter by Curator Donald Bowen to W.K., May 8, 1972; and the Exhibition Catalogue (March 22-April 23, 1972).

Chapter Fourteen—The Mass Marketing of Kurelek

1. See letter by W.K. to May Cutler, January 17, 1974.

2. Christopher Ondaatje talking with P.M., Toronto, December 11, 1982. Cf. letter by W.K. to Nancy Kurelek Black, December 9, 1975, where Kurelek refers to being besieged by buyers and visitors: "Being a public figure is pleasing but at the same time hard. I take it as the will of God and try to fulfill what it looks like He is expecting of me by putting me in limelight. One friend has accused me of growing egotism evident in the last quarter of my autobiography. That is another big danger I have to watch."

3. Ibid.

4. M.C. talking with P.M., Montréal, November 22, 1982.

5. William French, "May Cutler, publisher and tweaker," *Globe and Mail*, November 24, 1973, p. 34. When a fire gutted her company's premises in 1973 Bill wrote to express sympathy and to say that, in connection with the announcement

of the fire at a party for authors and booksellers, he had heard praise on all sides for Cutler's "courage, astuteness and fine personality".

6. Cutler, November 22, 1982: "In 1972, Bill wanted a book so much he would have let me do it without any royalty payments."

7. Letter by M.C. to W.K., June 14, 1971.

8. Cutler, November 22, 1982.

9. W.K., text for colored leaflet printed by The Art Gallery of Windsor for *A Prairie Boy's Summer*. Kurelek adds that the *Prairie Boy* books sweetly vindicated his long-standing disappointment regarding his inability to find listeners in the city school for his stories of farm adventures (see Chapter Eleven, unpaged). His gratitude to Cutler is found in many of his letters to her. Cf. June 12, 1977: "You opened up the world of publication for me which I'd hardly dared to dream of. . . . I owe a lot to you."

10. Letter by M.C. to Robert Fulford, September 14, 1976.

11. Letter by W.K. to M.C., March 13, 1973. In the same letter Kurelek praises the production quality: "It's a beautiful book you're making."

12. Cutler, November 22, 1982.

13. See W.K., *O Toronto*, Introduction by James Bacque (Toronto: New Press, 1973; General Publishing, 1978).

14. Letter by W.K. to M.C., September 11, 1973.

15. W.K., *O Toronto*, p. 40: "The My Lai incident in Viet Nam has come to represent in the public mind today the slaughter of innocent and helpless people. It's relatively easy to express indignation at injustices abroad, while staying blind to the wrong being done in our own back yard."

16. Letter by W.K. to M.C., September 3, 1974: "I count you as a friend."

17. See William Stephenson, "The Aesthetic Entrepreneur," *Financial Post Magazine* (February 1, 1983), pp. 01-05; and John Lane, "Growth the debt-free way," *Financial Times*, vol. 71, no. 19 (October 18, 1982), pp. 4, 7.

18. Stephenson, "The Aesthetic Entrepreneur," p. 01.

19. Ondaatje, December 11, 1982: "He'd talk to me for four or five hours. I was a real sounding board, certainly for money!"

20. The first four photo-prints were published in limited editions of 950, 950, 554, and 550, respectively; four scenes from *Kurelek's Canada* were published in editions of 300, namely *Newfie Jokes*, *Potato Planters Admiring Baby Killdeer*, *The Barn Dance*, and *Excitement of First Heavy Snow*. The Sporting series, in editions of 225 numbered impressions each (with ten artist's proofs), consists of *Volleyball*, *Tennis*, *Lacrosse*, *Hockey*, *Football*, *Tobogganing*, *Fishing*, *Hunting*, *Skiing*, *Sailing*, *Ice-sailing*, and *Golfing*. These photo-lithographs are high-quality photographs of the original paintings, and were printed at Herzig-Somerville in Toronto.

21. See W.K., *Map of Toronto*, first ten copies only: "Once a stern, foreboding Victorian town, Toronto in the Seventies blossomed into a city for people, lauded in song, and praised throughout the world for its vitality, humanity and excitement."

22. W.K., *Kurelek's Canada* (Toronto: Pagurian Press, 1975), Artist's Acknowledgement. See also letter by W.K. to C. Ondaatje, May 6, 1974, from Dublin; and the contract for the book, signed in October 1974.

23. See letter by W.K. to C. Ondaatje, May 6, 1974, where Kurelek expresses his dislike of *Kurelek's Canada* as a title. He used "The Happy Canadian" as the title of a projected film which was never completed.

24. Ondaatje paid $600 each for thirty paintings, $18,000 in total.

25. A.I. talking with P.M., Toronto, December 5, 1983.

26. Jeremy Brown talking with P.M., Toronto, December 8, 1983.

27. May Cutler talking with P.M., November 29, 1982. Cutler believes that Kurelek's confused finances and the long hours of work, through which he raised money, quickly contributed to his early death.

28. See letters by W.K. to M.C., December 13, 1974, and January 26, 1975. Written on the hand-labelled diagram is the following notation: "To whom it may concern: Every time someone adjusts my wording describing drawing fuel out of a barrel by suction they wreck the system laid out diagramatically below. I don't mind the words being changed as long as whats diagramed below still remains clear. The obvious alternative is simply to leave my wording alone. Then the readers who know the principle below will follow my story without difficulty." Kurelek obviously perceived the task of editing as cosmetic at best. Few things rated lower on his scale of valuable activities.

29. Letter by W.K. to C. Ondaatje, October 22, 1976.

30. Letter by W.K. to C. Ondaatje, January 29, 1976.

31. Ibid.

32. Letter by W.K. to a business associate of C. Ondaatje, October 22, 1976.

33. Letter by M.C. to editor Mary Harmon, November 16, 1973.

34. Letter by M.C. to W.K., December 4, 1973: "All I did was act as midwife." Cutler's letter to W.K. of February 8, 1974, reveals the roughness of the original Kurelek text for *Lumberjack* and her contribution to the final version.

35. See letter by W.K. to M.C., October 30, 1971.

36. Letter by W.K. to M.C., December 7, 1973. Cf. letters by W.K. to M.C., June 6, 1974: "the 2 moral references ... are much more important to me than the grammatical or factual errors. ... Its a beautiful book and Canada owes you a pat on the back for doing it." And February 25, 1974: "You've changed my original script so much that I'm wondering whether it wouldn't be more accurate to have the book coauthored something like 'story by William Kurelek as told to May Cutler'. That would be fine by me."

37. See letter by W.K. to M.C., January 17, 1974, where Kurelek emphasizes the importance of the "2 or 3 brief religious references" in *Lumberjack*. One such is in Chapter 25: "The windows were frosted over with a half-inch of art work by a better artist than I—He who gave me such talent as I have."

38. Letter by W.K. to M.C., February 14, 1974.

39. Letter by W.K. to M.C., February 1, 1974.

40. The twenty paintings for *A Prairie Boy's Summer* were sold to Hiram Walker and Sons, and loaned permanently to the Art Gallery of Windsor.

41. Letter by W.K. to M.C., September 18, 1974. Cf. letter by W.K. to A.I., September 19, 1974: "This farm is the best place yet I've worked at painting. The isolation is more complete than big city hotels. ... I bought a 3 speed bike and that and the phone is my contact with the outside world."

42. W. O. Mitchell talking with P.M., June 23, 1983. In the summer of 1977, Kurelek wrote to his sister Nancy to promise her a copy of the illustrated edition of *Who Has Seen the Wind* by W. O. Mitchell: "He's the one who composed the dedication [to *Prairie Boy's Summer*]."

43. W.K., as recalled by Mitchell, ibid.

44. Ibid. Although Mitchell refused gifts, he bought from the artist at the preferred rate for friends. Later, he accepted the gift of a small painting, *Field Mouse Taking a Chance*: "It was done with restraint too, there wasn't the shadow of a hawk, an image he liked incidentally. To him the hawk was satanic. ... The little field mouse was taking a chance and you pray that he will make it to the sanctuary of that next hole before a goshawk grabs him up in his talons." Mitchell remembers another Kurelek painting of an evangelical sect immersing converts in a baptismal rite outdoors, while a hawk prepares to swoop on a young partridge family. Bill had been upset by the news that some of his relatives had joined this sect; he believed them to be in deadly danger.

45. Letter by M.C. to W.K., September 24, 1974.

46. Kurelek died before the possibility of a second Nativity volume could be realized.

47. Letter by W.K. to M.C., June 6, 1974.

48. See letters by W.K. to M.C., November 6, 1974, and by M.C. to W.K., November 8, 1974.

49. See letters by W.K. to M.C., January (1975), and by M.C. to W.K., January 9, 1975.

50. M.C. talking with P.M., November 22, 1982.

51. "Montréal Revisited," exhibited December 10, 1975-January 8, 1976, at the Marlborough Godard Gallery, Montréal. To Kurelek's great disappointment, Cutler eventually declined to publish the Montréal series in book form.

52. Letter by W.K. to M.C., August 30, 1975.

53. Letter by M.C. to W.K., January 7, 1976.

54. Letter by M.C. to W.K., June 30, 1976.

55. Letter by W.K. to M.C., July 12, 1976.

56. W.K., *A Northern Nativity* (Montréal: Tundra Books, 1976), Chapter 20.

57. See letters by W.K. to M.C., August 24, 1976, and October 29, 1976: "Would it be possible for her [Nancy Kurelek Black] to get the royalties rather than me (if the book interests you)."

58. See letter by A.I. to W.K., June 9, 1976.

59. A.I. talking with A. Arnold (taped interview), April 26, 1978: "It's something I avoid like the plague."

60. A.I. to W.K., June 9, 1976.

61. See letters by A.I. to W.K., January 14, 1971, and by W.K. to A.I., January 12, 1972.

62. Letter by W.K. to A.I., August 16, 1971.

63. See letter by A.I. to W.K., December 6, 1973.

64. Many of Kurelek's sixteen Jewish paintings were composed by combining two or three archival photographs. Kurelek was also helped by Dr. Stephen Speisman, Archivist, Canadian Jewish Congress, Toronto. The artist chose to focus on scenes of Orthodox Judaism, a preference which Arnold connected with Kurelek's own religious orthodoxy.

65. Helen Worthington, "Catholic paints Canadian Jewish History," *Toronto Star*, November 17, 1976, p. E6.

66. W.K. and Abraham Arnold, Artist's Introduction, *Jewish Life in Canada* (Edmonton: Hurtig, 1976), p. 7. See also unpublished ms, "Artists Notes on His Drawings, Interpreting Ivan Franko's 'Fox Mykyta.'"

67. Bertha and Abraham Arnold talking with P.M., Winnipeg, May 2, 1982. A. Arnold stresses that Kurelek was open and "very tolerant".

68. Letter by W.K. to Michel de Kerdour, Québec City, March 5, 1976.

69. James Halpin talking with P.M., Québec City, July 8, 1983.

70. Vladimir Horik talking with P.M. by telephone, July 30, 1983.

71. Father Leo Letarte talking with P.M., Québec City, July 8, 1983.

72. Father Guy Bruneau talking with P.M., St. Nicolas, Québec, July 9, 1983. The religious joy of which he speaks may be seen in Bruneau's paintings in series such as "Canticles of the Sun" or "The Maya'ztec Festival". The latter has been donated to Concordia University, Montréal.

Cf. Father Michael Barida talking with P.M., Toronto, August 20, 1983: "Bill struck me as a Calvinist Catholic. ... The whole Orthodox tradition and its joy, incarnational joy, was entirely foreign to him. ... He was hung up on sin and its consequences. He had an inkling of the joy of the faith, but he felt so unworthy, not worthy to paint an icon." Kurelek did paint an icon of Our Lady and Child for St. Demetrius Church, at the urging of Father John Tataryn in 1975. In the resulting painting, Mary's expression was unpleasant and the total effect disturbing. Worse, Kurelek had made an error in the stylized position of Mary's hands. He had intended to depict them posed in blessing but had actually painted them set in a demonic position, the sign of the devil, according to Father Barida. The icon was hung briefly, then stored.

73. All of the paintings (uniformly sized, 20″ x 28″) in the Charlevoix series sold for $2,800. They were exhibited by Michel de Kerdour, Galerie d'art, Québec City, November 18-December 2, 1976. The French translation for the Kurelek texts was done by Professor Andrew Oliver, Trinity College, University of Toronto.

74. Kurelek later offered to paint a mural on the rear wall of the interior of the Catholic Church in Combermere, Ontario, circa 1976. His offer was refused by the church's priest and parish council. In the spring of 1977, Kurelek painted a mural on the wall of the side altar at Corpus Christi Church, Toronto—a Resurrection scene.

75. The $15,000 fee was much less than the amount that Kurelek's work would normally command at that time. The fee was paid directly to Kurelek's favorite charities in India.

76. See W.K., "Notes on the St. Thomas More College Mural," 1976. Most of the text has been published in a College pamphlet.

77. See letter by Father Alphonse de Valk to W.K., August 5, 1975.

78. See letters by W.K. to Father de Valk, August 7, 1975, and by Father de Valk to W.K., September 9, 1975.

79. The face of J. J. Leddy, a lay supporter of the College in its early days, was given to a figure dressed as a Chinese immigrant. The face of a priest for whom no other niche could be found was placed on a man wearing what Kurelek called an "outlandish Hawaiian sports shirt". See Kurelek text. Students, staff, and nuns (all recognizable locally) form the listening audience at the base of the mural.

80. Geralyn Jansen Hall talking with P.M., on tape, January 1983. Jansen also assisted with the scratching technique Kurelek used to depict grass or wheat. She says that the mural was done in mixed media, including poster paints, pencil crayons, and acrylic sprays.

81. Diary by Father Alphonse de Valk, CSB.

82. See Diary by Father K. J. Kirley; portions are reproduced in *The Chelsea Bulletin*, vol. IX, p. 5 (November 16, 1977), in a special Kurelek Issue. Cf. Kurelek: "Paintings may not have nearly the power to convert people that the printed or spoken word or even films have. But each believer has his or her role to play in the drama of mankind's salvation." (A2 174)

Conversations with Father Kirley provided Kurelek with material for the Irish series, painted in the spring and summer of 1976. Two paintings from the Irish series are reproduced in Murray, *Kurelek's Vision of Canada*, pp. 56,57. Critical reaction to the mural was almost uniformly enthusiastic, with one curious and bitter exception: see letter to the editor, *Prairie Messenger*, March 28, 1976, pp. 5, 14.

Chapter Fifteen—The Crusader

1. W.K., *O Toronto* (Toronto: New Press, 1973), p. 30.

2. Letter by W.K. to Dr. E. Wachna, February 13, 1972.

3. John Aitken, "The Noisy Revolution—Sex," *Weekend Magazine*, December 13, 1975.

4. Letter by W.K. to E. Peplinskie, December 25, 1975.

5. W.K., "Hushing the Noisy Revolution," *Weekend Magazine*, vol. 26, no. 15 (April 10, 1976), pp. 20-21.

6. In Jewish mysticism, sex serves as a metaphor for union with God; and in the Provençal love poetry of medieval France, the worship of an idealized beloved became fused with the cult of the Virgin Mary.

7. Form letter by W.K. to "Dear Friend," April 1976. Cf. letter by W.K. to K.S., April 23, 1976: "I had letters from right across the country urging me to write more rebuttals."

8. See Letters, *Weekend Magazine* (June 19, 1976), p. 14.

9. Donald DeMarco, "Artist or Propagandist?" *The Chelsea Journal*, vol. I, no. 2 (March-April, 1975). Cf. Barry Lord, *The History of Canadian Painting*, where Lord objects to hidden crucifixes in Kurelek landscapes and argues that dogma has affected his work adversely.

10. See letter by W.K. to Gloria Frolick, January 22, 1976; see also *Kurelek*, Winnipeg Art Gallery Catalogue, 1980, pp. 11, 23; and Gloria and Stanley Frolick talking with P.M., Toronto, June 19, 1982.

11. See Father Kevin Kirley, "Prairie Journal," vol. I (unpublished ms), p. 149: "I counselled him to agree to associate his name with the book only on condition that the author remove any reference which might be taken up by the pro-abortionists and used against the Right to Life movement. I suggested a change in the plot. ... He reflected for awhile, somewhat pained, and finally said that probably the abortion incident would have to stay because in real life it had happened and the book was based on real experience. He told me that he could influence the author because publication of her manuscript depended on whether he illustrated it or not. He wondered if it would be possible to change the abortion story into one that would attack the whole movement for greater freedom in this area, and at the same time it could become a story in defence of the unborn." See also Don DeMarco, "W.K. 'Message' Painter," *The Uncertified Human*, vol. 5, no. 9 (February 1978), p. 3. DeMarco, whose Pro-Life book entitled *Abortion in Perspective* was illustrated with seven Kurelek sketches, was impressed by the artist's love for life and by his integrity.

12. Letter by W.K. to children of 6B Class, October 16, 1975. Kurelek's references to *A Prairie Boy's Summer* as his first published writing is inexplicable, since it had been preceded by *A Prairie Boy's Winter*, *Lumberjack*, and other books.

13. Barry Callaghan talking with P.M., December 10, 1982.
14. Letter by W.K. to Michael Clayton, September 26, 1975.
15. Jacques Hnizdovsky, "Remembering Kurelek," July 1984.
16. Letter by K.S. to P.M., June 12-13, 1985.
17. See publications from C.O.H., the Center for Occupational Hazards, 5 Beekman St., New York, N.Y. 10038. See also Alan Bakes, "The State of the Art: Health Hazards, Conservation and New Materials: Bibliography," compiled for Visual Arts, Ontario, 417 Queen's Quay West, Toronto M5V 1A2; and Inge Langer, "Pursuit of art a deadly business," Ottawa *Citizen*, July 16, 1982, pp. 1, 31: "A recent study by the U.S. National Cancer Institute revealed the incidence of cancer in artists was two to three times higher than that of non-artists." Jean Kurelek firmly believes that her husband's cancer was caused by using sprays and other pigments in an airless space: see Lawrence Sabbath, "Seeing Hidden Evil: The Art of William Kurelek," *MD* (January 1985), p. 47.
18. Agnes Krumins talking with P.M., December 9, 1983.
19. Ibid.
20. Sylvia Chan talking with P.M., Toronto, June 20, 1983.
21. One of the paintings being copied in the 1970s had been inspired by a scene from Jerzy Kosinski's autobiographical fiction, *The Painted Bird*. Tricked by a boy, a soldier has fallen into a pit with starving rats; the child watches as the rats devour the man, and one another. Bill had meticulously executed both versions, one of which someone had commissioned. Callaghan remembers Bill showing him this work, and watching for his reaction. Bill himself said nothing, but smiled wryly.
22. To another assistant who worked for Kurelek briefly and proved unsatisfactory, the artist wrote (May 22, 1977) to defend his dismissing him by letter rather than in person: "I have never told anyone off [in person] in my life. I just haven't that kind of character and have always dreaded making enemies. In the past 20 years I have deliberately made it a policy to be friendly towards those who hurt me or tried to antagonize me...."
23. Letter by W.K. to Gordon Rayner, March 21, 1975.
24. Letter by W.K. to Mr. Dolphin, January 8, 1975.
25. Letter by Anna Balan to P.M., July 15, 1982.

Chapter Sixteen—Strange Prophecy

1. See letter by Stanley Frolick to P.M., May 10, 1985.
2. See letter by W.K. to Simon Kalba, September 2, 1977.
3. Ibid. As it turned out, Kurelek was forced to stay in a hotel in the nearby city of Chernivtsi and was transported daily by taxi to Borivtsi, a distance of forty-five kilometres each way.
4. Letter by W.K. to M.C., August 31, 1977.
5. Letter by Jean K. to O. and M. Kolankiwsky, undated (1977).
6. Letter by W.K. to Nancy Kurelek Black, August 21, 1977.
7. Letter by W.K. to Father A. de Valk, December 14, 1975.
8. See W.K., *The Ukrainian Pioneer*, Introduction by Mykola Kolankiwsky (Niagara Falls Art Gallery/Kurelek Collection, 1980), p. 7. Three of the five paintings were later donated to museums in Kiev. Kurelek worked on the drawings after returning to Canada, at home and in the hospital.
9. Cf. letter by W.K. to Simon Kalba, September 2, 1977: "If they let me bring out all I produce there should be 100 drawings and 6 paintings."

10. W.K., *The Ukrainian Pioneer*, p. 7.

11. Artist James Halpin viewed the 1977 Ukrainian drawings that October: "They were beautiful, fantastic! He was a *master* in drawing. His drawing style is like Ingres, like Degas."

12. The Kolankiwskys proceeded to Warsaw for the exhibition of "The Polish Canadians" which Kurelek had hoped to attend. In July 1977, for the annual Kurelek festival at their gallery near Niagara Falls, Kurelek had painted a series entitled "Temptation in the Desert."

13. J.K. talking with P.M., August 15, 1983.

14. Letter by W.K. to Jan Disselkoen, September 30, 1977, and to the Kolankiwskys, October 9, 1977.

15. *Death Fears Him Who Resists Her*, an undated Kurelek painting (mixed media, 13" x 6.5" high) was sold to a private collector as the artist's last painting. Its acquisition history is unclear. John Kurelek remembers that his brother was painting during his first days in hospital; later he drew but did not paint.

16. A palliative-care unit was opened at St. Michael's Hospital, Toronto, in April 1982. There was no such facility there in 1977, although there was a palliative-care nurse who was helpful.

17. Dr. E. J. Prokipchuk talking with P.M., Toronto, 1982.

18. Radio broadcast, "This Is My Story: William Kurelek," 1978.

19. J.K. talking with P.M., August 15, 1983; cf. letter by Jean K. to the Kolankiwskys, October 12, 1977, which notes that Kurelek remembered the past more than present happenings, a state which his wife found to be one of the most disturbing features of his illness.

20. Dr. D. W. Jirsch talking with P.M., Toronto, 1983.

Chapter Seventeen—Shifting Portraits

1. Dr. J. K. McConica, Kurelek Eulogy, November 7, 1977, Corpus Christi Church. Cf. Don DeMarco, "William Kurelek: 'Message' Painter," *The Uncertified Human*, vol. 5, no. 9 (February 1978), p. 4: "For Kurelek, life, art, and morality were indissolubly one."

2. Father K. Kirley, "William Kurelek. 1927-1977," *The Chelsea Bulletin*, vol. IX, no. 5 (November 16, 1977).

3. Jacques Hnizdovsky, "Remembering Kurelek" (unpublished memoir), July 1984.

4. Barry Callaghan talking with P.M., December 10, 1982.

5. See letter by W.K. to Dr. E. Wachna, February 13, 1972, where Kurelek praises Smith and Isaacs as the two who have helped him most after his parents; the latter, however, "were obligated to anyway."

6. Mrs. Sandy Kurelek Takacs talking to P.M., August 14, 1983.

INDEX

ARTWORKS AND PUBLICATIONS

Titles of books by William Kurelek are shown in CAPITALS

Index

EXHIBITIONS